PATTERNS OF NEGRO SEGREGATION

CHARLES S. JOHNSON

Professor of Sociology
Director, Department of Social Sciences
Fisk University

HARPER & BROTHERS PUBLISHERS

New York   London

This study was made possible by funds
granted by Carnegie Corporation of New
York. That Corporation is not, however,
the author, owner, publisher, or proprietor
of this publication, and is not to be understood as approving by virtue of its grant any
of the statements made or views expressed
therein.

To

M. B. J.

CONTENTS

PART I

PATTERNS OF RACIAL SEGREGATION AND DISCRIMINATION

PART II

BEHAVIORAL RESPONSE OF NEGROES TO SEGREGATION AND DISCRIMINATION

FOREWORD

This volume is one of the products of a Study which was announced
in the Annual Report of the President of Carnegie Corporation of
New York for 1938 in the following terms:

The Corporation has for some time felt the need of a general study of
the Negro in the United States, not only as a guide to its own activities,
but for broader reasons. It appeared to be essential that such a study be
made under the direction of a person who would be free from the pre-
suppositions and emotional charges which we all share to a greater or less
degree on this subject, and the Corporation, therefore, looked outside the
United States for a distinguished student of the social sciences who
would be available to organize and direct the project. It is a pleasure to
announce that Dr. Karl Gunnar Myrdal has been granted a leave of
absence from the University of Stockholm to enable him to accept the
invitation of the Trustees to undertake this work.

Dr. Myrdal arrived in New York in September, 1938, and remained here until the European situation made necessary his return
to Sweden in May, 1940. During this period he requested some
twenty American students of the Negro to prepare memoranda on
all the more important aspects of Negro life in America, and on
numerous minor ones. Most of these memoranda were unfinished
at the time of his departure, but the majority were completed by the
following September. Uncertainty concerning the date of Dr. Myrdal's return demanded reconsideration of the original arrangement
which provided that the right to use all materials collected in the
course of the Study should be vested in the contributors after the
main report was published. Because of the unavoidable delay in the
completion of Dr. Myrdal's own work, it was decided to facilitate
the publication of some of the memoranda in advance of the main
report, and the undersigned Committee was appointed to advise
in the selection of those contributions most nearly ready for publication. Dr. Samuel A. Stouffer of the University of Chicago, who
acted as executive officer of the Study during Dr. Myrdal's absence,
was invited by the Committee to serve as its secretary.

In general the memoranda were not designed for publication in
the form written. Contributors' instructions were to prepare work-

ix

ing memoranda rapidly and in a full and easy style which would make them most useful for Dr. Myrdal's purposes. Thus, by definition, they were not to be formal, balanced manuscripts ready for the printer and the public. The Committee found that every manuscript submitted offered significant contributions. In serving the purposes of the Study so well, the contributors necessarily subordinated their individual publication interests to the interests of the central project. This is evidence of unselfish team-play which deserves respect and commendation. The Committee, however, was pleasantly surprised to find an appreciable number of manuscripts so near the publication stage that it could proceed with plans for the prompt publication of a group of monographs in advance of the main report. Dr. Myrdal returned to the United States in March, 1941, and it is hoped that his own report may be released early in 1943.

Patterns of Negro Segregation is the essence extracted from many volumes of manuscript material collected in the field by Dr. Johnson and his staff. While many of the data were assembled in the course of the regular research program of the Department of Social Sciences of Fisk University, their presentation in this form was made at the request of Dr. Myrdal. The material is unique in its geographical coverage, in its scope, and in the fullness and accuracy of its detail. Dr. Johnson is one of the foremost students of race relations and the author of numerous books and articles which have long since won for him the great respect of his contemporaries.

The general *facts* of Negro segregation and discrimination are well known to everyone in the United States, but there is little realization of the great variations in customary interracial practices from one locality to another. In spite of the contrary evidence plentifully available to all who can see or hear, there is a widely accepted assumption that segregational practices are relatively simple and uniform, and that the white people who believe the Negro should be "kept in his place" are in close agreement as to just what that place should be. The divergence from reality of this assumption has long been known to students of race relations, but it has remained for Dr. Johnson to supply the essential documentation and the analysis of American discriminatory customs directed against the Negroes in this country.

Geographical differences in the patterns of segregation and discrimination should not be regarded merely as sociological curiosities; they are important to the individuals who experience them and are a key to the understanding of interracial relations. As though it were not enough for the individual Negro to know that the number of places he may go and the number of things he may do are severely limited by the white man's idea of propriety, whenever he is in an unfamiliar environment he must also be confused by uncertainty concerning the bounds of his confinement. Such uncertainty adds to the problems of personality development, produces behavior which may be mistakenly regarded as a personal affront by some white men, and increases the likelihood of interracial friction. The whole problem of Negro everyday living is involved. The white man too may be disturbed and bewildered by unfamiliar patterns when away from home, although in a much less serious manner. While it is impossible to defend racial segregation in a democracy, it may still be observed without any implication of such defense that human beings seem to prefer a definite and understandable social role to one that is ambiguous, even though that role be one in justice unacceptable. It is not unreasonable to expect that better knowledge will lead to better understanding of Negro-white conflict. Dr. Johnson has clearly demonstrated that specific customary rules governing interracial contacts are essentially symbols of white men's concepts of the relative social status of the two races. Further, he has made an inestimable advance by showing that they are fully as important as symbols as they are as specific prohibitions.

As earlier studies of the American Negro were too prone to gloss over variations in patterns of segregation, so they also tended to assume tacitly that the wide range and the subtlety of the Negro responses to segregation and discrimination could be adequately described in such simple terms as anger, annoyance, resentment and resignation. Indeed, it is not surprising that in a nation dominated by the white man the problem of the Negro's reaction to discrimination should be unconsciously neglected by scholars as well as by laymen. Furthermore, the subject is a delicate one for discussion and pertinent data have not been easy of access. The section of Dr. Johnson's monograph devoted to the specific behavioral adaptations which the Negro makes to specific discriminatory practices belatedly fills some of the gaps in the literature on this most serious problem of race relations in the United States.

SHELBY M. HARRISON
WILLIAM FIELDING OGBURN
DONALD YOUNG, *Chairman*

PREFACE

This book is based, in considerable part, upon the results of a study of social behavior in interracial contact situations in selected areas of the United States. As such, it represents services rendered and information supplied by many persons. To all of these the author acknowledges his deep gratitude.

From a wide range of these services it seems urgent to single out a few individuals for particular mention, not only out of a sense of gratitude, but, in a manner, as an explanation of the methodology of the study itself.

The field staff, so very largely responsible for the intimate interviewing and reporting, consisted of Mr. Lewis Wade Jones, Mr. Harry J. Walker, Mr. Joseph Taylor, Mrs. Edmonia W. Grant and Mrs. Anne DeBerry Johnson. To them belongs the credit for the warm breath of realism in the interviews upon which an important portion of the text relies. Miss Estella H. Scott provided long and meticulous assistance on the examination and analysis of the State laws and judicial decisions. Dr. Bingham Dai, out of a wealth of experience in the psychiatric field, was a stimulating and invaluable aid in the attempt of the author to interpret aspects of behavior of marginal types described in the second part of the text. In the task of classifying a very large volume of field data and racial attitudes as expressed in publications, and in other source documents, the work of Dr. Lewis C. Copeland, Mr. Preston Valien, and Mr. G. Franklin Edwards proved indispensable.

The first text of this study was critically read by Dr. Louis Wirth and Dr. Donald Young, both of whom made suggestions not only of detailed helpfulness, but of structural importance. Chapters were read critically by Dr. Eli S. Marks, Dr. Mark Hanna Watkins, Dr. Addison T. Cutler, and Mr. David Robeson and their suggestions have added to whatever value this volume may have. Dr. Robert E. Park, in this as in other of the author's work, has been a constant and invariably stimulating adviser.

An especial debt of gratitude is acknowledged to Mrs. Eleanor C. Isbell of the Social Science Research Council, who gave a final and painstaking editorial reading of the manuscript before publication. Her contribution was one rich in constructive additions to the text.

From the first stages of the field work to the completion of the text and reading of the proofs, the author has had the consistently efficient and indispensable assistance of Mrs. Bonita H. Valien.

This is more than a note of acknowledgments; it is a formal recognition of the contribution of the responsible persons to a study which is essentially a collaboration.

Always the obscured but vital and concerned partner in such an enterprise is my wife to whose patience, intimate counsel and constructive help in an infinite variety of ways, I am dedicating this volume.

CHARLES S. JOHNSON

Fisk University

INTRODUCTION

Historically, all race conflicts had their origin in the migration of races and the conquest of territories already inhabited by other races. Differences in culture usually provided the basis for a conflict in which the old and stable organization of social life of one people suffered profound disturbance or complete disorganization under the impact of a more dynamic civilization. In more recent times the essence of this impact has been the resistless economic imperialism of Western civilization, seeking raw materials, new markets, and *Lebensraum*.

The atomization of the culture and social organization of a subject race permits temporarily free exploitation of its labor and other resources. Inevitably, however, human and personal relations develop from these contacts and spin themselves into a nonrational web of interaction and interdependence. Political institutions, which follow economic penetration, seek to regulate the relations between the peoples of different cultural levels. This entire social structure derives its power and its prestige from the culture of the dominant race, which, in the meantime, supports its authority by rationalizing that its self-styled racial and cultural superiority afford natural and even divine rights of conquest and domination.

Thus the philosophy of conquest, nurtured in self-interest and reinforced by the accomplishment of physical domination, becomes a vital part of the whole institutional structure supporting the relationships. Subject races may take over the standards, taboos, and other cultural elements of the dominant group, including even the concept of their own inferior status. This, indeed, frequently happens in a slave, or caste, organization of society; and no urgent race problems arise as long as the subject races accept or rationalize their position. The symbols of authority, preserved in the etiquette of race relations and in the conventions, crystallize into customs, which are enforced by informal means.

Such a status quo, however, cannot be maintained indefinitely. The process of acculturation will inevitably cause a disturbance of fixed racial roles; for the influences of penetrating economic, political, and religious forces cannot be isolated; nor can these elements of a dominant culture divorce themselves from others which are bound up in the web of personal relationships. There is no avenue of escape from the social and biological consequences of contact. Mixed-blood populations and culturally marginal peoples emerge. Adoption of the dominant cultural standards and values produces new wants, new aspirations, and new ambitions among the subject peoples.

In modern times these new ambitions have been supported by the philosophy of human equality and freedom which are inherent in the culture of the West, in Christian doctrine, and in the equalitarian sentiments which gave rise to the American and French revolutions. They are likewise reinforced by miscegenation, which detracts from the prestige of the dominant race and produces among individuals in the two castes an interpersonal familiarity which contains the germs of equality. The subject peoples, then, become increasingly sensitive to the disadvantages of their debased position in the social structure, the consciousness of which is but the prelude to overt measures to change and improve their status. The race problem, thus, becomes largely a conflict between the conservative forces, bent upon maintaining the traditional status, and the efforts of the more advanced and self-conscious of the subject peoples to improve their lot. Under some conditions this struggle may take the form of nationalism; under others it may give solidarity and purpose to an active racial or national minority. In either situation the essential dynamics of race relations in a changing civilization are implicit.

The story of the Negro in America is that of a transplanted group, whose original culture has been disintegrated, and which is now in process of cultural assimilation into the American variant of European civilization. The democratic theory of government which obtains in the United States is, in principle, opposed to those racial and cultural assumptions which support the philosophy of imperialism. Markedly analogous and differing only in degree is the conflict of the equalitarian principle with traditional policy in connection with class and sex distinctions. At least three variables are involved in the relations of Negroes to the American institutions: the rate of acculturation and socialization of the Negro element of the population, the dynamics of technological development, and the maturing evaluations of the democratic theory of government and social relations.

This study is concerned with the current sociological aspects of patterns of racial segregation and discrimination with particular reference to the Negro in the United States. In the light of the historical processes noted above, the point of view of the study assumes a developing cultural process. The democratic principle has not yet found full acceptance or expression in the United States. In its initial opportunity, during the post-Revolutionary War period, democracy was deflected from its course by the rise of the planter "aristocracy," which offset even the vibrant, leveling, frontier influence. When the middle class became the custodian of democracy immediately following the Civil War, it ushered in an insistent capitalism which demanded a society no less stratified than the one which it had conquered. Capitalism could be fully realized only if the masses, who were not to share in the larger economic benefits emanating from it, could be pacified in the meantime. The solution was reached by providing the masses with an illusion of superiority in relation to a lower caste, the Negro group, and thus obscuring for a time the undemocratic tendencies of the total pattern of society. It is against this background of class and caste struggle, of a democracy defensive against the economic processes within its framework, that Negro segregation and discrimination must be studied and analyzed.

Segregation involves a process of differentiation and distinction. As a result of natural and social selection operating through free competition and conflict an individual or group in time acquires a habitat, a function in the division of labor, and a position in the social order. By such characteristics individuals or groups are distinguished and set apart. Physical separation of groups with different characteristics—whether accomplished by force, or through sanctions imposed by another group, or by the formation of a self-contained defensive aggregation for protection against unfamiliar ideas and customs, or for escape from ostracism and persecution—achieves the same purpose, that of the isolation of one group from the other.

There can be segregation, supported by the sense and conventions of social distance, without physical separation. This segregation may be self-imposed or imposed from without; it may not carry any invidious connotation; but in the isolation achieved the sense of social distance may be accentuated and reinforced by conceptions developing in each group regarding the other, for isolation and social distance inhibit communication which is basic to insight and understanding.

Social discrimination is "the unequal treatment of equals, either by bestowal of favors or the imposition of burdens." It carries with it the idea of arbitrariness, of unfairness, and of injustice. It involves the inclusion or exclusion of groups or individuals by an infinite number of arbitrary lines of demarcation drawn on the basis of the most varied marks of similarity or dissimilarity. Differential treatment of individuals based upon accepted differences in rank or status is the result of a similar process. This definition is important for this discussion because of the conflict between the theory of democratic institutions, which assumes equality, and the sanctions in the mores supporting and justifying unequal treatment of theoretical equals. Distinctions in law or custom, based solely upon race, which have the effect of imposing an unequal burden of restriction or other disadvantage are discriminatory and, to be understood, must be referred to the underlying schemes of social values prompting the distinctions.

Variations in regional background and organization of economic and social life are reflected in the character of Negro-white relations, in the methods of regulating these relations, in the nature of popular sanctions, and in the active philosophies which give meaning and form to the kind of relations that exist. These differences suggest a broad division between the southern region, in which the race tradition has its firmest rooting in the economic and social life, and the northern and border regions, in which there appear significant modifications of this basic race tradition. In short, the patterns of racial segregation and discrimination appear to vary according to the social and economic factors dominant in each region.

There is a wide range between the degree of acculturation of the "folk Negro" in the culturally isolated plantation areas of the South and the more sophisticated and educated Negro in the urban centers of the South or North. The folkways of the former have developed out of the necessity for individual and group survival. The Negroes of the plantation areas are so economically and socially restricted that the standards and values which give meaning to their behavior and cohesion to their social life evolve from the exigencies of their relative insecurity and do not necessarily represent the values and standards of the dominant group. In the urban areas the closer exposure to the material culture, traditions, ideas, and social habits of the dominant group and the more extensive participation in institutional and social life have accomplished a fuller measure of assimilation of the Negro. At the same time his anxiety concerning his status has been enhanced, since his expectations and aspirations have been enlarged and heightened by the knowledge that his society professes to embrace the democratic ideal. Between these two extremes of the Negro population are several cultural, social, and economic groups all of which are retarded by relatively low economic status and potentialities. Their consequent illiteracy, isolation, and lack of communication slacken the flow of culture and help to crystallize the most unfavorable marks of race. In all these groups acceptance by the dominant race on certain levels and rejection on others give rise to certain inhibitions and frustrations, which in turn promote insecurity and social maladjustment. When subject peoples identify their status and destiny with the inescapable fact of their race they become race conscious and take on the characteristics of a minority group.

It is important to keep in mind that the white population of America is by no means a homogeneous group. Social and cultural distinctions of a significant character stratify this population, and the divisions suggest the differential value of these groups as culture bearers. A wide gulf separates the urbane and cosmopolitan New Yorker from the wan and desolate relics of Western culture isolated in the mountains of Tennessee or the swampy marshes of Louisiana.

The culture of the South is perhaps less complex than that of New York, but it is complex nevertheless; and this may be attributed in large part to the diverse populations whose interactions have been responsible for the loss of some traits and the revamping of others, until there has emerged in the process something we call American, and southern. It is not English, nor Spanish, nor French, nor East European; nor is it distinctively representative of any of the peoples who settled America. Even in areas where there is a predominant concentration of one nationality group or another, the distinctive nationality traits which survive for a time are always changing. Maximum cultural lag and the survival of archaic traits with a minimum of change occur only in isolation so complete that a group of people is able to continue its behavior patterns indefinitely without influence from the outside. It is possible to study culture survivals in these isolated areas, as has been done in investigations of Appalachian mountaineers.

One element that distinguishes the South in its culture, philosophy, and population characteristics from other sections of the country is the presence of the Negro and his historical relationship to the white population. The significant fact about the distinguishable Negro culture is that it was developed out of the conditions of life found in America; but quite apart from the cultural specializations developed by the group in the simple struggle for survival, the presence and role of the Negro in the South have influenced in a pronounced degree the behavior, the thought forms, the philosophy and ideology, the political concepts, the sum of knowledge, the personal habits, the temperament, the morals and manners of the people of the South. This fact has great importance in any attempt to study the phenomena of Negro-white relations.

The Negro and slavery were largely responsible for the creation of the planter class which became the symbol of southern "aristocracy" and the center of a feudal social economy. Just as the Negro, slavery, and the plantation created the planter, they also helped to create the poor white. In the very nature of the plantation structure no white workers were needed. What was needed, or thought to be needed, was forced rather than free labor. As a consequence the non-propertied whites were pushed off to the barren hills to nurse their bitter resentments and to impoverish such cultural heritage as they had brought from Europe. These distinct social categories of the white population have responded differently to the presence of Negroes in the economy of the region; and these responses are a vital aspect of the complex structure of race relations.

There is a further consequence of this racial symbiosis, which is related to recent problems of the region and the nation. Just as the restriction of free competition in the ideological context of race and slavery contributed to the creation of the planters and the poor whites, historically, it created tenancy as a fixed status instead of the ladder to a free status of ownership; and this blight is upon the South today. Beginning with the assumption that southern tenancy was a necessary transition from the plantation under slavery to free labor in an economy of open resources, providing valuable discipline for the Negroes in their long process of assimilation, this category of agricultural labor took on the cultural characteristics of the Negroes' fixed role, and eventually drew into this status more whites than Negroes. Today nearly 60 per cent of the producers in agriculture in the South are tenants and sharecroppers. Where once practically all of them were Negroes, today over a million families are white and about seven hundred thousand are Negro.

There is little thinking in the South which the Negro does not in some way influence. Indeed, so profound is this influence that it shapes reactions on practically every social and political issue. Sometimes this influence appears in conscious thought, as, for example, when the retention of the poll tax is defended as a barrier to Negro participation in government; sometimes original motivations are forgotten but remain implicit in popular thinking and administrative planning on such subjects as education, labor legislation, and child labor. The conservatism, vague apprehensions, and feelings of insecurity engendered by such a setting inevitably limit the quality, character, and influence of social movements. It is, thus, not at all strange that the section should present a defensive emotional solidarity on many issues, and set itself indignantly and righteously against the rest of the nation.

Against this background of diverse cultural values, the study of the history and sociological implications of racial segregation and discrimination is divided into two parts. Part I deals with three aspects of the phenomena under consideration. It treats customs as codes and rules of conduct which become embedded in the conventions and the established racial etiquette, the unspoken imperatives of tradition, and the social institutions which define, for all practical purposes, the respective spheres of the two groups and the social mechanisms by which these spheres are kept inviolable. It deals, secondly, with the attempts to regulate race contacts and relations by legislation. Thirdly, it considers the definition of Negro status inherent in the racial orthodoxies, taboos, and stereotypes, and the interpretations of personal experiences and sentiments which combine to fashion the basic social attitudes and reactions of the members of the white society in their relations with members of the Negro group.

In Part II an attempt is made to describe and interpret the behavioral responses of Negroes to segregation and discrimination, their personal behavior in varying types of interpersonal relations with whites, and some of the psychopathological phenomena resulting from the efforts of Negroes to make satisfactory individual and racial adjustments.

This study is based in large part upon special investigations in selected areas in the United States which represent, according to their structure, organization, and traditions, different stresses and facets of the American biracial system.

The areas selected for intensive study were as follows:

The Rural South
Bolivar County, Mississippi
Poinsett County, Arkansas
Johnston County, North Carolina

The Urban South
Nashville, Tennessee
Richmond, Virginia
Birmingham, Alabama

Atlanta, Georgia
Houston, Texas

The Border Area

Baltimore, Maryland
Indianapolis, Indiana

The Urban North

Chicago, Illinois
New York, New York

In each of these areas systematic inquiry was made on a wide variety of social institutions. Personal experiences and racial attitudes of Negroes of recognizably different social and economic classes were secured through intensive interviewing, and were observed objectively in both normal and crisis situations. Attitudes of white persons were drawn from interviews and behavior observed in racial situations in cities from Maine to Arkansas.

The assembling and analysis of these materials has made possible a consideration of the exclusion of Negroes from group participation on the basis of race in so far as this factor can be isolated from other social and economic influences on the order of life to which Negroes in America belong.

Part I

PATTERNS OF RACIAL SEGREGATION AND DISCRIMINATION

Chapter I

SPATIAL AND INSTITUTIONAL FORMS OF RACIAL SEGREGATION

The most elementary form of racial segregation is the reservation, or preserve, which in American history is associated with the development of the frontier. This form may be distinguished from that involved in the more complex social processes observed in the spatial distribution of urban populations which, in the growing community, is occasioned by the inevitable division of labor. Both forms of segregation are based upon difference. The basis of the difference in the first instance is in respect to kind, and in the second, in respect to function.

Incompatibility of groups, whatever the cause, is a basis for segregation. The most familiar type of inharmonious contact leading to segregation is found in the relations between a dominant and a subordinate group competing as groups rather than as individuals within the same area. Examples of this appear at one stage or another in every instance of the association of alien groups. Culture, religion, and physical characteristics all play an important part in defining the group relations. The Indian reservations in North America, the kampongs of Java, the compounds of South Africa, the Jewish ghettos of Europe, the Chinatowns and "Little Italys" and "Black Belts" of the United States are all expressions of the social or racial policy of the dominant society.

Segregation may be described as a form of partial ostracism. The ostensible purpose of this ostracism may be the protection of one group or the other from the consequences of contiguity and physical contacts, or the artificial limitation of economic competition, or the isolation for whatever reasons, religious or personal, of the social worlds of the groups in contact. In a fluid and unstable society such as that of the United States segregation may be, for a period at least, a partial substitute for caste.

There are forms of segregation or group isolation which are

3

self-imposed. The purpose of such self-segregation may be to protect the group from the infection of strange or incompatible ideas and customs, or to achieve freedom in the exercise of some social functions, as in the case of a religious cult. Where there is no external compulsion, the limits and duration of the segregation can be regulated by the group itself, and no invidious distinctions of the segregated group need be implied.

A segregated immigrant community may perform the function of a cultural enclave in which the immigrant is at home and in which assimilation to the larger culture proceeds slowly. When cultural assimilation is achieved, the individual is less at home in this "cultural island" and in a generation or two may be lost in the larger society. This is the history of the European immigrant in the United States. But assimilation among the various racial and national groups in America proceeds at an unequal rate; and this diversity is due largely to differences in the culture and economic status of the groups and to the interest of the dominant or minority group in maintaining these distinctions. In the case of the white and Negro populations of the United States, the patterns of racial segregation and the intensity of the supporting sanctions vary markedly in different regions, in response to population ratios, and according to the historical and cultural backgrounds of the groups involved.

It is obvious that the policy of segregation which the American system of values proposes, merely to separate and to maintain two distinct but substantially equal worlds, is a difficult ideal to achieve. Any limitation of free competition inevitably imposes unequal burdens and confers unequal advantages. Thus, segregation or any other distinction that is imposed from without almost invariably involves some element of social discrimination as we have defined it. Residential segregation enforced by law is an obvious instance.

It is not enough for the purpose of the present study, however, to limit the concept of segregation merely to physical or spatial separation. Occupational segregation can be just as effective in maintaining an invidious distinction, but the separation is not necessarily spatial. So it is with many other types of relationship having the effect of restricting or qualifying communication between groups in contact. In order to distinguish and analyze certain less obvious aspects of the policy and practice of racial segregation in the United States, the term "segregation," as here used, includes all conventions and social ritual designed to enforce social isolation and social distance, and for this reason embedded in racial traditions.

The most distinct and clearly defined racial segregation is in the

South. Bound as it is by its static economy and its racial traditions and ideologies, it presents an environment which resists, with a considerable expenditure of human energy, the incorporation of the Negro population into the total life of the area. In the early years of the present century an experienced and discerning journalist from the Middle West traveled over portions of the southern and northern states for the purpose of recording, as objectively as possible, "the exact present conditions and relationships of the Negro in American life."[1] This was a period slightly more than a generation removed from the abolition of slavery and Reconstruction in the South. The older patterns of race relations, rooted in slavery and temporarily disturbed by the collapse of the formal structure of the institution, were apparently being restored and maintained with increased vigor. This is substantiated by Bertram Doyle who notes, in discussing the restoration of the etiquette of slavery in the South, that in a given locality both whites and Negroes have discovered and continue to observe the forms expected.[2] This appears to be the easiest adjustment making for tolerable relations. At the time of Baker's visit every southern state had enacted legislation requiring physical separation of the races in public and private institutions. Economic competition between the Negro and the emerging white worker, who was supported by the ballot, was acute in the cities. Atlanta, the most prosperous and promising of the cities of the "New South," had just experienced a most disastrous race riot which unquestionably had its roots in the economic competition of white and Negro workers. A new brand of politician had emerged from the ranks of the poor whites, long submerged by the planter-slave domination of the cotton kingdom; and these leaders were stimulating the emotions of the masses with bitter eloquence of speech with reference to a threatened "white supremacy." There was an outburst of overt conflict in the form of lynching. The average number of Negroes lynched each year in the first decade of this century was 115, with two peak years of 155.[3] The ties between master and slave, which in numerous individual cases had persisted for nearly a generation after the collapse of slavery, were rapidly disintegrating under the new order, without a reassuring remedy or substitute.

There had been no great migrations to the North, but a steady

[1] Ray Stannard Baker, *Following the Color Line* (New York: Doubleday, Page and Company, 1908).

[2] Bertram W. Doyle, *The Etiquette of Race Relations in the South* (Chicago: University of Chicago Press, 1937), p. 156.

[3] Arthur Raper, *The Tragedy of Lynching* (Chapel Hill: University of North Carolina Press, 1933), p. 480.

small stream of migrants out of the South to the larger cities. Although the Negro population in these northern cities was negligible when compared with the population in the South, these migrants found themselves inexorably pressed together in more and more exclusively Negro blocks and residence areas. They found better wages but also higher living costs. In contrast to the positive opinion of virtually every white man in the South the average white man in the North knew little, and cared less, about the Negro and rarely, if ever, discussed him. There was little professed segregation, but a subtle and persistent discrimination in practically all areas of life and particularly in the economic sphere.

There have been important changes over the past forty years in the basic economy and also in the cultural life of the people in all sections of the country. The changes have affected the Negro as well as the other elements of the population. The broad structure of race relations, with its separate social categories, is deep-set in the mores and has changed more slowly than other conventional social practices. Within the framework and policy of racial segregation are wide variations in local practice. In fact, the items of behavior demanded of Negroes and of whites in relation to Negroes, in order to conform to the conventions, have become so complex that it is difficult at times to follow them. This very complexity and uncertainty have become, for the Negro in particular, abundant sources of confusion and discontent. It is what a Negro traveler, Albon L. Holsey, had in mind when he described himself as "zig-zagging through the South."

Those states lying between the southern and northern states, and referred to as border states, play an interesting role in the realm of race relations. There are to be found many of the traits of the racially "solid South" and at the same time many of the practices of the northern states which violate the southern racial conventions and taboos. While practicing both segregation and nonsegregation, these areas are usually most explicit in labeling the segregation where it does exist. It is in these areas that attempts to reinforce custom with legal support have been most frequent, as, for example, in the matter of separate residential areas and a different scale of salaries for white and Negro teachers.

Since the border cities vary among themselves almost as widely as their practices vary internally, it is difficult to describe a fixed pattern. There are cities in this area with more and with less pronounced traditions and ideologies. The patterns of segregation and discrimination represented here, however, are typical of this marginal area. In Baltimore and Washington, D.C., for example, there is more rigid segregation and rejection of Negro patronage in the large department stores than anywhere in the South. In Washington the theaters are completely segregated. No Negroes, except those who pass as whites, can attend the theaters used by whites in the nation's capital. More of the government offices separate Negro workers and exclude them from the restaurant concessions in the buildings than accept them. There have been more changes in this practice since the beginning of the New Deal government under President Roosevelt than had occurred over a full generation before. There is segregation in the public schools, but none in local transportation, nor in the use of libraries, public buildings, and parks.

In such a border area, in which the institutional forces are so largely arbitrary and the total pattern of segregation so often broken by both planned and unplanned exigencies, the web of racial custom is confused and confusing. It is frequently necessary to be more explicit regarding segregative intent than in the South. Baltimore is one of the cities in which an attempt was made to effect complete residential segregation by race, only to have the law declared unconstitutional by the Supreme Court. Such a law is unnecessary in the South because the end is served by the fixed racial etiquette, as well as by the economic limitations of the Negro people.

In the northern cities there is no legalized and little overt racial segregation on a formal basis. In fact, however, there is considerable segregation and discrimination in this region.

If we attempted to classify institutions by degree of physical and spatial racial segregation, they would range themselves along a continuum, from those institutions in which complete segregation is supported by custom and prescribed by law to those institutions without differential treatment.

The most conspicuous forms of racial segregation are (1) in residential areas, (2) in educational, recreational, and other public institutions, (3) in quasi-public institutions or privately operated institutions under public control, such as railroads, steamship lines, streetcar and bus systems, and hospitals, (4) in private business establishments, such as hotels and restaurants under customary or legal mandate to prevent racial contact on a level implying social equality or permitting social intimacy, (5) in other private commercial and professional services, such as department stores, undertaking establishments, and doctors' offices.

RESIDENTIAL SEGREGATION

The racial segregation in residential areas provides the basic structure for other forms of institutional segregation. It is a result of social and economic selection, of the direct operation of racial sanctions, and of the internal pull and cohesion of a community, and bears a significant relationship to those impersonal forces operating in the growth of the city. Wherever there are Negroes in any appreciable numbers, in rural or urban areas, some form and degree of concentration of this population can be observed. The patterns of separation vary considerably as to details, but these may be reduced to a few general types.

The Rural South

Small Negro dwellings are scattered over the open country of the South, sometimes widely separated on plantations and at times grouped. Since most of the rural families are tenant families, and in the plantation areas most of the tenants are Negroes, the problem of segregation arises only where white families of approximately the same economic class are introduced. Most often the white and Negro families are grouped separately. Following the older pattern of the plantation, it is no violation of the principle of racial segregation if the home of a white planter, overseer, or commissary owner is surrounded by Negro dwellings. Where there are Negro owners they are most often found in small communities.

The Small Town

The small towns in the South show a more definite clustering of the Negro population. A good example is Laurens, South Carolina, one of the areas included in this study. The Negro residential communities in the township of Laurens appear to represent a semivoluntary isolation for a more satisfying and secure community life. One of the smaller neighborhoods, called "Possum Hollow," is significant because for more than half a century the Negro school has been located there. This little neighborhood, wedged closely between white districts, also contains two of the larger Negro churches. The new Negro high school, however, is located east of the business center and just beyond a paved street on which white people live.

A Negro neighborhood called "The 400" was once important because an academy maintained by the Baptist church was located there. The academy building has been repaired and is now used by an NYA housekeepers' training project. Another Negro neighborhood, "Stump Town," is composed of a small cluster of houses apparently isolated from the rest of the town.

It is an interesting fact that practically all the Negro neighborhoods in the small towns are located on the edge of town. There are usually no white residential areas beyond them. They are separated from one another by intervening white neighborhoods which have paved streets, street lights, water and sewerage connections which seldom reach the Negro residential areas. These areas, unlike those in the larger cities, are not "inherited" from white residents who have moved on to better areas, but were developed as Negro residential areas, or "quarters."

It is not uncommon in these small towns to find a block in the older and less desirable part of the main street, or on a side street, turned over entirely to Negroes for their small businesses and service establishments. The restaurant or barbecue stand, pressing shop, pool hall, barbershop, and similar services are located here.

The Back-yard Residence Pattern

A somewhat unique pattern is found in Charleston, South Carolina. The Negro population is scattered fairly uniformly throughout the city. Under an old custom, dating back to an early period in the history of this once aristocratic city, the homes of Negroes were located in the back yards of the wealthy white families. In more recent years there are larger proportions of whites who are not wealthy enough to have servants and larger numbers of Negroes who are above the servant level. The accommodation to racial proximity has persisted, and Negroes live in any section of town in which they can secure a dwelling, whether on the street or in the rear of a dwelling; and living in the rear carries no obligation to the white owner other than the rent. Frequently both front and rear houses are owned by persons other than the occupants.

The Isolated Community

In a few of the cities of the South there is a concentration of the Negro population which approaches complete segregation. The separation may be marked by a railroad track, stream, or other fixed barrier. Examples of this type of segregation are found in Tulsa, Oklahoma, and in Durham, North Carolina. Although both of these cities have active Negro communities with thriving businesses, they have the disadvantage of isolation from municipal improvement and protection. During the race riot in Tulsa, for example, a large portion of the Negro area was burned by mobs. In Springfield,

Illinois, however, where a similar incident occurred, the burning of Negro homes endangered the whites and was stopped by other white citizens. Durham has some of the best and some of the worst Negro dwellings in the South located on one long paved street, which is the main thoroughfare for Negroes.

The Urban Clusters

Most of the cities of the South contain at least one large Negro neighborhood with smaller clusters scattered about the city. Thus 75 per cent of the 43,000 Negroes in Nashville in 1930 resided in nine of the city's twenty-seven wards, in six of which they constituted over half the total population. Nevertheless, Negroes are found in all wards in Nashville. The same is true of Atlanta, but in this case Negroes are in the majority in only two wards, which contain two-thirds of the 90,000 Negroes in the city. The pattern of residential distribution is similar in other southern and border cities, but in northern cities the concentration is more intense and the dispersion less extensive.

Generally considered, the core residential sites of Negroes will almost certainly be found near the centers of cities in the oldest residence areas, where buildings are out of date, depreciated, difficult to keep in repair, and practically impossible to purchase because the area has only a limited residence value. The land, on the other hand, is potentially valuable for business, its tax rate is high, and its value usually beyond a figure convenient to the economic class which occupies the buildings. It is impracticable for investors to build new houses in the area, or to repair those already there, or to do anything that will increase the cost of maintaining them until the maturity of values. Rentals tend to increase when Negroes move in, as the last class to occupy an area; being less desirable than a white group of somewhat lower economic status, they are expected to pay more for the privilege of occupancy. This mass feature, in which there is a confusion of racial and economic factors, contributes to many of the problems of congestion, deterioration, health, and morals which are involved in the situation.

In the South the location of many Negro homes near places of employment (as domestics) has established a large degree of tolerance of Negro neighbors, and it is frequently possible for Negroes to purchase and improve property. Moreover, in many cities of the South Negroes have preceded white populations in sites desired as new developments and, owning property, have remained as these sites developed.

Border and Northern Patterns

In the border area one finds an uncertain mixture of traditions of both North and South, although there is a general attitude which requires the separation of the two races in residential areas. In Washington, D.C., while the Negro population is not huddled into one specific geographical area, there are many instances in which white people are found occupying one side of the street and Negroes the other.[4]

In northern cities the Negro population was a negligible factor prior to the large migrations from the South. Economically hard pressed, Negroes lived in sites abandoned by early white residents, along with or in close succession to other racial groups of similar or slightly higher economic status. With the sudden influx of new-comers and the overrunning of areas gradually associated with Negroes, reaction to expansion was acute. In many instances racial factors were given an importance much out of proportion to their actual place in the evolution of the properties in question. The Chicago race riot had as one of its aggravating causes this feature of the housing problem. Other cities have had similar if somewhat less violent experiences.

Although most cities contain an area in which the Negro population is so concentrated as to be regarded as the "Black Belt," there are few cities in which there is a concentration approaching complete segregation. In Chicago there are Negroes in 63 of the 75 community areas, but in only three did Negroes compose more than 75 per cent of the population in 1930. In the Black Belt they composed 91 per cent of the total population in 1934. In Richmond, at the time of Woofter's study, 53 per cent of the white people were in concentrated white areas and 25 per cent of the Negroes in concentrated Negro areas.[5]

In Dayton, Ohio, residential areas in which Negroes live are increasingly all-Negro. One Negro resident stated that when he came to the city twenty years ago there was only one other Negro in his block. Now the entire area is Negro. Restriction compacts were written into deeds in most of the better residential areas.

Acquiring of residence sites by new groups of imputed inferior status has been observed to follow a pattern described by Dr. Burgess as (1) *invasion*, beginning often as an unnoticed or general pene-

[4] William H. Jones, *Housing of Negroes in Washington, D.C.* (Washington: Howard University Press, 1929).

[5] T. J. Woofter, Jr. and Associates, *Negro Problems in Cities* (Garden City, New York: Doubleday, Doran and Company, 1928), p. 38.

tration, followed by (2) *reaction*, either the resistance, mild or violent, of the inhabitants of the community or the resistance resulting in (3) the *influx* of the newcomers and the rapid abandonment of the area by the old-time residents, and (4) *climax*, or the achievement of a new equilibrium of communal stability. In the case of Negroes this process is pronounced in the North.

It appears that there is on the whole greater concentration of the Negro population in the northern and border cities than in the cities of the South. In the main it can be said that cities have different types and degrees of segregation, determined by Negro-white population ratios, distribution of Negro employment, growth of the city, availability of low-priced properties, and local attitudes toward segregation.

SEGREGATION AND DISCRIMINATION IN EDUCATIONAL INSTITUTIONS

The most complete system of racial segregation appears in the schools. In fact, the school policy regarding racial separation is perhaps the most obvious index to the racial "climate" of a region. Seventeen southern states have separate school systems. In such border states as Indiana, Missouri, and Maryland, and the southern portions of Illinois and New Jersey, the policy is varied and uncertain. In the northern states there is no policy of racial segregation, but the residential segregation of the Negro population frequently achieves a corresponding racial separation. Racial separation in respect to the schools ranges from total and complete racial segregation, accompanied in the southern rural areas by systematic discrimination, to policies in certain northern metropolitan centers, in accordance with which Negro pupils and teachers alike are distributed without regard to race.

Schools in the South

The principle of racial separation in the schools, required by law in all southern states, affects both public and private schools at all levels. Not only are separate buildings and teaching staffs provided, but both Negro pupils and teachers are excluded generally from access to the equipment used by the white children and white teaching staff. There is no pretense of a unitary system since the Negro teachers have little or no contact with the white teachers or administrative officials.

This dual system, far from supporting separate but autonomous units, has the effect of a dominant system and a wardship, for Negro parents have little voice in determining or administering school policies for their children. The Negro school public is impotent, without authority and without responsibility. The situation fosters inefficiency and even graft. Parents and pupils lose interest in schooling and, as a matter of fact, are uncertain as to the values to be achieved. With but few exceptions the Negro children receive inferior units as their share in the system. The Negro teaching staff is discriminated against in pay, in provisions for advancement, and in equipment. The administrative authority is dichotomized and responsibility so placed that when white officials will not act the Negro administrators are restricted and cannot act.

Discrimination with respect to public educational advantages is greatly facilitated by racial segregation. Such discrimination arises chiefly in administration of the public-school laws, although a few states have enacted statutory discriminations against Negroes in the form of differential salary schedules for Negro and white teachers and in the provision of "out-of-state tuition scholarships" for Negro students. However, whether administrative or statutory, discrimination in education may be classified under two main categories: (1) an unequal allotment or division of public funds; (2) the denial to Negroes of certain facilities. For both of these categories adequate documentation as to discrimination can be adduced.

Public funds for educational purposes are furnished by federal, state, county, and municipal governments. Federal aid to state educational programs began in 1862 with the First Morrill Act; and the increasing interest of the federal government in this direction is indicated by the increase in funds allotted to seventeen southern states, from approximately five million dollars in 1922-23 to ten million in 1934-35 and sixteen million in 1935-36. The history of the distribution of these funds in the southern states has been one of almost continuous discrimination against Negroes. In the seventeen states receiving sixteen million dollars for Negro and white land-grant colleges in 1935-36 Negroes constituted 25 per cent of the total population between the ages of 18 and 21 inclusive; yet they received only 5.4 per cent of the total federal allotments.[6] Only one group of federal land-grant college funds was divided between Negro and white institutions in an equitable manner; these were funds authorized by the Morrill-Nelson and Bankhead-Jones acts, the only federal education laws which require a "just and equitable" division of funds between racial groups in separate schools.

The differences between what Negroes would have received if

[6] U. S. Senate Committee on Education and Labor, *Hearings on Federal Aid to Education Act of 1939* (S. 1305), March, 1939, pp. 204-209.

funds had been apportioned on the basis of population and what Negroes actually did receive in federal funds for vocational education in southern schools of less than college grade, from 1928 to 1935, ranged from $13,800 in West Virginia to $809,000 in Mississippi.[7] Oklahoma gave Negroes $9,000 more than they would have received on the basis of population apportionment and was unique in this respect. On the basis of their population, Negroes should have received $5,018,824 of the funds allocated to all the states. They actually received $1,926,682, the difference of $3,092,142 being diverted to white schools.

The distribution of state funds is, perhaps, even more discriminatory. Computed on the basis of current expenses, the annual cost per Negro pupil in average daily attendance in ten states during 1935-36 was $17.04; the cost per white pupil in the same states and year was $49.30. As can be seen from Table I, the range in cost per Negro pupil was from $8.75 in Georgia to $69.96 in Missouri; in cost per white pupil, from $28.66 in Arkansas to $78.23 in Maryland.

TABLE I

COST PER NEGRO AND WHITE PUPIL IN AVERAGE
DAILY ATTENDANCE, BASED ON CURRENT EX-
PENSES, TEN STATES, 1935–1936*

State	Negro	White
Missouri	$69.96	$59.78
Maryland	59.52	78.23
Oklahoma	50.32	42.78
Florida	22.83	64.82
North Carolina	16.77	36.25
Alabama	10.90	37.64
Arkansas	10.77	28.66
South Carolina	10.63	48.00
Mississippi	9.30	44.65
Georgia	8.75	42.53

* Statistics of the Education of Negroes, 1933–34 and 1935–36,
U.S. Office of Education Bulletin 1938, No. 13, p. 15.

Differences in per capita expenditures for Negro and white children take on added significance when related to the basic economy of southern areas. It is possible to present a summary statement of these differences for 1,104 southern counties grouped according to their dominant economic characteristics.[8] There are, for example, 551 cotton counties in most of which the plantation system has played a role. In 1930 the median expenditure for Negro teachers' salaries (the major expenditure for Negro education) in the cotton counties

[7] Ibid., p. 209.
[8] Charles S. Johnson and others, Statistical Atlas of Southern Counties (Chapel Hill: University of North Carolina Press, 1940).

was slightly over half that in other farm counties and about two-fifths that in metropolitan counties. Only 38 of the 551 cotton counties spent more than $15 per Negro pupil, and only 38 cotton counties spent less than $15 per white pupil.[9]

In cotton counties the median percentage of Negro to white per capita expenditure was 28; in other farm counties it was 47; in metropolitan counties, 46. In 39 cotton counties and 4 noncotton counties expenditures per Negro pupil were less than 10 per cent of those per white pupil; and in only 17 cotton counties were expenditures per Negro pupil over 70 per cent of those per white pupil. Outside the cotton counties the differential was somewhat less. In 26 per cent of the other farm counties the amount spent per Negro pupil was more than 70 per cent of that spent per white. The differentials are greatest where the Negro population comprises a relatively large proportion of the total.

Discriminatory allocation of public funds for education has its counterpart in actual diversion of funds earmarked for Negro schools. Raper points out that of $15,000 appropriated to the Greene County Board of Education by the Georgia state legislature for Negro children in 1928, about half was diverted to the white schools. In 1933 Greene County Negro schools received only $5,000 of the $21,000 appropriated for them. A similar situation obtained also in Macon County, Georgia.[10]

Discrimination in the allocation and diversion of public funds for education is necessarily reflected in differential salaries for white and Negro teachers. The average annual salary of teachers in Negro schools in 17 southern states during 1935-36 was $510 compared with $833 for teachers in white schools in the same states and year. Average annual salaries of teachers, principals, and supervisors in white and Negro schools in 1937-38 are available for 12 states. As shown in Table II, the average Negro salary ranged from $215 in Mississippi to $1,458 in Delaware, while the average white salary ranged from $620 in Arkansas to $1,650 in Delaware. It is significant and hardly fortuitous that in every state listed there was a differential in favor of white teachers, although in widely varying degree.

It should not be inferred that the unlisted states which have separate schools do not have wide differentials between salaries of white and Negro teachers. Tennessee and Kentucky may be taken as examples. For the scholastic year ending June, 1940, white male teach-

[9] *Ibid.*, pp. 24-25.
[10] Arthur Raper, *Preface to Peasantry* (Chapel Hill: University of North Carolina Press, 1936), pp. 310-311.

TABLE II

AVERAGE ANNUAL SALARIES OF WHITE AND NEGRO
TEACHERS, PRINCIPALS, AND SUPERVISORS, TWELVE
STATES, 1937–38*

State	White	Negro
Alabama	$ 827	$ 393
Arkansas	620	367
Delaware	1,650	1,458
Florida	1,146	542
Georgia	876	352
Louisiana	1,165	499
Maryland	1,623	1,308
Mississippi	630	215
North Carolina	984	674
Oklahoma	1,039	891
South Carolina	943	373
Virginia	1,025	558

* D. T. Blose and H. F. Alves, *Biennial Survey of Education in the U. S., Statistics of State School Systems, 1937–38*, U.S. Office of Education Bulletin 1940, No. 2, p. 137.

ers in county elementary schools in Tennessee received an average monthly salary of $83 as compared with $54 for Negro male teachers in the same type of school. In city elementary schools white male teachers received an average monthly salary of $130 as compared with $58 for Negro male teachers. Table III summarizes the situation for different types of schools in Tennessee.

TABLE III

AVERAGE MONTHLY SALARIES OF TEACHERS IN TENNESSEE SCHOOLS BY COLOR
AND SEX, 1939–40*

Type of School	White		Colored		All
	Males	Females	Males	Females	
County:					
Elementary	$ 82.86	$ 77.27	$ 53.96	$64.95	$77.14
High school	127.61	98.35	87.77	73.66	..
City:					
Elementary	129.89	92.81	58.42	64.06	92.28
High school	154.44	119.48	104.80	92.40	..

* State of Tennessee, *Annual Report of the Department of Education for the Scholastic Year Ending June 30, 1940*, pp. 126–127 and 170–171.

The situation in Kentucky has a somewhat different setting from that found in the other states having separate school systems. The Kentucky state constitution provides that there shall be no distinction in the distribution of school funds between the races; and the statutes provide that school districts shall pay teachers according to a schedule taking account of training, quality of service, experience, and other items approved by the State Board of Education.[11] In practice, however, the constitutional and statutory provisions are not followed. This is more apparent in the case of elementary-school teachers than high-school teachers and more apparent for elementary teachers in independent (urban) school districts than for teachers in county (rural) school districts. In the elementary schools in independent districts, for example, the average annual salary of 1,610 white teachers with an average of 101.33 semester hours of college training and 9.37 years of experience was $1,063, while that of 430 Negro teachers with about one-half year less of college training on the average and 1.35 years more of experience was $881, approximately 83 per cent as much.[12] The estimated salary discrimination in individual districts ranged from 5 to 59 per cent.[13] In districts where differential salary scales were found, superintendents were asked to indicate the reason. The answers generally represented merely the individual superintendents' personal opinions; but the majority gave difference in cost of living as their reason, while a few specified quality of service, public sentiment, and expediency.[14]

Absolute or partial denial to Negroes of many of the facilities afforded to whites is another result of discrimination in the allocation of public education funds. School transportation constitutes a notable example. In 1935-36, 48 per cent of the total number of pupils enrolled in public schools in South Carolina were Negroes; but they received only $3,642, or less than ½ of 1 per cent, of the $860,379 spent for transportation of pupils in that state.[15] Table IV shows the situation in nine states which reported the amount spent for transportation of Negro pupils in 1935-36. It can be seen that in only two states, Missouri and Oklahoma, do Negro pupils receive a proportion of public-school transportation expenditures approximating their proportion of the total public-school enrollment; and it is worth noting that the pattern of race relations in these two states

[11] Leonard E. Meece, *Negro Education in Kentucky* (Lexington: Bulletin of the Bureau of School Service, College of Education, University of Kentucky, 1938), pp. 103-104.

[12] *Ibid.*, pp. 110-111.

[13] *Ibid.*, p. 118.

[14] *Ibid.*, pp. 120-126.

[15] David T. Blose and Ambrose Caliver, *Statistics of the Education of Negroes, 1933-34 and 1935-36*, U.S. Office of Education Bulletin 1938, No. 13, pp. 26, 57; David T. Blose and Henry F. Alves, *Statistics of State School Systems, 1935-36*, U.S. Office of Education Bulletin 1937, No. 2, pp. 92-93 (advance pages).

TABLE IV

PERCENTAGE NEGRO OF TOTAL SCHOOL ENROLLMENT, AND
PERCENTAGE SPENT FOR NEGROES OF TOTAL TRANSPORTA-
TION EXPENDITURES, NINE STATES, 1935-36*

State	Percentage Negro of total enrollment	Percentage spent for Negro pupils of total transportation expenditures
Alabama........	35.1	1.7
Arkansas........	26.8	2.2
Florida.........	31.1	1.5
Georgia.........	38.3	0.5
Maryland.......	16.9	6.8
Missouri........	5.8	5.1
North Carolina...	30.9	3.5
Oklahoma.......	7.7	8.8
South Carolina....	48.5	0.4

* Blose and Caliver, *loc. cit.*; Blose and Alves, *Statistics of State School Systems, loc. cit.*

diverges significantly from that generally found in the southern states.

Denial of facilities extends in some instances to actual failure to provide basic instructional units. This is most clearly seen in the lack of high schools for Negro pupils in counties where Negroes constitute a substantial proportion of the total population. In 13 states having separate schools for Negroes there were 87 counties in 1938-39 which had no high school for Negroes, although Negroes constituted 12 per cent or more of the total population of each of these counties in 1940.[16] In 14 such counties Negroes constituted over 50 per cent of the total population and in 40 counties they constituted from 26 per cent to 50 per cent of the total population. Out of a total of 45,669 Negroes of high-school age living in these 87 counties, according to the United States Office of Education, four-fifths lived in counties where Negroes comprised 26 per cent or more of the total population.

Partial denial of high-school instruction is seen in those counties which provide high schools for Negroes but do not provide four-year courses in any such school within the county. In 12 states having separate schools for Negroes there were 115 counties in 1938-39 which fell in this class,[17] although Negroes comprised at least 12 per cent of the total population of each county. In 31 of these counties Negroes comprised over 50 per cent of the total population, and in 49 counties they comprised from 26 to 50 per cent. According to the

[16] Ambrose Caliver, "Secondary Schools for Negroes," *School Life*, 25:380 (July, 1940).
[17] *Ibid.*

United States Office of Education, there were 101,633 Negroes of high-school age in the 115 counties, more than 85 per cent living in counties where Negroes comprised at least 26 per cent of the total population.

In the light of this situation there appears to be substantial support for the contention that a large proportion of the Negroes of high-school age who are not in school are in that category because of the lack of high-school facilities in the counties where they live.

The situation with respect to graduate-study facilities for Negroes has received much attention in recent years because of a series of court actions brought on behalf of individual Negro students desiring training offered for whites but not offered for Negroes. Until relatively recent years the southern states had made no provisions for graduate or professional training for Negroes. Agitation by Negroes led to the adoption of "out-of-state tuition scholarships," widely varying in adequacy, purporting to enable Negro students in these states to attend graduate and professional schools in states not having separate school systems. The Gaines decision, rendered by the United States Supreme Court and discussed elsewhere,[18] declared this compromise not within the meaning of the "equal provisions" which a state owed its citizens within its own boundary. In attempting to comply with this decision the southern states have adopted widely varying techniques, including the addition of graduate work in existing Negro state colleges, the establishment of separate professional and graduate schools for Negroes, the part-time use of white state university faculty members by Negro colleges, and proposals for regional universities for Negroes to be supported by a group of states. The effects of the ramifications of this decision will not have run their course for some time.

In summary, then, race differentials in public education have their basic roots in administration of the public-school laws and in the discriminatory allotment of public education funds. This in turn is rooted in the inability or the unwillingness of the states having separate schools to support adequately a dual school system. The legality of racial segregation in public educational institutions has been well established by the courts, but the illegality of racial discrimination is coming to be equally as well established. Only when the offering to the Negro in separate schools, in funds and facilities, "from the primary grades through the graduate and professional level, is in truth the equivalent offered to the white students—then,

[18] See *infra.*, pp. 181-182.

and only then can it be said that in the separate school system there is segregation but not discrimination."[19]

Typical effects of racial discrimination in the rural schools can be illustrated by data from our field observations. Bolivar and Coahoma counties, located in the Mississippi Delta area, pay Negro teachers little more than they were paid fifty years ago. In 1889 average monthly salaries of white and Negro teachers in Bolivar County were $45 and $20, respectively. Today white teachers receive an average of $100 monthly; Negro teachers, $30. In 1934 in Bolivar and Coahoma counties there were only 51 buildings meant to serve as schools for Negro children, but 175 schools were being housed in churches, tenant cabins, lodge halls, and other makeshift locations. In these privately owned buildings there was no school equipment. In Bolivar County 110 of the 1,475 schools for Negro children were one-teacher schools, as were 56 of Coahoma County's 70 Negro schools. By contrast, the schools for white children were consolidated, well constructed, and well equipped.

Both of these counties have Negro county high schools which are the especial pride of the more benevolent planters. The Coahoma County Training School is an attractively designed institution set in the center of a large plantation development. The Bolivar County Training School is located at Mound Bayou, the one all-Negro town in the county. These schools, however, reach only a small section of the Negro population. The great mass of the youth are exposed only to such elementary schools as are available. In Bolivar County white schools operate for a period of nine months, while the Negro schools have terms of from four to seven and a half months, the majority being in session for a period of six months.

The situation has provoked comment from Negroes in the local community who have noticed these contrasts. One Negro, a small businessman in Clarksdale, in describing the schools, said:

Most of them have got a sorry building that's about to fall in. There is no convenience. There are no desks and most of the children have to study on benches. In some places they use the old plantation churches for school buildings. There are a few Rosenwald schools scattered about the county, and they are pretty good, but the rest of them are a disgrace to a civilized county.

Now the whites have all modern buildings with modern equipment. They have some big buildings and consolidated schools and good buses

[19] L. A. Ransom, "Legal Status of Negro Education Under Separate School Systems," *Journal of Negro Education,* 8:405 (July, 1939).

to haul the students. The colored school system can't even be compared to the white system.

In the town of Cleveland, Bolivar County, the contrast in the provision of plant and equipment for Negro and white schools is striking. The white school is a commodious building with a large gymnasium and is located on a large, well-landscaped plot of ground. The Negro school is of brick construction, but the upper story has been unsafe for use for several years. In fact, the whole building sags and has been condemned, but is still used. The school ground is small and grown up with weeds. When the school board was asked to repair the building it refused, explaining that the board could not do it because it did not own the property.

A striking exception to the common practice appeared in Johnston County, North Carolina, resulting largely from the presence of an influential, aggressive superintendent who set himself to provide better schools for Negro children. Some of his problems are described by a Negro teacher:

Whatever the county superintendent gives to white schools he'll give to colored schools, but the Board of Education is different. Why, they fought the building of that colored high school in Selma. They put up quite a fight, but the superintendent won out. You know he does not give colored schools the worn out things from white schools. When he gets something for Negroes he gets good new materials for colored and white. He may make some difference there, but he'll go pretty far with this equality business, even in subscribing to newspapers and magazines. He doesn't subscribe to only white magazines and papers, he subscribes to Negro newspapers and magazines for our colored schools.

The functional relationship between the Negro school and the farming system appears in various details of administration in the rural Negro schools. The signal for the closing of school in the cotton county is not a predetermined date, as in the case of the white schools, but the condition of the crop. The landlords watching the maturing crop are the ones who set the date. Neither the pupils nor the teachers nor the Negro principals know when the schools will open or close very far in advance of the signal by the landlords. In the spring and fall the internal school program is changed to accommodate the farming system. Chapel exercises, lunch hours, and recreational periods are either shortened or eliminated entirely in order that school may close at an earlier hour, to let children get away to the farms. The average length of the school year for Negro children in these areas, including these adjusted days, is 161 days. For white children there is a nine months' session of 180 school days.

In the southern cities under the policy of segregation the differences are not so great as in the rural areas, but disproportions are consistent, in buildings and equipment as well as in teachers' salaries.

In the city school system of Birmingham, Alabama, the average yearly salary of the white teachers is $1,466, and the average for Negroes is $682. In Richmond the maximum salary for Negro elementary teachers is $990, while the maximum for white elementary teachers is $1,620. The minimum salary for a Negro teacher in the senior high school is $810; the maximum, $1,350. The minimum salary for a white teacher in the senior high school is $1,000; the maximum, $2,001.60. There are no junior high schools for Negroes in Richmond. A report of the Richmond schools for 1935, based on average daily attendance, revealed that the average expenditure per white elementary pupil was $76.59 compared with an average of $43.72 per Negro pupil. On the basis of average daily attendance in the senior high schools, the average expenditure was $102.26 per white pupil and $59.58 per Negro pupil.

The secretary of the Urban League in Richmond declared:

There is no comparison between the white and colored schools here. A study of the public schools in Richmond showed that the value of equipment in Negro schools is $700,000 while the value of white school equipment is $7,000,000. Negroes get a proportion of one to ten, although we are 31 per cent of the population. Why, it is so bad that they used to separate it in the superintendent's report, but now it is not separated into white and colored. They think they are shrewd not to separate it, and I guess they are, because it's as hard as the deuce to get at this thing of comparison now.

On the whole the Negro teachers are less well prepared than white teachers. The salaries paid to Negro teachers offer little encouragement for able persons to enter the field. However, where the same academic standards are used as criteria for selection the differences are in the same direction. In spite of the superior academic rating of the Negro teachers compared with the white teachers in the public schools of Nashville, salaries of Negro teachers are from 20 to 30 per cent lower than those of white teachers, depending on the type of teacher and the principal.[20]

Border and Northern Schools

Baltimore and Washington have more nearly equal facilities for white and Negro students than any other cities in which there are separate schools. There are the same academic offerings and equally

[20] Tennessee State Department of Education, *Annual Report for the Scholastic Year Ending June 30, 1938,* pp. 116, 118, 128.

well-qualified teachers. The average salary of Negro teachers is about 85 per cent of the average of the white. Negro and white school-teachers have no contact in conferences or conventions. They are, however, members of the same teachers' union; but the Negroes rarely attend because they feel that white teachers are better protected against "left-wing" associations. There are white and Negro vocational schools. The local industries accept white and Negro graduates, but the city and labor organizations cause difficulties in the licensing of graduates. As a result the Negro school must offer special instruction in domestic and hotel work or shoe repairing; and many of the youth who normally would go into mechanical fields seek to go to college.

Provisions for higher education of Negroes in Maryland include an all-colored school in Baltimore for the training of colored elementary teachers; Morgan College which is subsidized by the state and is considered practically a state-supported institution for Negroes; and admittance of Negro students to the law department at the University of Maryland. The National Association for the Advancement of Colored People made a test case in Maryland and won for Negroes the right to attend the university to get training not offered in the existing Negro schools. Maryland both admitted Negro students to the university and offered them scholarships for out-of-state study.

Throughout most of the North there are no official policies of segregation in public schools; that is, the state constitutions make no provisions for separate school systems. However, the concentrations of Negroes in certain residential areas frequently create the same result as designedly segregated schools. The whole question of educational segregation and discrimination in the North is of further significance in the present context because there are many white Northerners and Southern whites living in the North who are convinced that separate schools are desirable despite the laws prohibiting them. Moreover, some Negroes support educational segregation on the following grounds: (1) that mixed schools attend only to the needs of the white group; (2) that the social discrimination practiced against Negro children in mixed schools is warping to their personalities; (3) that there are gains from segregated schools in increased administrative and teaching positions for Negroes; (4) that it is better to have segregated schools, fully controlled by Negroes, than mixed schools in which Negroes have no voice or administrative offices.[21] Negroes who oppose segregation do so

[21] Howard K. Beale, "The Needs of Negro Education in the United States," *Journal of Negro Education*, 3:10 (January, 1934).

largely on the grounds (1) that separate schools mean inferior schools for Negroes and (2) that Negroes can never participate fully and equitably in the life of the nation as long as they are forced to live a life apart, as a subject race.

Private schools in the North frequently practice discrimination. Negroes are usually excluded from private schools below the college level, from medical schools, and in some instances, from private colleges. In any of the colleges to which Negroes are admitted they are likely to experience forms of discrimination; most frequently they are excluded from private organizations such as fraternities; sometimes as a matter of institutional policy they are excluded from athletics or dormitories. On the whole, Negroes are ignored socially in a large number of colleges to which they are admitted.

The status of Negroes in northern schools varies markedly from state to state. In New Jersey, for example, there is evidence of a tendency toward an increase in separate schools, which has been observed since the turn of the century. Reid, in a study of the Negro population of the state, found that the number of separate schools had increased from 52 to 66 between 1919 and 1930; and Oak found that this number had increased to 70 by 1935.[22] In the same year Granger pointed out that northern New Jersey was not interested in separate schools, but from Princeton southward to Cape May every city or town with a sizable Negro population had a dual educational system for the grammar grades. In no town south of Elizabeth was there a Negro teacher in charge of a class including white pupils, but all-Negro classes sometimes had white teachers.[23] Although distinctions and discriminations have continued to increase in New Jersey, the courts have consistently rendered decisions against discrimination and segregation. An adverse decision was handed down against the Trenton board of education in favor of Negro pupils using the high-school swimming pool. Negro parents in Trenton, Camden, and Atlantic City have successfully insisted upon the right to send their children to the nearest school, even if white.[24]

In deference to the Ohio civil rights act the schools in Dayton are not segregated, but they are described as all-Negro and all-white schools. To facilitate this separation the argument of more jobs for Negro teachers was advanced. A school official born and reared in Virginia said:

[22] Marion M. Thompson Wright, *The Education of Negroes in New Jersey* (New York: Teachers College, Columbia University, 1941), p. 185.
[23] *Ibid.*, p. 184.
[24] *Ibid.*, p. 188.

Of course we have separate schools, although we don't call them that. We have a civil rights law, and we are not supposed to have any racial segregation, but we have what we call all-Negro schools. We are going to have some more separate schools soon.

In addition to the all-Negro schools, Negroes comprise about 50 per cent of the enrollment in two schools, 25 per cent in five or six schools, and about 10 per cent in five or six more. Since high-school pupils can transfer to any school in the city, the policy is to accommodate readily any Negro who wishes to transfer to the all-Negro high school and to make every effort to impose a rule of no-transfer if one should attempt to transfer from the all-Negro high school. There are no Negroes who teach white children.

In New Haven, Connecticut, Warner found no noticeable segregation or discrimination in the school system.[25] According to this writer, there are Negro children in four out of seven schools in the city, in none of which are they seated or classified by race. There is no distinction shown in school or class activities, such as glee club, school programs, class offices, and the like. In the senior high schools, however, social relations between white and Negro pupils tend to be much more restrained than in the lower grades. Where Negroes attend any school in considerable numbers, Warner reports that they tend to group themselves together and apart from the whites. The four Negro teachers in New Haven all teach mixed classes, some having few Negro children. It has been reported, however, that some Negro parents have objected to having their children taught by a Negro. The white and Negro teachers engage in social intercourse quite freely. The most conspicuous discrimination shown is in the reluctance of the school board to appoint Negro teachers in numbers even nearly proportionate to the size of the Negro population. There have been no appointments of Negro teachers in the junior or senior high schools.[26]

White and Negro teachers in New York are assigned without particular regard to racial composition of schools. In Chicago there is a stronger tendency to place Negro teachers in the schools having large proportions of Negroes, and also a tendency to transfer white pupils to other school districts if they object to attending a school with Negroes. In Philadelphia the elementary schools are virtually segregated but the high schools are not. In most of the other larger cities the number of Negro teachers is small.

[25] Robert A. Warner, *New Haven Negroes* (New Haven: Yale University Press, 1940), p. 277.
[26] *Ibid.*, pp. 278-280.

Chapter II

SEGREGATION IN PUBLIC AND QUASI-PUBLIC SERVICES

::

RECREATION

Libraries

Public libraries represent an area of extreme racial distinction, since these publicly supported institutions sometimes make no provisions for Negroes. Even where there is an attempt to provide a dual system the provisions are not equal, for although the Negro branch library may borrow books that circulate from the main library, Negroes do not have access to reference books.

In the rural sections and small towns of the South there are few library facilities for either race. In some places where public libraries are not provided, the white citizens form an association for supporting a small library, the services of which are limited to whites. The reading interests of some rural and village people are met by traveling libraries transported by truck. These are few in number and Negroes seldom come in contact with their services. At any rate there is a general presumption that these are for whites. It appears from the following remarks by a librarian in Alabama that lending books to Negroes presents something of a problem, for it is obviously not customary. She said:

When the state library sent the book-mobile down here the books were furnished from this branch, and I always accompanied the book-mobile. We traveled all over the county. The young woman working with me said, "What will we do if Negroes ask to rent books?" so I said, "I just don't know." Fortunately none of them asked for books except in one place. A white woman was looking at the books in the book-mobile and her colored cook came out and looked too. The cook picked up a book and said she would like to read it, so I just charged it to the white woman and let her have it. I put it in the white woman's name.

The librarian in a town in Johnston County, North Carolina, was

26

hesitant about circulating books among Negroes. Her comment, when asked about the matter, reflected her indecision:

I don't know just what the people would say about colored people using the books. The question has never come up, so I just don't know how they would feel about bringing it up. I guess they could if they asked to. I'm sure the colored teachers could use them, but I'm not so certain about the other people.

Generally, in small towns with publicly supported libraries Negroes are excluded from the privilege of borrowing books. In one town it was reported, "The library has no accommodations for Negroes and no books may be drawn by Negroes from there." An informant in Marked Tree, Arkansas, said:

They have a city library here but colored people can't take any books out. They won't let colored people go there unless they was sent by white people. I go up there to get books for the family I work for and to take back books. I never got any for myself, but I read all I get for the boss's family. They know me at the library and they treat me all right.

Prominent Negroes, such as schoolteachers, may be allowed to use books by some such exceptional means. The wife of the principal of a Negro school in South Carolina said:

Negroes can't borrow books under any conditions. We get them but we get them through a white lady friend who borrows them like she was borrowing them for herself and gives them to us.

In southern cities Negroes are supplied with books through a separate library, which is usually a branch of the main publicly supported library. Negroes are restricted almost completely to the use of facilities in this building and excluded from other libraries. Likewise, they are generally restricted to the use of books in the Negro branch, although in some instances it is reported that books may be secured from the main collection, but only through the Negro branch. The Negro branch of the public library in Nashville is operated as a branch under the charter of the Carnegie Library of Nashville. There is no segregation clause in the charter, but the common assumption expressed by library employees is that state and municipal laws provide for segregation and a statement in the bylaws of the library is unnecessary. The Negro library is conceived of as a branch library and is treated as such. Under the present administration books housed in the main library are available to Negro borrowers. Negroes who apply at the Negro branch for books housed in the main library may be sent there by the Negro librarian to get them; but Negroes applying first at the main library, without being sent by the Negro branch librarian, are referred to the Negro branch.

There are reports from one city of cases in which Negro students were allowed access to books in the main library, but were segregated in a small separate reading room. The librarian who reported this practice thought it was exceptional and not generally known to the public, and that if it were announced there might be a reaction forcing her to discontinue the practice. A Negro scholar in South Carolina, working on source materials in the state archives, was allowed to use the books called for, but in the basement. Another Negro student was permitted the freedom of an arrangement with the janitor to use books after library hours, while the cleaning was being done.

There is a freer use of public reference libraries in larger centers. No special provisions are made for Negroes in the use of the library of the state of Tennessee. The custom is for Negroes to be seated at one table when they come in. White readers who happen to be using this table at the time of appearance of the Negro are requested to move. The librarian shows courtesy and is helpful in finding material which has not been requested but which she thinks may bear on the subject in which the Negro reader is interested. Such readers are usually professional men, however, who are using the library in their work. One of the large private colleges in Nashville has made it possible in special circumstances for Negro students to work in its library if a number of books are desired. A table in the stacks is assigned to the student. Interlibrary loans also are made freely in this city.

In the State Library of Virginia there is a segregated table in the main reading room designated, "For Colored Readers." According to the librarian there is no discrimination otherwise. There are no separate toilet facilities for Negroes in the building; the races use the same toilets. Municipal libraries in Richmond are controlled by a city ordinance which provides that Negro readers shall have a separate branch. There is such a branch, but many Negroes in Richmond refuse to use it because of its inadequacy and the acute sense of discrimination which they feel. They may and often do borrow books from the white library through interlibrary loans.

In Atlanta no books housed in the central library or other white branches may be used by Negroes or the Negro branch. The librarian at the Negro branch stated, however, that the authorities are liberal in purchasing books requested at her branch. Recently requests by

Negroes for books of such special character as to have few readers have raised the question of securing such books through the main branch. It was decided that it would be better for the library system to buy the books for the Negro branch than to let them leave the main library. The Negro librarian is never invited to staff meetings, and must deal directly with the head librarian.

In the border and northern areas Negroes use library facilities freely. They sit where they choose and receive the same service given to white readers. While there is no segregation or discrimination in the use of facilities, Negroes in Baltimore felt that they were being discriminated against by the failure of the libraries to employ Negroes in any other capacity than janitor or servant, even in the branches which for the most part serve only Negroes.

Parks and Playgrounds

Facilities for public recreation are seldom provided by villages or rural communities. School playgrounds, ball parks, and fairgrounds practically exhaust the list; and in the South these are usually developed for whites only. Play facilities are not provided for Negro school children at public expense, and it is not possible for them to share in the use of equipment provided for white children. Negroes seeking space for recreation or picnics resort to churchyards or open spaces.

Negroes are excluded from the general public parks in all the southern cities visited except Richmond, where they are restricted to walking, sitting, and fishing. But even within these restrictions, Negroes in Richmond have a wide range of freedom as compared with other cities. There are no parks for Negroes in Birmingham; and in Atlanta, where Negroes were formerly permitted to use one of the parks for picnics, the privilege is no longer granted. They visit the zoo in one park in Houston on special days, but they understand that they are excluded from other facilities. In Nashville there are several small Negro parks located in or near the larger Negro communities. However, the Negro population, which is 28 per cent of the total, has for its use only 1 per cent of the total park area.

In the border areas parks are for the general public, although there are some restrictions upon their use by Negroes. They may sit in, walk through, and generally enjoy the use of the parks, except for the play facilities. Negroes have separate swimming pools, tennis courts, and other playground equipment, usually situated in one section of the park; play facilities for whites are in the opposite section. Concerts or programs given in the open air are attended by both races, and there is no segregation. In one case, a privately owned baseball park has segregated sections.

LAW ENFORCEMENT

Although the judicial and penal institutions deal with cases involving Negroes, nowhere in the South do Negroes share in directing, administering, or controlling these institutions. There are no Negro judges, few Negro officers of the law, and no Negroes serving in minor clerical positions in official agencies. In the rural counties visited there were no reports of Negroes serving as jurymen; and a Negro lawyer is still an anomaly in the small towns.

In the courtroom of the Johnston County courthouse Negroes sit only in the balcony. White people sit downstairs. Negro witnesses come downstairs only when called. When addressed in court they are called by their first names. Only in exceptional cases are they given titles such as "Mr." or "Mrs.," as in the case of whites. One local Negro physician seems to be an exception to this general rule, for he is accorded courteous treatment in this respect.

Rural Negroes complain generally that they are not given sufficient police protection. A Negro grocer in Poinsett County, Arkansas, said:

They don't have much of a police around here. They don't give a damn about the nigger. I remember the times when there was a guy in the mayor's office who used to fine you $14 every time you came up for something. They stuck many a nigger for that sum then. They don't give the nigger much protection. I let some white customers have some credit once, and they did not pay me. I tried to get the marshal to help me collect my money. He said that he could try but that he knew a white man's word would be taken in court before mine. He advised me to stop letting them have anything. That is what I did.

The remarks of a Negro farmer in Johnston County are also indicative of the predicament of Negroes before the courts of the white man:

The whites are a good bit ahead in court. They let the Negro know he's a Negro there. They call him a nigger, of course. They don't sit together. A Negro's word won't take like a white man's, unless he's got a mighty good reputation with the white people.

The accounts of Negroes whose appearance in court has been in the capacity of witnesses describe it as an unpleasant experience in which witnesses are intimidated; the words "nigger" and "darky" and various humiliating epithets are constantly employed. Conversations with rural Negroes reveal that Negroes mention as a particular matter of pride that they have never had to go to the courthouse or to jail.

There is another side to this picture, however. Negroes who have a white man upon whom to depend can frequently secure protection even when in the wrong. In such cases the Negro community's recourse to law is not effective.

If there are restricted provisions for Negroes in the county courthouses, the same cannot be said of the county jails. Ample provisions are made for them here. Those who commit offenses anywhere in the county, of a seriousness beyond the misdemeanor level, are brought to the county seat and lodged in the county jail. In the usual structural pattern a hallway runs the length of the building, dividing it equally. Quarters on one side of this corridor are assigned to white prisoners and on the other side to Negro prisoners. A Negro porter frequently attends the Negro side of the jail, even to the point of acting as key bearer.

In the jail in Richmond there are no observable differences between the quarters for whites and Negroes, although they are lodged in separate wings of the building. There are three tiers of cages for white men, identical with three tiers of cages for Negro men. At the time of the visit there were nine white women confined, and thirty colored women. The white women were in two small rooms and the colored women were in a large cage. The only discrimination observable was that Negro women and men, as trusted persons, were doing most of the work. White persons were not working in the building except as paid employees.

In Houston, as in other southern cities, the practice of Negro lawyers is largely confined to civil cases involving property or divorce; their criminal cases are few, especially those in which serious charges are brought against Negroes. No Negro jurors were found on the jury list; and there had apparently been no jurors of color in recent years, except for one Negro on the grand jury. A Negro professional man said:

We generally have a Negro on the grand jury here. In 1932 a Negro was being tried for some offense, and the court assigned a young white lawyer to defend him. This young fellow took his law seriously. He had no better sense than to try to win the case. He got a verdict of guilty. He appealed the case on the grounds that there were no Negro names in the jury box. The case was thrown out. Since then Negro names have been put in. I have received several notices, but when I go down there they use every means known to man to keep you from serving.

In Houston courtrooms Negroes are seated in the rear seats. Most of them crowd into the rearmost seats, hesitating even to take the seats which mark the beginning of their section. Cases are called in their turn regardless of the color of the defendant. All defendants are called by their first names, and no prefix is given to either white or Negro names. When a Negro defendant is not called by his first name he is usually referred to as "boy."

In Nashville courtrooms Negroes and whites sit on the same seats at times, but Negroes always discreetly leave a foot or more of space between themselves and the whites. The judges use the customary form of address—the first name, if the Negro has no title. Otherwise, his title of doctor, lawyer, or professor is likely to be used.

In the courtrooms in Birmingham the pattern of segregation does not yet appear to be firmly fixed. The Negroes have no definite place in which they are expected to sit, but they are not expected to sit in the same row of seats as whites. If the whites begin to fill in first, the Negroes are expected to give them leeway, but the opposite is also true. In the courts of this city the Negro attorney is treated with a great deal of courtesy. While he is seldom called "Mr." he is usually called "lawyer" or "counselor." He is given the protection of the court even when he is arguing against a white person. The Negro witness is given some respect in that most of the judges do not allow the word "nigger" to be used. There is more evidence of discrimination in the court building; there are separate toilet facilities and elevators for Negroes and whites. Although Negroes may not use the white elevators, the whites do use Negro elevators. This is in violation of the state law, but it has not been challenged.

To the Negro in the South the law-enforcing machinery is symbolized by the police. To the majority of the Negro population, in fact, the policeman *is* the law. For this reason it is impossible to understand either the differential character of public protection received by Negroes or the complex reaction of the Negroes to the law without analyzing the relation of the Negro to the police. The police in the southern cities are, for the most part, recruited from the white lower middle class, in which racial attitudes are firmly set. The low level of education and the social and economic insecurity of this class help to explain why, when the men are invested with formal authority, they are frequently as much concerned with the "superiority" of white status as with the dignity of the law. The authority to administer physical punishment and to kill a Negro without fear of serious censure gives special significance to their role as agents of the law in the South.

Lower- and lower middle-class Negroes are frequently exposed to the power of the police with or without warrant. The policy appears to be to control this class of Negroes by instilling complete fear; and policemen are indeed both feared and hated by lower-class Negroes. They are subjected to more frequent arrest and more severe treatment than whites and upper-class Negroes; reports are consistent on this point in all the cities.

Both Atlanta, Georgia, and Clarksdale, Mississippi, have curfew laws which are rigidly enforced for Negroes. Such laws also exist in other southern cities, and there are many stories about Negroes who have been unfortunate enough to encounter policemen on the streets after hours. In cities where there is no curfew it is a favorite sport of the policemen to relieve the boredom of patrol by accosting Negroes and subjecting them to ridicule and abuse. If a Negro shows resentment he may be beaten and arrested. The most benevolent and least rabid policemen are selected for duty around Negro schools and at gatherings where a policeman may be required.

Attitudes of policemen toward upper-class and upper middle-class Negroes and toward Negroes with known white connections are not as vicious as toward Negroes of the lower classes and those without influential connections. Middle- and upper-class Negroes have most frequent occasion to encounter policemen in traffic situations.

A Negro principal of a high school in a southern city, who went to the police station for information, described his experience as follows:

The white police here are like they are in most southern cities. When I was working on my thesis I went to the police station to get some information on crime. I saw one of the Negro policemen and arranged to meet him at the station. He took me in and introduced me to the chief of police. The first thing the chief said was: "Well, niggers commit more crime than white people." He told another cop to show "this nigger the files."

A middle-class Negro woman who had recently come to the South from the Middle West expressed surprise at the attitude of southern Negroes toward the police. To accept the evaluation of the police made by her new southern friends was disquieting. She said:

The strangest feeling I experienced in making my adjustment to the South was the realization that the policeman on the corner was not there to protect me. In Cleveland the policeman was my friend. He protected me from harm and did not in himself represent a threat of harm. From childhood I always liked policemen. They saw me safely across busy streets as I went to and from school. The presence of a policeman was always an assurance of protection. It was difficult for me to see the policeman as an enemy to be avoided. That realization left me with such a great sense of insecurity.

The relationship of the southern Negro population of all classes to the law is strongly conditioned by the police factor. So far as possible they stay away from any contact with the courts or the police. The safest policy is one followed by the woman who said:

I ain't been to court and the police ain't never said nothing to me. I don't care who they "try" at that courthouse, I ain't going to see. It's the wrong place for me to go. I don't have no business at the courthouse and the police don't have no business at my house. We stays our distance. They don't bother me and I don't bother them.

One southern informant, however, reported a recent incident in his city involving the arrest and punishment of a white policeman for "unbecoming conduct" against a Negro whom he had arrested. The punishment consisted of a public reprimand and a year on probation. This represents a modification of the usual pattern of unpunished police brutality.

A Negro newspaper editor, in speaking of the general practices of the police in the South, said:

When they arrest a Negro and take him to jail they usually beat him up. It just seems to be a practice here. I knew a Negro woman who was arrested because she got into a fight with her husband. The cops put her in jail and that night they turned all of those white prisoners in on her. I understand that is a regular practice. This woman had a white lawyer and he wanted her to win her case. She pled guilty, and when he asked why she pled guilty she told him that she could not stand another night in jail where they turned all of the white prisoners in on her. She was heartbroken and left the city and went North. She said she would never return to the South again.

In Richmond, which is fairly typical of the cities in the upper South, Negroes constitute 29 per cent of the population but are involved in approximately 55 per cent of the court cases. The police are said to be more prone to arrest Negroes than whites, and the Negro offenders are given more serious sentences. Until recently, the court proceedings involving Negroes were regarded as burlesque. A judge of superior quality took matters in hand, objected to white lawyers and witnesses referring to Negroes as "niggers," and in general introduced more dignity into the proceedings. Since 1936 there have been a few Negroes on juries. With all these changes, it was still possible for a competent observer to say:

A Negro prisoner just takes a chance as to how his case will turn out. His fate usually depends on his counsel. A good lawyer, one who argues well, may even get you acquitted when everything seems against you. The court decision is just a gamble. The police here are accused of being exceedingly brutal. Yes, exceedingly brutal. They will beat up a Negro on the slightest provocation. The NAACP started such a stink about public beatings when arrests are being made that they stopped that. Now they won't beat you until they get you to the station. They will not strike you at the scene of arrest; public sentiment will not support that.

In Houston there are five Negro policemen. They cannot arrest white men, only hold them. Contact with white offenders, however, is unusual except in cases of traffic violations and accidents. A Negro political leader commented on this system as follows:

They are supposed to arrest only Negroes. There are a lot of these pimps or stool pigeons who are given a privilege of carrying a gun, and they just do a lot of telling the police what is going on. If it was not for them I don't think that the police would even make an arrest here. The white police used to run in these Negro sections, but so many of them ran into bullets that they couldn't find who fired, they had to put Negroes out in these places.

A few other large cities in the South also have Negroes on the police force, but their powers are restricted as in Houston. Juries are with few exceptions composed of white men; and Negroes complain generally of the treatment they receive in the courts, and especially from the police. Civil rights are commonly disregarded at all stages of procedures against Negroes. More general still is the practice of treating Negroes as wards and disregarding formal etiquette in disposing of their cases.

RELIEF AND WELFARE

Eleemosynary institutions are not as well developed in rural areas and villages as in cities. Aid to Negroes from private and semipublic agencies is not systematic, and is more in the nature of alms than welfare. Negroes share to a greater extent in the benefits of public, tax-supported, welfare institutions, especially those supported by the state rather than by the local government. Here again the whites are cared for first and, admittedly, even they are not cared for very well. Negroes have profited greatly by the recent multiplication of public relief agencies. It appears that they receive most consideration from federal agencies, and receive less attention the farther the control of relief is removed from Washington. In the large southern cities many complaints regarding discriminatory practices are heard. At the various relief agencies there are usually separate waiting rooms for white and Negro clients; and the relief allocations are, as a rule, different in amount. The assumption is that Negroes require less or that they have learned to live more efficiently than whites of the same economic level. In the large cities of the South the proportion of Negroes on relief is larger than that of the whites mainly because there are more Negroes of marginal economic status, more unemployed, and fewer opportunities for Negroes in either regular or temporary work.

The various New Deal agencies employ Negroes, and the Works Projects Administration has sponsored many projects for Negroes in the areas visited. Some Negroes have been given employment on WPA street and road construction projects; but they do not regard employment of this kind as relief because their jobs are similar to those to which they have been accustomed, and the circumstances of the employment do not appear to have much significance. They have received loans from the HOLC for improving homes they own; and there has been no general complaint of discrimination in the granting of these loans. There are, however, no Negroes in the administrative personnel of the federal agencies; nor were there any clerks or case workers reported in the rural areas visited.

Social welfare work is concentrated in the larger cities, where it tends to become professional. On the whole Negroes apparently receive a larger share of relief in cities than in small towns, but complaints were heard in all the cities visited. The most general complaint is that they do not receive relief and welfare care in proportion to that given white people. It is also a common complaint that Negroes are not accorded fair and courteous treatment by white social workers. Organized relief, both private and public, is controlled and administered almost exclusively by white people. This exclusion from policy making and execution opens the way for far-reaching discrimination and a great deal of complaint and misunderstanding. It is said that white workers and administrators do not know the social situation in the Negro community and cannot deal justly and efficiently with Negroes. A social work executive gave this analysis of the situation:

The relief setup in the city is administered by the department of public welfare; every one of whose employees is white. The investigations of

Negro families are not thoroughly done. You know these young case workers can't understand Negroes; it's foolish to think that they can. Well, as a result many Negroes who are entitled to relief don't get it and some who don't need it get it. But Negroes get more than their share of relief here. I understand that 55 per cent of the relief clients have been Negroes. Negroes have got relief and white people have got the jobs. There are some WPA jobs available to Negroes, but they are far less than what they should be. If there is any position of control they think it should be held by a white person—no matter how incompetent that person may be or how well trained the Negro is. Negroes get social security when they are entitled to it, but the trouble is that very few are entitled to it, under the provisions. You know that domestic workers, farm, seasonal and professional workers are excluded from participation in social security. These classifications include most of the Negroes.

Government loans are very difficult to get at times. We have one agency as reference, the FHA. There they turn down Negro applications because they claim they are responsible for depreciation of property in adjoining neighborhoods. They gave as their reason for refusing a loan to a friend of mine that if something should happen to him there were no Negroes to whom they could sell the property. Then it is difficult for Negroes to meet the requirements for FHA loans. I think the farmers have a pretty tough time too, but it is kept under cover. I don't think colored farmers in Virginia participate freely in government loans. At least that is my understanding.

Where understanding between the races is lacking, consideration of the Negro's claim on relief is negligible and its administration is a farce. A Negro editor in Birmingham said:

There is no discrimination in social security because there is no chance for it. But there is plenty of it in the welfare department. They ask Negroes all sorts of questions and try to intimidate them. They ask questions that are not on the blanks, and they turn down many of them. They have some Negro social workers who are posted to turn them down. One of them told me about it. They favor the whites with relief. The whites embarrass every Negro who goes in there, and try to make them feel their poverty as much as they can.

A skilled tradesman in the same city said:

A couple of years ago I tried to get relief or a job. At the office building I had to go back in the alley and take the freight elevator. They just wouldn't let a Negro use the main elevators. When I got in there they talked rough. One little old white boy said, "What's your trouble, boy?" Then when I started to tell him he wouldn't let me talk. They asked all kinds of questions. They asked me if I had ever been in any trouble and if I ever took a drink. They was so mean I just got tired of it and walked out.

In the border and northern areas discriminatory practices follow political lines more often than racial ones. In some instances the personal attitudes of relief officials and workers may influence the situation quite apart from any question of policy. For example, the director of public welfare in one of the border cities is a former judge of the juvenile court and has long had the reputation of being very liberal and fair toward Negroes. In this city there were 4,161 cases receiving general public assistance in July, 1939. Of that number 2,026 were white and 2,135 were Negro, although Negroes comprise only one-sixth of the population of the city.

THE FEDERAL POST OFFICE

In the rural areas surveyed in this study there were no Negroes employed as mail carriers or clerks in any post office, although they were frequently employed as janitors. In Bolivar County, in which the all-Negro town of Mound Bayou is located, certain Negro leaders asked the Republican postmaster to appoint a Negro clerk, and it was understood that he would. But this postmaster died and a Democrat was appointed, so they gave up hope of getting any such appointment.

In regard to order of service the disposition of clerks at post-office windows is to recognize white people first and to give them more courteous treatment, but this rule is not rigidly followed. The practice is based upon the common assumption that Negroes are to be unobtrusive and deferential in the presence of whites. A Negro visitor in Cleveland, Mississippi, took a place in line with whites who were waiting for service at a post-office window. This was so unusual that it attracted the attention of both Negroes and whites. The surprised white people made no comment, but one of the Negroes who were patiently waiting until the white people were through remarked to the visitor, "You are a stranger here. I can tell by the way you do."

There is free delivery service with white carriers at some of the offices, but many Negroes as well as whites rent mailboxes in the post office in order to secure their mail more promptly.

Some Negroes have ideas about "Uncle Sam" and "the government" which they express when inquiry is made about the post office: "That's Uncle Sam, and he don't stand no fooling with"; "the government don't stand for this foolishness," the point being that they receive impartial service at the post office. Thus, an insurance agent in Bolivar County reported:

There used to be a practice of marking the "Mr." off of the Negroes' mail, but that was really against the law and some of the Negroes did not hesitate to let them know that they knew that they had no right to be doing anything like that. They cut that out. They don't like to mess with Uncle Sam. It is too bad if they do, too.

A more flagrant violation was reported in Laurens County, where it was said that Negro weekly newspapers mysteriously failed to arrive for distribution by agents selling them. There was no explanation; the papers simply "didn't come this week." Since some of these papers are from the North, it is considered inimical to good race relations for Negroes in the South to read them.

In the larger southern cities Negroes report little constraint on their behavior in the post office, which is one of the most formal of all the institutions where whites and Negroes meet. The majority of the complaints are in regard to the employment of Negroes in the postal service. Generally they are given prompt and efficient service. There is little deferential yielding in favor of whites on the part of Negroes; and ordinarily all persons await their turn in a common line, and the next in line is served, regardless of race. Conveniences in the lobby of the post office are used by Negroes and whites alike. There is no particular etiquette observed by Negroes. Custom seems quite weak as an agency of separation here; and there is little chance that it will be strengthened by legal provisions since the service is under federal auspices.

There are Negro postal carriers in several southern cities; and in Richmond there are more Negro than white carriers in the system. (There are 130 Negro carriers and only 30 white.) In an interview with the assistant postmaster it was revealed that most of the whites and Negroes who take a postal examination take the clerk-carrier examination. The whites are placed as clerks and the Negroes are placed as carriers. This is understood. They take the same examination and they get the same pay of $2,100 a year. The highest salary paid a Negro is that of a special clerk who receives $2,300 a year.

There are separate toilet facilities for Negroes in the post office in Richmond, although there are no signs to indicate this. A postmaster explained that there are separate toilets for persons of different occupational levels. The clerks and the carriers can use the same toilets, although in actual fact the clerks use the same toilets as white superiors. Asked if the Negro employees were told what toilets to use, the assistant postmaster said, "No, they are not told. They tell each other; they are clannish, you know; you don't have to tell them. They take care of that themselves. But it's best to keep them separate. It keeps down friction."

There are a number of Negroes employed in the post office in Nashville, in both the Local Post Office Division and the Railway Post Office Division. In the former there are two Negro carriers, five laborers, and thirteen custodians; in the latter, four Negro clerks and eleven laborers. From the reports of informants representing both sections of the service, it appears that whatever discrimination exists in work opportunities is more obvious in the Local Division. It has come to be expected that no Negro will be appointed to clerical work there, but in the Railway Division a Negro has a good chance. Seniority and efficiency are the main criteria here, and at present there are Negroes working in all capacities; some rank above whites in experience and seniority. Negroes and whites work side by side; and in one instance a Negro man and a white woman sort parcels at the same stall.

In the Local Division the laborers are given quite a bit of responsibility in the guarding of parcels inside the building. However, whites always have charge of a package to be carried outside the building, even if Negroes have had charge of the same parcel inside.

The relations between the races in the Railway Division appear to be cordial. Once, when a member of the white group died, a floral offering was collected from Negroes and whites alike. This procedure was duplicated when the deceased was a Negro. There is a common radio, purchased with funds pooled by both groups. In personal relations, the white workers usually refer to the Negroes by their first names. Negroes refer to white persons either as "Mr." or by use of last or first names. There are separate rest rooms for colored and white employees, but with approximately the same equipment; and there are common water fountains.

In the border areas Negroes are employed in post offices as clerks and carriers, custodians, laborers, and janitors. In Baltimore, at the time of the study, 334 of the 1,619 persons employed in the postal service were Negroes; but no Negroes were employed in the general delivery or registry sections, and no Negroes worked at windows.

PUBLIC BUILDINGS

Government institutions such as the courts, post office, and relief and welfare agencies are supported by the public presumably for both races. In the South wherever Negroes and whites are accommodated by the same institution in the same building various devices and practices have developed for maintaining the racial distinctions.

Office Buildings

Political functions in rural areas and small towns are centralized in the county courthouse, where the offices of county officials are centers of activity for county politicians and voters. Negroes are rarely involved in political activities, since it is generally recognized that "politics is the white man's business," and Negroes do not have the franchise. There are no Negro officials, and no Negroes in the garrulous groups loitering in courthouse halls and wandering in and out of offices. Negroes who visit the courthouse usually have business there; these are chiefly property owners making their annual tax payments and those who come to attend the sittings of the county court as litigants, witnesses, or spectators. In some towns they may be observed sitting in small groups on the steps or ledges of the building, apparently just because it is a place where people congregate.

Some facilities are provided for Negroes, indicating that they are expected to use the courthouse. There is a fountain marked "For Colored," and the one public toilet for Negroes is usually located in the basement. There are unmistakable indications, however, that the courthouse is primarily for the service of white men.

In one of the small county seats visited in this survey—Laurens, South Carolina—it was found that Negroes visited the city hall to pay city taxes and to pay for certain public utility services, but that few Negroes knew what was above the first floor in the city hall. A servant who had served Rotary Club dinners in the auditorium and a schoolteacher who had met there with a committee on tuberculosis control recalled that the city hall was used for such purposes.

In southern cities racial distinctions are fewest in federal and state buildings, but even in post offices, state capitols, and office buildings the racial etiquette is not relaxed in the presence of whites. Although Negroes are not excluded from these buildings, they are usually not welcome to loiter there and are restricted in the use of public facilities such as elevators. A discussion of typical situations will make the points of difference clear.

The Customs House in Nashville was formerly both the United States Post Office and the Customs House, but is now occupied entirely by auxiliary federal offices. There are twelve Negroes employed in the building, but not in any official capacity; most of them are janitors under the direction of a white custodian. There are separate facilities for white and colored employees, and a rather well-equipped rest room for colored employees. The rest rooms for the public, however, are used by both colored and whites, and the same is true of the water fountains in the halls.

In the State Capitol of Virginia there is no segregation of Negroes. There are no seats set apart for observers in the House of Representatives, nor in the Senate. The attendant explained that common use of all facilities is compulsory in the State Capitol. The races use the same facilities except in one instance: in the women's rest room there is a sign "White Only." An attendant explained that if anyone protested, the sign would probably be removed.

The only evidence of formal segregation in the capitol building of Georgia is the provision of separate toilets in the basement or on the first floor. Offices, elevators, and visitors' galleries in legislative chambers carry no signs indicating racial restrictions in their use. Toilets on floors above the basement carry only sex designations. Some of the office buildings in Atlanta have a separate elevator for Negroes. All Negroes must ride up in this elevator, but all of the cars will take Negroes down. Whites may use any elevator.

Public Auditoriums

Negroes are segregated at practically all public meetings in southern rural areas, especially at assemblies in public auditoriums. Such mixed meetings are infrequent, however, for Negroes do not participate in political affairs nor in civic or cultural activities which are the concern of most public meetings. Negroes may be allowed exclusive use of public auditoriums on certain occasions, but permission is granted with some reluctance on the part of whites, and usually some restrictions are imposed. Utilization by Negroes must not conflict with any programs of whites, and when Negroes arrive they are likely to find the private facilities, such as toilets, locked. It is often more comfortable for them to use church buildings for their meetings.

The farm agent in Johnston County, North Carolina, reported that Negroes and whites sit together at the meetings of farmers, and no attempt is made to segregate the races. This is clearly an exception to the general practice, however, for at other meetings in this locality and elsewhere the races are segregated and Negroes are often restricted to the balconies. Meetings of men only are less strict in enforcing segregation in all details than are meetings attended by white women. As a rule, Negroes are excluded from business meetings where matters involving both races are discussed.

In the cities there is freer use of public auditoriums, and more privileges were observed in Richmond than in any other southern city. A well-informed Negro social work executive explained:

Our city auditorium is rented; it is not free to anybody. Now there are occasions when it is free. The city has twenty-five nights a year at the Mosque. If your organization gets one of those nights, it is free. But the Mosque is privately owned and it is so beautiful that since we started using it people prefer it. Oh, it can be used for all kinds of affairs. Some nights it is used for whites and the next night for colored. Negro groups can get it easily. We have our commencement exercises there. We have the use of the auditorium rest rooms, cloak rooms, dance halls and everything. No difference is made in that respect.

The variety of practices in these buildings is indicated in the uses of the city auditorium in Atlanta. A schoolteacher explained this as follows:

There are three kinds of things given at the auditorium. There are all-Negro affairs, when Negroes take the whole house and have no contact with white people. Our high-school commencements and programs fall into this category. Then there are mixed things, such as the Marian Anderson concert this spring, when the auditorium was divided equally from the first floor to the top gallery, one-half for Negroes and one-half for whites. There were white ushers and colored ushers. The ushers were all college boys, and white boys from Emory and Tech would show a colored person to his seat if he happened to come up to him. The ushers stood together and talked together in a friendly fashion. The third kind of affair is the white affair, when provisions are made for Negroes in the gallery. I never go to those.

While Negroes may be allowed seats in a segregated section of public halls, they are not always sure of being able to keep their seats, as is evidenced in the experience of a Negro schoolteacher in Birmingham. She said:

I went to the city auditorium to see the Celtic basketball game. We went in the section they had for colored people. We had a comfortable seat, when suddenly here came a big rusty cop. He said, "Get up, nigger, and get over there in the corner where you belong." It made me hot, but there wasn't anything I could do. We just had to move.

The use of the public auditorium in Houston is somewhat typical of the terrific strain toward general segregation. An informant explained:

The city auditorium can be gotten by Negroes any time they have the money to pay for it. The Baptist church used it for its convention. The Sam Houston hall is the same way. The auditorium is used mostly for dances. Whites are permitted to come and sit in special sections, but they are not allowed to dance. The first time Duke Ellington or Fats Waller came here they put a rope across the floor and permitted the whites to dance on one side and Negroes on the other. After that they gave Negroes one night and whites the next night for dancing. On those nights they didn't have a section reserved for whites.

In the border cities Negroes do not suffer the rigid exclusion from city halls and stadiums that they experience in a number of southern cities. On the other hand, there is not the complete freedom from exclusion which exists in the North. Usually the border areas allow Negroes to use these accommodations, barring them only on certain occasions or from certain specified forms of entertainment. For example, in Baltimore the city-owned stadium is managed by a commission and can be rented. Negroes have rented it for a Tri-State Elks Convention and for pageants. Negroes ordinarily attend football games and concerts held in the stadium with no difficulty. They purchase tickets, and are not segregated. The only trouble has been in connection with concerts by the separate white and Negro city symphony orchestras. Only two concerts have been given, but it appears that the white patrons wish to have the audiences of the white orchestra restricted to whites. At the last benefit concert, according to a local police lieutenant, the tickets bought by Negroes had to be collected and the money refunded; white purchasers threatened to boycott the performance if this was not done.

TRANSPORTATION

All southern states have laws separating white and Negro passengers in all land and water transportation. When the statutes were enacted there was no indication that the airplane would ever become a common medium of transportation and so no present laws regulate interracial association on air passenger lines. The Negro traffic, however, has not yet reached sufficient volume to create an issue in this new means of transportation.

Laws regulating racial separation in land and water transportation are similar throughout the South. These laws stipulate that the separate accommodations shall be similar, in the sense of being nondiscriminatory, and the intent of the policy is to achieve complete separation; but neither of these objectives is achieved. There is separation but it is seldom, if ever, complete; and accommodations are seldom equal or similar.

Railroads

The varying volume of both white and Negro traffic imposes a formidable cost hazard for the railroads. Above the level of the plain railroad coach, the "separate but equal" principle would become definitely costly, if carried out faithfully. On trains with sleeping, dining, and club cars it would be necessary to provide sections of these special facilities for both whites and Negroes despite the small volume of Negro patronage, if the spirit and letter of the laws were observed. It seldom happens, however, that these are observed or that the car, or section of a car, for Negroes is substantially the same as that for whites. In attempting to allow for variations in traffic some flexibility has been introduced in practice. Where the volume of Negro traffic warrants, an entire separate car may be assigned to Negroes; but white men have no scruples about riding in the open Negro coach for the purpose of smoking, or conveying a prisoner, or visiting with train officials, for the Negro coach is the favorite spot for the congregation of white train functionaries, including the news vendor.

Trains consisting of three or more cars set aside from one-half car to a whole car for Negro passengers. On trains containing coaches, chair cars, sleeping and club cars, and a diner, the front half or all of the first coach immediately behind the baggage and mail cars is usually set aside for Negroes.

Where traffic is light Negroes may ride in a separate section of a car occupied by white people, but may be asked to move if more space is needed for whites. The cars provided for Negroes are almost invariably older and less well equipped, and frequently in such condition as to defy cleaning. Trains engaged in interstate transportation usually employ the divided baggage and smoking car for Negro passengers. The newer streamlined trains have separate but more comfortable accommodations for Negroes.

Railroad stations and terminals vary widely in provisions for segregation. The waiting rooms and toilets are always separate and, except in a few instances, disparate in equipment. The typical station has the Negro waiting room adjoining the baggage room, with a window aperture to the ticket agent's office. Negroes are served when they can get the attention of the ticket agent. The entrance to the Negro section is generally on the side or back of the station. Some stations have separate entrances and exits from trains, but this is cumbersome. It is simpler to leave it to custom to enforce a sort of caste etiquette in passing through the gates to trains. The rules and expectations vary. For example, at the Union Station in Atlanta Negroes may leave the waiting room provided for them and patronize the newsstand and lunch counter in the white waiting room. At the Terminal Station in the same city they cannot enter the white waiting room for any purpose, and they are denied use of facilities other than those provided for them specifically. The stationmaster stands at the entrance to the white waiting room and directs Negroes away if any attempt to enter.

In Houston the new Grand Central Station has a well-appointed waiting room for Negroes with well-kept rest rooms and a capably operated lunch counter. Entrances to the street and the train sheds make contact with white travelers unnecessary. The check room, however, is in the white waiting room and Negroes with bags or parcels to check are directed there. The newsstand, from which Negroes may make purchases, is also in the white waiting room. At the Union Station in Houston the Negro waiting room is an alcove off the white waiting room, with no separating doors between, but passage from the street to the waiting room is direct. While contact with white travelers is thus reduced, all entrances to trains are through the large white waiting room in which the ticket office is located, and to get to trains or to purchase tickets Negroes must go into the white waiting room.

In Richmond one railroad station provides a small waiting room for Negroes with a separate entrance at one side of the building. Negroes must use a long passageway to reach the gateway to trains. Another station has a bare and dirty little alcove, marked "For Colored," at the bottom of one stairway, so inadequate that little attempt is made to enforce the segregation. Negro passengers do not sit in the general waiting room upstairs, but await their trains standing near the train gates.

Only in exceptional cases are Negroes sold accommodations in Pullman cars; they are ordinarily obtained through some irregular procedure, such as having a white person purchase the reservation, or approaching a friendly railroad official who will sell the reservation without regard for the prohibition features of the laws. In some states legal provisions regulating accommodations for Negroes in Pullman cars are so phrased as to permit varied interpretation. Because of the heavy penalties imposed for violation of the explicit provisions of the state, trains entering Houston carry very few Negro Pullman passengers, and these only under most unusual circumstances. No Negro interviewed in Houston recalled an instance of Pullman accommodations being sold to a Negro leaving Houston; nor could informants who were interviewed in Birmingham recall any such sales. The late and distinguished James Weldon Johnson, a few years before his death in 1938, attempted to secure such accommodations. After engaging space over the telephone he called for the ticket and it was bluntly refused. No amount of argument or persuasion from him or several prominent citizens of the city could change, or obtain an exception to, the prevailing policy.

The Negroes who occasionally procure Pullman accommodations on trains entering Alabama are given "Lower 13," the drawing room; and this is interpreted as providing segregated quarters. Pullman accommodations are used without difficulty by Negroes entering Atlanta, probably because of the frequent use of this form of transportation by teachers in the various Negro colleges. The ticket offices in the Atlanta stations sell only coach accommodations to Negroes. Pullman accommodations are usually secured by telephoning the city offices of the railroad line on which passage is desired. The city office sells the reservation and instructs the station agent to deliver it when demanded. In Richmond Pullman accommodations are sold freely to Negroes.

When Congressman Arthur Mitchell was ejected from a Pullman car in Arkansas in 1937, he brought suit against the railroad and Pullman companies and eventually won a decision from the United States Supreme Court which, in effect, declared that the railroads would have to provide accommodations for Negro passengers in common Pullman and dining cars, if demanded, or provide a special Pullman and dining car. The practice of denying these accommodations has been considerably relaxed since this decision.

Meal service for Negroes varies on different railroad lines. In the recently inaugurated practice of serving Negroes in the dining cars on southern lines the separation is accomplished by curtaining off the two tables near the kitchen, and by making the call for Negro diners before the beginning or near the end of the regular meal hour. For example, some trains running through Alabama invite Negroes to the diner for the last service at each meal call. Trains in Texas have for some time served Negroes in the coaches where they ride, which practice is also observed in Georgia.

In actual practice there is no segregation on trains in the border area, and there are no "Jim Crow" trains. Pullman tickets are sold readily. According to the superintendents and public relations officials of the Pennsylvania Railroad and the Baltimore and Ohio

Railroad no discrimination is made. Negroes and whites sit where they choose in the waiting rooms of the Baltimore and Ohio and the Pennsylvania stations in Baltimore. Negro customers are served in the restaurant at the Pennsylvania Station. "They never try" at the Baltimore and Ohio Station.

There is an electric train which runs from Baltimore to Annapolis on which Negroes are asked to fill the car from the back and the whites from the front. These trains are operated by the Baltimore and Annapolis Railroad Company, and leave Baltimore from the Camden and the Baltimore and Ohio station. Negro informants report that they are asked to sit in the back of the coach on trains coming into Baltimore from points in Maryland; but when they leave Baltimore to go to those places they are not segregated. If this is true, the conductor takes it upon himself to set the policy, because each company states that it has a policy of "no segregation."

Intercity Bus Lines

When intercity buses were first introduced in the South there was apparently no plan to provide space for Negroes. In some places they accepted white passengers only. Thus, in North Carolina legal action was required to force bus lines to take Negro passengers. Only after experimenting with separate buses for the races did they finally set aside the back seats for Negroes. This is the general practice now. Usually no dividing line is made; the Negroes fill up from the rear, but it is not usual for them to be forced to move back or even stand as whites fill up from the front.

The bus terminals in small towns are frequently located in drug-stores, garages, cafés, or other business establishments where no special provisions are made for passengers. No separate accommodations are provided for Negroes, and they must adapt themselves to the circumstances and make themselves as inconspicuous as possible. Since it is not customary for Negroes to loiter in public places in the presence of whites, they usually wait outside. For example, drug-stores are used as bus stations in Johnston County, North Carolina. Negroes buy their tickets in the stores, then go outside and stand, or sit on benches. White customers may sit in the drugstore, but in practice both whites and Negroes occupy the seats provided outside. No signs for colored or white are on the benches. In Cleveland, Mississippi, the bus stops at a filling station where a small, comfortable waiting room is provided for white passengers, while for Negroes there is a bench in a small, poorly ventilated room which is also used as a storeroom for soft drink cases, beer cases, and tires.

For white passengers clean rest rooms (one for men and one for women) are accessible from the waiting room. A single toilet for Negroes is located in the rear of the building and is not accessible from the waiting room. In Jackson, Tennessee, on the other hand, the facilities for Negro passengers in the new Greyhound terminal are similar to those for whites, though smaller. In general, throughout the South the provisions for transportation of Negroes by bus are not equivalent to those for whites but are comparable with provisions made by the railroads.

In general there is no segregation of Negroes riding on buses going out of most of the border cities, although there are instances of segregation on buses going south. In Baltimore Negroes and whites use the same waiting rooms and toilets in the bus stations, but these arrangements vary from city to city.

City Streetcars, Bus Lines, and Taxicabs

Southern municipal ordinances require a separate section for Negroes in city streetcars and buses. The front seats in the car or bus are set aside "For White People" and the rear seats are assigned to "The Negro Race." The operator is empowered to regulate the space occupied by each race in accordance with the respective numbers of passengers. This system is subject to abuse since it permits the attitude of the operator to become a factor in segregation.

In Houston, as in many other cities, the buses have a movable sign designating the racial sections. In that city Negroes reported that they have had much greater freedom since buses were installed than when streetcars were in operation. There is a kind of customary arrangement which is expected not to be violated: In the Negro sections Negroes are assumed to have the whole bus with the exception of two seats in the very front. Often Negroes begin seating themselves just behind the two seats for whites. If it becomes apparent that the two seats will not suffice for whites, the Negroes will move a seat or two back, without being told by the operator of the bus.

The passengers on streetcars in Birmingham are segregated in a more definite manner. Large screens serve as partitions when clamped on the back of a seat to indicate the respective accommodations for white and Negro passengers. The unwieldy character of the screens and the reluctance of car operators to change them account for many abuses of this system.

In Richmond, Atlanta, and Nashville the personal inclination of the streetcar operator is eliminated from segregation. Signs in the cars notify white passengers to seat themselves from the front toward the rear, and colored passengers from the rear toward the front. The number of passengers by a sort of automatic process determines the line of separation. In Atlanta racial distinctions are also made in boarding the trolleys. The cars are operated by one man and, while all passengers enter from the front, Negroes are supposed to leave by the rear door only. A Negro going to the front door is usually told to go to the rear, but some operators of cars serving in Negro communities will allow Negroes to leave by the front door. Entering from one end only causes little friction or confusion. In fact, use of one-man cars has reduced friction; when the cars were operated by two men and the conductor attempted to take a hand in regulating the seating, there were frequent conflicts.

Policies regulating taxicabs differ from city to city. As a matter of fact, the policy is left largely to the cab company or individual operator, and the latter frequently takes any proffered fares. In Houston and Atlanta taxicabs operated by white drivers will not accept Negro passengers. In the latter city all the meter cabs are owned by one company. One set, called Harlem cabs, are operated for Negroes by Negro drivers; these are older and less substantial cars and appear to be those no longer used for white passengers. The understanding is that cabs operated by white drivers will carry only white people and the Harlem cabs will take only Negroes. Some of the white drivers, however, will pick up Negro passengers after dark, and some of the Negro drivers will take white passengers at night when the identity of the passenger is not readily recognizable. Conversations with taxicab drivers revealed that some Negro drivers take white passengers because they tip. Others think they are troublesome and not worth the risk of losing one's job. White taxicab drivers have a union and are paid forty cents an hour. Negro taxicab drivers are not admitted to the white drivers' union, and are paid $10 a week during the first year of employment by the company and $12 a week after one year's employment.

In Nashville, Richmond, and many other southern cities taxicabs operated by white drivers take Negro passengers as a matter of course. This situation is confusing to the Negro traveler since he is readily taken to his destination by a certain cab company in one city and refused transportation by it in the next. In those cities in which white taxicabs do not transport Negroes, there are usually other arrangements for handling Negro passengers. Most often there are cars operated privately by Negroes; the cabs stand at some distance from the station and the drivers spend their spare time around the Negro waiting room.

In the border and northern areas Negroes are privileged to ride wherever they choose on city streetcars and buses; and white or Negro taxicab drivers serve members of either race without discrimination.

HOSPITALS

The general pattern of segregation in hospitals requires the isolation of Negro patients from contact with white patients and, so far as possible, from contact with equipment used for white patients. Private hospitals either refuse to admit Negroes altogether, give them only emergency treatment, or if they are admitted, segregate them. Contact between white and Negro patients is avoided by admitting Negroes through the side or back doors and, in some cases, requiring them to use the freight elevator. Likewise, Negro visitors generally are required to use the back doors and the freight elevators, or even, as in one case noted, the fire escape. With the exception of the few Negro-owned and operated hospitals, public medical care in the South is controlled and administered by whites. The hospitals and clinics are staffed by white doctors and only rarely may Negro doctors serve on clinic staffs or even treat their own patients once they have entered these institutions.

In the rural areas and small towns of the South there are few hospitals of any kind and those that do exist are usually owned and operated by white people, who exclude Negroes except for occasional emergency cases. Thus, in Cleveland, Mississippi, Negro patients are not admitted to the hospital although it is supported in part by public funds. It is reported by Negroes, however, that they would be given emergency treatment in case of accident, but under no circumstances would they receive more than first aid. Negroes needing other treatment must go to larger cities where publicly supported hospitals provide regular segregated quarters for them.

Negroes seriously injured in automobile accidents while passing through or near small southern towns have in many instances been refused even emergency treatment at the hospitals. One of the most tragic losses to Negro educational leadership resulted from such a refusal in Dalton, Georgia, where Miss Juliette Derricotte, an internationally known educational and social leader, was injured in an automobile accident.

There are two privately owned hospitals in Smithfield, Johnston County, North Carolina: the Furlonge General Hospital is owned by a Negro physician and treats Negroes only; the Johnston County Hospital is owned and controlled by the white people in the county. Negroes are treated in Johnston County Hospital but are admitted only to the Negro ward on the basement floor. The nurses, who generally stay on the second and third floors reserved for white patients, are seldom in service on the first floor where the Negro patients are located, except at regular intervals when medicines are to be administered. Negro patients generally complain that they do not receive the same treatment from white nurses as white patients, but such complaints do not reach the ears of white people for fear that later treatment may be harsher still.

In all the southern cities visited discrimination in treatment and medical care was reported. While institutional practices vary, racial distinctions persist. In some places where Negro patients are received, it is required that some relative or friend stay with and attend them because the white nurses object to certain types of bed service.

All the large industrial plants in the Birmingham area operate hospitals for their employees, and these hospitals have separate wards for Negroes. Several of them employ Negro nurses, but no Negro doctors are on the staffs. Negroes report "fair" treatment in Birmingham hospitals, meaning "as good as you can expect from white people." When urged to comment on the meaning of "fair" treatment, one Negro informant stated:

If they are not too busy when you are taken out there in an emergency case they might get to you right away. If they are busy, you will have to wait until they get to you. They always look after the white emergency first.

I wouldn't send a sick cat to one of them. When I was working as a truant officer I was bitten by a dog. I went to a private physician. I had to go to the head of the welfare department [FERA]. The white woman in charge was very nice. She was as nice as white people can be. She sent me to the hospital. When I got there I had to wait a long time, and then I was sent to a white intern. He took me in a little room on one side. It looked like a storeroom. He told me to sit down and said that he wanted to look at my leg. My leg had a bandage on it, and the tape was stuck to the skin. He started tearing the bandage off. I asked him if he didn't have some ether to loosen the bandage with, and he said he didn't have any and that he could get it off without getting any. I was in this small room with the door shut. After he got the bandage off he refused to give me the Pasteur treatment. I got up and walked out. He followed me and called me everything but a child of God. He certainly did scare me. It is against the law to refuse the Pasteur treatment, but I never got it.

On another occasion my doctor told me that I would have to have an operation for appendicitis. The white woman at the desk asked me if I had ever been there. I told her that I had and that I had been refused treatment. She looked up my record. Then she talked to me worse than she would if I had been a dog. I just walked out.

In another case a boy was struck in the eye by a ball. He fell while he was on his way home. They took him to the white hospital. They kept him there in the waiting room from seven to eleven that night. The nurses and interns were sitting there eating sandwiches and talking and drinking Coca-Cola. The boy's leg was broken in two places. They jerked on his leg and then sent him home without setting it. They said I should bring him back in the morning. The next morning they took him upstairs and the staff physician gave him decent treatment. They never would have done a white case like that.

A variation of the general pattern was found in Richmond, where the majority of nurses are Negro. The medical staff of St. Phillips Hospital is exclusively white, as is the clerical staff, but the nurses, supervisors, and student nurses are all colored. The Negro physicians in Richmond feel very keenly that they are discriminated against because they can go no farther than the door of St. Phillips Hospital with their Negro patients. White physicians who are not members of the staff may bring patients into the hospital to be treated and may attend them personally.

In Nashville at the General Hospital, a publicly supported institution, the physicians and nurses are white, while the orderlies and maids are Negro. Negro patients are well treated in the hospital, and the Negro wards are clean and well kept. There are about two private rooms on each ward for Negro patients. Most of the Negro cases in the General Hospital are indigent persons or insurance cases. In the latter the insurance company defrays the cost of hospitalization and stipulates the hospital to be used. At Vanderbilt Hospital nurses and physicians are white. Services to Negro patients are regarded as good. Negro physicians say that the nurses and doctors at Vanderbilt are of a "higher type" than those at the General Hospital. While Negro physicians may not treat patients at this hospital, they are received courteously and cordially when they visit the hospital. The Hubbard Hospital of the Meharry Medical College, a Negro institution, is rated as one of the best in the South.

In the white hospitals of Houston all Negro wards are housed in separate wings of the buildings so as to be accessible without passing through white wards. Elevators carry patients and visitors directly to the Negro wards. Negro patients are always addressed by their first names in all the white hospitals. Clinics for Negro patients are held separately, and separate waiting rooms are provided for Negro patients and visitors in each of the hospitals. The Jefferson Davis Hospital is the only one that uses Negro doctors in its clinic. Two Negro doctors assisted by white interns, Negro nurses, and occasionally white nurses hold clinics each week at this institution. The nature of the relations here is evident from the remarks of a Negro doctor in that city:

We got colored nurses in the Jeff Davis Hospital by going at it gradually. Miss B—— who had finished nurse training at Flint-Goodridge, came back home, and she couldn't find anything to do. She asked me about work, and I told her that I could get her a job as maid at Jeff Davis. Well, she didn't want to take it because she said she had spent her money and time preparing herself to be a nurse. I kept after her. I told her that you never can tell what will happen. She went out there and took a job as a maid. Well, she got along so well and everybody liked her, that they started recognizing her ability and training as a nurse. They started giving her more duties of a nurse. Then they had some trouble out there about one of the colored patients, and his people took him out of the hospital. We have a colored paper around here called *The Informer*. The head of the hospital didn't want any publicity. I took the opportunity to tell him that the trouble with the Negro wards was that these white women just were not going to wait on colored patients and give them the proper service. He said, "Well, what can we do about it?" I told him to put Miss B—— on as a nurse. He said, "I can't do that. Why, everybody will object." I kept after him and he said he would do it, and see what happened. He sent word that they were to issue her a uniform and they did. There was a lot of objection for a while, but all of the white nurses liked her, and she got along fine with the doctors. Some of them were glad to see it. It worked out so well that the superintendent called me up one day and said, "Send me a couple more nurses." I sent him two and from that time on they kept on adding them.

Prairie View found that they didn't have enough clinical material to train their nurses. So we got the Jeff Davis Hospital to give them a six-month course. Miss B—— became the first supervisor of colored nurses.

I have clinics out there every week. The white interns, white nurses, and colored nurses assist me. We don't have any colored interns out there. I think I had the road open for one this year, but I couldn't just put in anybody. A Negro woman doctor has been coming down here, and has been assisting and observing in the clinics. Now the white girls out there, and the interns, are used to seeing Negro nurses. So it was easy to get her in. They thought a lot of her, and those white nurses thought it was just fine that she was a colored woman doctor. Now, I believe we could have gotten her in there as an intern. She married some fellow in the North and she is going to intern up there. If we could have got her in there we might have been able to open the hospital up to a couple of interns each year.

Baltimore may be taken as somewhat representative of the general practices in hospitals in the border cities. It has three kinds of hospitals used by Negro patients: (1) those that give Negro patients emergency treatment and send them to other hospitals, although preferring that even Negro emergency cases be sent elsewhere; (2) those which admit Negro patients to segregated wards; and (3) those serving Negro patients only. There are two of these and they receive subsidies from the city for indigent patients. The University of Maryland hospital has "Colored" and "White" entrance indicators in the stone doorway.

Chapter III

SEGREGATION IN COMMERCIAL ESTABLISH-
MENTS AND PROFESSIONAL SERVICES

....

HOTELS AND RESTAURANTS

Everywhere in the South there is rigid segregation and traditional discrimination in hotels and restaurants, for these personal service establishments perform functions associated with strong racial taboos.

Hotels

No Negroes are accommodated in any hotel in the South that receives white patronage. As a rule there are no hotels for Negroes in small towns, but Negroes seeking lodging may find a Negro boardinghouse where rooms of a sort are available. In the cities there are usually several small but questionable hotels for Negroes, but nowhere in the South is the segregation pattern relaxed, except perhaps in the instance of a white person stopping at a Negro hotel.

Whether as a cause or as a result of the meager and unsatisfactory hotel accommodations available, most Negroes who travel in the South stop in private homes. On one social level private homes regularly accept a few transient lodgers and may rely on them as the chief source of income, but these are not always safe places because they have little or no supervision. Travelers exchange experiences, however, and recommend places that are more acceptable or agreeable than others. On another social level there is a mutual understanding of the problem of hotel accommodations, and when one has to visit a city, any friend or acquaintance in that city readily accepts the person as a guest; or he may be accommodated by a friend of a friend. Negro schools with eating and sleeping arrangements will usually accommodate a few visitors, whether their visit has to do with the school or not.

Hotel functions have expanded to include their general use for meetings of civic, business, and professional organizations. While the taboo against the association of Negroes and whites in hotels as lodging places is definite and strict, the pattern of exclusion is not so clearly defined on the more formal institutional level. As Negroes come to be included in civic and business organizations, a strain develops between the mores and a practicable pattern of behavior in a new situation. The traditional color line still is insisted upon; and even in the largest cities mixed meetings involve a compromise of custom, if not of law. Hotel managers are not always willing to compromise, nor are officers of the law always willing to look the other way while Negroes and whites assemble or eat together. For the sake of the patronage of such gatherings, however, the management may permit Negroes to attend general meetings, but usually on condition that they use side doors and freight elevators and do not loiter in the lobby.

A few of the hotels in the large cities of the South permit interracial dining in private dining rooms on such special occasions and at least one hotel has extended the privilege to the general dining room. This was doubtless due in part to the pressure and prestige of the Southern Sociological Society, which is made up almost entirely of northern social scientists and has a rule that, when its Negro members are excluded from dinner or luncheon meetings, these formal meetings will not be held.

The strict policy of segregation and exclusion of Negroes from the hotels of southern cities for many years prevented a meeting in the South of the National Conference of Social Work, with a membership reaching several thousands. When this organization finally decided to accept an invitation to meet in New Orleans, it was necessary in view of the Negro membership to insist on certain guarantees: (1) Negroes should attend all meetings freely; (2) there should be no separate entrances or elevators; (3) there should be no segregation in seating arrangements of delegates; (4) on the part of the organization, if meetings were to be held at a time when meals were being served and Negro members were not allowed to share the meals in private dining rooms, the meetings would be dispensed with. It was not expected that the Negroes would sleep in the hotels or eat in the general dining rooms.

When the National Education Association, whose membership includes several hundred Negro teachers, met in New Orleans in 1937, the headquarters hotel objected to use of the formal entrance by Negroes and to their passing through the lobby. As a solution the hotel proposed a temporary ladder or stair leading through a side window. The Negroes objected, and only a few attended. One special program on problems of Negro education was canceled.

In the border cities there are separate hotels for whites and Negroes. Each race uses the establishments provided for its use; and Negro hotels generally serve only Negroes.

In Baltimore at Community Chest banquets, meetings of the Junior Bar Association, and similar gatherings Negro and white members meet together in white hotels and are served together. No discrimination is felt in these meetings. It was reported that the city's largest hotel first opened its doors to mixed meetings several years ago. It received a large amount of trade as a result of this liberal policy and other hotels changed their policies of exclusion. According to a local Negro attorney, "mixed meetings" can be held at all the hotels in Baltimore.

The hotels in Dayton stringently discourage Negro patronage. The manager of the best of the local hotels, conscious of the civil rights act, said that he did not object to a few Negroes at meetings, but private lodgings are never offered except in rare cases. He said:

We recently let Marian Anderson stay here, but it was all arranged beforehand, so that when she came in she didn't register or come anywhere near the desk. She went right up the elevator to her room and no one knew she was around.

In the North many of the hotels belong to syndicates or chains, and their policies are remarkably consistent. One or two Negroes, usually of national distinction, are accommodated on occasions at the well-known hotels, but in most cases some special arrangement has been made with the management. When this concession is made, the facilities of the hotel are limited to the room. There is no effort to conceal the intent to exclude these special guests from the rest of the facilities. Negroes attend meetings in most of the hotels without difficulty and on occasion, as members of a convention predominantly white, may for a limited period be extended most of the privileges of the hotel, including the dining room and lobby.

An ordinary applicant for a room will be met with the statement that no rooms are available. Civil rights statutes permit court action for proved discrimination. In such cases, if one can prove by witnesses that he was refused accommodations after being accepted by mail, he may receive damages. However, with the still small number of suits it has been easier for the hotels to pay the comparatively small damages than to change the present policy of exclusion.

Restaurants and Cafés

Discrimination in eating places may be regarded as a reflection of the taboo against interracial dining which is so pronounced in the South and in the border states. The exclusion of Negroes from eating places in the South is based upon the social implications and does not prevent white men, usually foreigners, from operating places strictly for Negro trade. In Birmingham, Memphis, and Atlanta there are several restaurants run by whites for colored patronage. These are inexpensive places where the quality of the food is of secondary importance in comparison with the quantity of liquor and beer that is dispensed. If such a place is of sufficient size to warrant additional help, some Negro who is known by the clientele is usually employed. Small cafés catering to Negro trade may also be operated by Negroes. Cafés catering to whites frequently have a side or back entrance for Negroes, and they are served at a table in the kitchen. At lunch counters and roadside stands they may buy a sandwich and a drink to be eaten some distance away.

In the business districts of northern cities Negroes usually eat in the more impersonal chain restaurants catering to large numbers of hurried workers; otherwise Negroes "pick their spots." The lunchrooms of department stores are as a rule open to Negroes. More expensive restaurants and the smaller and cheaper ones are likely to discourage Negro patronage in one way or another. Since it is a matter of individual management and the particular circumstances under which service is sought, it is never wholly possible to predict what may happen. Disagreeable incidents, especially if comparatively frequent, are enough to eliminate all except naïve or bold and aggressive Negro patrons.

In Chicago a middle-aged Negro bachelor with a comfortable income reported that he occasionally dines downtown when tired of the food in the Negro restaurants. He goes alone and is served in the dining rooms of two hotels without noticeable difficulty. On a recent occasion he went into a Michigan Avenue restaurant and seated himself. No one paid any attention to him for about thirty minutes. Then he asked for service, and was told that he would be taken care of in a short while. After waiting another half hour he left. He said:

I was plenty hot, but I didn't show it. When you show it you lose your point. That's what they are trying to do—make you hot so you'll cuss and start something; then they can have you arrested for disturbing the peace.

In another northern city a Negro attorney reported that he stopped at a small lunch car on one of the crosstown streets of a residence neighborhood to get a quick sandwich. The waiter said, "Brother, if you want to come back of the lunch counter we'll serve you." He did not go, and he did not eat. A law clerk from the same office went into a downtown restaurant for lunch. The waiter served him, but slammed the food down on the table before him and stood glaring. The law clerk ate unhurriedly, and when he had completed his meal he made a like gesture of slamming the exact change down on the counter. Not to be intimidated, he went to the same restaurant again the next day and continued to go until the discourtesy stopped. The manager discovered his presence had not injured his white trade and restrained the employees from further discourtesy.

In the effort to discourage Negro patronage and at the same time avoid suits for violating civil rights statutes, managers, waiters, or cooks may make the food unpalatable by filling it with salt, or even, as in a recently reported case, a violent emetic. Incidents were also reported in which bartenders and hotel managers insultingly smashed glasses after they had been used by unwelcome Negro customers. The simplest way of discouraging the return of an unwelcome Negro patron is to overcharge him. A businessman who frequently has occasion to visit the central business district of Chicago went into a public club for a drink. The bartender was reluctant to serve him, but finally served the 15-cent drink ordered and gave a bill for $1.25. The Negro protested that it was an overcharge and was told that they had the right to charge anything they liked. He asked for a receipt, and it was refused. Then he called a policeman, but the officer would do nothing about it. The manager threatened to have the Negro arrested for disturbing the peace. Then a white customer came up and volunteered to testify for him if he wanted to bring suit. He brought suit and won; but it cost him more in time and fees than he got in damages.

Occasionally some inconvenience can be caused restaurant owners, and this serves to make them more cautious. When a party of six Negro business and professional men stopped at a restaurant in a Chicago suburb, the owner informed them that he did not serve Negroes. They went to the near-by town of Robbins (an all-Negro town) in the same county, and swore out a warrant for the manager's arrest. A Negro deputy was sent to serve the warrant, and the manager was brought to Robbins for the hearing. Bail was set at the maximum of $500. The manager did not have the money and so was placed in the single little cell block of the Robbins jail. He remained there two and a half hours before the money was raised. His lawyer immediately got a change of venue, and the case was lost. One of the Negro parties to the suit said:

I got up and told the judge that I thought the case had been improperly settled. He said that we got what we wanted. He said we wanted to break up discrimination, and that is what we had done. No other white person wanted to spend a couple of hours in the jail over at Robbins, and he would promise us that there wouldn't be any more discrimination.

There are now several Negro lawyers in Chicago who specialize in handling these discrimination cases, and there are Negroes who are adventurous and "race spirited" enough to seek out places reported to employ discriminating practices. Judgments can be secured if they are careful to have witnesses and to avoid countercharges of disturbing the peace.

In New York it appears to be the middle-class type of restaurant that most often discriminates. A Negro writer who is frequently invited out with white friends said:

I use the restaurants downtown occasionally. I'm usually with white friends. I just don't patronize places if I'm doubtful. I'm not a fighter. It does something quite intense to me to have to fight my way past the color bar. I make it a point to go to places where I know I'll be served.

Instances are reported of small sandwich places that serve Negroes freely, but certain white customers, usually women, object to the presence of Negroes. A middle-class Negro housewife reported this experience:

I was in a cheap place where you can get a nickel sandwich and coffee, and a white woman came in and sat beside me before she saw my face. When she looked she threw up her hands and said, "My goodness," and moved to another seat. Another time I went to a five- and ten-cent store downtown. I sat by a woman and she picked up her dishes and moved.

Certain places make a practice of seating Negroes inconspicuously at back tables, but it is done with such grace that the real design is not detected unless a Negro expresses a preference for some other seat. The following story was told by a social work executive who has frequent conferences with other professional workers at lunch or dinner in a business district of New York City:

I accompanied my white friend to one of the better restaurants. He didn't see what happened, but I did at once. We entered and were received. The waiter seated my friend and then me. The headwaiter came forward to inquire if we were comfortable. Someone else had taken our hats. We were certainly getting the best of service. We ordered a turkey

dinner and it was some time being prepared. While sitting there a party
of eight came in—four men and four women. It was necessary to push
two tables together to accommodate them at one place. It was done very
quickly—no commotion.

I'm telling you these details so you can get the atmosphere of the
place—it's really quite exclusive. The ladies were seated and the men
were getting their seats. A tall red-headed man was taking his seat at
the end of the table when he looked up and saw me. I continued to look
right at him, because he appeared to be on the verge of a stroke, after one
glance at me. He summoned the headwaiter and I knew what was going
on. My friend's back was to their table, and he couldn't see it. I didn't
mention it as I was his guest and I knew he'd be disturbed if I were
made uncomfortable. Anyhow, at the opposite table there was quite a
conference. The women were consulted. They didn't turn and glare, but
eventually each one sent a gaze in my direction. I could see there was no
other space where a double table could be arranged.

What they did was to separate the party and sit four at a table, so
they could be at the other end of the room, away from me. I've told you
I'm not sensitive and it is so, but that was so obvious. Now, what makes
the trouble is that the headwaiter who was so gracious to us on our
arrival was somewhat inconvenienced by their shifting about, and if
Negroes go there again he may offer them a rear table.

A young public-school teacher, who has lived much in Europe,
and a friend, a sculptor of some distinction but discernibly a Negro,
went into a New York restaurant for dinner. This is his story:

One day we entered a restaurant downtown—quite an exclusive
place, and, after causing much excitement and concern, finally got service.
We ordered the same thing—something *en casserole*. We waited almost
an hour before it arrived. Both he and I noticed it looked peculiar and
different from the same dish served other places. When we cut into it
there was a hard crust of browned salt about one-half inch thick on top.
Naturally, the salt had gone through and the stuff couldn't be eaten.
I looked at my friend and he caught my look. We were aware that the
waiters and managers were watching us to see what we would do. We
pretended to be discussing something else and we decided we would not
send it back as they might remove the crust of salt and add something
worse—you know they will spit in food. I've heard that from kitchen help.
We decided to eat what we could and pretend to enjoy it. That was what
they didn't want us to do, so we'd be game enough to spoil their fun.
It was awful plowing through that food, but we did. They looked amazed
when they removed our dishes. They then served our dessert, which appeared and tasted all right. The entire day was spoiled.

The wife of a well-known surgeon, a beautiful and well-poised woman of taste, stated that she had visited a wide list of exclusive restaurants and had experienced difficulty only once. This was in an expensively equipped Chinese restaurant. She ascribed the failure of most of the places to discriminate to the fact that the patrons are of a type that does not make scenes and as a consequence the management would not do so. Her husband, on the other hand, was of the opinion that there is least difficulty in places where waiters are so busy they have no time to discriminate.

STORES

In the rural areas of the South the country store is the one universal meeting ground of the two races. Custom regulates social distance, and there is a common understanding that spatial propinquity does not imply social intimacy; hence signs for separating the races are not always necessary. In the larger towns of the South, and especially in cities where many specialized institutions perform the constellation of functions of the general store, the buying public is more heterogeneous and there is a great deal of variation in racial behavior, but there are rigid conventional patterns which may be broadly stated: Generally all the business houses fronting on the town square, or main street, are owned and operated by white people. Negro-operated businesses are usually found on back streets or in blocks conceded for Negro use. Negroes were served in all the business establishments of the towns visited for this study, except in cafés, barbershops, beauty parlors, and some amusement places. Grocery and dry-goods stores depend as much on the Negro buying public as on the white, a fact easily understood in areas where Negroes often greatly outnumber the whites.

In the cities of the South the treatment of Negroes in private commercial establishments is a matter of local custom, modified by the manner in which the manager and clerks interpret the strength of public opinion in a particular situation. Legal codes do not deny Negroes access to such establishments except where eating is involved, nor guarantee him the privileges usually accorded the white public. As a matter of fact, there is no uniform pattern of segregation and discrimination. The policies of stores vary widely, as do the relations between clerks and Negro patrons. One generalization can be made: In the interracial situation in trade relations there is constant uncertainty. One never knows quite how to deal with a new clerk or manager. Any breach of the racial etiquette, knowingly or unknowingly, or any new policy by manager or clerk can disturb the balance of relations established by personal understanding or customary expectations. Negroes exchange information on new business establishments in order to know what to expect. The larger and more exclusive stores prefer not to have large volumes of Negro trade, fearing that it will affect white patronage; but there is Negro trade in practically all of them. These better stores sometimes encourage the patronage of Negroes in the upper economic brackets, extend credit, and attempt to avoid offense in matters of fittings. At the same time they shunt both the mass Negro and poor white trade to their bargain basements.

Grocery Stores

Cleveland, Mississippi, provides an interesting variant of the small-town pattern. There are chain stores and also stores operated by Chinese, Italians, and Negroes. The bulk of the Negro population trades at three grocery stores operated by Chinese on the main business street. The Chinese stores are preferred to chain stores because Negroes are permitted more freedom and escape the traditional observances. On a Saturday night Negro farmers may be seen loitering in these stores, sitting around on the counters and benches engaged in unrestrained conversation. They wait on themselves, even to the extent of going behind the counters for articles. There is no particular racial etiquette to observe. As a result, the regular chain stores get little Negro patronage. Negroes who use them are usually upper-class persons such as schoolteachers, ministers, or others who by reason of their better economic position and education have achieved a status above the masses.

Least discrimination in the southern cities appears in the chain grocery stores. Here the clerks are most likely to place all relations on an economic basis and extend all services to all customers regardless of race. Negroes report that stores in which customers serve themselves offer fewer discriminatory practices than those in which customers must await the personal attention of a white clerk. The question of precedence of whites over Negroes does not intrude in self-service; it escapes another practice which Negroes find obnoxious—that of being offered inferior goods laid aside especially for the purpose. A Negro porter in a unit of a large grocery chain owned by a Jew in Houston said:

Colored people get right in line with all the other customers, and there ain't no difference made. If the checker tries to overlook a colored person and check a white person's stuff first, all you have to do is report him to the manager and the manager'll give him hell. One day in the store where I work the checker slighted a colored woman and waited on a white woman. The colored woman called the manager, and he told the checker that everyone was to be treated the same way, and not to let it happen again. We don't have much trouble like that because the checkers know that the boss won't stand for it. The porters carry the packages out and put them in the customer's cars. We carry packages for everybody, whether they are colored or white. We take them just as they come.

Personal contacts are unavoidable, however. The older counter arrangement still persists in the meat market, where each customer must be given personal service. It is here that Negro informants experience most embarrassment and more discrimination in chain stores.

The economic factor is observed to have some effect on racial taboos. Clerks do not insist upon addressing financially well-situated Negroes by their first names when this is resented. Such Negroes are called "Mr." and "Mrs." or "Dr." or nothing at all, instead of the commonplace "boy" or "auntie." Some of the variations in usage were pointed out by a Negro professional man in Richmond:

Except for this question of title, I think the Negroes are treated about like white people in the stores. Of course none of them want to give you the same service they give to white people, but competition for Negro trade is so keen that every store has to make some pretense at fair play. Negroes trade in the neighborhoods in which they live generally for groceries, and they are served in the order in which they arrive. It is just in the little niceties that discrimination is made in a grocery store. Now, of course, in a grocery store which is located in a white neighborhood a Negro customer may have to wait to be served, but I think even there that might be seldom.

The neighborhood stores are indeed somewhat better, according to some observations. There is more informality in carrying on business transactions. Some of the small neighborhood stores are run by foreigners who often allow themselves to be called by their first names. Relations are usually cordial in these stores, but the traditional distance is kept in most respects.

Department and Apparel Stores

In dry-goods stores in rural areas and small towns consciousness of race arises in sales of personal goods where touch is involved. Negro customers may not be allowed to try on goods or to use the private facilities. This distinction is intensified as the value of the goods involved increases. Again, it appears that in the better shops there is a feeling that the presence of Negroes makes a place unattractive; that if they must buy, they should be as inconspicuous as possible. As the quality of the stock carried increases and the buying power of the white patrons rises, there is a tendency to shunt Negroes toward the back of the store. They are not excluded entirely, however, except in the larger cities, where highly specialized stores can afford to cater only to a discriminating, and economically well-established, white public.

There appears to be little restriction on the trying on of hats, shoes, or dresses by Negroes in department stores of Johnston County. The clerks are subtle in arranging for separate fitting rooms for white and colored women, and the Negro women questioned on this point were not aware of the discrimination. The attitude of a shoe clerk in one of the department stores is that Negroes should have separate seats, and he tries to avoid fitting shoes on Negro customers, but he manages not to offend them, for competition is keen in Johnston County and the stores depend as much on Negroes as on whites.

In southern cities there is wide variation in the treatment of Negro patrons in department stores, women and men's clothing stores, and shoe stores. In the cities visited Negroes have favorite stores at which most of them trade because of the common belief that they are accorded fair treatment or at least meet less discrimination there than elsewhere. Likewise, there are stores that are known to be inhospitable to Negro trade and to discourage it. In most cities there are large stores that permit Negroes to make purchases across the counter but do not permit them to try on gloves, hats or dresses. The owner of a large department store in Richmond explained that he had no set racial policy, but he did have certain saleswomen who waited on Negro customers and tried to be especially friendly. These saleswomen are allowed to evade a request from an untidy Negro customer to try on garments; but the same policy holds for untidy whites.

The oldest and largest department store in Atlanta is a favorite store of Negroes because it has no restrictions on dealings with Negroes and makes no racial distinctions, except for the special rest room for Negro women which is located in the basement. Clerks are courteous and make a policy of using titles of "Mrs." or "Miss" in addressing packages or making charges to Negro customers. The proprietor is a Jew who determines the policy of the store and discourages any discourtesy to Negro patrons. Negroes are allowed credit, may use fitting rooms, and may try on any piece of apparel.

In shoe stores and in display sections of department stores it is a common practice to usher Negroes toward the back; and usually there are a few seats, separated slightly from others, where Negroes are expected to sit. Some stores have maids and porters assist with Negro trade in rush hours, but some of the higher-priced men's clothing stores have Negro porter-clerks who confine themselves to the Negro trade. A few of the larger stores have toilet facilities for Negroes, but these are located in the basement or adjacent to the men's toilet and are seldom well equipped. There were many complaints from Negroes that clerks attempted to sell them old or inferior goods; some reported a refusal to show certain goods. However, there were fewer complaints about difficulties in men's stores than in stores handling women's apparel.

Negroes make more use of neighborhood stores in Baltimore than in other cities. Even clothing is generally purchased in neighborhood stores because of the policies of the large downtown stores. The central business street of the Negro section is lined with small stores of all kinds: ladies' dress shops, men's shops, shoe shops, hosiery shops, hat shops, five- and ten-cent stores, etc. In no one store can a family be outfitted, but this can be accomplished by going to several shops. Most of these shops are owned by Jewish merchants, and they carry inexpensive lines of merchandise. There are a few small Negro-owned shops.

Most of Baltimore's leading department stores do not want or do not encourage the trade of Negroes. Stores are often crowded, but no brown or black face is observable, in spite of the fact that the Negro population amounts to 18 per cent of the total. The stores are of three types so far as policy toward Negro customers is concerned: (1) Most extreme are those, generally on Howard Street, which exclude Negroes completely. As soon as a Negro customer enters, she is approached by the floorwalker and advised that the store does not cater to Negro trade. (2) There are stores which allow Negroes to enter and buy articles across the counter, but do not allow them to try on hats, dresses, or gloves. (3) There are stores which accept Negro trade and allow Negro customers to try on dresses and hats. There is only one large downtown department store in this class.

There are no signs to indicate that Negroes are not wanted, and none to indicate to what extent they are allowed to trade. It would appear that Negroes must learn from each other's experiences just what is acceptable and what is not acceptable. Many managers voiced the opinion, "We have no signs. All Negroes in Baltimore know that their trade is not wanted. They know how far to go." But the Negroes interviewed had conflicting views about stores. From the white point of view, "Negroes never have traded on Howard Street" (the street of exclusive stores) ; but according to many Negroes this is not true. One said, "'We traded at some stores on Howard Street until the ——— Company came here about six or seven years ago. They started this policy of exclusion of Negroes." The truth seems to be somewhere between these two opinions. One store, which was established in 1858, never had much Negro patronage and now it has none. Since the policies of the stores are not recorded anywhere and the managing personnel changes often, it is not possible to discover when the policy of a store changed, or why, or how. Managers insist that they accepted the present policy when they were employed. Some Nergoes insist that the Housewives' League forced the managers to change their policies, but the managers insist that letters came only from individuals. The objective fact is that the Negroes do not patronize these stores.

In Indianapolis, another border city but with a slightly broader northern exposure, segregation policies are less strict on the whole, but there are variations in fitting practices. Some of the small shops have separate fitting rooms and rest rooms for Negroes; this policy permits discouragement of Negro trade without total exclusion. A housewife in a lower middle-class family said:

Some of these stores try to be exclusive. I went into one and the clerk acted like she didn't want to serve me. Finally she did, and I asked to try on a dress. She told me I could try it on over my dress I was wearing. Well, I couldn't tell how a dress would look that way, so I walked out.

Back of the policy is the belief, sometimes warranted, that the heavily oiled hair of many Negro women buyers soils hats and renders them unsalable and that some of the lower-class women neglect to take hygienic measures for cleanliness before seeking to try on dresses. The objection does not hold, however, for most of the Negroes who are actually able to buy in these stores. The policy can be regarded as a matter of hygiene and not as racial discrimination only when untidy whites also are discouraged, and when Negroes who are not objectionable in this respect are served.

Middle- and upper-class Negro informants in Indianapolis report experiences differing in character. One schoolteacher said:

I know of only one store that actually refused to permit Negroes [of her class] to try on garments. If they can prevent you from entering the store, without a scene, they will do it. Once when I went to the store a clerk finally came up, after keeping me waiting a long time. She asked what I wanted, and finally told me she had nothing big enough for me. I was determined to find out, so I got a friend who wears about size 12 to go down with me. The clerk then said they had nothing under $19, and unless we wanted to buy she would rather we not look at them. I told her we would not have come if we were not ready to buy. Her answer was, "Lots of you people have nothing to do but come in here and take up our time when you know you aren't going to buy." I was too mad to curse her. After trying on a few she said they wanted to repair the fitting room, and asked if we would come back the next week. I saw no reason for going back.

A well-known Negro businessman reported:

All of the large department stores serve Negroes without making any difference. Negroes are expected to use the same toilet facilities and drinking fountains used by the white people. I've understood that a few small shops have special fitting rooms for Negro customers. The kind of service you get in some of the places depends on your appearance and bearing.

For the border cities it is reasonable to conclude that in the smaller stores no discrimination is experienced in ordinary purchases across the counter; that there is a definite attempt at class discrimination among Negro customers in the large stores, but this sometimes extends to white customers; that in large stores in Baltimore and Washington there is total discrimination on a racial basis; and that in Indianapolis a less rigid policy of racial discrimination is influenced by the economic standing and appearance of the Negro customer.

In the northern cities, as a rule, neighborhood stores catering especially to Negroes are adequate to meet all ordinary requirements of lower- and lower middle-class groups. In these neighborhood stores Negroes not only receive courteous treatment, but occasionally they themselves become discourteous. A steelworker in Chicago said:

I do most of my trading with foreigners and Jews. All you have to do is holler, and they start moving.

The larger department stores in the downtown business districts, with few exceptions, serve all Negroes courteously. The character of the exceptions may be illustrated by the reports from Chicago. There were several reports of one large store which was attempting to discourage Negro patronage by slow and reluctant service and even by serving white customers first. A woman informant complained that at one department store the clerks were reluctant to fit gloves on Negro customers. An exclusive haberdashery discourages Negro patrons by making them wait for service. In larger shoe departments, it was asserted by some informants, Negroes were seated with their backs to the door to reduce their conspicuousness.

There are authenticated instances of discrimination in northern cities, but the range is limited and many contradictory experiences are reported. It might well be concluded that for the lower- and middle-class Negroes discriminatory practices are not acutely felt because most occasions for them are avoided; and for the upper middle- and upper-class Negro the treatment varies with the individual Negro and the individual white management or agent.

Five- and Ten-Cent Stores

Salesgirls in five- and ten-cent stores in the South are usually not discourteous in waiting on Negro patrons, but almost invariably wait on white customers first and have a customary way of dealing with Negroes that is different from the way they deal with whites. A Negro customer is approached with the query, "Something for you?" Occasionally a "thank you" is forthcoming when the sale is completed. The clerks always stand in a position dictated by the racial mores and exact a definite form of behavior from Negroes. A certain manner of speaking, or an expression so couched and intonated as to indicate the relative position of the Negro and the white person, may elicit a "yes, sir" from a Negro customer.

One modification of the pattern of service to Negroes appears in the avoidance of certain services that are regarded as special. A Negro investigator went into a five- and ten-cent store in Atlanta with the intention of making a purchase. As he entered the door he observed that a salesgirl was handing out tickets with which patrons could purchase a dish of ice cream at a reduced rate. The investigator was interested and approached the salesgirl in an effort to get the necessary ticket. She stopped issuing the tickets until the situation became embarrassing for the investigator and he moved on. The girl resumed her task. Several times later a similar effort was made to get a ticket, with the same result. From other informants who have frequented the store it was learned that Negroes are not given the privilege of these bargain prices on delicacies.

In all the downtown five- and ten-cent stores in Baltimore Negroes are accepted readily as customers. They are waited on with the automatic response taught the salesgirls. Negroes who were observed in some stores seemed at times to have to wait longer than white persons to be served, but this appeared to depend entirely upon the clerk. Negroes eat at the counters of five- and ten-cent stores where customers must stand while they eat, but they cannot eat at the tables or at the counters which have seats. In all cases observed the Negro was the last person to be served. At a new and modern five- and ten-cent store on Lexington Street there is no counter without seats. A Negro woman who asked for a bottle of Coca-Cola was refused service there. There are no fountains marked "colored," nor are there separate toilets.

Other Stores

Jewelry stores, shoe repair shops, optometrists and similar establishments differ from others in that the merchandise they sell has a more intimate character, requiring personal association and attention. In such places the circumstances and status of the customer determine the rigidity of etiquette.

The heterogeneous character of contacts in drugstores creates a confusing situation at times. Some contacts here are quasi-professional, some involve ordinary purchases, while some involve eating and drinking. The drugstore is a common meeting place for whites of both sexes, especially around the refreshment counter. Consequently, they have a different pattern of patronage from other stores. The use of the drugstore runs into the taboo against Negroes and whites eating and drinking together. Negroes are quickly waited upon so that they may go out quickly, and they may not get fountain or table service. They are sold ice cream, sandwiches or drinks, but they must be taken outside for consumption. There is usually no restriction on where they stand in the stores while waiting to be served, but instances were reported where zealous young clerks asked Negro patrons to stand at one end of the fountain while waiting to make their purchases. There were reports from small towns of instances in which Negroes could not even enter drugstores while white women were present.

Filling Stations

Service to Negroes at gasoline filling stations varies by sections of the South, and also by type of station. Stations which sell national brands of gasoline practice little or no discrimination in the sales service. Occasionally on the back roads there appears to be a casualness about the service, and inattention to the usual courtesies offered to white patrons.

Strangely enough, only a few stations have separate rest rooms for whites and Negroes. It is always a matter of speculation as to whether the Negro patrons may use the facilities or not. The uncertainty and the frequent embarrassment of Negroes who have sought the use of these rest rooms were serious enough to prompt the interracial committee of one southern state to inaugurate a campaign. The expense of providing four toilets and the rigidness of the architectural designs of the national service station systems have resulted in simply ignoring the Negro patron's needs in the physical arrangements and leaving to local custom or whim, or to national policy, the disposition of each emergency situation. Negro travelers on the highways are allowed the use of general rest rooms in some places and refused in others, depending upon conditions existing at the time and upon the apparent monetary advantage to the operator. Prosperous Negroes who are prospects for a substantial sale are permitted to use the facilities more frequently than not. Less prosperous ones seldom make the attempt. Local Negroes are not expected to use the rest rooms except in stations located in or very near Negro neighborhoods and catering to Negro trade.

Operators in most of the national systems of stations perform the courtesy services as a matter of routine; this is always the case if the automobile is one of good appearance. In individual cases there is pointed neglect of this service. Filling stations in Baltimore sell to Negro customers without question and automatically perform the extra services of windshield wiping and checking tires and water. All permit Negroes to use the rest rooms, although it is said that some are reluctant. No station has a "White Only" sign on its rest rooms.

AMUSEMENT PLACES

The chief amusement places in the South are the motion-picture theaters, swimming pools, skating rinks, bowling alleys, dance halls, and baseball parks. The exclusion of Negroes from most of these places patronized by whites is so universal and complete as to require no further elaboration. The issue of segregation arises only in the theaters and ball parks. There are segregated sections for Negroes in the ball parks—usually in the less favorable locations. Negroes may also rent parks in some places, for their own games. If they expect white spectators they must reserve a section exclusively for them, and this section must be in some desirable location. The same procedure is followed in the case of dance halls. Commercial dances with a Negro "name band," sponsored by Negroes, frequently advertise "A reserved section for whites."

Negroes attend the motion-picture theaters in all the towns visited, but are always segregated. The common attitude in this regard was expressed by a Negro businessman in Bolivar County:

If they did not let the Negroes go to shows here there would not be much for them to do, but go to church. They don't have anything to do. The Negroes can't even gamble like they used to do. This new mayor has closed all of that down. They make the Negroes go up in the balcony or "buzzard's roost," as they call it. It is close up there, and sometimes when the Negroes haven't had a bath yet, it is hard to stay up in some of them. They can go to all of the shows. The only other kind of thing they can go to here is the minstrel, and that doesn't come until the cotton picking season. Everybody goes then, but you have to sit in separate places. They always save the best seats for the white people. Even when these Negroes give something for themselves, they have a special section for the white folks, and do you know that they leave the best seats for them? These Negroes here have been kicked so much by the white folks that they like it, I believe. They would not know how to act, most of them, if they were not making the world comfortable for white folks. I know what I am talking about. That is so.

The town of Cleveland in Bolivar County has three motion-picture theaters. All of them have outside entrances for Negroes in the front of the building to the side of the white entrance. Each theater has a separate ticket window for Negroes, and in all cases Negroes are seated in the balcony. At one of the theaters visited in the course of this study, a white man frequently passed through the aisle of the balcony ordering Negroes to move to make room for others. This person always spoke gruffly and in a manner that would normally be considered discourteous. He would shout, "Move over there, boy, and give these girls some seats. Hey, you boy, did you hear what I said?" The "girls" referred to were middle-aged Negro women.

While the color line is always drawn in theaters, it is sometimes of a tenuous and shifting character. Thus a domestic worker in Marked Tree, Arkansas, said:

Colored go upstairs in the movie here. It is either too hot or too cold up there. Colored buy tickets at the side window. You just stand there, as a rule, until all the white people go in. They had a colored picture here, and they were to let colored people have the whole theater. The white people wouldn't let the colored have the whole building, so they had three shows. Not many white people went to see it.

When they fill up downstairs some of the white fellows come up and set with the colored. Most of the time they are just young fellows. Sometimes they come up with their girl friends. It's just like it always is— the white can come on your side, but you don't go on theirs.

In Johnston County, North Carolina, Negroes sit in a segregated section of the balcony, but they are separated from white balcony patrons only by an aisle. If the houses are crowded, Negroes and whites sit together wherever a seat can be found, but generally they seat themselves separately.

On "jack pot" nights, in one Mississippi town, Negroes are not admitted to the theater, although they may hold winning tickets for the money given away by the theater to attract patronage. After the jack pot a special picture is shown for whites and Negroes who want to come.

In all the cities visited the theaters either segregate Negroes or exclude them altogether. The usual pattern of segregation appears in the description provided by a Negro professional man:

In one of the oldest theaters half of the balcony is divided by a chain. When the white side fills up they push over into the colored side. They used to have special days for Negroes, but I understand now that it is open all of the time to Negroes. Negroes enter the theater from a side door, on a side street. They have a separate ticket window, and a colored girl selling tickets. Two of the large theaters have special midnight shows for colored people when a Negro stock company or some Negro movie comes here. They had a special show when Ivy Anderson was playing in some movie here not so long ago. She is a native of Houston. At one of the houses Negroes enter through a side door. At the newest theater they have to use the fire escape.

In some cases theaters have discontinued the "crow's roost" in the balcony and no longer accommodate Negroes, because of inability to compete with theaters operated by Negroes, or by whites for Negroes. A school official in Birmingham said:

There is one white theater that the Negroes can go to but must sit in the balcony. I never worry about going there. If I go, I am going to the Negro show. They don't have much like that in the way of amusement for Negroes around here. When you get away from the movies there is little that you can point out. They used to go in another show, where they had to go in through the back. That made the Negroes pretty mad, and they did not go very much. So few of them went that the management did not think it worth while to make arrangements for any of them.

In Richmond all-Negro houses have entirely displaced the attendance at white shows. This movement received its impetus in Richmond in 1934, when a Negro motion-picture house showing good pictures was opened. The situation is similar to that in Washington, D. C., where Negroes prefer the all-Negro theaters to the segregated sections of the larger white theaters. By 1937, when the last of five all-Negro theaters was opened in Richmond, the Negro population had been won from the white theaters altogether, and now no provision is made for Negroes to attend white motion-picture shows. The chain theaters for Negroes have been successful and are now found in many cities along the eastern seaboard.

In Baltimore Negroes generally attend all-Negro theaters, of which there are ten or more. Most of these are on Pennsylvania Avenue in the Negro residence section, and some of them are clean and attractive. None of the theaters are owned by Negroes. Negroes can go to three white theaters which have legitimate stage performances as well as motion-picture shows. In all cases they sit in the last rows in the balcony, but they use the common entrance to the balcony.

The local theaters in Dayton, Ohio, discourage Negro patronage. One theater manager said:

Of course, I have nothing against them, but I know that most of my patrons have. I don't want any migrant business, so I try to keep them from coming into my theater.

This theater has the general privilege of changing prices without notice, which is done if a Negro appears at the ticket window. If this fails to discourage their patronage, Negroes are ushered to an inconspicuous corner of the theater. On one occasion a Negro woman was pulled from the ticket line by an attendant.

BANKS

With a few exceptions in the South, the banks in cities as well as small towns accept the business of Negroes. While most banks accept deposits from Negroes, there are some which refuse to make loans to them, although Negroes who own land or other property that can be used as security can usually get loans on their own initiative. Bankers insist that Negroes whose property is considered a good risk can get loans just as easily as whites. Both white and colored sharecroppers who have no security have difficulty borrowing from banks. No signs segregating Negroes are displayed in any bank, but in some banks there is a special window to which all Negro patrons are directed.

PROFESSIONAL SERVICES

The majority of Negro professionals are found in the larger cities, and it is here that white professionals meet their greatest competition for Negro clients. However, the white professional man still dominates in all of the important fields. He has control of the judicial institutions, social welfare agencies, hospitals, and professional and business associations. Through his political power he can enact legal or professional codes to control competition in these fields. By far the largest volume of medical care for Negroes is administered by white doctors. The same is true of other professional services such as dentistry and law, the one outstanding exception being mortuary services.

Medical Service

Some Negro doctors were found in the rural places visited, but it appears that among Negroes there is still a decided preference for white doctors. This is due partly, no doubt, to the entanglements of the race system. Thus, for example, when white people send their Negro employees to a doctor, although Negroes pay the bills in the end, the Negroes feel compelled to go to a white doctor. A white man is a good reference in establishing surety for the doctor's bill, but such backing would not be given for treatment by Negro doctors. Significantly, it is taken for granted that Negroes do not get standard care in the hands of doctors, any more than in hospitals and other professional agencies, but complaints are made in bated breath. There is a fear that they may fare worse later.

The practices of white doctors vary in serving Negroes. In small towns Negro patients are not refused treatment, but white patients are usually served first. Some doctors have separate waiting rooms, but in some cases Negroes wait in the same room or give way to whites and wait outside. The same office is used for treatments, however. Only one instance was reported in which the doctor-patient relation is formalized and Negroes and whites are taken in turn.

There was evidence in some of the cities of direct and subtle pressure on Negroes to use white doctors. In large cities segregation and handling in the office follow about the same patterns noted in smaller places.

In some urban localities particular Negro professionals have sizable clienteles. In Richmond prior to 1929 about 48 per cent of the Negro population used Negro physicians. The proportion is less today than it was ten years ago; and according to one informed observer there is some justification for it in the experiences of the people using Negro physicians. The white physicians have both prestige and the best equipment, and these impress many Negroes when in critical condition. Nevertheless, Negro physicians in Richmond appear prosperous and insist that they have made progress in many ways. Most of the white physicians prefer to visit the Negro patient instead of having him visit the office. Two of Richmond's most prominent white physicians began their practice with Negro patients, but later found the practice embarrassing.

Interestingly enough, in a few instances it was observed that Negro doctors and dentists had white patients; and in two cases Negro doctors had white patients exclusively.

Mortuary Services

Very rigid segregation exists in taking care of the dead; there are parallel funeral establishments and cemeteries in all parts of the South. In one state the health code prohibits Negro morticians from handling white bodies. This once led to an embarrassing situation when the police unwittingly turned over to a Negro mortician the body of a white criminal who had blackened his face as a disguise. In most places the Negroes have organized burial policy associations, and it is through these organizations that Negro undertakers operate. Since the business is one of intimate personal service, there is little competition between white and Negro undertakers. As a result, this field is one in which Negroes are most successful.

There are occasional exceptions to the general rule of racial exclusion, and some white undertakers take Negro business. As a matter of fact, small funeral establishments sometimes seek it. Other exceptions occur in cases of prominent Negroes or those with sentimental attachments to white people. Such an exception was reported in Cleveland, Mississippi, where a white undertaker buried an old Negro "who always told the white undertaker that he had to bury him when he died." It was once customary for Negroes attached to white families to be buried in the same cemeteries, but in some instances Negro bodies have been removed, years afterward, to Negro cemeteries; this sentimental gesture has seldom been made in recent years.

Other Services

There are not many Negroes in professional fields other than teaching and medicine. As shown in Chapter II, there has been little yielding to the Negro in the legal profession in southern cities, and none at all in small towns. There is a belief among Negroes that a white lawyer can generally do more for a Negro than a Negro lawyer. In a court battle it is power that counts and one chooses a representative from the race where sovereignty resides. The clienteles of Negro lawyers, ministers, and teachers are limited to their own race.

Chapter IV

RACIAL SEGREGATION IN OCCUPATIONS AND INDUSTRIES

The basis of racial segregation in occupations is to be found in the fundamental concept of social classes. Historically, the stratification of society in the South was influenced by the presence of the Negro and by the acceptance of slavery as a system of organizing production. The early social thinkers of the South assumed the inevitability of permanent classes of persons for the performance of different types of work. Some work was regarded as degrading, but nevertheless had to be performed. The institution of slavery ensured the performance of the menial work and at the same time ordered the march of progress in the interest of the master class. This is the famous "mudsill" theory of the structural basis of society accepted by the social theorists of the slavery regime. Requiring but a low order of intelligence and little skill, menial labor had as its prime requisites vigor, docility, and fidelity. A category of workers to perform such labor was necessary for the existence of a class which could develop progress, civilization, and refinement. This theory, however, took no account of other classes in the white society; class was construed to be identical with race and color. While aiming basically at the production of property in slaves, in practice the theory created a false caste system on the basis of race, which made no adequate economic provision for the nonslaveholding whites who were actually the most numerous element in the population. Labor below the level of intellectual or managerial functions was stigmatized as degrading and as the exclusive province of the slave.

The literature and other records of the period show how shrewdly the slaveholders won popular support for a doctrine which benefited only themselves. They largely succeeded in persuading the nonpropertied whites that the interests of all whites in the Old South were the same. Although the poor white had no property, they argued, "he has the purpose and the hope to be rich before he dies, and to leave property to his children."[1] It was landownership that gave a person status. However small or barren the plot, an owner felt that he had a mystic stake rooted deep in the land and in the nation's freedom of fee simple ownership. If a man could not own slaves he was still proud and free if he could own a patch of land. Even if he was hungry and without clothes, at least he was better than the slaves and free Negroes who formed the laboring classes.

The plantation system did not require whites in any large numbers, and the lack of industries limited the growth both of a middle class and of white-collar workers. The "tarheelers" and "sand hillers" of the Carolinas, the "crackers" of Georgia, the "red necks" of Alabama, the "wool-hats" of Mississippi, the "piney woods folks," the "swamp dwellers" of Louisiana, together with others of the lower middle and lower classes, felt the brunt of the slave system. While the planters lived in the rich river bottoms, the poorer whites lived in the hills, nursing their illusion of a common destiny by virtue of a common color. The two classes seldom came into contact where dangerous economic contrasts could be made. The interclass struggle, hatred, and antagonism of the poorer whites were mitigated both by this geographical segregation and by the consoling rationalization of a superiority to the black labor that was controlled by the planters.

The situation had two significant consequences: (1) the labor of the South—at first only the arduous and unskilled labor but later the semiskilled and skilled work as well—came to be performed very largely by Negroes under the "protection" of the institution of slavery; (2) the potential white laboring class was left to work out its own destiny outside the basic economic system of the region. Whatever class bitterness was generated against the more fortunate classes of the population was deflected to the Negro slaves with whom the poor whites could not live and for whom they could not advocate freedom. An incident of this situation was the development of a slave artisan group that effectually retarded the growth of free laboring classes and labor consciousness in the South.

OCCUPATIONAL PATTERNS OF FREE WHITES AND NEGRO SLAVES

Of the slave artisans the historian Jernegan says: "Whatever the shortcomings the weight of evidence shows that there was a great increase in numbers; that they were more valuable than untrained slaves, and much sought after; that they competed with free white labor especially in the towns; and they were the most important

---

[1] William S. Jenkins, *Pro-Slavery Thought in the Old South* (Chapel Hill: University of North Carolina Press, 1935), p. 286.

agency in the commercial development of the South."[2] From the
frequency of advertisements for escaped slave artisans, it appears
that they were fairly numerous in the population. Moreover, there
are records of protests from white workers over the use of skilled
slaves by owners, notably as carpenters and brick and stone masons.
In the inventories of estates are records of Negro factory hands,
accounted as being worth about $200 a year plus maintenance.

Cases reported by Catteral[3] reflect the frequent presence of Negro
slave artisans in comparatively high positions. For example, in
Columbia, South Carolina, in 1850 a Dr. Sill brought suit against
a railroad company for hiring a Negro of 25 years of age, "skilled in
the business of attending a drug store."[4] In Columbia, Tennessee,
in 1858 two Negro slaves were barbers, acting for themselves with
the permission of their masters. They earned enough money to be
involved in litigations about lending money for interest, through an
agent; in one case the amount involved was $2,424.77.[5] Another
Tennessee case in 1856 concerned the payment of $2,000 for the
hire of 22 Negroes as ironworkers.[6] In North Carolina a Mr. Bost
willed in 1857 "that my sons . . . have my mill . . . and also my
Negro boy, George, the miller."[7] In the same year Gardner and
Masters, in "a co-partnership in the business of making, distilling
and selling turpentine in Georgia," hired a number of slaves and
purchased others for carrying on the work. An argument concerning
the worth of a certain 18-year-old Negro brought out the testimony
in a Tennessee court in 1855 that he had been worth $640 in hires
during the past six years. The judgment was that if he could command a hire of $150 a year he was worth no less than $1200.

Although there are no reliable data on the occupational classification of slaves by states, some independent censuses of cities are available. When a census of Charleston, South Carolina, was taken in
1848,[8] the population of approximately 40,000 persons was about
equally divided between whites and Negroes (slaves and free); and
the data may be taken as typical of occupational distributions in

[2] M. W. Jernegan, "Slavery and the Beginnings of Industrialism in the American
Colonies," *American Historical Review*, 25:220-246 (October, 1919).

[3] Helen Tunnicliff Catteral, *Judicial Cases Concerning American Slavery and
the Negro* (Washington, D.C., 1929), Vol. II.

[4] *Ibid.*, p. 418.

[5] *Ibid.*, p. 528.

[6] *Ibid.*, p. 562.

[7] *Ibid.*, p. 215.

[8] John Dawson and H. W. DeSaussure, *Census of Charleston* (Charleston, 1849),
pp. 21-30.

similar urban areas. The male manual laborers are classified by color and occupation in Table V.

TABLE V

SLAVE, FREE NEGRO AND WHITE MALES IN MANUAL OCCUPATIONS,
CHARLESTON, SOUTH CAROLINA, 1848*

Occupations	Slaves	Free Negroes	Whites	Total
Skilled artisans...............	421	122	634	1177
Mechanics....................	45	2	182	229
Semiskilled..................	131	41	73	245
Domestic and personal.........	1948	18	23	1989
Unskilled....................	838	19	192	1049
Apprentices..................	43	14		57
Other.......................			55	55
Total.....................	3426	216	1159	4801

* Ulrich B. Phillips, *American Negro Slavery* (New York: D. Appleton and Company, 1918), p. 403.

Slaves comprised 71 per cent of all manual laborers, 36 per cent of the skilled artisans, 98 per cent of the domestic and personal service workers, and 80 per cent of the unskilled laborers. In his classic volume on Negro slavery Phillips says that "the repugnance of white laborers toward menial employment corresponds with the traditional predilection of householders for Negroes in a lasting tenure for their intimate services and gave the slaves a virtual monopoly of this calling."[9] This occupational pre-eminence, however, did not stop with the menial category. Together with the free Negroes the slaves held a strong position in carpentry, masonry, coopering, painting, plastering, shipbuilding, tailoring, and baking.

The racial division of labor is suggested in a comparison of the occupational distribution of the population in a typical slave state with that in a typical free state in 1860. The federal census of occupations in 1860 does not include slave labor, but gives the occupations of the total white population. In the typical slave state of Mississippi and the similarly agricultural, free state of Iowa the foreign-born represented very minor proportions of the total white population. Of the gainfully employed whites in Mississippi, 6 per cent were professional persons; 62 per cent were managers or proprietors of farms or other establishments; 11 per cent were skilled and semi-skilled workers; 3 per cent, clerical workers; 17 per cent, laborers; and 1 per cent, personal and domestic servants (Table VI). Com-

[9] Ulrich B. Phillips, *American Negro Slavery: A Survey of the Supply, Employment, and Control of Negro Labor as Determined by the Plantation Regime* (New York: D. Appleton and Company, 1918), p. 402.

pared with the occupational distribution of the total white population
in Iowa, the proportions of professional workers, farm owners and
managers, and white-collar workers in Mississippi were decidedly
larger, while the proportions of skilled, semiskilled, and unskilled
workers and of domestic and personal servants were considerably
smaller. This suggests that in Mississippi the lower grades of work
were being performed by the 436,631 Negro slaves. They were the
ordinary and prime field hands, blacksmiths, carpenters, wheelwrights, and masons on the plantations, and in many instances the
leased artisans in the towns. They were also the servants in households, taverns and hotels, and not infrequently helpers and workers
in the mills and factories of this predominantly agricultural state.

TABLE VI

NUMBER AND PERCENTAGE DISTRIBUTION OF GAINFULLY-EMPLOYED WHITE POPU-
LATION BY OCCUPATION, IOWA AND MISSISSIPPI, 1860

	Iowa		Mississippi	
	Number	Per cent	Number	Per cent
1. Professional and semiprofessional workers	8,524	4.6	5,476	6.0
2. Proprietors, managers and officials	6,851	3.7	3,269	3.6
3. Farmers and farm managers	88,960	47.6	53,539	58.8
4. Clerical, sales and kindred workers	2,644	1.4	2,251	2.5
5. Craftsmen, foremen and kindred workers	21,179	11.3	7,490	8.2
6. Semiskilled workers	6,382	3.4	2,350	2.6
7. Service workers, except domestic	355	0.2	267	0.3
8. Domestic service workers	7,001	3.7	790	0.9
9. Laborers, except farm	27,202	14.6	7,972	8.8
10. Farm laborers	17,729	9.5	7,585	8.3
Total	186,823	100.0	90,989	100.0

In the North Negroes had no such monopoly on work, whether
unskilled or skilled. Northern industry was attracting its labor from
Europe, a cheaper source in the long run; and the white laboring
class acknowledged itself as such. The relatively few Negroes of
the region, although free, were employed in the less responsible occupational positions. There were a few successful caterers, tailors, and
dressmakers who served a wealthy white clientele; but the majority
of the Negro workers, when employed at all, were in domestic service
and in the ranks of common labor.

THE INFLUENCE OF EMANCIPATION ON OCCUPATIONAL PATTERNS

The political upheaval of the Civil War and Reconstruction was even more deeply an economic upheaval. It brought about a reorganization of the artificial occupational structure and a redefinition of the Negro's occupational status in the light of the newly acquired status of the white workers and the loss of the traditional status of the white master class. The barriers to free movement between classes were lowered.[10] In the strictly plantation areas the transition from slavery to share-tenancy did not seriously change the position of the Negro worker but, characteristically, it did not adequately take into account the white agricultural worker. One of the first clear evidences of the collapse of the artificial occupational stratification on the basis of race was in the gradual but inevitable sifting of the white farm workers down to the class level of the Negroes.

The first efforts of the white population to control the competition between Negroes schooled in slavery and white workers appeared in the Black Codes. These attempted to re-establish the traditional social order whose economic base had been annihilated. In the cities and small industrial towns of the South the emerging white workers, armed with the ballot and led by shrewd politicians and demagogues from the forgotten classes of the past, met the competition with slavery-trained Negro labor by direct legislation and the pre-emption of new industries such as cotton textiles. The legislation demanding complete segregation of workers in certain industries destroyed the principle of free competition by imposing the financial burden of dual overhead costs for manufacturers. The cotton mills, which came to be the most prominent manufacturing industry of the South, were developed with a fervent concern for the neglected poor whites and, by social as well as economic and political design, excluded the Negroes from all but the most menial labor. Skilled crafts, which were less effectively controlled by industrial organization, remained an open field for racial competition until they fell under the control of white labor organizations which attempted to practice the same racial exclusion policies. The only area where occupational differentiation of Negro workers was free to take place was in work and services for other Negroes; and this in time contributed to the social class stratification of the Negro population.

In spite of restrictions, changes in the occupational alignment of white and Negro workers began shortly after the abolition of slavery.

[10] Edgar T. Thompson, "The Planter in the Pattern of Race Relations in the South," *Social Forces,* 19:251 (December, 1940).

As early as 1880 census data on occupations indicated that white workers were increasing their proportions in skilled occupations in the building trades, in which Negroes had formerly held an important position. The one outstanding industry of the South, textile manufacturing, drew all except its most menial labor from rural whites. Jobs which were in the range of political patronage, including such unattractive ones as scavenger and garbage collector, which might have been considered "Negro jobs" from the character of the work, became increasingly jobs for unskilled whites who were potential voters. Barbershops and other public personal services operated by Negroes for white patronage began to decline in numbers. By 1890 Negroes in the United States as a whole were distributed in some numbers over all occupations from agricultural labor and domestic service to the professions; but the great bulk of the working population, 88 per cent, was in the two lowest groups, agricultural labor and domestic service (Table VII). Adding those employed in

TABLE VII

PERCENTAGE DISTRIBUTION OF GAINFULLY EMPLOYED NATIVE-BORN WHITES AND NEGROES IN SELECTED INDUSTRIAL OR OCCUPATIONAL GROUPS, UNITED STATES, 1890 AND 1930*

	1890		1930	
	White	Negro	White	Negro
Professional service	4.6	1.1	8.0	2.5
Trade and transportation	16.2	4.8	21.9	10.5
Manufacturing and mechanical trades	25.1	5.6	27.5	18.6
Domestic and personal service	17.1	31.3	6.6	28.6
Agriculture and mining	37.0	57.2	23.2	37.5
Other occupations	..	..	12.8	2.3
Total	100.0	100.0	100.0	100.0

* Adapted from *Negro Population in the United States, 1790–1915*, U. S. Bureau of the Census, Table 20, p. 526, and *Negroes in the United States 1920–1932*, U. S. Bureau of the Census, Table 7, p. 290.

the manufacturing and transportation industries, where 80 per cent were in unskilled jobs, the proportion in the unskilled class was approximately 97 per cent.

Nevertheless, two factors distinguished the position of Negroes from that of an occupational caste: (1) although their largest proportions were in the lower occupational brackets, they shared this level with whites, native and foreign-born; (2) they were not rigidly restricted to the lower levels. Varying proportions were in skilled, clerical, managerial, and professional occupations.

THE RACIAL DIVISION OF LABOR IN 1930

Any attempt to determine the present division of labor by race must consider, first, the extent of Negro inclusion in industry and, second, the distribution of the Negro group by occupational levels of work. Negroes constituted 11.3 per cent of the gainful workers of the United States in 1930. As in 1890, the Negro workers still had their heaviest concentrations in the unskilled branches of industry and agriculture, and in domestic service positions, but the proportions at the higher occupational levels had increased.[11] Nearly two-

TABLE VIII

INDUSTRY OR SERVICE GROUPS IN WHICH MORE THAN TEN
PER CENT OF EMPLOYEES WERE NEGROES, 1930*

Group	Per cent Negro
Turpentine farms and distilleries	75.2
Fertilizer factories	60.4
Domestic and personal services	38.6
Saw and planing mills	25.1
Fish curing and packing	24.3
Cigar and tobacco factories	22.9
Laundries	19.5
Agriculture	19.0
Livery stables	19.0
Charcoal and coke works	18.6
Hotels, restaurants, boardinghouses, etc.	16.8
Cleaning, dyeing, and pressing shops	15.2
Other specified mines	15.1
Water transportation	15.1
Brick, tile, and terra-cotta factories	14.8
Construction and maintenance of roads, streets, sewers, and bridges	14.1
Sugar factories and refineries	14.0
Other woodworking factories	13.6
Forestry	13.1
Stockyards	12.9
Not specified industries	11.9
Slaughter and packing houses	11.2
Iron mines	11.1
Other food factories	11.1
Not specified metal industries	10.7
Quarries	10.5
Garages, greasing stations and automobile laundries	10.5
Steam railroads	10.3

* W. S. Woytinsky, *The Labor Supply in the United States*, pp. 50-64.

[11] The occupational hierarchy, furthermore, has taken on a significant division: the upper half of the occupational pyramid, including Negro professionals, pro-

thirds of all Negro workers were now employed in agriculture or various types of domestic and personal service (Table VII).

Examining first the 126 different industries, branches of industry, and service groups in which the 1930 census classifies the gainfully employed population, Negro workers are found in every group.[12] Table VIII shows the particular groups in which Negroes comprised more than 10 per cent of the total workers, while Table IX sum-

TABLE IX

Chief Industry or Service Groups in Which Less Than Five Per Cent of Employees Were Negroes, 1930*

Group	Per cent Negro
Professional service (except recreation and amusement)	4.7
Clothing industries	4.5
Metal industries (except iron and steel)	2.6
Textile industries	2.2
Paper, printing and allied industries	2.1
Advertising, banking, insurance and real estate	1.7
Leather industries	1.6

MISCELLANEOUS "NEW" INDUSTRIES

Automobile factories	4.0
Electric light and power plants	2.6
Rayon factories	2.4
Automobile agencies, stores, and filling stations	2.4
Air transportation	2.4
Rubber factories	2.1
Electrical machinery and supply factories	0.8
Telegraph and telephone	0.7
Radio broadcasting	0.7

*W. S. Woytinsky, *loc. cit.*

marizes the chief groups in which less than 5 per cent of the workers were Negroes. The industries shown in Table IX represented a total of 10,162,527 workers, 21 per cent of the nation's total. Yet they employed only 307,440 Negroes, less than 6 per cent of all Negro gainful workers. The industrial or service groups in which Negro numbers are most strictly limited are: (1) those which represent new technical developments, such as radio, rayon manufacturing, electrical machinery, rubber fabrication, airplane construction and service; (2) those which involve large amounts of white-collar work, such as telegraph and telephone systems, advertising agencies, bank-

---

prietors and managers, and clerks, represents work performed for the Negro group, and is the basis of the class divisions within the Negro population; the lower half of the pyramid, including skilled, semiskilled, unskilled, and domestic workers, represents work performed, for the most part, for whites.

[12] W. S. Woytinsky, *The Labor Supply in the United States* (Washington: Social Science Research Council, Committee on Social Security, 1937), pp. 50-64.

ing and brokerage; (3) those in which the working force is fluid and promotions from lower to higher positions are logical and frequent, as in automobile factories, electric light and power plants, and railroad transportation; (4) those in which there is contact with the public in the capacity of salesmen or skilled operatives, such as clerks in stores, meter inspectors, street car, bus and subway conductors and motormen; (5) certain food industries which do not involve canning, such as butter, cheese, condensed milk, and candy manufacturing, and bakeries; (6) industries located in areas in which few Negroes live, such as lead and zinc mines, furniture factories, carpet mills, woolen and worsted mills.

In the industries in which there were many Negroes they were almost wholly in unskilled occupations. Altogether there were 64 general industrial or service groups in which at least half the Negro workers were engaged in unskilled labor, while at least half the white workers were above that level. These 64 fields accounted for 55 per cent of the total Negro working population in the United States.

In industries in which there are few Negroes there are varying proportions in the semiskilled and skilled occupations depending upon the character of the industry. There were 38 general industrial or service groups[13] in which at least half of the Negro workers were employed in capacities above the unskilled labor category. These industries accounted for 12 per cent of the total Negro working force. The largest numbers were in cigar and tobacco factories; independent hand trades; truck, transfer, and cab companies; wholesale and retail trade; professional service; recreation and amusement; and laundries. More than half of the Negro employees were skilled or white collar workers in seven groups: suit, coat, and overall factories; automobile repair shops; postal service; insurance; real estate; professional service; and recreation and amusement.

A valuable study of occupational changes among Negroes in Chicago, made under the auspices of the Works Projects Administration and supervised by Cayton, illustrates the changing occupational pattern of the Negro.[14] Using 1890 census data as a base, the occupations of Negroes were studied by districts through 1930. In 1890, 54 per cent of the Negro gainful workers were in domestic service or employed by hotels, large restaurants, and rail-

[13] *Ibid.*
[14] Estelle Hill Scott, *Occupational Changes Among Negroes in Chicago,* Report of Official Project 665-54-3-336, WPA, H. K. Seltzer, Director, District 3, 1939.

roads. Only 7 per cent were in skilled, clerical, managerial, or professional positions. Outside the field of domestic and personal service, unskilled positions were largely filled by foreign-born whites who comprised 72 per cent of the unskilled workers. Negroes had their introduction to industry in 1890 when they were used to break the stockyard strike.

By 1910 Negro males were found in some numbers in 166 out of 178 industry or service groups and Negro females in 37 out of 42 groups. There had been intense competition with the foreign-born while native whites moved steadily into the upper brackets.

By 1920, following the migrations, Negroes comprised 11 per cent of the laborers in manufacturing and mechanical industries compared with only 3 per cent in 1910. Nevertheless, they remained below the foreign-born in mass occupational level; and the foreign-born, in turn, below the native whites. By 1930 the proportion of Negro unskilled workers was about double that of the foreign-born whites, and six times that of the native whites.

Native whites were found at all occupational levels in both periods, but were relatively concentrated in the three top categories. In 1890 they dominated the professional and white-collar classes, had a relatively large proportion of proprietors and managers, and a relatively small proportion of skilled and unskilled workers. The foreign-born formed an intermediate group between the native whites and the Negroes with few professionals compared with native whites, and, compared with Negroes, less than half the proportion engaged in unskilled work. The foreign-born, however, had a larger proportion of skilled workers. Three-fourths of all boot- and shoemakers and repairers, blacksmiths and wheelwrights were foreign-born, while less than 1 per cent were Negroes. The latter were heavily concentrated in the unskilled class, with relatively fewer semiskilled workers than either the native or the foreign-born white, and negligible proportions in any higher class. The Negroes exceeded the other nativity groups in the servant classes, and the foreign-born exceeded the Negroes in the other unskilled classes.

By 1930 the pattern had changed significantly, reflecting the experience of Negroes in occupations in northern cities. The native whites had increased their proportions in the professional and white-collar classes and decreased their proportion in unskilled fields to the smallest proportion in any category except professional. They clearly had a monopoly on the preferred and status jobs. The foreign-born whites had begun to develop a professional class, continued to command the skilled and semiskilled fields, and had a sizable proportion of shopkeepers, presumably serving the requirements of their own cultural backgrounds. While the Negroes still had their largest proportions in unskilled work (both domestic service and labor), they had pushed into the skilled field and had developed their own professional class and some business; proportionately, they had almost as many semiskilled workers as the foreign-born, and over half as many white-collar workers.

CURRENT FACTORS IN THE RACIAL DIVISION OF LABOR

A general tendency in occupational differentiation has been the use of Negro workers for heavy types of unskilled manual labor and the use of white workers where machinery is involved. Back of this practice is the assumption that the Negro race is mentally, culturally, and temperamentally ill-adapted to work with machinery. However, the number of highly skilled Negro workers found in plants where the management does not share this assumption suggests that performance in this line is more a matter of opportunity for training than of native ability. The historical association of Negroes with arduous, routine, and directed work is perhaps the basis of the persisting conception that this is exclusively their sphere. This belief is bound up with the whole complex pattern of race and class status, group competition, and the struggle for economic and social security. Some occupations are an important structural element in the social class hierarchy. Attributes of these occupations have important implications for the division of labor in a dynamic society. If the economic structure of the nation were rigid and simplified, the relationships would be more clearly defined, self-enforcing, and hereditary, i.e., they would have the characteristics of an occupational caste structure. But impersonal forces are constantly operating to alter these relations, thus making necessary their constant redefinition within an ideological framework which is itself changing slowly. Some of the factors operating to preserve this moving equilibrium merit further consideration.

"Status" of Work

Characterization of work as menial may determine its acceptability to white workers. Work once done by Negro slaves still carries a certain social stigma. Scrubbing the floors of public buildings is not generally acceptable to white women in the South, although it is in the North. The use of white uniforms for street cleaners and scavengers, or the fact of municipal employment, can change the status of such work enough to make it acceptable to white men; this is occurring with considerable frequency in the South.

Wages

An important distinction is preserved, particularly in the South, between wages for white and for Negro workers. This wage differential is usually taken for granted because of the difference in the types of work done in the past. It is also based on the assumption that whites and Negroes have fundamentally different living standards and requirements. Wage differences are now so well established in custom that they are frequently maintained where work is identical, with the conviction that this is necessary to preserve the superior social status of the white worker. This practice of employers is not only in the interest of morale within the plant, but also a matter of white employee expectation, and even demand. Numbers of white workers, in commenting upon the minimum wage rates established by the Fair Labor Standards Act of 1938, expressed the fear that Negro workers would "get out of their place" if they received much more money than they were accustomed to having. One of the difficulties of effective labor organization in the South has been the unwillingness of white workers to agree to the principle of equal pay, even when it was apparent that lower pay for Negroes depressed standards for white workers.

Separate wage rates for Negroes are thus in a sense a fixed tradition. Although rates for white workers are inadequate for a comfortable level of living, Negro rates are expected to be lower. The pressure of economic depression forced numbers of white workers to accept Negro jobs, at Negro wages. An upward change in wages can make a job more desirable for white workers, who promptly attempt further to increase the prestige of the work by having all Negroes excluded from it. There has been some support for such action in the attitude of certain employers who have declared that if they "have to pay white man's wages" they may as well hire white men. Instances have been noted of wage increases that have not changed the occupational pattern, but in these cases some other factor has usually controlled the selection and retention of Negro workers.

Economic Dislocation

In times of work shortage it is expected that there will be increased competition for jobs. Uncontrolled, this competition can, conceivably, retard the advance of workers to improved wages and conditions of labor. Where organized labor aids in bargaining, some gains can be retained for a group strong enough to enforce its claims. Where the racial factor is conspicuous several results are possible: There may be direct group competition with the ultimate elimination of the weaker by the stronger; the separate interests may operate to make ineffective the organized demands of one group or the other; or there may be downward bargaining for work and wages, which is disastrous to the welfare of labor generally. All these results have actually occurred. What is most serious at present is the fact that technological development in industry tends to make permanent the decreased labor demand and increases the competition of workers for available jobs. In this situation the Negro workers have felt the impact of new conditions in industry more keenly than any others excepting perhaps the group of resourceless, superannuated workers.

Where the objective is profit it is scarcely to be expected that sentiment will play a major role in determining wage policy. If lower wages mean greater profits without impairing the product or arousing public hostility to it, that fact will frequently have more weight with employers than a sentimental race or sex preference. Marginal workers, whether Negro, European, or Mexican, have ultimately the alternative of adjusting themselves to lower wages or of reducing their opportunities for working at all. In the past the greatest security for Negro workers has been in jobs where wages were chronically low. Unless there is some assumed superiority for certain types of physical labor, as existed until very recently in longshoring or the open-hearth sections of iron and steel, any important change in the conditions of employment is likely to impose a redefinition of the occupational pattern.

Changes in Duties Associated with Jobs

Types of work not usually performed by Negroes may for economy be combined with their regular work. For example, when to a porter's duties are added those of a part-time clerk, or when a wagon or truck driver is given the task of soliciting or collecting, the work automatically falls into the province of white workers. Some employers have avoided a clash with custom by stressing the least essential features of a position. A Negro messenger may frequently perform highly responsible duties in connection with the handling of money and do clerical work as well, as long as he is given the personal service title of messenger. His pay may or may not be changed. Again, a porter may be a shipping clerk provided he retains the title and pay of a porter; but if these are changed, the status is no longer that of a Negro job.

Managerial or Supervisory Functions

One of the most persistent elements of the racial orthodoxy has to do with positions of authority, however insignificant in point of actual control. A considerable waste has been incurred in the multiplication of unskilled white inspectors and subforemen of unskilled work being done by Negroes, in response to community expectation. When it is necessary to combine any supervision with unskilled work, it becomes definitely a white man's job. The practice is supported not only by popular insistence upon this occupational hierarchy, but by the frequently expressed conviction that Negro workers can be controlled only by the prestige of white foremen.

Exceptions have been made as circumstances permitted tests to be made, as for example, in the Negro educational system which at one time was believed to be manageable only by white principals. There have also been many exceptions to the common practice in southern industries where Negro contractors supervise white skilled and unskilled workers, where skilled Negroes direct the work of white apprentices, and where Negroes fill the role of foremen over white and Negro workers although without the title.

Control over Work by Labor Organizations

Twenty years ago there were many Negro organizations of plasterers, bricklayers, and carpenters in southern cities, for the simple reason that Negroes were established in these trades ahead of white workers. Having received the first charters, the Negro groups held local positions of advantage with reference to general organization. There are today few such organizations of Negroes and their bitter complaint is that their white fellow workers, once in sufficient numbers to control the distribution of work, have gradually pushed them out of the unions.

The practice of restricting Negro membership in labor unions has been prevalent in the past in the North and West and is often cited by Negro nonunion workers as the reason for their fear and distrust of labor organizations. This attitude is not by any means characteristic of labor organizations generally, since there are unions which, as shown in greater detail hereinafter (pp. 97 ff.), not only do not countenance racial discrimination, but impose a substantial fine on individual members or local organizations attempting such discrimination.

Improvements in Industry Removing Disagreeable Features of Work

Negroes are preferred for certain types of work which white workers find disagreeable and leave quickly. The Negro workers, more or less compelled by a limited range of occupations to accept any work without complaint, are assumed to be contented, and even happy, regardless of the nature of work. The heavy pungent dust of tobacco; the dust and odor of fertilizer plants; the dampness, stench, and gore in slaughtering plants; and the blistering heat of the open-hearth section of steel factories are still "protected" for Negro workers. There are notable instances of direct displacement of Negro workers where improvements have been introduced which removed a part or all of the disagreeable features of work.

Change in Fashion

The fashions in personal service have changed in many cities, and instead of the genial Negro waiters and bellmen, most of the large hotels in the South have white bellmen and white waiters or waitresses. The Negro busboys, porters and, less often, cooks have been retained.

When the fashion of bobbing ladies' hair opened a new range of work for barbers, it delivered the coup de grâce to the Negro barber with white patrons. In one southern city an ordinance was passed prohibiting the Negro-operated shops from serving women.

Eligibility for Promotion

Much of the work performed by Negroes by its nature does not lead to higher ranges of employment. Some employers have expressed the view that there is greater ultimate economy in hiring a person who can work from the bottom up, being promoted as he demonstrates his fitness. A notable case in point is the contention of the Brotherhood of Engineers and Firemen that, since under the present custom Negro firemen cannot be promoted to engineers, they should be discharged or replaced by whites. There are increasing numbers of white college-trained men who are willing to begin their careers by performing the less desirable work, on the chance of subsequent promotions.

Pressure of Employment Agencies and Organizations

Periods of work shortage or other job-limiting circumstances have prompted some white pressure groups to invade spheres of work customarily performed by Negroes. This can be urged, under a partial view of the labor situation, as a "civic" duty. In university centers positions held by Negroes have been sought for students working their way through school. In one southern city a roadhouse recently discharged twelve Negro waiters and hired white college students on the insistence of the placement office of the college; in another city a string of cafeterias employing Negro waiters objected to their affiliation with a labor organization and took on white college students instead. The "odd job" of firing furnaces in homes during the winter months lends itself conveniently to the time of students, and numbers of them, needing work, have been aided in locating these jobs by college employment offices.

In other cities civic and social welfare organizations have been concerned with the numbers of white women who were in moral danger because of their need of work and money. Such organizations have canvassed stores employing Negroes as stock girls, and physicians' offices employing Negro girls for light cleaning, sterilizing instruments and answering the telephone, and urged the use of white girls in their places. These activities have often been naïve and thoughtless, but other types of organizations more definitely racial minded have urged upon employers the policy of hiring no Negroes until all whites have been employed. A pamphlet of one such organization asserts that "this is a white man's country and must forever remain . . . We are not going to sit idly by and see white men discharged from their jobs for no other reason than they belong to the white race and see his or her place taken by niggers." It cannot be said that this sort of campaign has met widespread approval or support.

Political Pressure

In New Orleans, a port in which Negroes have great difficulty in voting, a recent effort was made to restrict the employment of longshoremen—the occupation having the largest number of Negroes receiving wages above the common labor level—to persons who were voters. In Richmond it has been a matter of local pride in some quarters that the municipal payroll for the whole range of skilled and unskilled work does not contain the name of a single Negro. Again, it should be noted that situations of this type, while serious enough for workers in the cities involved, are not the rule.

Personal and Emotional Factors

Changes in management may bring shifts in personnel which are occasioned by the personal tastes and whims of employers. A disagreeable experience with an individual Negro may have consequences affecting many other Negroes. There are strong personal likes and dislikes for Negro men and women in service positions of large establishments.

RACIAL SEGREGATION IN LABOR ORGANIZATIONS

The segregation of Negroes in labor organizations follows fairly closely the pattern of segregation in industries; and as frequently as not, labor unions are responsible for the exclusion of Negroes from certain occupational areas. The various labor organizations may be classified as follows: (a) organizations composed exclusively of white workers in fields in which no Negro workers are employed; (b) organizations of white workers which expressly exclude Negro members by provisions in their constitutions or rituals; (c) organizations that admit Negroes to membership, but do not encourage them to join; (d) organizations which admit Negroes, but only to separate locals; (e) organizations that admit Negroes freely and impose penalties for any discriminative practices; and (f) exclusively Negro organizations in fields in which few or no whites are employed, or fields in which white unions so effectively bar Negro membership as to force the creation of independent unions.

Labor organizations developed in the North, of course, much earlier than in the South. Immediately following the emancipation of the Negro, the National Labor Union at its first session in 1866 faced the problem of the new labor position of the Negro. It finally decided to encourage their organization and to urge their inclusion generally among the ranks of labor, sensing the danger to the labor movement in their unorganized competition.[15] The action, however, was scarcely more than a moral gesture of wishful thinking since the various local and national unions followed their own sentiments in the matter and so generally excluded Negro workers that in 1869 the first Negro protest organization, the Negro National Labor Union, was formed in Washington, D.C. In a memorial to Congress this organization referred to the exclusion of Negro workers and apprentices from industries and trade unions as "an insult to God, injury to us and disgrace to humanity."

The Knights of Labor, which followed the National Labor Union in the decade from 1870 to 1880, had many Negro members, numbers of whom were skilled workers. At the height of its power the organization is reported to have had as many as 60,000 Negro members. The first organizations in the iron and steel industry, the Sons of Vulcan and the Associated Brotherhood of Iron and Steel Heaters which later combined to form the Amalgamated Association of Iron,

[15] Ira D. Reid, *Negro Membership in American Labor Unions* (New York: National Urban League, 1930), p. 23.

Steel and Tin Workers, barred Negroes from membership.[16] Competition developed between white workers and skilled Negroes trained in the South; and logic dictated their inclusion. The records indicate that they followed the white workers on strikes and generally lived up to union regulations. The test of the rank and file came when white workers in a crisis situation refused to work with Negroes and the latter, disillusioned and discouraged, began to desert the unions.[17]

The changing and expanding industrial organization of the country compelled a change in the type of labor organization. This led to emphasis on craft organization, which at first neglected Negro workers because their largest numbers were in unskilled work, and later excluded them more deliberately despite occasional pronouncements of the national labor councils against the policy. The most constructive, even though inadequate, solution of the impasse was the encouragement of separate local unions and separate central bodies of Negro workers.

Southern white labor responded to the labor movement from the beginning with an acute consciousness of the "race problem." As a result of the position of Negro workers in skilled crafts in the South, some of the first local charters were granted to them. Later, however, as white skilled workmen came into the ranks the Negro union members lost control of the organizations, and eventually in many instances lost their membership as well. To the southern white worker a labor organization was more a fraternal association than a bargaining agency. In the early efforts of the white railroad workers to perfect their labor organization, for example, the exclusion of the Negro was of first concern. Spero and Harris[18] quote a member from Louisiana as declaring in one of the general sessions that "the firemen of the South have a great work to do without crossing the color line." The alternatives for coping with the situation of efficient Negro workers with seniority rights in the railroad industry were: (a) to take the Negro in, "teach him and educate him, thus, to fight discriminatory practices on a united front," or (b) to force the railroads to eliminate the Negro from train and engine service. The latter alternative won out.

New Orleans has been an important shipping port for over a hundred years. The dock companies have employed both whites and

[16] Horace R. Cayton and George S. Mitchell, *Black Workers and the New Unions* (Chapel Hill: University of North Carolina Press, 1939), p. 73.

[17] *Ibid.*, p. 75.

[18] Sterling D. Spero and Abram L. Harris, *The Black Worker* (New York: Columbia University Press, 1931), p. 285.

Negroes since the days of sailing vessels, but the Negro worker has held a slight edge in the preferences of the shipping companies. When the longshoremen were finally organized, separate unions were established. The labor agreement appears, on the surface, to guarantee equal treatment. White workers, however, have insisted from the beginning that it was their traditional right to select the places in which they worked in loading and unloading ships. Usually this has been on the starboard side of the ship nearest the wharf. As Spero and Harris point out, this form of Jim-Crowism worked no actual hardship, but it was an indication of the absence of real labor solidarity. The foremen who assign work are themselves members of the white union; and although they are supposed to divide the work equally between the two races, the Negro workers usually come out short in the end and invariably get the more difficult jobs.

In Jackson, Mississippi, as late as 1928 there were white members of the Bricklayers Union originally chartered to Negro bricklayers. The white workers complained that their families objected to their meeting with the Negroes; and not wishing to "force the issue of social equality," the Negroes gave way to the demand of the whites for a separate local. The granting of this charter has had the effect of reducing drastically the number of employed Negro bricklayers. The original local, which was predominantly Negro, is no longer in a position to bargain with contractors for work; and Negro bricklayers applying to white foremen for work assignments have been compelled to take only what was left after all white bricklayers had been given jobs. There is no redress; the white foreman is responsible only to his own local.

In general, labor organizations in all but a few of the southern and border states either exclude or segregate the races; and in the northern states, where mixed unions are more often the rule, most of the older organizations tend to discourage or exclude Negro workers. The exceptions to this rule are significant, however, and represent fields in which Negro workers have become fairly well entrenched as, for example, in mining, in iron and steel manufacturing, and in slaughtering and meat packing.

The most important of the newer developments away from segregation and exclusion are found in the industrial unions. Just as craft organizations in an earlier period of the organized labor movement tended to supplant general labor groups, the industrial unions, following the further development of American industry, are tending to supplant the craft unions. Since the industrial union takes into account all classes of labor, the Negro workers who are still very largely unskilled have an added importance and are being given more consideration in the new type of organization.

The prevailing forms of segregation in labor organization are the (a) separate, independent locals, (b) Negro auxiliary locals—usually subordinated to the nearest white local, and (c) pseudo-local labor unions for Negroes with restricted privileges. The last-named type, created merely to protect the wage level of the whites, comprises labor organizations which deny to members of their Negro units the privileges of transferring to white locals anywhere, holding office, or being represented in conventions or conferences except by white men. The Blacksmiths and Helpers, for example, have ruled that members of a Negro auxiliary may not be promoted to the rank of blacksmith or admitted to shops where white helpers are employed. The Brotherhood of Maintenance of Way Employees requires that members of a Negro local must be represented in the Grand Lodge by members of the white lodge. The Sheet Metal Workers have ruled that Negroes may not be admitted to the white union, and that they may secure separate local charters only with the permission of the white local. Any auxiliary local organized without the consent of the white local must come automatically under its jurisdiction.

Although there are isolated exceptions and occasional changes in practice, existing labor unions fall into our broad classification by racial policy as follows: (1) Labor unions which exclude all Negroes by special clauses in their constitutions or rituals: locomotive engineers; aeronautical workers; railway carmen; railway and steamship clerks; railway expressmen, trainmen, and firemen; train dispatchers; yard masters; masters' mates and pilots; switchmen; railroad telegraphers; railway mail clerks; dining-car conductors; sleeping car conductors; railroad station employees; wire weavers; boilermakers; machinists; commercial telegraphers.

(2) Unions which exclude Negroes completely as a matter of custom, but without exclusion clauses in their constitutions: plumbers; electrical workers; rural letter carriers; and flint-glass workers.

(3) Unions which require separate locals: hotel and restaurant employees; sheet-metal workers; railroad maintenance of way workers; motion-picture operators; textile workers; tobacco workers; barbers and journeymen; blacksmiths, drop forgers, and helpers; musicians; longshoremen; molders; federal employees.

(4) Unions which expressly prohibit racial discrimination: miners; teachers; ladies' garment makers; fur workers; subway construction workers; employees in maritime shipping agencies. The

organizations under the CIO in the automobile manufacturing and rubber fabrication industries do not discriminate; but so far the industries most completely organized by the CIO are not those in which the largest numbers of Negroes are employed.

(5) Independent Negro unions, largely in railway transportation or allied fields: Pullman porters; redcaps; transport workers; postal employees; colored railway trainmen; dining-car employees; train porters, brakemen, and switchmen; colored locomotive firemen; also plumbers, ship workers, sheet-metal workers.

RACIAL SEGREGATION IN A SOUTHERN INDUSTRY: PATTERN AND PRACTICE

So far, occupational and industrial segregation have been treated in terms of general patterns, which are necessarily only approximate and somewhat abstract. A better understanding of the operation of the policy of segregation may be gained from an examination of a single industry as a unit of organization. In the tobacco industry[19] the race factor has a long history, heavily freighted with the social traditions of the South and with the protective sentiments of the white and Negro workers who have been in actual or potential competition. The issue of race dictates the wage differentials in the industry, effectively prevents any sustained organization of labor, restricts internal plant adjustments, and more often than not duplicates physical facilities and increases overhead costs.

The racial division of the working force in the tobacco industry is a part of the general culture and social life of the area and is respected as an institution in itself. When changes in economic patterns and in industrial and technological adaptations occur, they must make adjustment to the deeper lying traditional attitudes concerning race, which, of course, change less rapidly and less suddenly.

The racial sentiments supporting segregation in this industry are fully shared by the workers, especially by the white workers who regard the practice of segregation and its attendant attitudes as essential to their own security and to their racial as well as economic status. The Negro workers, more or less resigned to their station, seek whatever security they can gain from a less exacting wage scale, from the uncomplaining performance of disagreeable tasks, from casual personal relations with employers, and from the occasional benevolent sentiments of the more influential elements of the white population.

[19] The areas covered in this study were Richmond and Danville, Virginia; Durham, Winston-Salem, and Reidsville, North Carolina; and Louisville, Kentucky.

Division of Occupations

In carrying out the traditional racial policy, segregation of workers is practiced in most of the plants, but the form varies widely. The most common and widespread form of segregation is that which follows the racial division of occupations. The Negroes perform most of the work up to the point of manufacture, and the white workers most of the work from fabrication to marketing. That this occupational segregation is more a matter of race and custom than of skill and capacity is suggested by the fact that there are some white stemmers in Louisville, and some Negro "making machine" operators in Winston-Salem and other cities. All the supervisory posts are held by white workers except in Louisville, a border city, where there are some instances of Negro foremen over Negro workers. White workers hold practically all the jobs classified as standard crafts, and Negroes hold practically all the jobs regarded as menial.

Physical Segregation

Various types of physical segregation are found in the industry. In many of the Richmond plants there are entirely separate buildings for white and Negro workers. In Winston-Salem, Durham, and Reidsville segregation is effected by allocation of Negro and white workers to separate parts of buildings, or to different workrooms even when performing the same tasks, or to separate sides of the same room, or even to separate rows in the same room. The principle of racial separation is at least preserved symbolically. In two cities the segregation is effected by having separate white and Negro groups on day and night shifts, using the same machines. In one instance the Negro workers had the preferred shift.

Separation by Special Tasks

Not all processes are easily adapted to strict racial separation, but their uneven work requirements mean that Negroes are used on certain aspects and whites on others. For example, in one plant Negroes "sacked" while whites "booked" on the same machines; and in another Negroes "tagged" while whites "changed the knives"; and in still another plant Negroes were hopper feeders on machines operated by white men. When a heavy and a light task, or a pleasant and a disagreeable task, are combined in one operation, there may be racial segregation with respect to tasks, without spatial separation.

There are other conditions under which spatial segregation is not feasible, as when two processes are so closely related that they must be performed in the same room. A Negro may be given a machine at the end of a room in which all other operatives are white. In one case noted, the spirit of segregation was honored by providing separate doors to the same workroom.

Race Relations

It is interesting to note that although practically every form of segregation is employed, in each case the particular form is regarded by white workers as natural, and by the Negro workers as traditional; and relations in the plant rest with a certain finality upon this basis. Moreover, with respect to certain types of segregated work the rationalizations in terms of special racial abilities and instincts are made and accepted by the workers themselves, although these assumptions are frequently contradicted in fact by other instances. A white worker, in referring to a type of heavy, dirty work usually performed in his plant by Negroes, said:

The niggers handle the dirty work. A white man wouldn't get in there. The niggers always done the heavy, hot work. *They stand it better.*

However, white workers were performing these same tasks in Louisville without complaining. A Negro prizer in Winston-Salem, commenting upon the heavy work connected with his job, said of his white fellow workers:

Yes, they work alongside of us, but they do the light work and we do the heavy work. *They couldn't do the kind of work that we do.* We go carrying around iron racks weighing from 90 pounds up. *That would kill the whites.* They tell me that the white man does the work in St. Louis where they work all whites, *but these kind of whites couldn't stand this work, no sir!*

It was believed by a white worker in Richmond that it would cause a race war if a Negro were put on a machine; but there actually were some Negroes on machines, not only in Richmond but in other cities.

To preserve proper relations it was deemed most important by the white workers that Negro workers should "keep their place," with respect both to social distance and to work status. At a Durham plant a white worker objected to the fact that white and Negro "packers" worked together on the same task. He said:

You see, the southern man knows how to get along with the niggers. If they don't stay in their place you take a club and kill 'em. Of course they shouldn't work together this way.

Another white worker, a union member, further revealed the status motive in the present racial attitude of some white workers when he said:

> I wouldn't work with niggers on the same kind of work. I don't think a nigger ought to make as much as a white man. It just won't do. Give a nigger a little money and he's a "big Ike" right then. He'd want to come in the same cafes you do. You can't reason with a nigger when he's got a little bit of money in his pocket.

Just as there were many forms of segregation without conspicuous difficulty in race relations, there were instances of absence of segregation without evidence of friction. In Winston-Salem there were divisions of plants in which whites and Negroes worked side by side as pickers, cappers, machine operators, and stemmers. Again, during the Christmas rush, it has been customary to have groups of them work together. Recent economic maladjustments have prompted compression or reorganization of tasks, resulting in the breaking of the racial alignment. Where particularly strong foremen willed it, arrangements have been changed in either direction; and none of these rearrangements appears to have provoked any abnormal situation. Two significant comments on this modification of traditional policy were made. Said a worker in one of the Winston-Salem plants:

> The poor whites and niggers is worked together, up at No. ———. They is using the poor whites to whip the nigger and the nigger to whip the poor whites. If the poor whites sort of get out of line, they fire them and put niggers in their jobs, and they do the niggers the same way.

The observation by a Negro worker was to the effect that they are all "equally hard off and can't complain."

In Winston-Salem there had been an instance in one plant of the displacement of a white gang by Negroes, and in two other plants the shifting upward of a Negro to a more skilled task alongside white workers without changing the designation of his task or his pay.

One situation making for tolerance of a nonsegregated working arrangement is work shortage, which, however, results frequently in the displacement of Negro workers. Types of work long regarded as "Negro jobs" are being increasingly sought by white workers; and these workers not only make no objection to, but seek, apprentice opportunities among Negro workers. This is very pronounced in Louisville, where a Negro remarked about a newly mixed gang:

> No white man did my kind of work till lately. They just like us, kinda poor and they want to stay. They all want to keep a job here now, and they's all right. The other superintendent didn't let white men come down

on our gang, but this one does. He's from South Carolina. Sometime they send white men down to work on our gang when they ain't nothing doing much on another floor.

The problem of what jobs Negroes should have and what jobs whites should have in the tobacco industry has at least three aspects: (1) The Negroes need the jobs they have always had as a livelihood. (2) Whites, unemployed at former occupations, are seeking jobs in the tobacco industry. (3) The employer is interested in securing adequate help at least cost. The principles of seniority and skill have favored the continued employment of Negroes in their old jobs; but as new jobs have developed Negroes and whites have been employed as stemmers. This factor has tended to reclassify stemming as a "white" job. In most places all machine operators and cigarette makers are white. In many cases strictly Negro jobs have been reduced to mere cleaning and such heavy work as handling hogsheads. The Negro worker is by tradition to "stay in his place," but his fixed place is being continually narrowed.

The employer's problem, to get the most work done at least cost, is complicated by another race differential. Whatever a Negro earns at a given job, according to the prevailing tradition a white worker should get more. Whatever the general standard of living of the Negroes, that of the white workers is expected to be higher. There is, of course, no real reason why an employer should pay higher wages to white workers when he can get the same work done for less by Negroes. He is, however, continually faced with the pressure of white workers for jobs, and with their insistence that Negroes be paid less. The employer is not, of course, wholly the passive victim of the white workers' racialism. There are frequent instances of a deliberate "divide and rule" policy, as suggested in the observations of the workers. The existence of the wage differential usually exerts a downward rather than an upward pressure on wages as a whole. Even if individual employers have had no part in the instigation of racialism, employers as a class have seen some profit in the fact that it exists.

Chapter V

OCCUPATIONAL DISCRIMINATION IN A NATIONAL EMERGENCY

The beginning of the American program for the defense of democracy against the organization of economic resources by the racially self-assertive totalitarian powers forcefully challenged for the first time the traditional occupational policies concerning Negro workers in the United States. The emergency demanded a sudden and drastic shift from normal production to high-geared production of war materials. Attention was focused upon types of industries requiring new skills, and as a result old working relationships were profoundly disturbed. Millions in defense contracts were earmarked for the manufacture of aircraft, ships, machine tools, and other items. It was estimated by the Bureau of Labor Statistics that between April, 1941, and April, 1942, approximately 1,400,000 additional workers would be required for these industries. Shipbuilding alone would require some 323,900 additional workers; aircraft, 408,000; ordnance and machine tools, 291,000; and construction and other defense industries, 384,000.[1]

To meet these requirements the government initiated a program of vocational training through pre-employment, refresher, and supplementary courses. Out-of-school youth, rural and urban, were trained in these vocational courses. The Works Projects Administration and the National Youth Administration turned their programs to this end. Engineering colleges and the Apprenticeship Unit of the United States Office of Education fashioned their programs around the national emergency, placing apprentices in various approved plants with government funds.

It was not long, however, before it became apparent that an artificial element was dangerously restricting this all-out program of

---

[1] See testimony of Sidney Hillman, associate director general of the Office of Production Management, before the Committee of the House of Representatives investigating national defense migration, on July 15, 1941 (Office of Production Management, Labor Division, P M 729, Release July 15, 1941).

industrial preparation for defense. The traditional racial policies in both northern and southern states were thrown into sharp relief. In spite of the critical need for workers, skilled and unskilled, qualified Negro applicants were refused employment in industries manufacturing a wide array of defense materials. In airplane plants there were no Negroes employed above the level of menial labor. Nor were they employed in chemical industries, nor in machine-tool plants; and their numbers were held to a minimum on the various jobs connected with the construction of hundreds of plants and military camps. At Wichita, Stearman Aircraft, a division of Boeing, received government orders for $5,713,389 worth of planes, and another Boeing plant had an order for $2,041,947; but the total number of Negroes hired in the two plants was three, of whom two were porters and one was a cook. The Westinghouse Manufacturing Company, which had government contracts totaling over $8,000,000, had three Negro workers in a total force of 800 in its Baltimore plant. The Glenn L. Martin Company of Baltimore, the Colt Arms Company of Hartford, the Spartan Aircraft Company of Tulsa, General Motors and the White Motor Company in Cleveland, all with large government contracts, employed no Negroes.

The Tampa Shipbuilding and Dry Dock Company, with contracts from the Maritime Commission exceeding $17,000,000, indicated that it was willing to employ qualified Negroes; but the International Boilermakers Union, with its constitutional clause restricting membership to "members of the white race," objected.[2] Negroes had formerly comprised 50 per cent of the company's working force, and helped to organize it, but they were left stranded when a closed-shop agreement was secured. Similarly, a Boeing Aircraft branch agreed to accept Negroes if they were members of the Aeronautical Mechanics Union No. 757, with which the company had a contract; but this union also has a clause barring Negroes from membership.

This discrimination has not been limited to defense industries, as numerous recent studies have shown. The New York State legislature appointed a committee to study the condition of the Negro urban population in the state; and in 1939 it reported "growing discrimination against the employment of Negroes in New York in any but menial and unskilled jobs."[3] Financial and mercantile enterprises, employing hundreds of thousands of white-collar workers,

[2] Walter White, "It's Our Country Too," *Saturday Evening Post*, December 14, 1940.
[3] "Restrictions in Employment of Negroes in New York," *Monthly Labor Review*, 49:360 (August, 1939).

would not hire Negroes in trades and related occupations. With the exception of the garment and fur trades and related industries, there were no openings for Negro labor in the vast array of urban factories. Department stores used them only as elevator operators, cleaners, and cafeteria and kitchen workers. In Rochester out of 35,120 employees in private firms only 70 were Negroes. The largest firm, manufacturing photographic equipment and supplies and employing 16,351 persons, had one Negro porter and 19 Negro construction workers engaged by a subsidiary corporation. The largest insurance company in the state, with more Negro policyholders than all Negro companies combined, had not a single Negro in its force of over 20,000 employees in New York State alone.

The anomalous situation induced by racial discrimination, with more men wanted than could be found among whites and simultaneous unemployment among Negroes has been dramatized by several of the liberal journals. In the June 27, 1941, issue of the news magazine *Friday* several full pages were devoted to a case cited as typical of an able-bodied Negro American. This issue quotes the Negro as saying:

Everywhere you hear there is a shortage of labor technicians for national defense. What supreme irony. I am a Negro American, 30 years old. I am registered under the Conscription Act. Any day a Draft Board may put me in uniform, hand me a gun. The ranks of death are open to me, but the ranks of life are tightly closed. Though I am a chemical engineer, a graduate of famous Cooper Union, I am not wanted. I can always get a job as janitor. . . . Their democracy is color bound. It stops at a black skin.

The Negro commentator pointed out that an executive of the plant which manufactured the famous Sperry bombsight was a member of the New York State Defense Council; but the Sperry Company steadfastly refused to employ a single Negro worker. Attention was called to Southern California's aviation industry, which employed less than 12 Negroes among its 60,000 workers. The Wright Aeronautical Works and the Brewster Aircraft Company would have no Negroes. The Nashville branch of the Vultee Aircraft Company openly asserted:

. . . we do not now believe it advisable to include colored people with our regular working force. We may, at a later date, be in a position to add some colored people in minor capacities such as porters and cleaners.

In discussing this matter with some of the members of the Board of Education, they have advised that they are considering starting courses in occupations which colored people would experience no difficulty in obtaining employment. These courses, I believe cover such subjects as auto repair, construction work, cement finishers, molding, etc.

The newspaper *PM* has cited, with evidence, scores of examples of racial discrimination and exclusion in industries holding large government contracts. The Consolidated Aircraft Corporation of San Diego, for example, with millions of dollars in war contracts employed no Negroes; and the Board of Education of that city in a spurt of collaboration had ruled that no Negro could take vocational courses without first getting a letter from a local employer saying that he would be employed. One article carried a reproduction of an advertisement by the Swallow Airplane Company's training division: "Men selected for training must be white Americans over 18 years old, physically fit."[4] *PM* also published a long list of companies holding defense contracts and refusing to employ Negroes;[5] cited the fact that 97 per cent of the metal trades industries in New York would not employ Negroes;[6] sent a competent reporter out with a qualified Negro applicant and noted the consistent and inflexible method of rejecting an applicant who had all other qualifications except the one of color.

In May, 1941, sixty prominent white Americans, including Governor Lehman of New York, Lieutenant Governor Charles Poletti, Dr. Anson Phelps Stokes, Mr. Lessing Rosenwald, and Father Ryan, drew up a pointed public statement reminding industrialists and workers alike of their obligation to the principle which they professed to be defending, in these words: "Concern for democracy in Europe lacks reality and sincerity if our plans and policies disregard the rights of minorities in our own country."[7]

Despite government sponsorship, the various vocational training programs for Negroes lagged in practically every state and were notoriously weak and belated in the southern states. Early in 1940 the National Defense Advisory Commission attempted to discourage the prevalent practice of artificially restricting Negro employment; but the commission discovered that it was not enough to request industries to include Negroes on an equitable basis. In spite of its pronouncement, the discriminations remained effective as late as September, 1940. Dr. John W. Studebaker, the United States commissioner of education, who had been charged with the direction of

[4] *PM*, May 14, 1941.
[5] *PM*, May 16, 1941.
[6] *PM*, May 7, 1941.
[7] *PM*, May 7, 1941.

the national program of vocational education, was presented with evidence of consistent misinterpretation of policy in the southern states: The state directors of vocational education insisted that Negro trainees must be taken from WPA rolls, although in setting up the WPA rolls previously they had generally refused to register Negroes as skilled or semiskilled workers. The prevailing policy had been to register Negroes only for jobs that the directors assumed they were likely to get; and these were limited to common labor or domestic service. A further rule was that persons to be trained must have jobs waiting for them before they would be considered eligible to receive training. However practical or rational such local regulations seemed to be, their effect was the exclusion of Negro trainees. In September, 1940, the United States Office of Education and the National Defense Advisory Commission were compelled to issue a statement urging that there be no racial discrimination in the training program, which was meant to train persons in anticipation of industrial needs not necessarily existing at the present time. At the same time the National Defense Advisory Commission made public a statement of labor policy, which included a protective clause asserting that workers should not be discriminated against "because of age, race, sex or color."

The official pressure for equitable inclusion of Negroes in the defense program produced striking, and in one sense disconcerting, evidence of the strength of the opposition to any such policy. The weakness of the antidiscrimination pronouncement of the National Defense Advisory Commission was revealed when the comptroller general ruled that there is no statutory authority for the insertion of a nondiscrimination clause in a government contract for performance of public work. Judge William Hastie, dean of the Law School of Howard University and civilian adviser to the War Department, recommended that the National Defense Advisory Commission make a study of "persuasive and coercive procedures" that might be adopted to end discriminative practices.

The National Association for the Advancement of Colored People conducted a survey of employment on defense projects in December, 1940, and disclosed that Negro carpenters were being refused employment on construction projects in many cities. The association cited two projects at Fort Dix, New Jersey, and three Florida cities which barred both skilled and unskilled Negro workers. At Fort Dix three out of 350 carpenters were Negroes. In Newport News, where Negro skilled and semiskilled workers were being barred from work on government contracts, the contractors had issued an ultimatum that Negroes would not be used unless they were members of labor organizations. In turn the labor organizations had said that they would be considered for membership only if they were willing to pay a union fee of $100. The regular fee for bricklayers, according to a Negro applicant, was only $32.50. The local white unions did not admit Negro members and looked with disfavor on separate Negro unions. After a succession of protests to the Virginia State Employment Office and the United States Housing Administration, this situation was eventually corrected.

In conference at Savannah the Brotherhood of Railway Engineers and Firemen recently proposed that the more than 2,000 Negro railway firemen and hostlers eventually be deprived of their jobs. The railroads have been paying Negro and white firemen the same wages, although Negroes cannot become engineers. Because of this, the union is insisting that the railroads cease employing Negroes as firemen and fill all subsequent vacancies with whites.

An amendment of the National Labor Relations Act to prohibit race discrimination by labor organizations has been proposed. In the hearing before the House Labor Committee it was suggested that the amendment be modeled after the recently enacted amendment of the New York civil rights law. In New York State the bill introduced by Representative Flynn sought to deny recognition to, and to penalize, labor organizations which discriminated because of race, color or creed; it won the approval of the judiciary committee but was opposed by the American Federation of Labor's Railroad Union.

A decision of the District of Columbia Court of Appeals in January, 1940, held that a labor union may limit the rights of its Negro members without trespassing upon their constitutional rights. According to this ruling, where Negro members of a union constitute a minority in numbers, they are deprived of no constitutional rights if for the purpose of collective bargaining they are represented by all whites. Thus, although Negro members have a right to vote, their votes are not effective as long as they remain a minority; and issues are decided by the majority in favor of its own interests as a racial group.

The steps taken by the government in its effort to curb the discriminatory practices that were actually holding back the emergency program and at the same time threatening to disintegrate morale among the various minority groups in the population have been without precedent. When the United States Office of Education began its program of vocational education for defense industries, to be carried out in the public schools of the states through the state offices of education, it announced that "In the expenditure of Federal funds for vocational training for defense there should be no discrimination on account of race, creed or color."[8] In October, 1940, the legislation expanding the program of training contained the following provision: "No trainee under the foregoing appropriation shall be discriminated against because of sex, race or color; and where separate schools are required by law for separate population groups, to the extent needed for trainees of such groups equitable provision shall be made for facilities and training of like quality."[9] According to Robert C. Weaver of the Advisory Commission to the Council of National Defense, these statements represented the first instance in which the federal government had specifically prohibited discriminatory practices in the expenditure of federal funds for vocational education of less than college grade. The Labor Division of the Advisory Commission, in its announcement of its labor policy, stated that "workers should not be discriminated against because of age, sex, race or color." It went another step in securing from the official leaders of the American Federation of Labor and the Congress of Industrial Organization a commitment that these two labor organizations would carry out the commission's nondiscrimination policy.[10]

On June 12, 1941, President Roosevelt addressed a memorandum to William S. Knudsen and Sidney Hillman, who were jointly in charge of the Office of Production Management, stating that complaints had repeatedly been brought to his attention that available and much-needed workers were being barred from defense production solely because of race, religion, or national origin. He emphasized that these complaints about exclusion were being brought at a time when labor stringencies were appearing in many areas, and fully qualified workers were being turned from the gates of industry because of specifications entirely unrelated to efficiency and productivity. He pointed out that discrimination against Negro workers had been nation-wide, and that other racial, national, and religious minority groups had felt the effects of discrimination in many localities. He referred to this situation as a matter of grave national importance, calling for immediate action. He placed his whole support, as chief executive of the nation, behind the statement of the Office of Production Management that "all holders of defense con-

[8] Supplementary statement to Miscellaneous 2400, N.D. 1, U.S. Office of Education, August 15, 1940.
[9] H. R. 10539, First Supplemental Civil Function Act 1941.
[10] Robert C. Weaver, "The Defense Program and the Negro," *Opportunity,* November, 1940.

tracts are urged to examine their employment and training policies at once, to determine whether or not these policies make ample provision for the full utilization of available and competent Negro workers. Every source of labor capable of producing defense materials must be tapped in the present emergency." Further, he placed on the Office of Production Management the responsibility for taking immediate steps to facilitate the full utilization of the nation's productive man power.

When there was still no important indication of a disposition on the part of either industry or labor to modify racial policies, Negroes under the leadership of A. Phillip Randolph, head of the Pullman porters' organization, and Walter White, executive secretary of the National Association for the Advancement of Colored People, planned a demonstration for jobs in the form of a march to Washington by ten thousand protestant Negroes from all parts of the country. The nation's capital, already overcrowded with defense workers in government offices, viewed this threatened protest march with alarm as well as indignation. The leaders of the movement were made aware that the President, while deeply sympathizing with the desire for increased employment, opposed the contemplated pressure tactics as unwise and untimely. He agreed to issue an Executive Order against discrimination; and three days before the scheduled date the leaders called off the demonstration.

An Executive Order, issued to all government departments and agencies concerned with vocational training programs for defense production and to all contracting agencies of the government, specified that special measures should be taken to assure the administration of training programs without discrimination because of race, creed, color, or national origin; and that all defense contracts thereafter negotiated should include a provision obligating the contractor not to discriminate against any worker because of race, creed, color, or national origin. The President also established in the Office of Production Management a Committee on Fair Employment Practice that would receive and investigate complaints of discrimination in violation of the provisions of this order, and take appropriate steps to redress grievances found to be valid. The committee was organized with three white and two Negro members under the chairmanship of Mark Etheridge, a well-known southern liberal and managing editor of the Louisville *Courier-Journal*.

The appointment of Robert C. Weaver to the Labor Supply Branch of the Office of Production Management, under Sidney Hillman, had been intended to assure adequate consideration of Negro workers in all phases of the labor recruitment program. The Labor Supply Branch had adopted three measures in its efforts to curb destructive racial discrimination: (1) It had announced that the policy of the Defense Training Branch of the Office of Production Management would be to train Negroes in selected occupations in communities where there had been no employment opportunities for them. (2) It had instructed the United States Employment Service to assume responsibility for exhausting the available labor supply within a locality before resorting to recruitment or training of labor from outside the locality. This included the responsibility for exerting every effort to place available workers from minority groups. (3) It passed on to its regional offices copies of the President's Executive Order of June 25, 1941, reaffirming the policy of full participation in defense of all persons regardless of race, creed, color, or national origin, and directing certain action in furtherance of that policy.

Spokesmen of the Catholics of America advised the Catholic population to give full support to the efforts of the President and of the Office of Production Management to integrate Negroes into the employment and training phases of the national defense program. This advice was given in a series of editorials in leading Catholic publications, one of which stated: "The present emergency demands an immediate reform. The age-old pattern of anti-Negro prejudice must not become a part of our national defense program. To allow this would be a grave injustice to loyal Americans. It would endanger national unity. It would seriously impair the international influence and prestige of American democracy. Democracy must function democratically."[11]

Racial occupational patterns appear to change only under the stress of abnormal conditions; and three important factors are operative: (1) amount of experience; (2) extent of labor scarcity; (3) presence or absence of political pressure. Some modification appears to have resulted from the wholly unprecedented volume of official concern about racial discrimination in defense industries, as evidenced by the number of firms hesitating to take chances with their defense contracts, whether in the end the President and the Office of Production Management could do anything about them or not. The Grumman Aeronautical Engineering Corporation of Bethpage, Long Island; the Republic Aviation Company of Farmingdale, Long Island; and the Curtiss-Wright Company's Buffalo plant began training and employing Negro workers. The Briggs Manufacturing

[11] *Interracial Review,* March, 1941, p. 36.

Company in Detroit and the Sperry Gyroscope Company (manufacturers of the famous bombsight) decided to include Negroes in their working forces. The United States Cartridge Company announced on August 1, 1941, that it would employ some 3,000 Negroes in supervisory, skilled, semiskilled, and unskilled categories. The St. Louis Ordnance Plant, then nearing completion, proposed to include an equitable number of Negroes in its force. On the same date the Radford, Virginia, ordnance plant of the Hercules Powder Company hired its first 100 of a contemplated 1,000 Negro workers for skilled, semiskilled and maintenance jobs. Procter & Gamble gave assurances at its Wolf Creek ordnance plant, Milam, Tennessee, that 20 to 25 per cent of the total employees of the plant would be Negroes.

Negro women got their first chance as gas mask assemblers in the Edgewood Arsenal in Maryland. One of the largest parachute manufacturers in the country placed Negro women on parachute assembling work in Manchester, Connecticut. The State Employment Service Offices have reported some success in placing them in defense industries in such unusual occupations as sheet-metal workers, press operators, jewelers, sign painters, and assemblers of electrical goods.

In July, 1941, Sidney Hillman reported that as a result of the field operations of agents from his office more than 2,500 Negro carpenters were employed in the construction of military camps at wages ranging from $8 to $12 a day; and that at the same time thousands of colored brickmasons, plasterers, cement finishers, painters, plumbers, roofers, and power-saw operators, and many more unskilled workers were given employment in this construction program, although of course for only a limited period.[12]

In spite of its dramatic flair, this official pressure has not profoundly influenced the fundamental occupational patterns by race. Employers who have been unaffected by the action of the Office of Production Management, by the President's appeal or the operating principle of democracy have pointed out that the government itself has set a precedent for both segregation and discrimination, and that many of its departments continue these practices as the most satisfactory policy. The Secretary of the Navy announced officially that Negroes could be accepted in the United States Navy only as mess attendants. He added that he regretted the situation, but said, "That is the way it is." With the passage of the National Conscrip-

[12] Office of Production Management, Labor Division, P M 797, Release July 29, 1941, pp. 3-4.

tion Act there flared up promptly what *Time* described as the Army's
Number One social problem: "What to do with Negro officers and
Negro enlisted men."[13] The War Department issued a statement,
following President Roosevelt's talk with certain Negro representatives, to the effect that Negroes would get the same kind of military training as whites, but they would get it in *separate* Negro outfits. This was presumably an enunciation of the "separate but equal"
principle of racial segregation regarded as both just and socially expedient in American society. There was, however, no indication that
the Army or any other regular branch of government recognized as
discrimination the very general practices of unequitable segregation,
or the disregard for Negroes where strict but equitable segregation
was impracticable or impossible.

Only four Negroes have ever been graduated from West Point to
date, and none from Annapolis. In 1940 the Army had only two
regular Negro line officers: Colonel Benjamin O. Davis, command-
ing officer of Harlem's 369th Coast Artillery (National Guard),
later promoted to general; and Captain B. O. Davis, Jr., his son,
whose first assignment was not with the Army but as a military instructor at Tuskegee Institute, a private school. After training there
for the Air Corps, he advanced rapidly from captain to major to
colonel. Prior to the 1940 military emergency the Army had only
four Negro regiments, two of cavalry and two of infantry, and all
of them were officered by white men. The first expansion of Negro
outfits included a regiment of engineers, a regiment of field
artillery, and twelve truck companies.

According to the statistics released by *Time*, only about 10 per
cent of the 400,000 drafted and enlisted Negroes in the Army in
World War I saw overseas combat service. The four separate regiments, the 369th, 370th, 371st and 372nd, distinguished themselves
as combat troops; but most of the regiments were pioneer infantry.

The War Department announced on October 15, 1940 that Negroes would be given training in aviation as "pilots, mechanics and
technical specialists." At the time of the announcement the only air
training for Negroes was being given by the Civil Aeronautics
Authority. At a hearing of the House Appropriations Committee
Representative Ludlow of Indiana called attention to an act of
Congress requiring that facilities be made available for the training
of Negro airplane pilots for the Army. When Congressman Ludlow
asked General Marshall, chief of staff, what had been done to carry

[13] *Time*, October 28, 1940, p. 19.

out the mandate of Congress, he was told that "there is no such thing as colored aviation at this time."

In August, 1940, the Chicago *Tribune* noted editorially[14] that the first requisites of a military flier are quick nervous responses, a superior sense of balance, excellent muscular co-ordination, a good sensory apparatus, and a sound body; in short, the qualities which make good athletes, together with physical and moral courage. In all these respects, the editorial argued, Negroes have given ample demonstration of their fitness. "The record of the Negro athletes," it stated, "provides a rich resource which ought not to be lost to the country through prejudice." In conclusion it said: "This record suggests that the country would lose less by refusing to train Harvard, Yale and Princeton men for the flying corps than by refusing to train Negroes."

The operation of the "separate but equal" principle of dealing with the Negro minority in the armed services may be summarized as follows: In the past most of the Negro regiments have been designated as service rather than combat units; few Negro reserve officers are being used, and few are being trained; practically all the Negro regiments are officered by whites, and the War Department insists that white officers have proved satisfactory for the regular army Negro regiments and contemplates no change; promotions of Negroes above the rank of lieutenant are drastically restricted; Negro doctors, dentists, and nurses are not being used, except in negligible proportions; no Negroes at all are accepted in the Marine Corps; and until limited openings were made recently, the only Negroes in the Navy were mess attendants.

The policy with respect to the utilization of Negroes as civilian employees in welfare, morale, and clerical work has not been defined by the War Department; and clerical applications have been rejected. In the administration of the Selective Service Act through state boards, various policies have been adopted by the states. Negroes have been included on these boards in northern states where there is a significant Negro population, and in three border and southern states. In other southern states the inclusion of Negroes on the boards is regarded as fantastically out of the question. The request by a group of representative Negroes in Nashville that Governor Cooper of Tennessee consider the appointment of qualified Negroes to the local selective service board was impatiently and explosively rejected by the governor, who warned them that Negroes expected too much. He announced that "this is a white man's coun-

[14] Chicago *Tribune*, August 8, 1940.

try" and expanded this remark by explaining that white men had developed America, and Negroes had come on the scene after all the work had been done. He was not in favor of Negroes on the selective service board because "some white boys might refuse to let Negroes examine them and that would cause trouble." Gratuitously he added that he was not in favor of Negroes attending the University of Tennessee nor of their riding in Pullman cars.

The traditional aspects of the racial occupational alignment are in constant conflict with the newer technology, tempo, and organization of American industry as it functions in a capitalistic system based upon free labor and competition; in a dynamic society it is essential that there should be enough fluidity to prevent crystallization of race status and occupations. Changes in industrial organization can create new occupations as swiftly as other occupations are destroyed; and so long as change is possible occupational stratification along racial lines is considerably more difficult. It is certain that there will always be problems associated with readjustments and redefinitions of roles.

There are indications that labor is recognizing the limiting character of certain types of economic segregation. In Birmingham, the center of the southern coal and iron industry, white and Negro workers in recent years have modified drastically the policy of separate labor organization. With less emphasis upon the social and status aspects of association in labor groups, these workers are now organized in more than a hundred "mixed" unions. A similar trend appeared in the first effective efforts of the sharecroppers and agricultural laborers in Arkansas, Alabama, and Tennessee to organize for mutual security. At least in those fields in which the Negro working force is a significant proportion of the total, the indications are that in the future less emphasis will be placed upon race competition and more upon the solidarity of class interests.

Chapter VI

THE RACIAL ETIQUETTE IN PUBLIC CONTACTS
AND PERSONAL RELATIONS

In addition to the formal and statutory regulations governing race relations, during slavery there grew up a body of conventional and ceremonial forms, a kind of racial etiquette or code. The character and function of this racial etiquette as it developed in the South has been well described by Doyle on the basis of the abundant literature of slavery.[1] Master and slave were able to live together in a most intimate household relationship so long as the proper social ritual was observed. This code continues to regulate the more intimate and personal contacts of the races, although it has been in process of modification ever since emancipation. The function of this racial etiquette is to define and maintain the social distances essential to a class or caste system in which one race is assigned to a "superior" and the other relegated to an "inferior" status.[2] Park observes that the etiquette turns out to be at the same time "a principle of order and an index to the stability of the society in which it exists."[3]

A factor contributing to the basic equilibrium of biracial association in the South since emancipation has been the ceremonial observance of the traditional forms of racial deference which recognize the historic status of the two groups. Circumstances and sentiments may change, but so long as traditional racial etiquette survives there will be little friction. The most serious of the racial problems in the South have been precipitated by the failure or the unwillingness of Negroes to conform to the code and the whites' insistence on its observance as the only condition on which Negroes might hope for toleration.

The shadings of etiquette reflect the class and caste consciousness of both whites and Negroes. A lower-class white man will recognize upper-class white men with a certain degree of deference; and he will recognize different classes of Negroes with certain degrees of

[1] Bertram W. Doyle, op. cit.
[2] Ibid., Introduction by Robert E. Park, p. xviii.
[3] Ibid., p. xix.

distance. He does not expect a Negro professional man to tip his hat to him any more than he expects a Negro of his own class to call him by his first name in the presence of another white man. He may, however, insist upon recognition by upper-class Negroes of his superior status as a white man in situations in which an upper-class white man would not consider recognition of the traditional caste distinction important.

There are situations within the legal and institutional structure separating the races in the South which permit a considerable degree of personal intimacy between whites and Negroes; but that intimacy is permissible only when both parties know what can and what cannot be done and the appropriate social distances prescribed by racial etiquette are maintained. Thus, while Negroes and whites are required by law and custom to travel in separate coaches in common carriers, a white person and his Negro servant, in conformity with the code governing these associations, may sit, eat or play together. The Negro "mammy" lived on terms of closest association with members of the white family, wet-nursing, spanking, kissing, and sleeping with the children and continuing this intimacy as they grew to adulthood.

This chapter will delineate the changing forms of the etiquette of race relations in the rural and urban South and the modifications found in the border and northern sections of the country.

The southern rural areas represent a stable, if not a static, culture. Change is slow; and custom and tradition exercise strong control over social relationships generally. Under the circumstances the traditional understandings, which control race relations and the sanctions by which they are enforced, take on an inflexible and sacred character.

Urbanization, on the other hand, is destructive of tradition. Large numbers of people living together require the impersonal regulations imposed by laws and ordinances, and the special regulations and regimentations demanded by the necessities of large-scale industry and commerce. Also, city populations are generally less homogeneous than those in rural areas. People in cities come from different cultural backgrounds, bringing with them different traditions; and these traditions modify one another in contact. Cities have, or seem to have, "personalities" which are complexes of the variant cultural backgrounds of the inhabitants; yet customs and relations conform finally to the organization of economic and material interests. In metropolitan cities there is a more detailed division of labor than in the rural communities from which the urban populations come. This changes the social structure from one of dependence upon the moral order, or upon persons, to one of dependence upon an impersonal and mechanical economic order. There is more social stratification and greater freedom of contact but less security for individuals.

The difference between a folk culture and an urban civilization, as Louis Wirth points out, is that between the *conubium* and the *commercium*, i.e., a society based on kinship and kind and one based upon territorial solidarity and commercial relations. This distinction is important for an understanding of the different patterns of race relations in rural and urban areas of the South, and in the predominantly rural South compared with the prevailingly urban North. Even though basic racial distinctions are recognized in both instances, the etiquette undergoes modification in the course of the transition from rural to urban society. A strong current making for disorganization of patterns runs along with an equally strong current tending to redefine the Negro's place in the urban community.

The changing structure and conditions of urban life tend to confuse current conceptions of the role and sphere of the Negro and make successive redefinitions necessary. Frequently these definitions are in conflict with the city's economy or bound up with the concerns of other interest groups. For example, traditional racial etiquette demands that Negroes calling at the homes of white persons should go to the rear. However, in cities increasing numbers of persons live in apartments that do not have back doors. Similarly, the introduction of one-man streetcars required a redefinition of the etiquette of entrance. The increasing number of exceptions to regulations imposed or implied by original taboos and traditional patterns have resulted in modifications of customs. Some taboos entirely lose their force, and new patterns are evolved to take the place of the old.

In the process of urbanization class divisions develop in the Negro population and take on importance for both races. Only in the city can professional classes be supported; and only in the city can a middle class develop. This class stratification plays a part in the determination and operation of patterns of race relations. Different classes of the Negro population make diverse responses to the mosaic of racial taboos and restrictions and place different emphases on its various aspects.

The racial climate changes gradually from the South to the border areas and from the border areas to the North. Broadly, the etiquette follows the institutional patterns; and the uncertainty of institutional patterns makes the etiquette equally uncertain. In the border areas the etiquette is expected to control relationships not regulated by

law. There are no laws, for example, against Negroes and whites
eating in the same restaurants in the border areas; but they seldom
do; if they do, it is more likely to be because whites eat in Negro
places. In private there are frequent instances of interracial dining;
and this is not seriously regarded as a violation of the taboo. As
has been noted, there is no legal segregation in streetcar transportation, but custom enforces it rather generally in buses and on local
railroad trains and, to some extent, in actual seat selection.

Relations in the border areas are more impersonal than in the
South and on the whole less strictly bound by racial conventions.
Discrimination in services may be punishable by law in some spheres
and upheld in others. Negroes are not disposed merely to seek the
security of their own group institutions; there is enough aggressiveness and absence of fear of drastic reprisals to support demands for
a substantially higher type of racial isolation. If a public institution
is needed, the Negroes may demand it from tax funds and support
their case by a judicious use of the franchise. If private concerns
attempt to impose inferior goods or services, Negroes feel free to
force improvements through the strength of their purchasing power.

In the northern states the burden of segregation is shifted completely; and racial attitudes are reflected in the character of support
of existing legislation prohibiting segregation or discrimination.

CASUAL CONTACTS IN PUBLIC PLACES

In rural areas where common folk of both races are always in
close contact, Negroes keep their distance with meticulous regard
for convention, fearful of getting involved in a situation that might
bring latent animosities to the surface. For the "poor whites," with
whom they are in most frequent contact, the Negroes have neither
admiration nor respect. During moments of release of tension the
more articulate Negroes may express downright contempt for the
crudities of these members of the superior race. One woman who is
a cook for a wealthy family complained:

When you walk through town on Saturday you just as like as not have
somebody spit tobacco juice on you. I think them crackers do it on
purpose, but everybody's spitting, white and colored, so you can't tell.
There's so many of them on the sidewalks chewing tobacco and dipping
snuff it's hard to get through without some of them spitting on you. You
ought to see these country women. You can see white women and colored
sitting on the benches out in front of the clothing store with their breasts
hanging out feeding their babies. They buy bananas and frankfurters and
eat them all up and down the streets.

There may be latent hostility but no overt expression of it on the streets of small towns. All seem to be too glad to get to town where they can see each other and talk. When they address one another the Negroes say "Mr. Jim" and the whites say "Jim," but they get along. In the country stores the Negroes hang about in little clusters, or lean on the counters, nibbling fruits and nuts. Later arrivals of the other race tacitly concede a bench near the stove to the group that first takes possession of it.

In a rural county in South Carolina it was observed that relations were more stable and more cordial than elsewhere. There was less overt hostility and more willing acceptance by Negroes of their customary role in the community. Whites and Negroes jostled one another about in the pursuit of their respective interests without a suggestion of the animosity that such acts of presumption on the part of Negroes are believed inevitably to provoke. A Negro inhabitant made the following comment on the situation:

Them niggers and white folks push each other about till it's a shame. On Saturday night when all the country folks come in town, white folks has to walk around them if they going to get anywhere. Them what knows one another stands around and talks and walks around together. Everybody knows me. When I go to work nearly everybody I pass hollers at me, "Hi, Tobe! How you Tobe?"

Wide variations in etiquette were observed in Johnston County, North Carolina, which is in the upper South outside the plantation area and hence under the influence of a code somewhat more liberal in its formal attitude toward Negroes. This attitude is related in various subtle ways to the economy and history of the area. A Negro schoolteacher pointed to individual variations:

Some white people speak to you on the streets, some grunt, and some ignore you. It is an individual issue.

There is also wide variation by class position. Upper-class whites are less custom-bound than middle- and lower-class whites. In fact, they achieve a certain distinction from their freedom in respect to interracial personal relations. There is also a stronger inclination in the upper South to give recognition to class differences in the Negro population. Middle-class Negroes are most insistent upon observance of the racial etiquette; but upper-class Negroes expect to be more or less exempt from the terms of the code as it applies to ordinary Negroes. The variation in the rigor with which the code is enforced is best illustrated in the attitudes of Negroes regarding public contacts. One of the most respected Negroes in Johnston County had this to say about contacts in public places:

It's pretty fair here. We don't go to their [white] things unless we're invited. When it's for both we go along and we're always treated fairly well.

Negroes would never venture into a mixed meeting without an invitation. In the mixed meetings the "common run of Negroes" are not accorded the same recognition as the doctors and professors who are the rural Negro elite.

In southern cities racial contact has many automatic checks and limitations; although the Negro lives in a segregated world, a certain *modus vivendi* has developed and defines racial boundaries. As has been noted, in public or semipublic institutions there is complete segregation of the Negro. Other public services provide separate sections for Negro use or have regulations which keep members of the two races separated. The points of most frequent contact are thus limited to the streets and highways, stores and markets, and employer-employee relationships.

The different social classes of the Negro population have somewhat different areas of exposure to contacts with whites. The lower economic classes are not concerned with highway etiquette because they do not own cars. Nor do they often encounter whites in voting, in public buildings, or in the more exclusive stores, as do Negroes of the upper classes. The upper-class Negroes avoid contacts with white workers and with other lower middle-class whites, such as court officers, policemen, insurance collectors, etc. There is little or no problem of proper titles of respect for the lower economic groups of Negroes who do not expect them. These titles of respect, however, are more important to upper-class Negroes than the indignity of segregation itself.

An informant who was a day laborer in Birmingham, with a rural background, had no trouble because he "didn't claim any rights." An office building porter explained his immunity by saying that he did not get into places where he would "have to be bothered." Similarly, a Pullman porter living in Atlanta in describing the way in which he meets white people said, "Going about the street I go about my business. I don't pay nobody no attention."

This tolerance is taken for granted, and such Negroes are more likely to denounce than to defend one of their number who lets his temper or indiscretion get him into trouble. In a city market in Birmingham a Negro and one of the clerks quarreled over a sales ticket that had been lost. A fight ensued in which the Negro was severely beaten. Other Negroes in the market continued their shopping without comment or interference. A white woman observing the incident went to one of them and said, "If I were a Negro I'd certainly stop trading in this place, if I couldn't do anything else." The Negro made no reply and did nothing.

Generally speaking, there is no problem in casual public contacts if the Negroes do not make themselves conspicuous by their aggressive behavior. Situations arise in which self-segregation by race is expected but in which there are doubtful areas. This is true, for example, in streetcars and buses with movable signs for the separation of the races. There is such a diversity of means of effecting this segregation that it is unsafe at times for a Negro to get involved unless he knows the local customs very well. A Negro who is unacquainted with the local policy can easily get into difficulty if this lack of acquaintance is interpreted as insolence or indifference to the custom, which often happens.

In Houston a young Negro woman boarded a crowded streetcar in the Negro section. There were no whites in the car, and the only unoccupied seat was one near the front. After she had occupied the seat for some time, a young white woman got aboard and asked that she be given a seat. The operator of the car asked the Negro woman to give up her seat. She declined to move unless she was given back her fare. This was refused; and when the woman persisted in keeping her seat the police were called and she was arrested. Other Negroes left the car in protest. At the trial the Negro woman was found guilty, but when the company sensed that under the circumstances serious punishment would affect its Negro patronage, it sought to have the fine suspended. The line had noticeably lost Negro patronage after the incident; but its capacity business was restored when the company's attitude became generally known among the Negroes.

The problems of casual relations in public places in urban areas are not so much those of physical contact as of status; and the Negroes most affected by this are those of the middle and upper classes. The principal of a high school in one southern city said:

I don't see any difference in whites and Negroes in public places. I have had no experience with white people on the street or in places like the city hall. They don't know your name there and they just don't pay any attention to you; and I don't pay any to them.

Several informants expressed the opinion that it was unwise to spend much time talking with whites in public. "If you have a lot to say to them, they are going to be asking a lot of questions that you will not want to answer. That will put you in a bad spot."

In the border areas race relations in casual contacts at least are reduced to individual problems. Some race-conscious whites regard it as improper to stop on the street and converse with Negroes; but others do so, and little attention is paid to it. In public contacts generally there is merely indifference: "Negroes go their way and white people go theirs." In all the border cities there are Negro residence districts where the common meeting places of the group are located; and there is little interference with their manner of life by outsiders. White persons visiting or passing through these districts seldom seek to arouse resentment by discourtesies or conspicuous racial arrogance; they are usually there for business or service, and any incivility or rudeness would militate against their mission.

In the northern cities there is also indifference in casual contacts; but the latent attitude back of the behavior is less a matter of mere tolerance than it appears to be in the border areas. On the crowded subways, in the streets, and in popular gatherings, whether at a baseball game or in a public meeting, there is little manifest objection on the part of whites to contact with Negroes. Individual instances of objection may occur; but in general civil and personal rights in these places are taken for granted.

In contrast to the southern and border areas, the questions regarding contacts in public places were considered slightly ridiculous by informants. In Harlem, the Negro section of New York City, and in the South Side area of Chicago, where the great bulk of the Negroes live, the state of mind regarding freedom of action is more often one of aggressive self-assertion than of subservience and apology. This may be traced to the fact that more of the emancipated classes of both Negroes and whites are found in northern cities. The majority of Negroes living in northern cities, however, have little or no contact with white persons, except in matters relating to business or work.

RACIAL ETIQUETTE ON THE HIGHWAY

The automobile is a technological innovation which has disturbed many of the traditional patterns of association, caused some modification of the established mores, and presented new problems of interracial etiquette. The highways themselves are new areas of exposure and contact. At first Negroes were expected to operate automobiles for whites, but not to own them. Later, ownership by

Negroes was tolerated, but they were not expected to own large and pretentious cars. Negro ownership of any type of car is no longer questioned except in the smaller towns. When Negroes were operating cars for whites, they were identified with the whites and accorded the rights of the road. When driving their own cars they were expected to maintain their role as Negroes and in all cases to give whites the right-of-way. Obviously, this made for much uncertainty and confusion, because it is impossible on the highway to make these distinctions without investigation. Furthermore, the driving of automobiles involves impersonal traffic regulations, the observance of which is essential to safety; and as one informant pointed out, any attempt to introduce the racial etiquette is likely to involve traffic regulations:

Some of them don't like it when you don't wait for them to get away first, but where there is a lot of traffic you can't bother with them because you tie up traffic and that would be worse.

The Negroes are careful, however, to avoid situations which suggest a challenge of the racial prerogative of the white motorist, whether the latter is right or wrong. They know that they will have to pay in many special ways for any mishaps. If they drive a new and expensive car, they must be able to keep it out of the way of malicious whites in cheap cars who would get satisfaction out of damaging the new car. If there is a collision, the Negro does not expect to get paid for damages to his own car, whether entitled to them or not. White women drivers are an especial concern of the Negro because many of them pay little attention to any of the traffic regulations when a Negro is involved. One Negro observed humorously but ironically:

These white women act like they think these brakes is colored too and just naturally stop dead still when they sees a white woman busting into a open highway without stopping. They look up and sees you colored and keep going like it's a disgrace to stop at a stop sign to let a nigger pass.

If there is any doubt about whose turn it is to make a move in traffic, the turn is assumed to be the white person's, especially if the driver is a white woman. With white men the Negro may sometimes indulge in "bluffing" in traffic. He may appear to be driving with a minimum of caution, when in reality he is employing a great deal of skill. He attempts to obtain his traffic right by innocently driving his rickety car very close to the shining body of the white man's automobile. They both know that in the event of a collision about all the white man can get is personal vengeance, which might give him a measure of satisfaction but would not repair his car. The

Negro seldom actually touches a car, but he gets close enough to prompt the white driver to weigh the advantages of arbitrary racial assertion at the cost of a smashed fender or radiator.

In North Carolina in the upper South there seems to be less concern about the "racial right-of-way" on the highways. A Negro school principal said:

I've looked for them to show signs of that on the highways, but I've never had or seen a concrete case. You pass like anybody else. They're very fair about right-of-ways in town, too. They seem to obey the law. Usually you are by before they know you are colored anyhow. If I have the right-of-way I take it.

Another informant thought the highway etiquette was largely a personal matter, depending on the temperament of the individuals. Another noted that class differences were reflected in the highway etiquette:

There's not very much argument about passing white people's cars unless it is Sunday evening and some poor country white folks is in a car. He may curse at you, but white folks generally don't pay any attention to you on the road. We take our right-of-way when our time comes. They better not try running in front of a truck.

The highway etiquette functions in southern cities only in areas where some arbitrariness of behavior is possible. White pedestrians occasionally appear to expect Negro operators of automobiles to give them the right-of-way. It is sometimes expected that Negro operators will wait at intersections until all white persons pass. Negro drivers of heavy trucks complain of the apparent carelessness or indifference of white woman pedestrians and motorists.

A Negro doctor in Houston described a situation that has contributed to the confusion of traffic rules and the racial etiquette. He said:

A lot of the Negro drivers don't give a darn about the white man or any other man if they are in a car. They just drive and have everybody afraid of them. They drive pretty fast, but are usually good drivers and they just bluff people out of the way. The whites would stay mad if they waited around for these Negroes to give them the right-of-way.

Police officers may enforce the racial etiquette by arresting Negro car owners on exaggerated charges of speeding or reckless driving and, in doing so, make every effort to humiliate Negro occupants of cars. A Negro physician in one city experienced serious physical violence over an incident that would ordinarily be regarded as trivial. He inadvertently passed a stop sign and was hailed by a traffic officer, who shouted, "Say, nigger, what in hell you doing there?" The physician, who was a small man of unprepossessing appearance, began to apologize; but the officer, swearing louder with each sentence, drew his club and struck the physician over the head, fracturing his skull. Learning that the Negro was a physician, the officer abated his abuse but continued to insist that there had been provocation. The physician reported the case to the chief of police, who said he would look into it, but nothing further happened. Associates of the physician urged him to sue the city for damages, but he refused, fearing that if he won he would be marked for more serious trouble later.

The insistence on the racial right-of-way in spite of traffic regulations has resulted in so many problems and accidents that it is increasingly difficult to maintain the etiquette. Some Negroes get satisfaction out of this impersonal defense of their position, and in some cases might be suspected of concealing aggressive impulses behind the menacing power of their machine. One man said:

It seems to me that the white pedestrians are worse than the white motorists. If a white pedestrian sees a Negro driving he doesn't think of stopping, because he thinks, "This nigger won't hurt me." But they are improving. The more they get hurt the quicker they will realize that it doesn't make any difference about the color of the driver, the machine will not fail to hurt just because you are white.

Court cases have resulted from conflicts between the racial etiquette and traffic regulations. The evidence has frequently revealed that the Negroes were strictly within the law, even though they ignored the racial etiquette, and they have won their cases in court.

In the South the etiquette extends to passing automobiles on the highways and in city traffic; but in the border areas questions of right-of-way arise only in cases involving individuals with strong racial biases which are not fully supported by local custom. A Negro police officer in Baltimore said:

I've never heard of a case where a white person resented a Negro passing him on the highway just because he is a Negro. That may happen but I've never seen any evidence of it.

Obviously, it would confuse traffic seriously if racial etiquette were introduced on the highway.

The racial factor is of so little importance on northern highways that a Negro may often be the aggressor in an accident without more serious consequences than would be involved in a conflict between persons of the same race.

Negroes are not expected to use tourist cabins in the border states or in northern areas near large Negro population concentrations. In parts of New England, in the upper tier of northern states, and in the western or mountain states these accommodations are used with only occasional question.

In the casual contacts, the racial etiquette prescribes only a weak ritual for observance in the South and none at all in the North. The difference between the etiquette and legal "rights" is that the weight of customary practice is on the side of the etiquette; and it reflects the traditionally observed racial distance between the two groups.

ENTERING OF WHITE HOMES BY NEGROES

In the rural South almost without exception a Negro is expected to enter white homes by the back door, unless he is a domestic close to the family, or has been invited to come in the front door by the houseowner. This invitation is more likely to be forthcoming if the Negro has some work to do in the house or is carrying some heavy article which could best be deposited in the front of the house. Negroes who wish to escape the customary treatment on going to a white person's home make use of the avoidance technique: they make it their business to see the white person on the street or at his office. Any business that a white man has with a Negro can ordinarily be transacted in one of these two places. There is no reason or excuse for a Negro to call at a white man's home except on business, for social calls are taboo. In a Mississippi county a Negro chiropractor with an almost exclusively white clientele said:

You got to go in through the back yard. I always go in the back door when they send for me.

Lower-class Negroes have no occasion to go to a white man's home except to work; and other Negroes, when they resent this back-door requirement, find ingenious ways to avoid the issue. A retired farmer and restaurant keeper in Mississippi uses this strategy:

I go up to his gate and ask him if I may speak to him for a minute. He is usually too lazy to come out to see you and he will tell you to come on in. In that case it's all right to come in the front. If not, he will come out to meet you and talk. They won't hardly ever tell you to go 'round to the back, because they'd have to go 'round there too.

The rigidness of the general pattern, however, is evident in the assertion of another informant in Mississippi:

I don't know of a Negro here that the white folks all don't expect to come to their back door. He had better have a good excuse if he goes marching up to the front door.

Then, reflectively, he added:

I tell you it's a funny place, this South. I hear you don't have to do that up North. I never did go up there, but I am hoping that I can get some money so I can make it up there. This place is all right, in a way, but a man has to be less than a man to get along most of the time.

In a South Carolina county the expectation regarding entering of white homes admits of exceptions within the general pattern of white paternalism. The few Negroes who violate the etiquette in this respect do so under the privileges of this loose paternalism. Some of these Negroes in a spirit of bravado interpret such violations as matters of personal pride. Thus, an elderly Negro woman school-teacher who observed all other aspects of the etiquette said:

I only go to my friends' houses, and I go in the front door. They don't expect anything else of me. I don't know the way to the back door. If I had to go to the back door, I wouldn't go.

Significantly, she added:

When a person has to go to a white person's house on business and doesn't know them he would go to the back door, but I haven't had to do that yet.

In a North Carolina county the upper and more secure white classes make some distinctions between classes of the Negro population. It occasionally happens that a Negro professional or school principal finds it necessary to visit a white person in his home; and although it is customary for Negroes to go to the back door, one school principal said he had entered one or two white homes by the front door. He said:

Recently I was talking to a white man about my baby sucking his thumb. He told me he had some medicine that had stopped his baby and insisted that I go to his house and get the bottle from his wife. He phoned his wife and told her I was coming. I thought about the question as I drove up, and wondered if I would be asked to the back door. When I drove up his wife was standing at the side door with the bottle. Then I knew she expected the side-door entrance.

Visiting a well-educated and friendly white official born in the South, this Negro found that he was expected to come to the front door and, on entering, to sit down in the library.

Another informant, a moderately successful farmer, said:

Some recognize you at the front door and some don't. Ordinarily it don't make any difference what they are worth; just some do and some don't.

In the cities the general assumption is that Negroes calling at white homes will enter by the rear, but there are two modifying factors: occasions requiring such contact are practically limited to cases involving servant relationships; and class differentiation within the Negro group introduces a distinction in the occasions for home contact. As a result the general policy regarding rear-door entrance holds for Negroes whose errands are associated with service, while exceptions occur in other contacts involving middle- or upper-class Negroes; although this depends also upon the class, temperament, and level of security of the white persons involved. On the rare occasions when a Negro goes to the home of a white person for other than a service purpose, unless the relationship is well defined and understood, problems may develop. A Negro finds it more comfortable to meet the white person in his place of business, or to talk with him by telephone. A Negro of the servant level never meets this problem unless rare chance takes him to the home of a lower-class white.

As in rural areas the occasions when Negroes of the upper and middle classes enter white homes are usually connected with school business, health, religious or interracial work. Such interests are so selective of persons that the incidence of unpleasant experiences is reduced. Servants with instructions to direct all Negroes to the back entrance, especially white servants, may insist upon the etiquette with less discretion and more racial discrimination than the employer. A Negro social work executive in one of the cities of the upper South made this observation:

I find that the well-dressed, well-bearing Negro—one whose general bearing is that of a man to be respected—a businessman above the average, will be admitted to the front door without question.

But this does not always work. When a Negro, however well dressed and well bearing, is unknown to the white person or to the servant in the house, a problem situation may develop. A Negro school supervisor in Birmingham said:

I always try to avoid going to a white man's home. Any business that I have with him I try to do at his office. If I can't do it there, I don't usually get it done. It happens that they invite you to their homes once in a while. If they do that, they will expect you to come in the front door. It is the rule that Negroes, locally, are expected to go to the white man's back door if they go to his house at all. Most of the Negroes who would not relish going to the back door would probably not go to the house at all unless they could not get around it.

In Nashville a Negro physician reported that in spite of the local expectation that Negroes will go to the back door, when an occasion arose for consultation on a school health program with a school board executive in her home, he went with some trepidation to the front door, was admitted by the maid to the parlor, and was courteously treated by the woman when she entered. On another occasion when he had car trouble in a suburban section and needed to telephone, he went to the front door of a strange house and was treated with similar courtesy.

In Houston another informant, a school principal, explained that in his limited contacts of this kind he always went to the front door. However, there is evidence that this is not a wholly common experience, even for Negroes of this class; because he could reconcile himself to going neither to the front door nor to the back, another Negro principal refused to attend a meeting in the home of a white school official. Our informant said:

Much of this kind of discrimination and feeling is in the Negro. They are so accustomed to going to back doors, taking off their hats, and bowing and scraping to white people that they don't know what else to do. These older principals wouldn't think of going to the front door.

Whites who object to Negroes coming to their front doors refrain from inviting upper-class Negroes to their homes. There is as much concern about the comments of neighbors as about upholding the principle. A white family that permitted this could easily be made to feel the silent or vocal censure of the neighbors and, if not well established and influential, could be made extremely uncomfortable. Friendly visits between whites and Negroes occur on rare occasions in all of the southern cities. In such cases members of both races incur risks. It is safe to say, however, that occasions for such contacts have been gradually increasing, and interracial contacts are attracting less attention than in former years.

In both border and northern areas the racial etiquette is frequently overshadowed by considerations of social class. Most Negro-white contacts in private homes involve work or business and the same rules hold for Negro and white visitors to white homes. The great majority of such Negro visits are related to work and, thus, they are expected to go to the back. One notable difference between the South and the border and northern areas is that no upper-class Negro whose mission is one of business or friendship is expected to call at the back. This etiquette is self-enforcing since no friendly or social relations could be sustained between whites and upper-class Negroes under this condition; when one must take the servant role and go to the back he is no longer upper class. The occasions for business or social contacts, however, are limited; and deviations from the general pattern are usually handled by some avoidance device.

ENTERING OF NEGRO HOMES BY WHITES

The corollary of an accommodation situation in which Negroes in most situations are not expected to enter a white man's front door is that a white man may enter a Negro's home through either door and should never be expected to come to the back door. Most whites who have occasion to go to the home of a Negro enter the front door; this applies to salesmen as well as businessmen. Even white hucksters and peddlers expect to deliver goods through the front doors of middle-class Negro homes, but seldom find enough profit in the practice to keep it up. In the case of salesmen the problem for Negroes is not one of keeping whites from entering the front door, but of discouraging them from showing signs of disrespect after they enter. These whites often keep their hats on. The Negroes have a mild form of control: they can refuse to buy; but frequently they need the goods and must accept the practice with as little embarrassment as possible.

In rural communities lower-class whites usually go to the front door of Negro homes. This is resented by the Negroes; but to avoid the reputation of being "uppity" or "too smart niggers," they either accept the situation or make it as difficult as possible for this type of white person. Thus one informant, speaking of lower-class whites entering his front door, said:

Well, they do come to my front door. If somebody else is in the house most of these peckerwoods will get them to answer them there. But me, that is the big reason I stay around here on the back so much. I never answer the door. If they get in this house or get any answer when I am here they sure will come to my back door. I bought and paid for this place, and I am proud of it. They can treat me here like they want to treat me if I come to their house.

This is one of the more subtle ways of getting some revenge for having to go to the white man's back door. A few Negroes tell the "poor whites" to go to the back door when they call or not to call at all.

A Mississippi informant made an interesting distinction between classes of the white population and indicated the courtesy expected of white persons when Negroes knew and kept "their place":

These peckerwoods for the most part don't like to give respect to the Negro's home. There are some of them that come here and talk till times gets better, but they never show any courtesy. They wouldn't pull off their hats if they had to. Of course, some people that stand for something would respect your place. Mr. B——, the superintendent, is one of these persons. He respects you and he seems to think that Negroes ought to stay in their places.

The average white person's manner of entering Negro homes carries implications which are resented by Negroes of all classes more bitterly than any of the other discriminative practices. It is an invasion of privacy and, in a sense, a searching out of the Negro in order to show discourtesy. In some instances whites open the door and walk in without knocking. When they fail to wipe their feet and "slosh mud over the floors" of Negro homes, it is interpreted by the Negroes as assuming that all Negro homes are dirty and a little more dirt won't hurt.

Salesmen eager to get Negro trade will sometimes remove their hats. A Negro barber in Mississippi estimated that about two out of a hundred do this. In Johnston County there is less freedom in entering Negro homes and more occasions on which men remove their hats as a gesture of respect to the home. The question that stands as the test of respect for the Negroes is whether or not the white person will sit down after he enters. Because it is suspected by some whites that middle-class Negroes expect them to remove their hats upon entering Negro homes, there is growing reluctance on the part of these whites to enter at all. Sometimes they call the Negro outside or to the car in which they are riding.

White persons may visit their servants' homes and appear at ease there. There are few other occasions for calls at Negro homes except to sell something or collect insurance. A woman informant said:

Some act like they're afraid to sit down and others act like they're at home. I have had them to take off their hats—insurance agents do.

This woman judged white people by their ability to be at ease inside a Negro home.

In the cities the most common white callers in Negro homes are salesmen, insurance agents, collectors, inspectors, and agents of various concerns. As in the rural areas, they all feel free to enter any Negro home by the front door. The great majority of Negro homes in southern cities are those of the lower economic levels, generally Negro servants or laborers. The white men make a point of not removing their hats, and the white women make a point of not sitting down. They call the Negroes by their first names. The average Negro family of this class expects this type of behavior. A Negro domestic said:

No white people come here except collectors. They just walk right in, if the door is open, and call me "Freddie." They have never called me anything else.

Regarding this practice a Birmingham miner said:

They don't care what you doing. They bust in and don't knock. They don't pull off their hats or nothing. I don't say nothin'. All I can see is that a colored man ain't much,—when they got everything. What can a man do when it's like that? Nothin' that I can see. This is a white man's country, and there ain't much that we can do.

It is above this level, among the middle- and upper-class Negroes, that the expected behavior is sometimes modified because of the Negroes' concern about status and respect. This is not always taken into account by white visitors, either through ignorance of the distinction or because of the inflexibility of their racial codes. These Negroes go as far as possible to make visits by whites to their homes unnecessary. A schoolteacher in Birmingham said:

If we have pleasant relations with a white person we give them as little chance to spoil things as possible. For that reason we make little occasion for them to have to come to our houses. Most of the bills that I incur I take care of them at the offices of the places. I have no collectors coming here. Most of the crackers that would act nasty at your house, and would not respect it, do not have the chance to come to my house. If they come here and I haven't sent for them, I tell them where they are to get off. They have no right to come to my house and misuse me. I don't remember that I have had any trouble with them lately.

This matter of respect becomes a point of great concern with Negroes of the middle and upper classes; and after unsuccessfully employing every convenient device to avoid contact with whites, they face the situation directly and sometimes aggressively. Occasionally they succeed in correcting the situation because white visitors usually have an economic purpose, and protest carries some weight when backed by the ability of the Negroes to refuse to buy goods. Insurance agents in some southern cities have modified their behavior to the point of acceptability because their failure to accord "respect" gave the competing Negro agents of Negro companies one of their strongest sales arguments. Collectors who receive commissions lose money when a Negro, out of resentment of bad manners, elects to pay his bills at the office or by mail.

Some employers apologize for their white employees in such situations, but in terms of the etiquette. They explain that the men have known nothing else, and it would be a hardship for them to have to remove their hats in a Negro home. It would be embarrassing for the employers to have to tell a white employee to do this. They hope the Negroes will be broad-minded and understand. This satisfies a few of the Negroes but not all. The economic pressure exercised by middle- and upper-class Negroes has been effective enough in some cases to encourage Negroes of lesser status to insist on the ordinary courtesies. A Houston informant who said that only white salesmen came to his home noted that all were very courteous. He remembered only one recent unpleasant incident: when a laundryman came into his house and kept his hat on, the informant protested without effect. He said nothing more to the man but called the management of the laundry and explained why he was discontinuing the service.

There are middle-class Negroes who are not aggressive enough to insist upon correction of behavior, and who meet the issue by complicated rationalization. A barber in Houston made this explanation:

When they come to my house I always accord them the very best of treatment, though they be the biggest white persons, who know how to accept courtesy, or the biggest cracker in the place, who is uneasy when anybody shows courteous treatment toward him. I get a certain pleasure out of making them feel uneasy.

It is a different and more difficult problem when the white person can reinforce the etiquette with the support of police authority. As a rule the police make no attempt to recognize the differences between classes of the Negro population and derive personal satisfaction from failing to make the distinctions expected. It is dangerous for Negroes to challenge this "disrespect" on the part of police officers, but occasionally it is challenged successfully. A Negro doctor told of an encounter with an officer of the law who called at his home for information on a case involving a Negro boy, the son of a servant in the family. The officer called about four o'clock in the morning, and the doctor answered the door in his bathrobe. The officer's greeting was "Hello, boy, where is Will?" In reply the doctor said that he was Dr. Doe, and that he thought the method of address was improper. The officer became angry, informed him that "niggers" were not supposed to "talk like that to the law," insisted on searching the house without a warrant, and pushed in to look around. The Negro sternly told the officer that he was a physician and knew exactly how far an officer could go, and that he would make "plenty of trouble" if the officer attempted to go any farther without a search warrant. The officer left after looking casually around the first floor. A week later a young white woman came to the informant's house and said that a colored nurse had told her that the doctor was very sympathetic and would help her get some morphine, which her condition demanded. She was very timid and appealing. He informed her that he never handled narcotics and did not have a license. The physician is convinced that the woman was an agent sent by the officer in an effort to trap him.

REMOVING OF HATS BY NEGROES

It is difficult to generalize in regard to the removal of hats. In public places most Negroes do not remove their hats when they are talking to white persons. It is customary for whites and blacks to remove their hats when they go into offices. Where there are ladies present, whites remove their hats. Negro women are not referred to as "ladies"; they are just "women." Negroes remove their hats when there is a white woman around, especially if they have occasion to talk to her. While it is true that there is ostensibly nothing racial in this pattern, it has certain racial implications. Failure to remove one's hat when talking to a white woman may be interpreted as an intentional insult; and this can easily threaten the security of the Negro concerned. A Mississippi Negro tenant succinctly described this expected gesture of deference:

Naturally niggers take off they hats around white people. Some places they could get away without taking them off but they don't know it. Sometimes white people make you take off your hat.

The gesture is so generally expected that most rural Negroes take no chances and remove their hats at any contact with a white person. Upper-class and urban Negroes try to restrict the removing of their hats to situations in which women are present. In the lower rural South when there is some question about the expected etiquette, upper-class Negroes leave their hats behind if they can, or affect extreme courtesy as a character trait that makes no racial distinction, or pretend to themselves and other Negroes that carrying their hats in their hands is a matter of comfort rather than subservience.

In urban places Negroes are expected to remove their hats in office buildings, elevators, and hotel lobbies. There is, however, no demand that they remove their hats in casual street conversations, although those who do are praised and sometimes rewarded for this courtesy. Such persons, however, are contemptuously referred to by other Negroes as "bowing and scraping Uncle Toms." When there are ladies in elevators, all men are expected to remove their hats. There are the following racial distinctions with respect to this gesture of deference: Negro men are expected to remove their hats when no women are present, and white men are not expected to remove theirs if only Negro women are present.

Lower- and lower middle-class Negroes in cities frequently remove their hats whenever they are around white persons. A Birmingham newspaper man said:

They are just used to it. I don't believe they would have to do it if they didn't want to. It's just a part of the southern Negro.

A skilled laborer felt that removing the hat was as imperative as applying titles of respect:

White people expect it, and when I go where they want me to take off my hat I do it just to keep out of trouble. In some of these elevators they tell you to take off your hat. I don't know which ones, because I never kept my hat on to find out.

It was reported in the Kansas City *Call* that a county police officer in Texas slapped a young Negro motorist because "he failed to remove his hat when talking to a white man."[4] This type of incident happens occasionally but is not common.

There have been two important modifications of this form of etiquette in southern cities. Lower-class Negroes distinguish between the whites to whom this type of respect is due and those to whom it is not; and upper-class Negroes, especially the younger ones, find ways of successfully avoiding the act in all situations except those involving women.

EXPECTED MODE OF ADDRESSING WHITES

In a crowd where there are other whites present, white persons regardless of class are expected to be referred to as—"Mr." On

[4] Kansas City *Call*, August 1, 1941.

jobs where Negroes and whites work in close contact and there are few of either, a Negro often calls a white man by his first name, but not if there are many others present. A white man who is not addressed as—"Mr." by a Negro is likely to lose status with his white associates. Where there is a choice facing the white man, the status loser is the Negro. According to the etiquette all whites, from the plantation owner down to the lowest "peckerwood," are—"Mr." to all Negroes in the rural South. An Arkansas informant said:

The poor crackers want you to say "Mr." more than the rich white people do. I know that they would hate it more if you didn't say it to them than the rich people would. I speak to all of them in the same way.

It is in the matter of according titles of respect that the Negro may estimate differences in the quality of whites. Negroes can avoid according this respect as cleverly as they avoid other situations; and among themselves they make use of terms not at all designed to indicate respect. A middle-aged Negro farmer said:

The people of the better class I always show respect and keep in position to ask a favor. The poor ones I don't call anything. If I have to say anything I just walk up and start talking. They can't demand respect and they can't give me anything.

Other Negroes take no chances on even the lower-class whites. Another farmer said:

I call all of them Mr. So-and-so. You can't tell when one of them crackers is liable to rise up and get to be somebody around here. They can get you then if they start gunning at you.

A lower-class white occasionally tries to bolster his ego by demanding that Negroes say "sir" in answering him. Policemen almost invariably use their authority to enforce respect and deference which is not always sincerely felt by Negroes in their power.

In referring to one white person in conversation with another, a Negro is always expected to use the title—"Mr." It is merely another feature of the racial code. "After all," one man reflected, "they don't care how big a red neck the white man, he is still more than a nigger. If they don't do that they think the nigger will soon get out of his place." Negroes do not object to showing respect for whites who are above them in economic status, but it irritates them to have to say—"Mr." to a "poor white." Contemptuously but cautiously an informant in Mississippi said:

These old peckerwoods—clay eaters—want you to call them "Mr." though they ain't got a thing but a lot of tobacco to go in their jaws. They don't care how bad they look, they think they are better than the Negroes around here. That's the thing that makes me sick.

This rule of etiquette may be enforced informally by the authority of a court. During a trial in a North Carolina township the judge stopped the testimony and asked why the Negroes did not call the white men "mister."

The younger whites and Negroes call one another by their first names and seem to be less self-conscious about it than the older people. Students of colleges and institutions generally are requiring less formality and more freedom; and this is having some effect on the traditional codes.

The etiquette regarding modes of addressing whites is similar in cities; but in the more impersonal setting there are both more ways of avoidance by Negroes and fewer whites who insist on being addressed formally.

EXPECTED MODES OF ADDRESSING NEGROES

All Negroes in the South know that they will not be called "Mr." or "Mrs." With few exceptions they expect to be called by their first names in most places and situations. Occasionally the men are called by their last names; and this is regarded as a limited effort to show respect on the part of the whites and, as such, is considered an improvement. A Negro whose name is not known is called "boy" if young and "uncle" if old. A young Negro woman is called by her first name if known, or hailed anonymously as "You, there," or some such vague designation, if unknown. An older woman is called "auntie." These are regarded as titles of address "without prejudice." The command address used by petty officials, police, overseers, and similar white persons with any semblance of authority is simply and bluntly "nigger."

A Negro professional man is occasionally called "doctor," or "doc," but most often by his last name. Where public courtesy is demanded, any Negro of status who cannot be addressed by his first name without giving great offense is called "professor." "Sir" seems to be a fairly general term and one not always used in recognition of status. It has been observed that "Yes, sir" will be used with the same person who has been called "boy."

The pressure for omission of certain titles of respect is so strong that in the presence of white persons Negroes are reluctant to use a title when referring to other Negroes. Instead they say "Brother Smith" or "Sister Jones." A lumberyard laborer suggested the finality of this custom when he said:

They don't call none of them niggers around here by no "Mr." I never been called "Mr." but once by a white man, that I can remember, and that was when I was visited by a northern white man who used to work with my son.

An observant old farmer in a Mississippi county said:

They call them big niggers around here by their last names, and if they like them pretty well they might get around to calling them "Mr." when they die and they have to put it in the papers. They will get around it if the Negro is a teacher or doctor or something like that.

These generalizations can be made about the use of titles of respect in addressing Negroes in southern cities: All Negroes are addressed without titles except when some special or compelling circumstance makes it necessary to modify this policy. Such special circumstances include public introductions before Negro audiences; relations in educational or religious matters; and business conversations with upper-class or economically secure Negroes where any other practice would result in loss of an important volume of business. Otherwise, only a few whites, usually those who are socially or economically secure, can freely use titles of respect in addressing Negroes. This taboo is deep-seated, involving in a complicated manner the status, self-interest, and self-conception of the individual white person.

In some instances the conflict between rational judgment and emotionally charged taboo results in a type of compromise utterly incomprehensible to one unacquainted with the customs of the area. In circumstances demanding some gesture of respect the etiquette demands that the white person carefully avoid using the titles "Mr." or "Mrs.," but it is permissible to employ the titles "doctor," "reverend," or "professor" whether appropriate or not.

It is easier to solve the problem of titles for men than for their wives because middle- and upper-class Negro women never permit their first names to be known. They use either initials or their husband's names; and this makes address difficult without using the title "Mrs." The wife of a well-to-do Negro businessman went into a department store in Atlanta to inquire about an account. The clerk asked her name and she said, "Mrs. William Jones." The clerk insisted on her first name and, when she refused to give it, declared that the business could not be completed without it. It was a large account; and the manager, to whom appeal was made, decided that "Mrs." was simply good business and not "social equality." In another case a business house wished to reach the wife of a Negro doctor but could not call for "Mrs." Smith. The caller asked, "Is this

the residence of James Smith, the colored doctor?" and was told
that it was. "Well, then, I want to speak to his wife" was the reply.

A Negro social worker in Richmond recalled an experience in one
of the national chain stores which suggests a conventionalization of
avoidance:

I noticed that every time I went into one of the stores the clerk called
me "doctor," so I decided one day to ask about it. The clerk told me
that in their training schools they teach their clerks to call Negro men
who are well-dressed "doctor." He said it quite broadly and innocently,
I must admit. He seemed to think that Negro men would be glad to be
called "doctor." They didn't know that most of us feel like a fool having
somebody call us doctor when we have not earned the title. They rarely
ever give a title to a colored woman.

When the exaggerated titles of "doctor," "professor," "reverend" are not used, it is understood to be a gesture of respect when
the last rather than the first name of a Negro man is used. Most
Negro schoolteachers in the city systems are so addressed by school
officials. The women teachers try to avoid occasions on which their
names would be used, because they are almost invariably subjected
to great embarrassment by being referred to by their first names,
before their pupils and associates. The insistence upon the use of first
names without titles serves to select for positions of responsibility
those Negroes willing to accept this usage. It frequently happens that
superior individuals who accept segregation as an institution refuse
to accept this personal and unnecessary disrespect for their personalities and positions, and they seek positions elsewhere. In the educational system of southern cities there are a few white men, with
advanced education and contacts outside the region, who will under
some or all circumstances employ the titles "Mr." and "Mrs." in
referring to Negroes.

There is a type of marginal situation in the use of titles of respect
which is confusing and also an indication of the modification of the
mores. It sometimes happens that friendships develop between whites
and Negroes of the professional classes. On this level respect and
association prompt the dropping of formal titles and the use of first
names. In fact, it is a fairly common practice for persons informally
in association to use first names. In this case the dropping of the title
by a white person addressing a Negro is not complete unless the title
is dropped by the Negro in return. This type of situation was interestingly described by a Negro professional in one of the cities:

Sometime ago I was at a meeting where social problems were being discussed. It was a bit informal, I admit. A very important man presided; he is the president of a bank and the president of the chamber of commerce. He introduced the speakers by name and evidenced much friendliness and real intimacy. He called them John Smith and James Howard—both white men—by name without a title when he introduced them. It seemed to be something of the relationship of players on the same football team—easy comradeship. I began to squirm, because I wondered how he was going to fit me into the picture. Well, he talked a few minutes about problems of Negroes, and then said, "But Frank will tell you about that." Everybody looked to see my reaction, because all of the workers know that I give them titles and expect a title. I smiled, and after about two minutes of delay, I gave my report. In it I asked to speak to the chairman after the meeting. And after the meeting I talked to him quite frankly. I told him that he and the other two men are good friends, very intimate. They go out together socially, enjoy dinner parties and all that sort of thing, and I could see where he would feel free to introduce them as he did. But as to me, there is no such strong friendship or suggestion of intimacy, and if such were suggested he and some others would be offended. I told him that to avoid any misunderstanding or misinterpretation I had rather that he address me as "Mr. Smith." He took it rather nicely and apologized. We have had many contacts since and he has always been very careful. Sometimes I think because of this talk we have become even better friends than we would have if I had let it pass.

The etiquette carries over into newspaper usage and correspondence. Titles are not used commonly in news references to Negroes. There are occasional exceptions and some interesting devices to avoid the use of titles without giving offense. Several southern newspapers carry a page or column of *News of Interest to Colored People.* Since whites are not expected to read this, the Negro correspondents may use titles and have them printed. One newspaper adheres to the etiquette more rigidly than the others and uses "Madame" instead of "Mrs."

In reporting an event involving no obvious segregation and individuals who are not known to the editors, it is safer to use titles for all or to omit all titles. In cities in which there are Negro colleges with mixed faculties, newspaper editors frequently telephone the college to inquire if an individual is white or Negro in order to handle the title problem properly. When the celebrated contralto, Marian Anderson, appeared in concerts in Tennessee, the critics were hard put to find an acceptable mode of referring to her in articles which paid tribute to a superb voice and manner. One used "Anderson"; and another, "Marian."

Formal salutations in letters also fall under the etiquette. When a letter is being addressed to a person known to be a Negro, "My dear" and "Sir" are self-consciously omitted. The letter begins simply "John," or there is no salutation at all; and the envelope carries no title for the name. A prominent Negro woman, president of a state parent-teacher organization in Louisiana, wrote the governor regarding a question of public concern. She received a reply from the governor's secretary addressing her, without formal salutation, simply as "Huggins." Unless accounts are kept separately by race, or there are markings to indicate race, conformity to the etiquette becomes expensive; and it is being ignored with increasing frequency by the larger businesses and by less provincial persons.

THE TABOO AGAINST INTERRACIAL DINING AND DRINKING

The proscription of interracial dining is one of the strongest of the taboos and is rarely broken in the South, for eating together carries a strong suggestion of social intimacy which is universally banned. In fact, the question of interracial dining seldom arises because it is so thoroughly prohibited and severely punished by ostracism of the white and labeling of the Negro. The operation of the taboo in public dining places has already been discussed. The taboo in private relations is best illustrated in two incidents. A party of four white men and a Negro guide went out in a boat to spend the day fishing. At noon they all ate; but for the comfort of the party a stick was laid across the boat between the Negro and the whites, and lunch and conversation took place without strain. Again, a Negro schoolteacher was entertaining a group of white school visitors when mealtime arrived. No other facilities being available, he offered them dinner. They ate willingly enough and to prove their friendship insisted that he get a small table and eat in the same room.

When a white person is alone, he is less scrupulous about preserving the integrity of the taboo. It is, of course, possible to eat together in private homes; but upper-class Negroes hesitate to do this in their own homes even when the white person is an outsider or "liberal" and does not feel bound by the custom. All informants agree that Negroes working in white families never eat with any members of the family. When whites visit Negro acquaintances, who are usually servants or former servants with a reputation for being exceptionally good cooks, separate accommodations are expected even though the food is furnished without remuneration.

An undertaker in Arkansas, giving his views on the prevalence of interracial dining, said:

I have never heard tell of colored and white eating together in this section. If it happens don't nobody know nothing about it.

A farmer observed that he had never eaten with any of the whites, although on various occasions lower-class whites came to his home to eat. He would prepare separate tables. "These crackers," he said, "don't go in for that." A compress worker employed with whites noted that they took their lunches to another side of the plant:

They were good to me and would give me anything that they had left that I wanted, but they would not eat on the same side of the plant with me. Somehow they don't like to eat with a nigger.

A Negro insurance agent who belongs to the more favored economic classes felt the insult implied in the taboo, but accepted it as part of the South:

They seem to think it would make the food poison if a Negro ate with them. They don't say anything about what is the case when the Negro woman in the kitchen fixes the food. It is foolish to me, but I don't let it worry me any.

In South Carolina there were Negro families who reported experiences which suggested eating together without the usual social implications. In one of the towns a Negro laundress who lives next door to a white family makes ice cream and invites her neighbor in to share it with her. This is reciprocated when the white neighbor makes ice cream. According to this informant, an old white man who does odd jobs comes into her kitchen and says, "Mayme, what you cooking?" He sits down in the kitchen and eats at the same table. Her husband resents the familiarity of both the woman and the man. The wife said:

He gets so mad he cusses. He'd come to dinner and see him and turn around and go back and wouldn't eat his dinner. He'd say, "I can't eat a square meal for looking at them damned old po' white folks."

In the upper South there are "cultural islands" where white and Negro teachers have frequently eaten together without feeling the pressure of the taboo. In Johnston County poor whites and Negroes eat together and apparently think little of it, if they know one another and no extra whites are around. In the cities of the middle and upper South the more liberal of the teachers and social and religious workers eat together at private and semiprivate affairs.

In the border areas the taboo against interracial dining may be broken without serious social consequences; but few eating places outside the home are normally and easily available for this type of association. Consequently, it is limited largely to formal meetings of social, educational, religious, and occasionally, civic groups. The status of the whites, however, is not as seriously affected by this association as it would be in the South.

In the North there is a wider range of facilities for interracial dining; when it occurs, it causes little thought or comment. It is regarded as a personal matter. In the city the impersonal character of associations, the wide variety of secondary relations, and the broad anonymity of individuals and groups tend to weaken the pressure of white group censure of this behavior. However, as has been noted, the discriminating practices of certain establishments can lead to situations of such intense embarrassment to both white and Negro parties as to reduce the number of such associations and to arouse consciousness of the taboo itself. This is, of course, an indirect manifestation and support of the etiquette.

There is more freedom in drinking than in eating together both in the South and in the North. The cafés and "joints" operated by Negroes are frequently visited by lower-class whites looking for excitement and liquor. They will not only drink with Negroes, but on occasion, out of the same bottles. In the stores some of them sit around consuming soft drinks with Negroes. Drinking together, however, is not confined to lower-class whites. One Negro informant gave this account:

When I worked at the compress there was some bosses who liked to drink. They didn't have legal whisky and it was hard to get the stuff. I always could find what I wanted. I would go and get the stuff and we would all be on the job just as drunk as we could be. We would all drink together. We would even drink out of the same bottle. Now and then one of them would stop to think about the fact that they were drinking after a nigger, and they would tell me to get something to put mine in. If not that, they would tell me to wait until they had got all they wanted out of the bottle and then they would hand it to me.

This practice is reported to be fairly common among lower-class whites and Negroes in rural North Carolina. The whisky is usually illicit and the drinkers are bound together by a common guilt, which apparently outweighs the taboo.

PLAYING TOGETHER

Negroes and whites do not as a rule indulge in recreational activity together. Adults may go fishing or hunting together, but in most cases the Negro is in a partially servile role. At least this is true in the small towns. White and Negro children in the country sometimes play together while they are young, but not after they reach adolescence. There are interesting exceptions to this rule in some areas where local white baseball teams play against the local Negro team in practice games. In one county where this occurred some persons were of the opinion that these games would continue only so long as the distribution of games won favored the white team.

In the cities the spontaneity of youth sometimes bridges the line of race, and white and Negro children play together at baseball or in other informal games; but since playgrounds and other institutions are conspicuously segregated, occasions for spontaneous play are restricted.

In the border areas, where such segregation is less universal, playing together by white and Negro children, when it occurs at all, is in mixed neighborhoods and occasionally in formal contests between neighborhood or athletic organizations representing different racial groups. Most of our informants agree that early childhood relations, however free in play associations, become more distant and infrequent in the adolescent years; and by late adolescence or maturity the youths have found their play interests in their respective racial groups.

In the northern areas there is less race consciousness in play, but the informal segregation in residence areas virtually amounts to formal institutional segregation. White and Negro children appear to play together naturally in the public schools, but it can be observed that spontaneous social cliques tend also to be racial cliques. There is little carry-over of early interracial play associations into the social life of maturity. The most commonly cited "playing together" in mature sports is "prize fighting."

RELATIONS BETWEEN THE SEXES

Instances in which white men have had sex relations with Negro women are common topics of discussion. However, in the social framework of the southern region there is no place for the discussion of sex relations involving a white woman and a Negro man. Even a rumor of this kind threatens the security of the Negro. Whenever the subject was mentioned, Negro informants gave knowing glances which meant only one thing—they knew that such behavior was possible in the setting, but they would not divulge it even if they knew all the facts.

Cases involving white men and Negro women were cited without hesitation. On the basis of information that can be verified one may say that sex relations between Negroes and whites, about which the community knows, continue—although not as frequently nor as widely as in former years. These relations are usually between Negro women and white men; but there are instances involving Negro men and white women, if the statements of informants can be accepted. However, such information is not in the possession of the community as a whole; it is almost exclusively a Negro possession. Should it become widespread, true or untrue, "race relations" would be seriously disturbed. This fact is indicative of the general pattern of interracial sex relations in the South.

The taboo on relations between Negro men and white women is enforced by swift punishment. In fact, any mutual desire is denied by the racial orthodoxy as unnatural and impossible. Thus, any sexual contact, or attempted contact, is interpreted as rape and punished accordingly. The unofficial punishment for rape of a white woman in the South is lynching. In recent years only six or eight lynchings have occurred annually over the entire South, and only part of these were for rape, attempted or suspected. This, however, does not tell the whole story. In Poinsett County, Arkansas, a few years ago a Negro man was accused of trying to keep company clandestinely with a white woman. He had been seen around the store where she was employed. On one occasion they met briefly in the shadow of a railroad underpass. Two white men came along as they were holding hands; and the girl, known in this small county to everyone, gave a cry of alarm. The Negro ran but was later arrested and severely beaten by officers. In court he protested that he did not try to attack the girl; he had been "going with her" for three years. A mob threatened to lynch him, but the sheriff warned that he would shoot the first to make the attempt. The Negro was sentenced to prison for ten years.

In 1935, in this same county, a young Negro half-wit was lynched for molesting a white girl. A Negro woman schoolteacher, commenting on this affair, said:

I blame the colored people for that because they knew that boy was abnormal and they should have had him sent away somewhere. No, they let him stay around, and people like that can cause all of us a lot of trouble.

Negro men apparently have been deeply impressed, even though somewhat confusedly, by the rigor of the unidirectional taboo on sex relations. One Negro in Bolivar County, Mississippi, said:

I am not going to be weak enough to let them catch me wondering too strong what all the noise about white women is. They don't look any better to me than them good-looking colored women that the white men has. I tell you, I don't know what the difference is. One thing, though, they won't get to barbecue me about trying to find out down here.

In rural areas, especially in the lower South, the early practice of "keeping" Negro "second wives" has been continued by white men longer than in the cities. The cases of two Negro women will serve as examples. The first woman owns a considerable amount of property, as ownership goes among Negroes; and she has reared two children of her white paramour, a man of moderate wealth in the community. She lived in his household and was referred to as the cook but could always afford to hire a person to do the cooking and other housework as well. At meals they all sat down together. Whites and Negroes called her by her first name; but she had few close friends and sought none beyond her household. When the man died, he left her the property and provided for sending the children away to school. At her death the property will go to the children. She moves about the town wearing a gray wig, like a neglected ghost; but she has money and gets what she wants, although she no longer has any means of enforcing her wishes.

In the same county is another woman known only by her first name, Mary. She is the active "second wife" of a member of one of the prominent families. Although the man does not spend much time in the county, he stays with her whenever he visits there. She now has a fading attractiveness and lives by herself in a neat little cottage that stands alone, across a field from the Negro community. She is seldom seen outside her yard. It is rumored that she is not allowed in the business part of the town.

In the several areas the various towns have sections where young white men go to meet colored women. The women are experienced prostitutes who favor white men because they occasionally have more money. Sporadically the white community flares up and attempts to stamp out the places, but they appear again as soon as the excitement abates.

Negro men resent these relations between white men and Negro women but are rarely able to take any effective action. In a Mississippi community a white man who made a practice of visiting a Negro woman nightly was irritated when the Negro man living next door turned on his porch lights to investigate as the white man's car drove up. The visitor blinked his headlights, signaling a command to the Negro to turn off the porch lights. The Negro was stubborn on this occasion and refused. The following day the Negro woman came over and threatened trouble from her visitor if the Negro did not stop interfering in her affairs. With the quiet backing of her paramour she swore out a warrant and had the Negro arrested. At the trial the Negro told the full story. The court was indignant because a white man's name had been brought into the case, but the Negro was released. He had secured a good white lawyer; and it was difficult to find ground for imprisonment in turning on porch lights.

A school supervisor in one of the counties complained that "most of the good-looking Negro women go with some white man." In another county in which there are evidences of such relations, an informant, pointing out two mulatto children who were passing by, volunteered this comment:

The husband in that family is as dark as night and the wife not much lighter. But you see the kids are almost white. What do you make of that? They are the spitting image of the man who runs the garage across the tracks. They are his children. Even her husband knows that. He would not dare say too much about it, though.

The impression that the practice of sex relations continues in its old form, particularly in the rural areas, is definitely gained from the common reports, from observation of covert familiarities, and from the presence of young mulatto children.

In one community a school principal, attempting to visit two of his mulatto students, was met at the door by a white man who informed him that the children lived with their mother, a dark woman, on the other side of the house. This man was the father of two of the woman's four children. In Johnston County many informants referred to illicit relations between servants in the homes and male members of the white households. A reputable physician remarked that knowledge of contraceptives reduced the incidence of issue from the relations and named several domestics whose knowledge of preventive measures had not been successful, if employed. A middle-aged carpenter said he had always provided well for his wife, and she had not fallen in the trap of white seducers. He thought all colored girls should behave as his wife did. He said:

Our girls will get too friendly with white men sometimes. I do everything I can to stop them from doing that. I talk to them lots of times and tell them not to do that, that's not the way, but some of them will go ahead anyhow.

He put no blame on the white man, however, and expressed the view that if only the colored girl would refuse the white man, all would be well.

The taboo on interracial sex relations is strong in the border area and continues, although seemingly somewhat abated, in the northern area; at least the taboo is more often violated in the North. Violation in the border area may lead to a critical situation involving violence or drastic ostracism. Social distance is such that associations which might lead to intermarriage are made conspicuous by their unnaturalness. Such relations must be carefully guarded and on a clandestine level. Further, as in the South, they are more frequent between white men and Negro women. Insurance agents; house-to-house salesmen; lower-class employers; occasionally heads of homes in which Negro women work as domestics; and young white men, usually of the lower middle or lower class, seeking adventure on the level of commercial or semicommercial prostitution, are most often involved. The stronger popular sentiment against sex intimacy involving Negro men and white women has the further support of the police who, without benefit of specific racial laws, find ways of raiding any quarter suspected of harboring or permitting this transgression of the most sacred of taboos.

In the North interracial sex relations are limited and controlled by both white and Negro groups. There is greater freedom of contact than in the other areas, and a larger proportion of associations involve white females and Negro males. Since interracial marriages and common-law unions are also more frequent, the associations, while much limited and frowned upon in practice, are not as dangerously unnatural as in the South or in border areas; and this applies especially to the Negro residence districts in northern cities.

Class differences appear in the matter of sex association. Upper-class Negro women refrain from this type of intimacy out of pride of status. The types of white women most frequently involved are lower middle- and lower-class young women who associate with Negroes in their work. Many of these women are of foreign extraction, but some northern and southern native-born are also included. Occasionally white women of well-known and upper-class families marry Negro men. Such women lose status among their more conservative friends of both races but are not generally ostracized. The situation for the girl is in many respects similar to marriage out of her social class. There is a wider range of class among the Negro men involved in these associations. The pressure, however, from both Negro and white groups seems to strengthen the taboo. Only a small proportion of the white population is in contact with the Negro population in the North. On the other hand, most of the Negro population is in contact with members of the white group at some level. Sex relations, when they occur, follow roughly this differential incidence of class contact.

One check on the freedom of normal personal association between members of different races and sexes is the popular presumption that any such contact is motivated by the prospect of sexual intimacy, and usually with the intent to avoid the social inconveniences of inter-racial marriage. In the two larger northern cities studied there are several hundred known cases of mixed marriages and many more common-law unions. Some of them involve upper middle- or upper-class persons of the respective groups; but for the most part these unions are from the lower middle and lower classes, or the so-called Bohemian elements. In some instances these associations constitute a small society of their own, since they are limited by both white and Negro groups.

TYPICAL REPORTS OF SOCIAL RELATIONS IN THE NORTH

Several types of experience may be cited as portraying the different forms which racial etiquette assumes in social relations in the North. There is, first, the experience of a social worker who has come into professional contact with numerous white groups. His home is located outside the congested Negro center of one of the large cities; and all his neighbors are white. When he meets white acquaintances on the street or in gatherings, they stop for a word or two of conversation. Men acquaintances, when accompanied by women, tip their hats and pass on. He does not expect an introduction because this would be, in his judgment, poor taste. "Most Negroes," he says, "aren't always conscious of the difference between a slight and good taste. It's all a part of their inferiority complex." Regarding the visiting of white homes he said:

Frankly, I think the visiting in each other's homes socially is the exception. There is a lot of it done, I'll admit, but when you think of the great numbers of people living here who have never been to visit a white family, I think the instances are exceptional. Now, last night my wife and I were invited to the home of a white neighbor to play bridge. There were several couples there. We were the only Negroes. They served a delicious supper, and the affair broke up early in the morning. We usually return the courtesy and have our white neighbors in for bridge, too. Everyone is quite free of any race consciousness.

On the other hand, I don't drift into their homes to chat or play cards unless I've been invited for a particular occasion. Living where we do you would be expected to be taken into some of the social life. I never urged it. They gradually took us in themselves. When we first came out they were simply indifferent. There was no attempt to stone our house or to insult us. They soon learned that we were capable of looking after our own business; that our friends who visited us were cultured, interesting people, and the first thing we knew they were inviting us to visit and to join a club. I've never bothered with any.

The limitations on these relations are suggested in this informant's cautiousness about contact without invitation, and the problems involved in contacts with the friends of the family which had made the first friendly gesture.

The second case is that of the wife of a real estate man well established in the social life of the Negro community. She said:

Things aren't like they were several years ago. Some people won't admit the amount of prejudice that exists here. I feel certain that the feeling against Negroes is far more intense and dangerous than it was, say, fifteen years ago. I don't have any white people visit me now at my home. I did once—rather extensively, but we do a lot of things when we are younger.

She recognized a certain freedom of association among the "lower class of people, especially the so-called Bohemian group" and said that they frequently "intermarry and lead a loose life." She disapproved of this type of intermarriage and association; she condemned a certain Negro professional man who associated with an uneducated white girl, saying that he was afraid to marry her because he knew it would ruin him with his Negro friends and patrons. This prosperous woman's only important contact with whites is as a member of the board of a social institution. All other members are white women, and most of them are wealthy. She goes to their homes for meetings. On several occasions when she has gone to one of the exclusive apartment houses, she has been escorted to the freight elevator. She telephones her hostess who has to inform the elevator operator that her visitor is not a servant.

A third case is that of a young woman living in Greenwich Village. She is tall, of light complexion but distinguishable as a Negro, masculine and slightly rakish in manner. She had this comment to make about her relations in the Village:

Most of the people living down here have their interests—they are artists, poets, theatrical people and the like. I was on the subway one morning reading a book. A man sitting near me had a copy of the same book and got interested. I didn't know him, but I believed he was one of my neighbors because I had seen him almost every morning. We got into conversation, and I learned he was a writer. I told him of my poetry. Later he invited me to dine, and I accepted.

As time went on we became good friends. Later, after eating out at restaurants, I discovered he enjoyed home cooked meals. So do I. We began marketing together and coming here to my place to cook. After a good dinner we would smoke and read together for hours. I never asked him much about himself. I don't even know if he was married.

I like to have people feel that within my home they find relaxation and spiritual satisfaction. He doesn't come here so often now. I had to stop him because he got to be a nuisance. He'd come too often.

After this recital of personal experiences a woman visitor and friend, who also had lived in Greenwich Village, mentioned the usual Negro problem of securing an apartment in that section. This latter informant, a mulatto of lighter complexion, said with a touch of realism:

I went all over the place trying to find an apartment. My companion during this time was a girl slightly darker in complexion than I. As long as my friend was with me I couldn't get anything. Finally, I decided just to get a couple of rooms in a boardinghouse and stay by myself. After two months I was sick of it. I couldn't have my friends in because I was afraid they would make me move. The bathroom was on another floor, and everybody used it. The people there seemed to be an awfully cheap crowd of whites. They were shouting in the halls all night, and men would run in and out of my room to show me some "new creation" or to read poetry, until I almost went nuts. I was very glad to move back to Harlem.

In different classes the etiquette is different. A steelworker gave this account of social relations:

The white man is a fellow that you got to forever keep your eyes on. It matters not where you are, in the South or in the North, if push come to shove he will try to make it hard for you. They don't tell you here that you got to respect them, but they make it so that you have to come to them in a pinch. My best advice to anybody in getting along with them is to keep out of their way.

There is a difference between here and the South, like having to call them "Old Boss" and that kind of stuff. You don't have to bow and scrape to keep from being kicked in the breeches, but it ain't much different when you see what little a Negro can get to do here. They will grin in your face and pal with you and all that kind of stuff. I have a lot of them that I guess if I did not know any better I would call my friends, but I know better. They will accept you when they are down and you can help them along, or something. They will not hesitate to do anything on your level then. But let them get the things they want, they are through with you. There are plenty of these old foreigners who are good for that kind of stuff.

There is some of most anything here you want to see between the Negroes and the whites. Some of these Negroes do what white folks say that a Negro will do. They can get plenty of white women and they will go with one at the first opportunity. I don't know what makes it, but the white woman don't hate the black man nearly as much as the white folks make on. Me, I think the Negro women are pretty, and they are as clean as you will find.

Negroes living in the North react differently to the dominant patterns of relations. Some of them who have grown to maturity in the South find that they are not prepared for the greater social freedom which the North is reputed to offer. They continue the habits learned in the South with but slight modification. The final case offers a picture of a significant type of response to the northern pattern of racial etiquette. The informant, a lumber planer who has lived in Chicago about ten years, said:

I came here so that I would have nothing to do but live where I would not be bothered. This is the thing that I have been able to do. In Texas, where I was born and reared, the Negro had to do the thing the white man thought was best for him. That is, they might let you do a thing, even a little thing like going in a front door, or they might not do it, and you did not have any rights. Here they might get mad for your doing what you want to in a case like that, but that is about all that they will do.

Until I came up here in 1929 I had never shook a white man's hand, and I have not done anything like that until this day. I don't have any occasion to. I know plenty of Negroes here who I have seen shaking hands with white people, but I never have done it. I don't know how I would feel doing it now, after knowing that I was not supposed to do it for so many years.

To tell you the truth, most of the things that I did not do down South I don't do here. I never did eat with one of them down there, and I have not done it here. I always eat at home, and if I happen to eat out at all I eat at a restaurant where the white people don't even come. I am not going to one of their big places down town. I don't imagine it would make any difference in eating with them, because if I was hungry, they would not even be there as far as I was concerned. I believe it would be the same way with them if they would just go on and eat. They will worry themselves to death trying to keep the Negro down.

The most frequent complaint on the part of Negroes is not about the restriction of social relations by etiquette but the restriction of economic privileges. This is prompted by direct and indirect refusals of white men to work with Negroes, and by objections to being served by them as clerks or as employees of public-utility companies. Latent race sentiment frequently appears among white and Negro workers in competition for jobs and is employed as a measure to fend off such competition. In this respect the white worker has an advantage, because he can use the issue of race to support him in group and individual competition.

Chapter VII

THE EVOLUTION OF RACIAL LEGISLATION

Law is only one of the agencies of social control, but it exercises the vital function of ensuring the stability and uniformity of customary practices approved by the dominant society. In a social order in which difference in race implies differences in quality and social preroga- tives, a legal structure defining *expected behavior* in race contacts is a response on the part of the dominant group to the threat of dis- organization of the traditional social order. At first, control of racial contacts was maintained by social sanctions without benefit of law. The status of the Negro under slavery was gradually defined in cus- tom under the economic imperatives of the New World order of life. While the institution of slavery itself soon had the support of law, for a long period only the racial etiquette, deeply entrenched in the customary practices of the region, prescribed and regulated the be- havior of subordinates and superiors in their mutual relations.

The emancipation of the Negro slave, followed by the sudden theoretical assumption of the full status of citizenship, occasioned a profound disturbance of the social equilibrium. Freedom, with the implication of equality, introduced a new and formidable problem into the still immature democratic concepts of a large part of the nation. In the stage of acculturation of the freedmen, with the weak- ened authority and prestige of their former masters and with the collapse of legal and political support of slavery, it became necessary to reinforce custom with a legal framework designed to define racial spheres of living and to regulate racial contacts. Habits and attitudes that had developed in both races during the long years of slavery could not be transformed overnight. Moreover, the interests of whites and Negroes were found to be in fundamental conflict. The races had become classes, whereas they had formerly been castes. The Reconstruction years following the Civil War produced a pro- found and bitter reaction on the part of southern whites. The attempt politically to force a legal framework of equality upon a customary order incompatible with it met with no success whatever.

SOCIAL AND ECONOMIC FOUNDATIONS OF RACIAL LEGISLATION IN THE SOUTH

The social institutions and racial traditions of the South were fairly adequate for the regulation of race relations prior to the collapse of slavery; and these customs were built upon clearly defined concepts of the respective roles of white persons and Negro slaves. These concepts developed from the economic and social stratification inherent in the slave economy. In a large measure the slave system brought about the plantation, as the most economical productive unit, and the staple-crop agriculture of the southern region with the subsequent reign of "King Cotton." Slavery also created several distinct socioeconomic classes for each of which particular conceptualizations arose and became crystallized. At the top of the economic scale was the master and planter-owner; and at the bottom were the slaves, themselves classifiable into at least two groups: "house servants" and "field hands." The house servants were in closer contact with the masters and benefited from the humanizing influences of this intimacy. They were frequently members of the primary household group, and so regarded themselves; they were exposed to the refining influences of life in the big house and looked with considerable contempt upon the poor whites and Negro field hands who performed the rough manual labor on the plantation. The latter were in contact only with one another and the overseer, who developed them as labor units and nothing more. Between these extremes were the poor whites, the free Negroes, and the middle-class whites who consisted mainly of small planters, proprietors, and professional persons.

The master class in its ideal role adopted an attitude of benevolent paternalism toward the Negro slave but had only contempt for the incompetents who were known as the poor whites. This contempt was reflected in the Negro slave's attitude toward this disadvantaged class. On the other hand, the poor white's resentment against his more fortunate white brother was deflected toward the Negro slave who was at least an instrument in the poor white's impoverishment. This antagonism was intensified by the consciousness of racial identity theoretically entitling them to benefits enjoyed by other whites. The Negroes were immune to this hostility so long as they remained slaves and recognized their inferior role in a society of dominant white masters and other whites whose color conferred status without effective power. As a rule, the free Negroes had an economic advantage over the poor whites but were considered their social inferiors.

Racial and cultural differences between southern whites and slaves were translated into terms of unquestionable superiority and inferiority. The subordinate position to which the slave had been assigned was reflected in every detail of his life. He knew his place and, according to the stereotype, had no desire for independence or for any type of equality or freedom. This subjective interpretation cannot, however, be accepted as historically correct; for the sporadic uprisings and rebellions among slaves indicate that many Negroes failed to conceptualize their race as inferior or permanently subordinate to the white race. The idea of equality or, at least, freedom seems implicit in the rebellions against lower caste status.

In the ideal tradition of slavery masters often assumed a paternalistic attitude toward their slaves. This meant that the slave was assumed to be incapable ever of achieving intellectual maturity; and his conduct and decisions in all phases of his existence were consequently dependent on the judgment of the master. Even though many upper-class whites honestly believed that Negroes should not be confused and harassed by education, either because of alleged lack of innate capacity to learn or because of the absence of any need for learning, many slaves became literate in the households of their masters. Religion among slaves was encouraged; and limited provisions for their spiritual needs were generally made.

In the area of social relations slaves were expected to marry slaves, usually on the same plantation. The prohibition of intermarriage between Negroes and whites in the South represents the first instance in which group sanctions were supported by a legal framework. Tennessee[1] passed its law prohibiting miscegenation as early as 1822; and North Carolina,[2] in 1838-39.

THE DEVELOPMENT OF LEGISLATION TO REINFORCE CUSTOMS, 1865-1867

The reassuring doctrine of white supremacy was challenged during the period of Reconstruction. Disorganization of the economic and political system in the South brought the threat of a loss of traditional dominance. In considering the development of the legal structure governing race relations in the South it should be remembered that there were two rather distinct periods of political reconstruction, characterized by Lewinson as follows:

[1] Acts of Tennessee, 1822, Ch. 19, Sec. 1.
[2] Acts of North Carolina, 1838-39, Ch. 24.

The first lasted from the end of the war until 1867. This was the Presidential Reconstruction, carried out by the States, under Lincoln's and Johnson's supervision with few conditions and not seriously interfered with by the national agencies until the second stage approached. The second stage was Congressional Reconstruction, lasting from 1867 to 1876, carried on by the Republican politicians of the National legislature and forced on the unwilling South in detail by national agencies and national partisans.[3]

During the first period of Reconstruction the southern states enacted legislation designed to continue the subordination of the Negro despite his technical emancipation. Eight states passed the famous Black Codes in a deliberate attempt to define the expected behavior of Negroes so as to coincide as nearly as possible with that which characterized the Old South. These laws were enacted after the close of the Civil War and before either the Reconstruction legislation or the ratification of the Fourteenth Amendment placed certain humane limitations upon state statutes.

The restrictions imposed by the Black Codes upon participation by Negroes in certain occupations served to keep the ex-slave economically dependent upon the plantation owners and to preserve selected occupations for the whites. The Alabama statute, enacted in 1867, stated that no free Negro should be licensed to keep a tavern or to sell spirituous liquors; and that no free Negro should be employed to sell, or assist in the sale of, drugs or medicine.

There were more extensive stipulations in the South Carolina[4] law, which was passed in 1865; its regulation of occupational pursuits obviously emphasized the intent to re-establish control over the Negro's person. Contracts for one month or more were to be put in writing, attested by one white witness and approved by a judge or magistrate. If the period of work was not mentioned, it was until the 25th of December following the making of the contract. Wages, if not mentioned, were to be fixed by the district judge or magistrate. Any Negro at least ten years of age, having no parents living in the district, and not an apprentice might make a valid contract for a year or more. If the servant received only board and clothing, a written contract was unnecessary. Labor on farms was also minutely regulated. All time lost, if not occasioned by the master, and all losses caused by neglect of duty might be deducted from the servant's wages. Food, nursing, and other necessities for the

[3] Paul Lewinson, *Race, Class and Party* (London: Oxford University Press, 1932), p. 18.
[4] Laws of South Carolina, 1865, pp. 295-299.

servant while absent from work on account of sickness or other cause might also be deducted. Even visitors of servants could not be invited or allowed to come on the premises without the master's consent. The master was not liable for voluntary misdemeanors of the servant. It was considered the master's duty to protect the servant from violence at the hand of others. The master had the right to command the servant to aid him in the defense of his own person, family, premises, or property.

In the same year Mississippi[5] passed a similar law which stated in part that all contracts for labor of free Negroes, freedmen, or mulattoes for a period longer than one month should be in writing, attested by two disinterested white persons in the county where the labor was to be performed, and read to the Negro by some officer. It was the duty of the civil officers of Mississippi, and the option of every other person, to arrest and carry back to his employer any Negro laborer who had left his place of employment; and the person making the arrest was entitled to a fee of five dollars plus ten cents per mile from the place of arrest to the place of delivery. This fee was to be paid by the employer and deducted from the wages of the Negro.

In the southern cotton states the landlord-tenant laws, which generally date from the post-Reconstruction period, do not appear from the wording of the texts to be racial laws; but they too were designed primarily to establish control over the persons of Negro tenants on whose labor the plantation system of cotton production depended. It was assumed that white agricultural workers would eventually become owners or leave agriculture. The laws have been effective chiefly in restricting the agricultural role of Negroes. At the time of enactment practically all Negroes in the agricultural system were tenants.

The movement of Negroes from state to state was regulated by law in several of the southern states. In 1865 South Carolina[6] passed a statute prescribing that no person of color should migrate to or reside in the state unless within twenty days after arrival he entered into bond with two freeholders for his good behavior and support. If he failed to execute the required bond, he had to leave the state within two days or be liable to corporal punishment.

Stringent vagrancy laws formed a considerable portion of the Black Codes of the Presidential Reconstruction period. Penalties were imposed upon Negroes who could not support themselves or

[5] Laws of Mississippi, 1865, pp. 86-90.
[6] Laws of South Carolina, 1865, p. 271.

who were found assembling unlawfully. The Mississippi[7] vagrancy law of 1865 specified a long list of vagrants, including any freedmen, free Negroes, or mulattoes over eighteen years of age found without lawful employment or business, or illegally assembling, on the second Monday in January, 1866, or thereafter. The law also defined as vagrants white persons assembling with freedmen, free Negroes, or mulattoes on a basis of equality, and those engaging in illicit relations with freedwomen, free Negroes, or mulattoes. Negroes could be hired out for nonpayment of fines, but there was no such provision for whites.

The beginning of the present segregation policy can be traced to the period of the Black Codes. Three states, Florida, Mississippi, and Texas, had transient "Jim Crow" laws; and southern states which made any provision at all for the education of Negroes demanded the separation[8] of the races in schools. Tennessee[8] in 1865 enacted a law which stipulated that it was unlawful for white and colored persons to attend the same school. The Florida[9] statute of 1865 declared that it was a misdemeanor for a person of color to *intrude* himself into any religious assembly of white persons, or for any white person to intrude upon the assemblies of colored persons. South Carolina[10] extended its separation policy in 1865 in a law declaring that persons of color could form no part of the state militia.

Legislation regulating the behavior of Negroes in the courts, as witnesses, complainants, defendants, and jurors, formed an interesting phase in the development of the legal framework redefining the status of Negroes after emancipation. A North Carolina[11] law passed in 1866 declared that persons of color were competent witnesses only in cases in which a Negro was accused of a crime or had a specific interest in a dispute. An Alabama[12] statute of 1865 declared that Negroes could testify only in open court and only in cases involving a freedman, free Negro, or mulatto. Similar regulations appeared in the Florida[13] constitution and in Mississippi[14] laws in 1865, and in the Texas[15] constitution and a Virginia[16] law

[7] Laws of Mississippi, 1865, pp. 90-93.
[8] Laws of Tennessee, 1865-66, p. 65.
[9] Laws of Florida, 1865, p. 25.
[10] Laws of South Carolina, 1865, p. 275.
[11] Laws of North Carolina, 1866, Ch. 40, No. 9.
[12] Laws of Alabama, 1865-66, p. 98.
[13] Constitution of Florida, 1865, Art. XIV, Sec. 2.
[14] Laws of Mississippi, 1865, p. 83.
[15] Constitution of Texas, 1866, Art. VIII, Sec. 2.
[16] Laws of Virginia, 1865-66, pp. 89-90.

in 1866. In Tennessee,[17] on the other hand, Negroes and Indians were classified as competent witnesses in 1865.

There was comparatively little legislation about the Negro as a juror during this period. In Tennessee[18] in 1866 and in Mississippi[19] in 1867 freedmen were not deemed competent to serve on petit or grand juries. In 1867 Arkansas[20] passed a law which granted certain rights to Negroes but nevertheless implied that they were not to sit on juries.

Invidious differences appeared in the punishments meted out to whites and Negroes in most of the southern states. According to a South Carolina[21] law of 1865 a person of color who assaulted a white woman or had intercourse with her by impersonating her husband was guilty of a felony. In the same vein, Alabama[22] exacted graver punishment for fornication and adultery between whites and Negroes than between members of the same race. An interesting variation appeared in the West Virginia[23] statute which penalized only white persons concerned in illegal sexual relations. (This is the only state which has such an act at the present time.)

Southern states which had not passed laws prohibiting intermarriage before the Civil War did so during the early period of the Black Codes. The individual laws exhibited rather wide variation in types of marriages prohibited. Likewise, there was wide variation in the severity of punishments for white and Negro parties to illegal marriages and for persons performing the ceremonies. Furthermore, there were differences in the amount of Negro blood required to bring persons within jurisdiction of the marriage laws.

During the period of passage of the Black Codes redefining the role and expected behavior of the Negro in his new estate, no southern state permitted the Negro to vote on equal terms with white persons; and only Tennessee permitted Negro suffrage on a restricted basis.

An examination of the laws of Tennessee, North Carolina, Virginia, Arkansas, and Louisiana reveals that legal regulation of the behavior of Negroes in these states, which represented either the upper or the newer South, was less stringent than in other southern states. This difference in legislation no doubt reflected the accept-

---

[17] Laws of Tennessee, 1865-66, p. 24 (26).
[18] Laws of Tennessee, 1865-66, p. 24.
[19] Laws of Mississippi, 1866-67, p. 233.
[20] Laws of Arkansas, 1866-67, p. 99.
[21] Laws of South Carolina, 1865, p. 27.
[22] Pace and Cox v. State, 1881, 69, Ala. 231.
[23] West Virginia Code (1931), c. 48, Act 1, Sec. 19.

ance by these five states of the plan of rehabilitation for seceded states set forth in President Lincoln's proclamation in December, 1863. The remaining states were the cotton states of the lower South and contained the larger proportion of the Negro population; they were uncompromising and remained in the Confederacy until the bitter end. During their brief period of relative autonomy these states enacted laws covering more relationships and punished their violations with greater severity, than did the other five states.

STATUS AND LAW IN TRANSITION, 1867-1876

The second stage of Reconstruction began in 1867 and lasted until 1876. In an attempt to stay the rise of southern power Congress repudiated the policies of the previous period, extended the program of the Freedmen's Bureau, and declared that representatives from states which had previously seceded from the Union should not be admitted to Congress until it extended to such states the right of representation. Then, in a swift move, came the Fourteenth Amendment, which granted "equal protection of the law" to Negroes, draped the mantle of federal citizenship around freedmen, and thereby set the stage for Negro suffrage. The negative response of all the southern states to this amendment, perhaps more than anything else, prompted Congress to pass the first series of Reconstruction Acts in 1867. They declared the existing governments in the Confederacy illegal and established military rule under federal army officers. These acts were followed by the Fifteenth Amendment in 1869 and a second series of Reconstruction Acts, which have often been referred to as the "Force Bills." Federal troops were stationed at strategic points in the South to enforce these stringent measures. The influx of carpetbaggers from the North and the shifts in policy created by these acts were accompanied by the ascendancy of a strong Negro political machine in the South.

The impact of these changes during this phase of political reconstruction brought revisions in the legal systems which had evolved from 1865 to 1867. In all the southern states some measures were repealed. Prohibition of intermarriage was omitted from the Mississippi[24] Code of 1870 and from the Arkansas[25] Code of 1874, and removed from the statute books of Louisiana[26] in 1870. With the exception of Mississippi, the states which legally permitted intermarriage between the races during this period were those which had

[24] Charles S. Mangum, Jr., *The Legal Status of the Negro* (Chapel Hill: The University of North Carolina Press, 1940), p. 242.
[25] *Ibid.*, p. 241.
[26] *Ibid.*

taken advantage of President Lincoln's offer of rehabilitation. In this most intimate area of relationship, tradition and custom in the lower South were evidently strong enough to preserve the essence of white supremacy and to act as a bulwark against change.

In 1869 a Georgia court held invalid a prewar statute preventing anyone with one-eighth or more Negro blood from holding public office.[27] The requirement of racial separation in the schools of Louisiana[28] was suspended by an article of the constitution of 1868; and in the same year the public schools of South Carolina[29] were opened to both races. According to Booker T. Washington, the University of South Carolina was opened to Negroes during the first years of Reconstruction.[30] For a period Richard T. Greener, a Negro graduate of Harvard, was librarian.

Changes also appeared in laws affecting Negroes in the courts. In 1870 South Carolina stated that rights in court should not be affected by race or color. The legal provision stated:

Wherever authority has heretofore been conferred by law upon any free white person or persons to institute any suit or proceedings, or to prefer any information or complaint in any matter, civil, penal, or criminal, the same rights shall be enjoyed by, and the same remedies applicable to, all persons whatsoever, regardless of race or color subject to the same conditions, and none others.[31]

In 1867 Mississippi[32] extended to Negroes the right to testify in court, the same as whites. The Texas[33] legislature which convened in 1871 enacted a law forbidding exclusion of any witness on account of color. In 1867 Virginia[34] repealed its law which declared that Negroes and Indians could testify only in cases in which a Negro or Indian was involved, and colored persons were declared competent to testify "as if they were white." Tennessee[35] gave Negroes full rights in respect to jury service in 1868.

Under the stress of this new regime, which threatened to disintegrate southern tradition and law, visible signs of anxiety and bitterness increased. Individual indecision and class differences among

[27] *White* v. *Clements,* 39 Georgia, 232 (1869).
[28] Constitution of Louisiana, 1868, Title VII, Art. 135.
[29] Constitution of South Carolina, 1868, Art. X, Sec. 10.
[30] Booker T. Washington, *The Story of the Negro* (New York: Doubleday, Page & Company, 1909), p. 38.
[31] South Carolina, 335—Rights in Court Not Affected by Race or Color, Civ. C. '22, 291; Civ. C. '12, 3924; Civ. C. '02, 2821; G.S. 2168; R.S. 2297; 1870 XIV, 338.
[32] Laws of Mississippi, 1866-67, pp. 232-233.
[33] Laws of Texas, 1871, p. 108.
[34] Laws of Virginia, 1865-66, pp. 89-90.
[35] Laws of Tennessee, 1867-68, pp. 32-33.

the white population were almost wholly dissolved in the surge of the "Solid South." Its resolute purpose was inescapable; and that purpose was to build up an energetic defense against the imminent social and political equality of the Negro, to curb the rise of the freedmen with a united front. Its immediate course was directed toward the restoration of its political strength, which had been unreservedly weakened by the Reconstruction Acts. Barred in a large measure from political activity, the southern whites turned to extralegal means of regaining control; and so the Ku-Klux Klan and similar organizations appeared throughout the South to intimidate and repress the Negroes, and to restore the prestige of southern whites.

DEVELOPMENT OF RACIAL LEGISLATION IN THE SOUTH SINCE 1876

As the "White Man's party" gradually grew, the South again had unequivocal recourse to law in redefining the status and position of Negroes and whites. Many of the measures which had been repealed during Congressional Reconstruction were rewritten into the state statutes under restored home rule; and new laws were enacted. Some of the first of these were laws designed to disfranchise the Negro, i.e., the so-called "grandfather clauses" and similarly restrictive measures. Legislation restricting interracial association flourished, particularly toward the close of the century.

Restriction of the Franchise

The grandfather clause in the Louisiana Constitution of 1898 stipulated that one might register permanently before September 1, 1898, (1) if he was entitled to vote in any state January 1, 1867; (2) if he was the son or grandson of such a person and 21 years of age or over in 1898.[36] The North Carolina revised statutes of 1905 permitted one to register permanently before December 1, 1908, if entitled to vote January 1, 1897, or if a lineal descendant of such a person.[37] The grandfather clauses were obviously a convenient device for excluding Negroes from the right to vote and at the same time permitting illiterate and nonpropertied whites to exercise the franchise. These clauses were declared unconstitutional by a Supreme Court decision in 1915; and since then the restriction of Negro suffrage has been left to devices of intimidation and circumvention, with popular and official sanction.

[36] Gilbert Stephenson, *Race Distinctions in American Law* (New York: D. Appleton and Company, 1910), p. 327 (chart).
[37] *Ibid.*, p. 333.

In 1890 Mississippi required that voters should be able to read and interpret the Constitution;[38] and South Carolina imposed the same regulation.[39] In a similar manner tax and property requirements supplemented or supplanted the literacy rules and grandfather clauses. Such requirements were not considered apart from the permanent registration clauses but were utilized as additional safeguards for the "purity of the polls." The southern states which enacted poll tax requirements were Alabama, Florida, Louisiana, Mississippi, North Carolina, South Carolina, Tennessee, Texas, and Virginia. North Carolina, however, removed the poll tax from her suffrage qualifications in 1920. The effectiveness of the poll tax regulation was measurably assisted in Alabama, Mississippi, Louisiana, and Virginia by stipulations that there would be no proceedings to collect the tax until three years overdue.

The property prerequisites were stated in terms of the number of acres owned and/or the value of the land. Thus, Alabama required an applicant for registration to be an owner "in good faith in his own right" or the husband of a woman who is an owner:

The owner in good faith in his own right, or the husband of a woman who is the owner in good faith, in her own right, of forty acres of land situate in this state, upon which they reside; or the owner in good faith in his own right, or the husband of any woman who is the owner in good faith, in her own right, of real estate situate in this state, assessed for taxation at the value of three hundred dollars or more, or the owner in good faith, in his own right, or the husband of a woman who is the owner in good faith, in her own right, of personal property in this state assessed for taxation at three hundred dollars or more; provided, that the taxes due upon such real or personal property for the year next preceding the year in which he offers to register shall have been paid, unless the assessment shall have been legally contested and is undetermined.[40]

Georgia required 40 acres of land or $500 worth of personal property in the state.[41] Both Louisiana and South Carolina required $300 worth of property and payment of personal taxes.[42]

A comparison of the number of Negro registrants in Louisiana in the national elections of 1896 and 1900 will illustrate the striking effect of this aspect of the new state constitutions. The reports of

[38] *Ibid.*, p. 328.
[39] *Ibid.*, p. 325.
[40] Rep. Atty. Gen. 1922-24, pp. 299, 300. Applies State v. Birmingham, etc., Ry. Co., 182 Ala., 62, 77, 80, 475.
[41] Stephenson, *op. cit.*, p. 301.
[42] *Ibid.*

the secretary of state[43] reveal that 130,344 Negroes registered in 1896 compared with only 5,320 in 1900. Negro registrants were in the majority in 26 parishes in 1896, but no parish showed a majority of Negro registrants in 1900.

Legal Restriction of Physical and Social Contacts

Many laws applying to practically all areas of relationship between the races were enacted to continue the safeguards against a breakdown in informal contacts. These included attempts to regulate contacts in public places and institutions, on common carriers, at work, in intermarriage and adulterous living, and contacts affecting property rights, especially with reference to residential segregation. The more recent developments in legal regulation of residential and school segregation are treated in detail in the following chapter. In this section the main trends in legislation covering racial contacts in other areas are briefly summarized and illustrated.

Legislation designed to regulate social contacts on common carriers has had several significant characteristics: In the first place, separation was made mandatory on all types of common carriers in use at the time of legislation. Second, penalties were imposed both upon the offending persons and upon the officials who failed to see that the specifications of the law were carried out. The third general characteristic of this legislation was the provision for *separate* but *equal* accommodations. Conductors were empowered to adjust seating arrangements whenever it was necessary to accommodate unusual numbers of either race. In the fourth place, the laws declared that signs must be provided to designate the separate accommodations for the two races. Exceptions were made in the laws to permit conformance to the exigencies of master-servant relations, which were adequately regulated by the existing conventions. The general segregation measures did not apply to nurses and other classes of Negro servants so long as they were in the company of their employers.

The racial separation law of Mississippi[44] provides a comprehensive illustration of the provisions of this type of legislation. With respect to common carriers, this law makes the following stipulations:

Railroads

1. Every railroad . . . shall provide equal but separate accommodations for each race . . . either by separate coach or compartments. The

---

[43] Lewinson, *op. cit.,* p. 81.
[44] Laws of Mississippi, 1904, Ch. 99.

conductor may assign seats and compartments, and has the right to refuse passage to any person refusing to obey.

  (a) Accommodations need not be identical but should be of the same kind.

  (b) White passengers compelled to ride in a Negro coach may recover damages. (Unless there is an unexpectedly large crowd.)

  (c) A carrier is liable to damages if the conductor's enforcement of the separate coach law is done in an offensive manner.

Street Railways

(1) Must provide equal but separate accommodations:

  (a) May provide two cars

  (b) May partition section of a car

(2) Must have a sign 8"x12" which indicates seats for whites and colored. If the sign is posted, it must be visible from all parts of the car.

  (a) Refusal to sit where assigned makes the offender liable to a fine of $25.00 or thirty days imprisonment.

  (b) The officer of any company insisting on seating passengers in a compartment set aside for another race is liable to a $25.00 fine or thirty days imprisonment.

  (c) An officer may refuse to carry a passenger who refuses to sit as assigned.

  (d) Refusal to provide separate compartments by an officer or employee of a company makes him liable to a $25.00 fine or thirty days imprisonment.

  (e) The Act does not apply to nurses attending children of another race.

There were, however, certain variations in the "Jim Crow" legislation of the early years of the twentieth century. A Virginia law,[45] for example, stated that Negroes might be excluded from Pullman quarters.

In 1922 Mississippi[46] expanded her "Jim Crow" legislation to include taxicabs. The statute declared that it was unlawful for the driver of a motor vehicle for hire to carry white and Negro passengers at the same time, except in the case of a white person accompanied by a Negro servant. This section of the law does not apply to interurban vehicles designed to carry more than seven passengers. It leaves to custom the regulation of a possible reverse of the situation in which a Negro might be accompanied by a white servant or subordinate.

Among the provisions which had been repealed immediately after

[45] Laws of Virginia, 1904, p. 129.
[46] Laws of Mississippi, 1922, Ch. 217.

the close of the Civil War and which were now rewritten into the laws of the various states were the regulations concerning inter-racial sex relations. Thus, the statute of Arkansas[47] prohibiting intermarriage reappeared in the revision of 1884; the present form of the law prohibiting intermarriage in Louisiana[48] was enacted in 1894; and the Mississippi[49] miscegenation law reappeared in the 1880 codification.

This type of legislation was aimed at controlling one of the in-evitable biological and social consequences of contact. In the south-ern states, during slavery and for a period thereafter, miscegenation was fairly common; and in many instances the sex relationships were of a more than casual nature. Legislation designed to curb misce-genation has always been more severe in its penalties for Negro men than for white men. Similarly, there has been caution and discretion in the enactment of laws providing penalties for concubinage, which in the South would most commonly involve white men and Negro women. However, in 1911 concubinage between the races was made a felony in Arkansas by the act which stated:

Concubinage between a person of the Caucasian or white race and between a person of the negro or black race is hereby made a felony, and whoever shall be convicted thereof in any court of competent jurisdiction shall, for each offense, be sentenced to imprisonment at the discretion of the court for a term of not less than one month nor more than one year in the penitentiary at hard labor.[50]

Segregation in public places, in various types of penal and mental institutions, and in public schools was given renewed or new or-ganized sanction through the medium of the law. In some instances, as in the Arkansas statute of 1901, the provision for a separate reading room for colored people at the state library implied an ac-knowledgment and extension of rights and privileges for Negroes, even though they were extended through the framework of segrega-tion legislation.

Legal provision for segregation in penal institutions had originated with the early manifestations of interest in penal reform. The Ala-bama law[51] of 1875 had made it unlawful for a jailer or sheriff having charge of white and colored prisoners before conviction to imprison them together in the same part of the jail or other place

---

[47] Mangum, op. cit., p. 241.
[48] Ibid., p. 242.
[49] Ibid.
[50] Acts of Arkansas, 1911, p. 295.
[51] Laws of Alabama, 1875-76, p. 285.

of safekeeping, provided there were enough space for separate confinement. The 1884[52] law, amended in 1931,[53] reads as follows:

It shall be unlawful for white and colored convicts to be chained together or to be allowed to sleep together; and it shall be unlawful to chain together or to confine together in the same room or compartment, male and female convicts. Whenever in the judgment of the governor and the board, it is practicable to do so, arrangements shall be made for keeping white and colored convicts at separate prisons, and they shall not be allowed to be kept at the same place.

Beginning in 1890 the white and colored convicts of Georgia[54] were not to be confined or work-chained together, or chained together going to and from work, or at any other time; in 1908[55] the races were separated in work on state prison farms. Arkansas[56] and North Carolina[57] passed similar laws during the period.

North Carolina[58] also passed a law in 1899 which segregated the colored insane and inebriates in state institutions. The law reads as follows:

The State hospital at Morgantown and the State hospital at Raleigh shall be exclusively for the accommodation . . . of white insane of the State, and the hospital at Goldsboro shall be exclusively for the accommodation . . . of the colored insane and inebriates of the State.

A Louisiana statute passed in 1908, which required separate saloons for white and colored persons, represents a comparatively new group of segregation laws. However, this situation had been regulated by custom in several southern cities.

In Mississippi[59] in 1900 the legislature permitted the Ladies' Auxiliary Cemetery Association (white) to remove the remains of a Negro state official to a Negro cemetery.

New Orleans added a new legal note when it segregated Negro and white prostitutes in separate districts in 1900. This law was declared invalid in 1917.

Missouri[60] incongruously took one of the stereotypes seriously when it decreed that chicken stealing was a felony subject to imprisonment for five years or a fine of $200.

[52] *Ibid.*, 1884-85, p. 192.
[53] *Ibid.*, 1931, p. 166.
[54] Acts of Georgia, 1890-91, p. 213.
[55] Acts of Georgia, 1908, pp. 1119, 1123.
[56] Acts of Arkansas, 1903, pp. 3, 160.
[57] Acts of North Carolina, 1909, C. 832, ss. 1, 2.
[58] *Ibid.*, 1899, C. 1, ss. 3, 4.
[59] Laws of Mississippi, 1900, p. 171.
[60] Laws of Missouri, 1903, p. 161.

Mobile passed a curfew law for Negroes in 1909. The following news item appeared in an Associated Press report of July 21, 1909:

Mobile, Alabama—The commissioners today established a curfew law for Negroes. Commencing tonight, all the blacks must be at home or in bed at 10 p.m. Any of them caught wandering at large will be locked up. This action is due to an epidemic of hold-ups perpetrated by Negroes.[61]

As an example of the extension of segregation legislation, South Carolina in 1917 advocated segregation in certain types of commercial amusements:

Tent shows are to maintain separate entrances for different races. Any circus or other such traveling show exhibiting under canvas or out of doors for gain shall maintain two main entrances to such exhibition, and one shall be for white people and the other entrance shall be for colored people, and such main entrances shall be plainly marked "For White People," and the other entrance shall be marked "For Colored People," and all white persons attending such show or traveling exhibition other than those connected with the said show shall pass in and out of the entrance provided for white persons, and all colored persons attending such show or traveling exhibition shall pass in and out of entrance provided for colored persons. Any circus or other such traveling show exhibiting under canvas and failing to comply with the provisions of this section shall be deemed guilty of a misdemeanor and, upon conviction, shall be fined not more than $500. The sheriffs of the counties in which such circus or traveling show shall exhibit shall be charged with the duty of enforcing the provisions of this section.[62]

Separation policies also sought a sure footing in industrial plants where whites and Negroes were employed. A Texas law of 1915 declared that

the operator, owner, lessee, . . . of any coal mine shall provide a suitable building . . . for use of persons employed in mine for washing themselves and changing their clothing when entering or leaving the mine. The baths and lockers for Negroes shall be separate from those of whites, but may be in the same building.[63]

In the same year South Carolina passed a similar law regulating racial contacts in cotton textile manufacturing establishments. It stated that it was

unlawful for any person, firm or corporation in business of cotton tex-

[61] Stephenson, op. cit., p. 276.
[62] Cr. C. 1933, 166; 1917, XXX, 48.
[63] Acts of Texas, 1915, p. 100.

tile manufacturing in this state to allow or permit operatives, help, and labor of different races to labor and work together in the same room and to use the same doors of entrance and exit at the same time, to use and occupy the same pay ticket windows or doors for paying off its employees. . . . This shall not apply to employment of firemen as subordinates in boiler rooms, or to floor scrubbers.[64]

Other types of public places frequented by Negroes such as theaters, inns, hotels, and lodging houses, were subjected to segregative measures in Alabama,[65] Virginia and Arkansas. The Virginia statute reads as follows:

It shall be the duty of any person, persons, firm, institution, or corporation, operating, maintaining, keeping, conducting, sponsoring or permitting, any public hall, theater, opera house, motion picture show or any place of public entertainment or public assemblage which is attended by both white and colored persons, to separate the white race and the colored race, and to set apart and designate in each such public hall, theater, opera house, motion picture show or place of public entertainment or public assemblage, certain seats therein to be occupied by white persons, and any such person, persons, firms, institutions or corporation that shall fail, refuse or neglect to comply with the provisions of this section shall be guilty of a misdemeanor and upon conviction thereof shall be fined not less than one hundred dollars nor more than five hundred dollars for each offense.[66]

The Arkansas statute is an example of the effort to regulate relations in a sphere of association which had been relatively free from race-conscious feelings, namely, race-track and legalized gaming operations. The statute reads:

All persons, firms, companies or corporations operating any plant, track or establishment where gaming is legal under the laws of the State of Arkansas, are hereby required to segregate the white and colored races, and to set apart or designate at each plant, track or establishment separate, equal and sufficient seats, betting and all other accommodations for the accommodation of the white and colored races.[67]

[64] Cr. C. 22, 167: 1915, XXIX, 79: 1916, XXIX, 706.
[65] Laws of Alabama, 1919, p. 843.
[66] Virginia—Chapter 73A—Title 15A, Regulation of Public Hall. Separation of Races—1796a (1926, pp. 945-946).
[67] Act 230 of 1937, Arkansas, Sec. 1.

Chapter VIII

RESIDENTIAL AND SCHOOL SEGREGATION
BY LAW

LEGISLATION CONCERNING RESIDENTIAL SEGREGATION

Various efforts have been made to secure legal regulation of residential segregation. Economic factors are involved in this problem. Economic selection of the population always results in some segregation without legal regulation; and since residence areas undergo many changes, any freezing of racial areas by legislation would constitute an interference with the "laws of changing property use." In some areas it has been considered desirable to have Negroes of servant status live near the homes of employers, segregated chiefly by social distance. Nevertheless, several cities have attempted, under the general framework of city planning and zoning, to fix separate residence zones for the races.

State and Local Government Action

In 1890 San Francisco passed the first race segregation ordinance of this sort; but the ordinance, which required all Chinese inhabitants to move from the area theretofore occupied by them to another part of the city, was declared void in court, as a violation of the Fourteenth Amendment and the treaty with China.[1] About 1910, southern cities began enacting segregation ordinances. In 1912 the Virginia legislature attempted to legalize residential segregation by decreeing that city and town councils might make segregation districts:

Any city or town may, by a recorded vote of a majority of the members elected to the Council thereof, or if there be two branches of such Council, by a recorded vote of a majority of the members elected to each branch thereof, adopt an ordinance dividing such city or town into dis-

[1] Warren B. Hunting, "The Constitutionality of Race Distinctions and the Baltimore Negro Segregation Ordinance," *Columbia Law Review*, 11:24 (1911). Quoted in Mangum, *op. cit.*, p. 140.

tricts . . . the boundaries whereof shall be plainly designated in such
ordinance, and which shall be known as segregation districts.[2]

Four types of segregation ordinances have been defined by Stephenson.[3] The first, called the Baltimore type, designated all-white
and all-Negro blocks in areas where both races live. This type was
copied by Atlanta, Georgia, and Greenville, South Carolina. The
second type, illustrated by the Virginia law, designated separate districts for white people and for Negroes and made it unlawful for
either race to live in the other's districts. Both Roanoke and Ports-
mouth took advantage of this law and divided their territory into
segregation districts.

The third type of ordinance, introduced in Richmond and later
copied by Ashland, Virginia, and Winston-Salem, North Carolina,
undertook to legislate for the whole city. A block was declared white
if a majority of the residents were white, or colored if a majority of
the residents were colored. Clothed in expressions of solicitude for
the public welfare, it was ordained by the Council of the city of
Richmond:

1. That in order to preserve the general welfare, peace, racial integrity, morals, and social good order of the city of Richmond, it shall be
unlawful for any person to use as a residence any building on any street
between intersecting streets, where the majority of residences on such
streets are occupied by those with whom said person is forbidden to
intermarry by section 5 of the Act of the General Assembly of Virginia
entitled: "An Act to Preserve Racial Integrity," and approved March
20, 1924, or as the same may be hereafter amended; provided, that nothing in this ordinance shall affect the right, existing at the time of the
passage of this ordinance in any person, to use any such building as a
residence.

2. Any person violating the provisions of this ordinance shall be
liable to a fine of not less than one hundred dollars nor more than five
hundred dollars, recoverable before the police justices of the city of
Richmond as the case may be, each day's violation to constitute a separate offense.

3. That all ordinances or parts of ordinances in conflict with the
ordinance be and the same are hereby repealed.

4. This ordinance shall be in force from its passage.[4]

This ordinance did not apply to white business enterprises operating
in Negro neighborhoods.

[2] Laws of Virginia, 1912, p. 330.
[3] Gilbert Stephenson, "The Segregation of the White and Negro Races in Cities,"
South Atlantic Quarterly, 13:1-18 (January, 1914).
[4] The Crisis, 36:131 (April, 1929).

The fourth, or Norfolk, type was more general than the other three types and applied to mixed as well as all-white and all-Negro blocks, the color of the block being determined by ownership as well as occupancy.

In order to avoid illegal specifications of a discriminatory nature, practically all ordinances made the statute apply to white and black alike, and insisted that the purpose of such ordinances was to prevent disturbances and so facilitate better relations between the races. Thus, the preamble to the Virginia statute reads:

> Whereas the preservation of the public morals, public health and public order in the cities and towns of this commonwealth is endangered by the residence of white and colored people in close proximity to one another . . .[5]

Booker T. Washington, reacting to the attempts at segregation, saw clearly much that was behind these early ordinances:

> In all my experiences I have never yet found a case where the masses of the people of any given city were interested in the matter of segregation of white and colored people; that is, there has been no spontaneous demand for segregation ordinances. In certain cities politicians have taken the leadership in introducing such segregation ordinances into city councils, and after making an appeal to racial prejudices have succeeded in securing a backing for ordinances which would segregate the Negro people from their white fellow citizens. After such ordinances have been introduced, it is always difficult, in the present state of public opinion in the South, to have any considerable body of white people oppose them, because their attitude is likely to be misrepresented as favoring Negroes against white people.[6]

In 1915 the question of the constitutionality of these segregation ordinances reached the Supreme Court, in the Harris case. This case originated in Louisville, Kentucky, where whites had brought action against a white landowner who had defiantly sold his property to a Negro. Under the Louisville ordinance the Negro was not allowed to occupy the property as a place of residence. The Supreme Court decided that the ordinance was unconstitutional because it violated the due process clause of the Fourteenth Amendment by interfering with the right of the property owner to dispose of his real estate.[7]

---

[5] Stephenson, "The Segregation of the White and Negro Races in Cities," *South Atlantic Quarterly,* 13:3.

[6] Booker T. Washington, "My View of Segregation Laws," *The New Republic,* 5:198-199 (Dec. 23, 1915).

[7] Mangum, *op. cit.,* p. 142.

Following the Supreme Court decision in the Louisville case, various municipalities attempted to circumvent the decision. [New Orleans devised an ordinance prohibiting members of either race from establishing a residence in a preponderantly Negro or white residential area without first securing the written consent of the majority of the persons residing in that particular area.] The State Court, in upholding the ordinance, held that it was not a violation of the Fourteenth Amendment by reason of the "consent" provision and that the act was merely a zoning ordinance within the power of the police department.[8] The Supreme Court, however, in its opinion written by Chief Justice Taft, held the law unconstitutional on the authority of the Louisville case.

These efforts to create "black ghettos" were effectively halted by the Supreme Court in the case of *Buchanan* v. *Warley*.[9] In this case a white seller of residential property sought enforcement of a contract made with a Negro purchaser, who relied on an ordinance similar to those discussed above as a defense since the property was located in a block in which there were eight residences occupied by whites. Both the Kentucky trial court and the Court of Appeals of Kentucky had held the ordinance valid and a complete defense. With Mr. Justice Day speaking, the Supreme Court unanimously held the ordinance invalid on the ground that it violated the Fourteenth Amendment in depriving the seller of the right to dispose of his property as he chose.

As late as 1935 attempts to evade the Supreme Court decision were still being made. The governor of Oklahoma tried to force residential segregation in Oklahoma City through the use of emergency military power; but the State Supreme Court held the ordinances unconstitutional.[10] While there is no state action that can be employed to prevent Negroes from residing in neighborhoods occupied by a predominant number of whites, and although the United States Supreme Court has consistently declared all such ordinances unconstitutional and thereby invalid, municipalities still sporadically attempt to initiate plans to keep the races separated, in order to preserve the general welfare, racial integrity, morals, and good order of the municipalities.

[8] *Tyler* v. *Harmon*, 158 L. 439, 104 S. 200 (195), 160 La. 843, 107 So. 704 (1926).

[9] *Buchanan* v. *Warley*, 245 U.S. 60, 38 Sup. Ct. 16 (1917). Two convictions under similar ordinances which had been upheld by state courts were reversed in deference to this decision. *Twine* v. *City of Clifton Forge*, 124 Va. 781, 97 S.E. 310 (1918); *Glover* v. *City of Atlanta*, 148 Ga. 285, 16 S.E. 562 (1918).

[10] *Allen* v. *Oklahoma City*, 175 Okla. 421, 52 Poe (2d) 1054 (1933).

Restrictive Covenants

The most recent, and for a period the most effective, means of circumventing the unconstitutional segregation ordinances is through the restrictive covenant. This is essentially a private contract entered into by white residents of a given neighborhood to regulate the disposition of their property and, incidentally, to regulate the complexion of the neighborhood. Such covenants may be contained in deeds from sellers of residential property or mutually entered into by groups of property owners. In a sense this is a social extension of the principle of zoning, which has held the favor of municipal associations. No statistics are available as to the extent of the use of this device, but unquestionably it is the only current method of restricting areas in which Negroes live which has any semblance of legal support, especially in northern and border cities.

Without judicial sanction, of course, these covenants can never achieve their purpose. Injunctions, however, have proved a potent means of limiting the areas in which Negroes may live. In some instances, races have been specified in the covenants; and various communities have included among undesirables Orientals, Mexicans, "Balkan" races, and South Europeans, as well as Negroes. The Supreme Court of the United States decided in 1926 (*Corrigan* v. *Buckley*) that these covenants and agreements do not fall within the provisions of the Fourteenth Amendment because a deed is the action of an individual and not of a state.

The individual states, however, are not in agreement on the matter of validity or invalidity, except that total restraints on alienation are considered void if they are unlimited as to time. Covenants preventing alienation to Negroes for various periods have been upheld by the courts in the District of Columbia, Georgia, Louisiana, Missouri, and Maryland.[11] The Maryland case[12] was decided as late as 1938. In the West, a Colorado decision in 1937[13] held a covenant preventing alienation of property to Negroes to be void, but covenants restricting occupancy by unwanted social groups have been held valid, whether such covenants were contained in deeds or in property owners' agreements. The Illinois intermediate appellate court appears to have approved both covenants restraining alienation to Negroes and occupancy covenants.[14] These decisions reach back, perhaps, to the racial friction in Chicago following the in-migration

[11] Mangum, *op. cit.*, pp. 147 ff.
[12] *Meade* v. *Dennistone*, 173 Md. 295.
[13] *Chandler* v. *Ziegler*, 88 Col. 1.
[14] *Burke* v. *Kleiman*, 277 Ill. App. 519 (1934), and *Lee* v. *Hansberry*, 291 Ill. App. 517 (1937).

of Negroes beginning in 1917. The resultant disturbances included numerous meetings of whites to prevent Negroes from occupying or even buying in certain designated "white" sections, and frequent bombings of residences of Negroes and white real-estate dealers who were known to sell or rent property in exclusive sections to Negroes. The Chicago Commission on Race Relations has described these bombings as follows:

From July 1, 1917, to March 1, 1921, the Negro housing problem was marked by fifty-eight bomb explosions. Two persons, both Negroes, were killed, a number of white and colored persons were injured, and the damage to property amounted to $100,000. Of these fifty-eight bombs, thirty-two were exploded within the square bounded by Forty-first and Sixtieth Streets, Cottage Grove Avenue and State Street. With an average of one race bombing every twenty days for three years and eight months, the police and the state's attorney's office succeeded in apprehending but two persons suspected of participation in these acts of lawlessness. One of these . . . was released on a $500 bond. At the writing of this report, one year after the arrest, there has been no trial. Another man was apprehended, questioned, held under surveillance for two days by the police and finally released.[15]

LEGAL SEGREGATION IN THE SCHOOLS

Legislation making separate schools mandatory was perhaps the most universal historically; and all southern states now have laws segregating the races at all levels of education.[16] Tennessee's[17] school segregation law goes back to 1866. North Carolina's constitution of 1875 provided for separate schools with "equal opportunities for each race."[18] In Texas the constitution of 1876[19] made provision for racial segregation in educational institutions, and a law in 1879 specified separate schools for white and colored children over six years of age. It further stated, in a dubious spirit of nondiscrimination, that a

school house constructed in part by colored parents or guardians . . .

[15] The Chicago Commission on Race Relations, *The Negro in Chicago* (Chicago: The University of Chicago Press, 1922), pp. 122-123.

[16] There are state constitutional provisions for separate public school systems in the District of Columbia and the following seventeen states: Alabama, Arkansas, Delaware, Florida, Georgia, Kentucky, Louisiana, Maryland, Mississippi, Missouri, North Carolina, Oklahoma, South Carolina, Tennessee, Texas, Virginia and West Virginia. Other states which do not provide segregated schools by their constitutions but which, nevertheless, have provisions for separate schools in certain sections are: Illinois, Indiana, New Jersey, Ohio, and Pennsylvania.

[17] Laws of Tennessee, 1865-66, p. 65, Sec. 7.

[18] Constitution of North Carolina, 1875, Art. IX, Sec. 2.

[19] Constitution of Texas, 1876, Art. VII, Sec. 7.

shall not be used for white children without the consent of trustees of the district, and a like rule shall protect the use of school houses erected in part by voluntary subscription of white parents or guardians for the benefit of white children.[20]

In Mississippi the statute of 1878 required that white and Negro pupils should not be taught in the same schoolhouse.[21] Virginia segregated the races in educational institutions in 1882.[22] In South Carolina separate schools were required by the state in 1895.[23]

Segregative measures relating to attendance and other school problems in the southern states have been revised and refined from time to time. In 1919 Georgia passed a law which stated:

It shall also be the duty of said board of education to make arrangements for the instruction of the children of the white and colored races in separate schools. They shall, as far as practicable, provide the same facilities for both races in respect to attainments and abilities of teachers and for a minimum of six months' length of term time; but the children of the white and colored races shall not be taught together in any common or public school.

Free tuition: Colored and white children separate. Admission to all common schools shall be gratuitous to all children between the ages of six and eighteen years residing in the subdistricts in which the schools are located. Colored and white children shall not attend the same school; and no teacher receiving or teaching white and colored pupils in the same school shall be allowed any compensation at all out of the common school funds.[24]

Mississippi in 1924[25] provided for separate examinations for Negro and white applicants for teaching licenses. Four states, Florida, Kentucky, Oklahoma, and Tennessee, have laws making it a punishable offense to allow white and Negro students to be educated together in any school, college, or other institution, public or private. While Virginia still has white teachers in Negro schools, Florida makes it a criminal offense for teachers of one race to instruct pupils of another; and West Virginia requires that all teachers in Negro schools must be Negroes. The most famous case of segregation on a higher educational level involved Berea College in Kentucky, a school founded by the American Missionary Association and engaged in the coeducation of the races. These laws which purport to

[20] Acts of Texas, 1879, p. 181.
[21] Laws of Mississippi, 1878, p. 103.
[22] Laws of Virginia, 1881-82, p. 37.
[23] Constitution of South Carolina, 1895, Art. XI.
[24] Acts of Georgia, 1919, pp. 323, 331.
[25] Laws of Mississippi, 1924, Ch. 283.

make provision for separate but equal accommodations have until recently been regarded as falling within the requirements of the Fourteenth Amendment.

In spite of the verbal provisions, "separate but equal," there has been gross discrimination in actual provisions for the two races, as has been shown; and some legislation specifically provides for unequal payment for white and Negro teachers. Only recently have these statutes prescribing unequal pay for teachers been tested: In Maryland a test case was brought to challenge the constitutionality of the unequal salary scale for white and Negro teachers. When the authorities sought counsel on this matter, they were advised that the statute was invalid.

In many southern states institutions of higher learning were established for Negroes to extend the opportunity for advanced education and at the same time to provide continuity in the separation policy. Thus we find the appearance of such state institutions as the Virginia Normal and Industrial Institute in 1887[26] (later called Virginia State College for Negroes) and Prairie View State Normal and Industrial College for colored teachers in Texas, established under an act of 1879.[27] As the education of Negroes has proceeded, the separate and limited Negro colleges have become more and more inadequate; and there have been increasing demands for facilities for study on graduate and professional levels, where these are not provided in existing Negro institutions.

Of the seventeen southern states with separate school systems, Missouri was the first to provide graduate and professional training for Negroes at state expense.[28] An act passed in 1921 authorized the Board of Curators of Lincoln University, the state-supported college for Negroes, to arrange for the attendance of Negro residents of the state at the university of any adjacent state to take any courses which were offered at the University of Missouri, but not at Lincoln. Reasonable tuition fees were to be paid by the state; and beginning in 1929 Missouri has made biennial appropriations of from $5,000 to $15,000 for such tuition aid. Kentucky, Maryland, Oklahoma, Tennessee, Virginia, and West Virginia have followed Missouri in providing this type of scholarship aid. Amounts available for this purpose vary with the states. For example, the Maryland annual appropriation was $40,000 in 1938, $25,000 of which was desig-

[26] Code of 1887, Virginia, Sec. 1506.
[27] Acts of Texas, 1879, p. 181.
[28] Rufus E. Clement, "Legal Provisions for Graduate and Professional Instruction for Negroes in States Operating Separate School Systems," *Journal of Negro Education,* 3:142-149 (April, 1939).

nated specifically for scholarships; while the $2,500 for which the Tennessee act provided was to be secured from the regular appropriation granted to the Agricultural and Industrial College for Negroes in Nashville.[29]

The state colleges for Negroes in Louisiana, Texas, and Virginia offer work that is listed on the graduate level. This work is, of course, at present inadequate for the educational needs of Negro students. For instance, at the Virginia State College for Negroes at Ettrick, in 1938, eighteen graduate students were enrolled for graduate work in eight departments. Prairie View, the state college for Negroes in Texas, began its graduate work by offering courses in agriculture, education, and one or two other fields. Georgia and North Carolina have given definite recognition to the problem, have held various conferences, and have sought some legal solution of the difficulty within the local mores. The District of Columbia has Howard University, which offers professional education for Negroes, and graduate work leading to the degree of Master of Arts. The states which had no provisions for graduate or professional training for Negroes at the time of Clement's survey in 1939 and have not recognized the need are: Alabama, Arkansas, Delaware, Florida, Mississippi, and South Carolina.

The discrimination described has been challenged in the state courts as well as in the Supreme Court of the United States. Most far-reaching in its effects was the case of *Lloyd Gaines* v. *University of Missouri*. Gaines, who held an A.B. degree from Lincoln University, was denied admission to the Law School of the University of Missouri on the ground that admission of a Negro would be contrary to the constitution, laws, and public policy of the state. Instead of applying for scholarship aid to study elsewhere, Gaines sought a writ of mandamus to compel the curators of the University of Missouri to admit him. The Circuit Court denied his petition and the State Supreme Court affirmed this judgment. The case by writ of certiorari reached the Supreme Court of the United States, which denied the right of the curators of the university to exclude Gaines, declaring that what would otherwise be an unconstitutional discrimination within the state could not be justified by resorting to opportunities elsewhere (scholarship aid). The court held further that, although the curators of Lincoln University had a discretionary obligation to reorganize that institution so that it would afford Negroes of the state an opportunity for training equal in standards to that of the University of Missouri, such an obligation was not

[29] Clement, *op. cit.*

sufficiently mandatory to relieve the state of the charges of illegal discrimination in the opportunities provided for the legal education of Negroes.

This decision in the Gaines case had a recent precedent in the Maryland case of *University* v. *Murray*.[30] When Murray, a citizen of Baltimore and graduate of Amherst College, applied for admission to the Law School of the University of Maryland, the registrar denied the application because Murray was a Negro. Murray then applied to the courts for a writ of mandamus to compel the Board of Regents to admit him to the law school on the ground that his exclusion because of race was unconstitutional. The court signed a writ ordering the institution to admit Murray upon compliance with the necessary formalities. The registrar and the Board of Regents appealed to the highest court in the state, the Court of Appeals, which held that the trial court had properly issued the writ of mandamus in Murray's behalf. The Court of Appeals declared that the state must provide equal educational facilities if it resorted to the separation of the races; and an out-of-state scholarship to Howard University, for example, would not only impose additional expense on Murray but would deprive him of the opportunity, offered law students at the University of Maryland, of specializing in Maryland law .

It was after this decision that Kentucky and Virginia without litigation began providing funds for scholarship aid outside the state. Maryland increased its annual scholarship appropriation by $20,000 and made substantial grants to the state training school for Negro teachers, Bowie Normal, and to Morgan College of Baltimore.

Another recent Maryland case, *Margaret Williams* v. *Baltimore*,[31] touches the heart of the issue of the separate school system. This case arose out of an attempt to compel Baltimore County, with eleven high schools for white children and none for Negroes, to provide one for Negroes. At the time of the suit Baltimore County paid the city of Baltimore tuition for Negro residents of the county who attended high school in the city; but before the county would pay the tuition of any student, he was required to pass a comprehensive examination to prove his ability to do high-school work. In 1935 only 64 out of 128 Negro students who took this examination passed, and these figures, apparently, were typical. It was claimed that the county seldom, if ever, appropriated enough money to cover the tuition of the students who applied.

[30] 169 Md., 1936.
[31] Henry J. McGuinn, "The Courts and Equality of Educational Opportunity," *Journal of Negro Education,* 8:150-163 (April, 1939).

Margaret Williams, plaintiff in the action, petitioned for a writ of mandamus to compel the Baltimore County Board of Education to admit her to the white high school at Catonsville. Her attorneys claimed that the examination which the plaintiff had failed to pass should not disqualify her from entering high school because the examination was not authorized by law nor required for the children of both races. It was further contended that the Maryland law does not require separation of pupils in the public schools and, finally, that the law was so administered that it did not provide equality of opportunity for members of both races. The Circuit Court, where the action was begun, held that the Board of Education had the power to determine the basis upon which students may enter high school, and the examinations given by the board were adjudged to be fair. The petition was therefore denied; and this decision was sustained by the Maryland Court of Appeals. It held that the attorneys for the petitioner erred in seeking to have her admitted to a school for white children; and that the remedy for refusal to admit the child, after her failure to pass a legally authorized but defective examination, was a better test to determine whether she was qualified.

The actual object of the lawsuit—to force the county to build a Negro high school—scarcely came before the court under this action. Baltimore County did subsequently, however, allow ten cents per day for transportation of Negro students to and from Baltimore City, and increased the amount available for tuition in its high schools.[32]

It is significant that these influential court decisions have been rendered in border states, lying between the southern states, where numerous contacts between the races are prohibited by law, and the northern states, where much of the racial legislation is designed to prevent and combat discrimination. The legislation of the border region often reflects its marginal geographic position in making *optional* many practices in respect to racial contacts.

The educational laws of Indiana are an example of legislation which makes educational segregation optional. A statute of 1869[33] required the trustees of district schools to organize separate but equal schools for Negroes. If there were not enough Negroes in one district to warrant a school, two or more districts might be consolidated for that purpose. If there were not enough Negroes within a reasonable distance, then the trustees might provide such other means of educating colored children as would employ their proportion of the

[32] McGuinn, *op. cit.*
[33] Laws of Indiana, 1869, p. 41.

school funds to the best advantage. The constitutionality of this law[34] was tested in 1874, in one of the most exhaustive cases on the subject. A Negro father applied for a mandate to compel the white school to admit his children. The court held that the separation of the races in schools did not violate the federal and state constitutions; that the common schools were based upon state legislation, were domestic institutions and, as such, subject to the exclusive control of the constituted authorities of the state. The federal constitution did not provide for any general system of education to be conducted and controlled by the national government, nor did it vest in Congress any power to exercise general or special supervision over the states in matters of education. Under the constitution of Indiana the common-school system must be general, uniform, and equally open to all, but uniformity would be secured where all schools of the same grade had the same system of government and discipline, the same branches of learning taught, and the same qualifications for admission. The court said:

In our opinion the classification of scholars on the basis of race or color, and their education in separate schools, involve questions of domestic policy which are within the legislative discretion and control, and do not amount to an exclusion of either class . . . there would be as much lawful reason for complaint by one scholar in the same school that he could not occupy the seat of another scholar therein at the same time the latter occupied it, or by scholars in different classes in the same school, that they were not placed in the same class, or by scholars in different schools, that they were not placed in the same school, as there is that black and white children are placed in distinct classes and taught in separate schools.[35]

In 1877 the statute of 1869 was amended to read:

The trustee or trustees of such township, town or city, *may* organize the colored children into separate schools of the township, town or city, having all the rights, privileges, and advantages of all other schools of the township, town or city: Provided, that in case there may not be provided separate schools for the colored children, then such children shall be allowed to attend the public school with white children; Provided, further, that when any child attending such colored school shall, on examination and certificate of his or her teacher, show to trustee or trustees of any township, town or city, that he or she has made a sufficient advancement to be placed in a higher grade than that afforded by such colored school, he or she shall be entitled to enter the school pro-

[34] Cory v. Carter, 1874, 48 Indiana, 327, pp. 362-363.
[35] *Ibid.*

vided for white children on a like grade, and no distinction shall therein be made on account of race or color of such colored child.[36]

Under these laws making segregation optional in educational institutions in Indiana there are a variety of practices and a difference in application on various educational levels. White and Negro children often attend the same school until they reach high school. Then all Negro children are sent to Negro high schools, and all white children attend white high schools. One of the schoolteachers in an Indiana city pointed out that the city purchased school buses to transport Negro children who lived too far from Negro schools, and who otherwise might expect to go to the white high school in the neighborhood. There are some neighborhoods where a few Negro children do go to the white school in the district. It is left with the principal of the school to decide whether or not he will admit a Negro to his school.

In the northern states there are no legal provisions for the segregation of races in education; and in some of the states there are laws specifically prohibiting segregation and discrimination. For example, in New York, the education law of 1910 provides that:

No person shall be refused admission into or be excluded from any public school in the State of New York on account of race or color.[37]

In Illinois the law provides that:

Any school officer or officers, or any other person, who shall exclude or aid in excluding from the public schools on account of color, any child who is entitled to the benefits of such school, shall be fined upon conviction, not less than five or more than one hundred dollars.[38]

In spite of the presence of legislation prohibiting segregation in the schools of some states with southern exposures, such as New Jersey and Illinois, in practice segregation is accomplished in some localities through administrative measures.

[36] Laws of Indiana, 1877, p. 124.
[37] Laws of New York, 1910, c. 140.
[38] Laws of Illinois, Statutes, 1896, III, p. 3730, sec. 292.

Chapter IX

"CIVIL RIGHTS" LEGISLATION PROHIBITING RACIAL DISCRIMINATION

THE BORDER STATES

The conflicting racial views of the North and the South met in the border states, with the result that uncertain patterns of race relations are more the rule than the exception in this marginal area, as has been illustrated in the case of racial segregation in Indiana schools. These states have enacted both legislation *restricting association* between the races and legislation which *prohibits discriminatory* practices on account of race, thus further confusing the patterns of race relations.

The legislation which prohibits discrimination in certain border states is often ineffective in the face of regional differences that cannot be overlooked in practice. Although it is against the law to discriminate between white and Negro passengers on public accommodations, there is actually much discrimination; and effective segregation can be accomplished by means other than law. The streetcar system can be segregated to a large extent by running cars connecting two Negro districts. Some Negro border residents have complained that bus companies consistently practice discrimination, by assigning Negro passengers to the less comfortable seats, for example. Similar indifference to the letter of the law appears in other types of public accommodations in the border states. The civil rights laws have been ineffective in altering the custom regarding the admittance of Negroes to hotels and restaurants. Such situations are often aided and abetted by judges who refuse to accept the priority of law over customary practice.

THE NORTH

In direct contrast to the segregative racial legislation of the South is the legislation which prohibits racial discrimination in the northern states.[1] This legal framework began to take shape after the Supreme Court declared the Federal Civil Rights Bill unconstitutional in 1883. The states north of Mason and Dixon's line then began to enact state civil rights bills as guarantors of the right to liberty and the pursuit of happiness. Economically, of course, the industrial North had pursued a course far different from that of the agricultural South. In the North the growth of capitalism, the influx of European immigrant labor for the expanding industries, the growth of cities and land transportation systems, and the increasing emphasis upon the "rights of man" to education and personal freedom helped to sow the seeds of political democracy; and it was reflected in the racial legislation.

The meticulously detailed character of the legislation prohibiting segregation and discrimination is illustrated in the New York laws of 1881 and 1935, dealing with the right of equal accommodations in public places:

Section 1. No person shall be denied the full and equal enjoyment of the accommodations, advantages, facilities and privileges of all hotels, inns, taverns, restaurants, public conveyances on land or water, theaters and other places of public resort or amusement, because of race, creed or color.

Section 2. Any person who shall violate the foregoing section by denying to any person, because of his race, creed or color, full enjoyment of any of the accommodations, advantages, facilities and privileges hereinbefore mentioned, or by aiding or inciting thereto, shall for every such offense be deemed guilty of a misdemeanor, and punished accordingly.[2]

The New York Law of 1935 reads:

All persons within the jurisdiction of this state shall be entitled to full and equal accommodations, advantages, facilities and privileges of any places of public accommodations, resort or amusement, subject only to the conditions and limitations established by law and applicable alike to all persons. No person, being the owner, lessee, proprietor, manager, superintendent, agent or employee of any such place shall directly or indirectly refuse, withhold from or deny to any person any of the accommodations, advantages, facilities or privileges thereof, or directly or indirectly publish, circulate, issue, display, post or mail any written or printed communication, notice or advertisement, to the effect that any of the accommodations, advantages, facilities and privileges of any such place shall be refused, withheld from or denied to any person on account of race, creed or color, or that the patronage or custom thereat, of any

[1] Throughout this chapter the laws of New York and Illinois are cited as typical of this legislation in northern states.
[2] Laws of New York, 1881, I, p. 541.

person belonging to or purporting to be of any particular race, creed or color is unwelcome, objectionable or not acceptable, desired or solicited. The production of any such written or printed communication, notice or advertisement, purporting to relate to any such place and to be made by any person being the owner, lessee, proprietor, superintendent or manager thereof, shall be presumptive evidence in any civil or criminal action that the same was authorized by such person. A place of public accommodation, resort or amusement within the meaning of this article shall be deemed to include inns, taverns, road houses, hotels, whether conducted for the entertainment of transient guests or for the accommodation of those seeking health, recreation or rest, or restaurants, or eating houses, or any place where food is sold for consumption on the premises; buffets, saloons, bar rooms, or any store, park or enclosure where spirituous or malt liquors are sold; ice cream parlors, confectionaries, soda fountains, and all stores where ice cream, ice and fruit preparations or their derivatives, or where beverages of any kind are retailed for consumption on the premises; drug stores, dispensaries, clinics, hospitals, bath houses, barber shops, roof gardens, music halls, race courses, skating rinks, amusement and recreation parks, fairs, bowling alleys, gymnasiums, shooting galleries, billiard and pool parlors, public libraries, kindergartens, primary and secondary schools, high schools, academies, colleges and universities, extension courses, and all educational institutions under the supervision of the regents of the State of New York; and any such public library, kindergarten, primary and secondary school, academy, college, university, professional school, extension course, or other educational facility, supported in whole or in part by public funds or by contributions solicited from the general public; garages, and all public conveyances operated on land or water, as well as the stations and terminals thereof. Nothing herein contained shall be construed to include any institution, club, or place of accommodation which is in its nature distinctly private, or to prohibit the mailing of a private communication in writing sent in response to a specific written inquiry.[3]

Laws Punishing Mob Violence

In some of the northern states there are no laws dealing with mob violence and lynching, but these are regarded as violations of civil rights and liberties stipulated by law. In Illinois, where outbreaks of mob violence have occurred, the following suppressive act was passed in 1905:

Be it enacted by the People of the State of Illinois, represented in the General Assembly: That any collection of individuals, five or more in number, assembled for unlawful purpose of offering violence to the person or property of any one supposed to have been guilty of a violation

[3] Laws of New York, 1935, c. 737.

of the law, or for the purpose of exercising correctional powers or regulative powers over any person by violence, and without lawful authority, shall be regarded and designated as a "mob."

Serious injury.—The term "serious injury," for the purpose of this act, shall include any injury to property which shall cause damage to the owner thereof, or any injury to the person which shall temporarily or permanently disable the person from earning a livelihood.[4]

This act was amended in 1931 to read as follows:

Damage by violence—Penalty—Action against municipality. Any person or persons composing a mob under the provisions of this act, who shall by violence inflict material damage to the property or serious injury to the person of any other person upon the pretense of exercising correctional powers over such person or persons, by violence and without authority of law, shall be deemed guilty of a felony, and shall suffer imprisonment in the penitentiary not exceeding five years; and any person so suffering material damage to property or injury to person by a mob shall have an action against the county, park district or city in which such injury is inflicted, for such damages as he may sustain to an amount not exceeding ten thousand (10,000) dollars.

Heirs of victim may recover from municipality. The surviving spouse, lineal heirs, or adopted children of any such other person or persons, who, before the loss of life, were dependent for support upon any other person who shall hereafter suffer death by lynching at the hands of a mob, in any county, park district or city in this state, may recover from such county, park district or city, damages for injury sustained by reason of the loss of life of such person, to a sum not exceeding ten thousand (10,000) dollars.[5]

The Right to Serve on Juries

Important among the early court rights assured to Negroes in the North was the right to serve on juries. In New York this right was granted to all persons regardless of race, creed, color, or sex, in the Civil Rights Bill of 1895 and reaffirmed in 1938:

No citizen of the state possessing all other qualifications which are or may be required or prescribed by law, shall be disqualified to serve as a grand or petit juror in any court of this state on account of race, creed, color or sex, and any person charged with any duty in the selection or summoning of jurors who shall exclude or fail to summon any citizen for any of the causes aforesaid shall, on conviction thereof, be deemed guilty of a misdemeanor and be fined not less than one hundred dollars nor more than five hundred dollars or imprisoned not less than

[4] Laws of Illinois, 1905, p. 190.
[5] Laws of Illinois, 1931, p. 454.

thirty days, nor more than ninety days, or both such fine and imprisonment.[6]

Protection in Industry

The antidiscrimination legislation of the northern states also
includes protective laws in industry. They apply particularly to
public utilities and contractors for public works and public buildings.
The New York law of 1933 declared:

It shall be unlawful for any public utility, as defined in the public
service law, to refuse to employ any person in any capacity in the operation or maintenance of a public service on account of race, color, or
religion of such person.[7]

In Illinois an act relating to civil and legal rights of persons was
approved in 1935. It dealt with discrimination in hiring persons for
work relief:

It shall be unlawful for any agent, appointee or employee of any State
commission or governmental subdivision of this State or of any county,
municipal or political subdivision thereof or of any Park District or
Forest Preserve District to either directly or indirectly discriminate or
cause to be discriminated against any person or persons in this State on
account of race, color or creed in the matter of hiring persons for work
relief projects.[8]

The most recent protective statutes are those which seek to enforce
fairness in the administration of the New Deal government's efforts
to control unemployment and provide work relief. An Illinois act,
approved on July 8, 1933, prohibits discrimination and intimidation
on account of race or color in employment under contracts for public
buildings or public works:

Race or color discrimination prohibited in contracts for public works.—
1. No person shall be refused or denied employment in any capacity on
the ground of race or color, nor be discriminated against in any manner
by reason thereof, in connection with the contracting for or the performance of any work or service of any kind, by, for, on behalf of, or for the
benefit of this State, or of any department, bureau, commission, board,
or other political subdivision or agency thereof.[9]

The provisions of this act were deemed automatically incorporated
in contracts and were applicable to independent contractors providing for any of "the said work or the performance of any of the said

[6] Civil Rights Bill of New York, 1895, Ch. 114.
[7] Laws of New York, 1933, Ch. 511.
[8] Laws of Illinois, 1935, p. 707.
[9] Laws of Illinois, 1933, p. 296.

services, or any part thereof." The act further provided for deduction from the compensation payable to the contractor by the state, and for recovery by the injured person, if such discriminatory practices occurred.

Protective racial legislation has been extended in New York to the point of forbidding discrimination by life insurance companies on account of race. This restriction is clearly set forth in the law of 1935:

Discrimination against colored persons prohibited.—1. No life insurance corporation doing business within this state shall make any distinction or discrimination between white persons and colored persons, wholly or partially of African descent, as to the premiums or rates charged for policies upon the lives of such persons, or in any other manner whatever; nor shall any such corporation demand or require a greater premium from such colored persons than is at that time required by corporation from white persons of the same age, sex, general condition of health and prospect of longevity; nor shall any such corporation make or require any rebate, diminution or discount upon the amount to be paid on such policy in case of the death of such colored persons insured, nor insert in the policy any condition, nor make any stipulation whereby such person insured shall bind himself, or his heirs, executors, administrators and assigns to accept any sum less than the full value or amount of such policy in case of a claim accruing thereon by reason of the death of such person insured, other than such as are imposed upon white persons in similar cases; and any such stipulation or condition so made or inserted shall be void.

2. No life insurance corporation doing business in this state shall reject any application for a policy of life insurance issued and sold by it, or refuse to issue such policy after proper application therefor, nor shall any lower rate be fixed or discrimination made by it in the fees or commissions of its agents for writing such a policy, solely by reason of the applicant being wholly or partially of African descent. A violation of any of the provisions of this subdivision shall be punishable by a fine of one thousand dollars.[10]

Recent Pressure for Civil Rights Legislation

Negroes did not compose a very large proportion of the total population of the northern states prior to World War I. The small numbers kept the racial problems below the threshold of attention; and the northern states were thus more objective about the question of human rights. The migration of a million and a half Negroes from the South, beginning about 1915, increased racial awareness; and this was registered in modifications of customs concerning free

[10] Laws of New York, 1935, Ch. 736.

association and civic participation. Although these northward population movements included thousands of whites whose racial attitudes
were fashioned by the traditions of the South, the modified racial
practices of the North did not result in supporting laws. An important reason for this was the fact that the Negro migration enfran-
chised hundreds of thousands of Negroes who could not vote in the
South. Their voting strength was for the first time significant and
effective. In some sections Negroes now hold the balance of power.
These new Negro voters have not only supported candidates who
promised to vote for civil rights legislation; but they have elected
increasing numbers of Negroes to the state legislatures, and the
bargaining power of these Negro representatives has helped to make
civil rights provisions effective.

The National Association for the Advancement of Colored People
has stimulated some of this legislation, and legislators are constantly
under pressure from the Negro press. During 1940 a committee
appeared before the Resolutions Committee of the Democratic National Convention and demanded a plank on the Negro in the plat-
form of the Democratic party. The lynching in Brownsville, Tennessee, which resulted from the fact that the Negroes there had
signified their intention of registering and voting in the 1940 elec-
tion, was cited as an indication of the need for federal action against
mobs. This committee also suggested the inclusion of Negroes in all
branches of the armed services and urged the abolishment of the
poll tax as a qualification for voting in the "lily-white" primaries.
The Pittsburgh *Courier* also launched a fight against discrimination
in the armed, and other defense, services of the nation. Readers'
opinions on such questions as the Anti-Lynching Bill have appeared
in other Negro papers; and the following excerpt from an editorial
in the Philadelphia *Tribune* sounds a note which is a familiar one
in the Negro press:

> There are two paramount things for which colored Americans should
> fight unrelentingly. First, foremost and always they should fight to pro-
> tect America's democracy. . . . The second thing for which colored
> citizens should fight with equal fervor is their full rights as American
> citizens.[11]

Custom and Law in the North

The fact that civil rights laws in the North are continually being
tested in the courts indicates both the need for such laws and the
reluctance of some individuals to change their customary practices

[11] Philadelphia *Tribune*, September 7, 1940, p. 4.

to conform with the requirements of the law. Northern proprietors have used numerous devices for effecting exclusion of Negroes while still remaining just within the letter of the law. For example, accommodations may be refused Negroes on "purely personal grounds" rather than on account of color. Managers of restaurants are required to do no more than instruct their waiters "in good faith" to afford all persons equal accommodations and full enjoyment of all privileges. If they have so instructed their employees, the managers are not liable under the law. It is not uncommon for a theater manager to say that the house is "sold out" if a Negro asks for an orchestra seat.

In Chicago when a school district becomes heavily populated with Negroes, the white children are given a transfer to attend another school, predominantly or wholly white. In Chicago, also, the accidental violation by a Negro youth of an "imaginary" but customary racial segregation boundary on the lake front precipitated a race riot in 1919 which resulted in 38 deaths and 537 injuries of white and Negro participants. There is still tension when these lines on the beach are threatened. The list could be greatly extended.

In several areas of contact between the races there are discriminatory and segregative practices against which no legislation has yet been enacted, as, for example, the restrictive covenants found in residential areas of northern cities. These covenants are an evasion of the legal prohibition of racial segregation. In some areas distinctions are made by common understanding. For example, one informant in New York stated that "they don't put Negro doctors on the staff of white hospitals," and "in private white hospitals Negroes are put in wards together." Thus there are areas of racial contact which are governed by custom rather than by law in the northern states, and the practices are molded in a discriminatory pattern.

Chapter X

THE IDEOLOGY OF THE COLOR LINE

The traditions of racial segregation and the complex codes regulating social contact between the races are given meaning by the attitudes, sentiments, beliefs, and opinions of the dominant society. Together these constitute a dynamic racial orthodoxy or ideology which rationalizes the race system and provides a philosophical bulwark for it. In its total effect the ideology defines the color line more certainly than either the laws or the customs. It is in this sphere that we must seek the explanation of the behavior of whites in their social relations with Negroes.

As in the case of institutions and practices, these attitudes and beliefs vary according to socioeconomic background and experience; and there is a pronounced regional differentiation in emphasis, and even marked variation within regions. Education, the range of communication between various classes of whites and various classes of Negroes, the ideology in regard to religion or labor or basic democratic theory, all contribute to differences in fundamental racial beliefs. However, back of the prevailing orthodoxies, taboos, and general patterns of white behavior toward Negroes, there is the dominant thread of beliefs held with more or less intensity and articulated in the sentiments here presented.

The social orientation of the beliefs of whites about Negroes is most apparent in the tenets that serve to rationalize and support the etiquette in interracial situations. Here it is obvious that the dogmas constitute something more than folklore or a creed of faith; they form a charter for social conduct.

THE NEGRO'S PLACE IN SOCIETY

The color line is so often defined implicitly by reference to the Negro's place that it will be revealing to present first the white man's interpretations of the Negro's role and status. A Savannah lawyer remarked:

We think of them as inferior because we have them in the house as servants. We have always had caste in the world.

Thus the black man is still conceived in the traditional role of servant. A Charleston housewife declared, "They make perfectly delightful servants. I wouldn't have any other kind." The secretary of the chamber of commerce in Shreveport, Louisiana, who had lived in the deep South only six years, was asked if he had changed his ideas about Negroes since he came South. He replied:

No, I just had to become accustomed to the southern ways of treating them. In the North there is a race problem, but not in the South. You just get accustomed to treating them in the southern way, or rather you learn from others. You treat them here as servants. They realize they are subservient and not equal to white people. They say the happiest person in the world would be a cross between a Jew and a Negro; the Jew would always have a dollar and keep it and the Negro would always be happy if he had one.

Social stratification is still rationalized in terms of theological dogmas, but it should be noted that in the minds of some, economic and religious doctrines can hardly be separated. An official of the Arkansas industrial welfare commission offered the following apologetic statement:

The Negro in his place is really an assistant in the South. He's what the Lord Almighty intended him to be, a servant of the people. We couldn't get along without them.

A former mayor of a North Carolina town also thought of Negro labor and subordination in the same breath:

This is a cotton belt and it is essential that we have Negro labor. When our own runs low, we import it. Our attitude is that the white man is superior and the colored are looked on as servants.

In Norfolk a clubwoman remarked:

They should be free, but they are more capable of the domestic arts than the fine arts. All human beings are fashioned to certain places, and theirs is utilitarian rather than artistic. It's due to their savage background and slavery. I may be all wrong. After centuries of civilization they may compare.

The manager of a machine shop in Newport News, while speculating on the Negro's place in southern society, said:

I explain it in this way. A mule is made to work; a horse is made for beauty. The Negro is the working man of the South. Plenty of Negroes here are much better than the whites. But as a class that is not as true for white people about being the workers. Take the tribes in Africa; some show civilization back in the Middle Ages. We have some savages here who pull the whole race down. Though we have some elegant ones, very wealthy, some are genuine blacks and you can't see much change in them. Those with some white blood show thrift and other white traits.

On the other hand, a rabbi in a Georgia city was very critical of the racial system and its mores:

The Southerners think the Negro should be hewers of wood and drawers of water. You often see a white foreman with the colored workers doing all the carpenter work and then the foreman does nothing but cuss out the "damn niggers." They think the Negro is dirt beneath their feet, and all they want to do is get rid of them. That's the attitude of the working class. It starts from selfish competition; that's where the trouble will come for a long while.

The "caste" position assigned to the black man, who is expected to be "submissive, humble, and subservient in his attitude toward white people," has an interesting effect on social sympathy. The question "Wouldn't it be humiliating to you if you had to ride on the Jim Crow car?" was asked a judge in a Georgia town. He replied:

We can't tell if it is to them because we think of their slave backgrounds, of their happy, carefree nature. That isn't true of many of them, but I imagine the average is probably happiest when he is waiting on white folks and wearing their old clothes. In that way they have more contact with white people and look up to them. We can't get away from the idea in the history of the Negro as a subservient race, from the prejudice that this is the white man's country and that the Negro will not be allowed to have equal share in making laws. It's unfair and undemocratic. We say that his father was a slave and degraded and we don't have to associate with him. But he does have the same legal rights and it can only be prejudice that keeps those rights from him; it's not reason, but emotion.

The stereotyped picture of the "former condition" is firmly fixed in the social consciousness of white people. They frequently compare the slave and the freedman, and there are still hints that the *ancien régime* might have been the Golden Age.

THE JUSTIFICATION FOR SEGREGATION IN INSTITUTIONS AND PUBLIC PLACES

Racial segregation in the social institutions of the South, particularly in the schools and churches, has long been an accomplished fact; and there is little active discussion of this subject by either whites or Negroes. When sentiment is expressed it is more often in relation to physical contact as such. Even on this question sentiment differs. There is aversion to contact when conceived as an objective racial fact; but there is favorable or even warm response to contact when conceived in terms of relations with particular Negroes, where the racial etiquette controls social distance between white master and Negro servant. It is assumed that the separation of whites and Negroes is natural. A minister in Waycross, Georgia, explained that it was very necessary that the state and local laws demand segregation:

While these laws have often been discriminatory and usually can't be defended as Christian humanitarianism, yet the principle lasts that there must be separation. Suppose you had a white girl in a class of forty colored boys. The girls may be taught by their fathers that it is necessary to maintain white purity. But these boys without it and marked by the servant-master relationship will get the idea as many did after the War that they can propose not only marriage but anything else to a white woman.

A school official in New Orleans explained that Negroes are gregarious and naturally tend to segregate themselves. A housewife in Greensboro, North Carolina, feared that if white and colored children attended school together they would "form friendships, and I don't want colored children in my home."

Since segregated schools are accepted as a part of the order of nature they are seldom questioned, and it is sometimes difficult to find a rational justification for them. A frequently expressed rationalization is the belief that Negroes have a disagreeable body odor. A rabbi in a Georgia city, whose family had lived in the South for several generations, thought that this odor alone made separation worth while. He asserted that when walking along the street, "if a Negro has been that way fifteen minutes before I can tell it." He added that he did not notice this in New York, nor with all of the Negroes in the South.

Other explanations offered as the basis for segregation in public institutions are: physical and racial aversion, uncleanliness, criminality, lack of morals, and ineducability. The beliefs that Negro children would contaminate white children and that the mental difference requires separate treatment are frequently held. A school official said that the colored child's mind was always two years behind that of the white. A railroad mechanic in Georgia, who did not think that education would be either possible or useful, remarked:

He's got a thick head, he can't get further. A little education is a poor thing, and that's all the further the average nigger gets, and that ruins him.

In the North, where racial segregation in schools is not universal, the question of contact in schools becomes an issue wherever Negroes appear. The entrance of Negroes into white schools brings a clash of opinion. There were Northerners who expressed the fear that contact in school might lead to dangerous associations. Thus a woman in Germantown, Pennsylvania, explained when asked about the schools:

I admit there is a problem in the schools. It is quite a different thing for me to meet them and for my children to grow up with them. It is different in the public schools. Then parents can say to their children that they must learn to pick their friends. But in the Friends' school we practice the Christian doctrines and the only thing is to treat them the same way. After the children get about twelve years old, the problem comes up, because we do not want our children to marry colored people. It wouldn't hurt their feelings if there had been no companionship from the beginning, but where they grow up friends and then have to draw back when they get older, it can't help but hurt them. There is no reason why they shouldn't marry except that they wouldn't be happy together.

Other racial dogmas, similar to those heard in the South, are offered in support of the idea of separate schools. One woman said, "The white children couldn't adopt anything from the colored children." A principal in Atlantic City, New Jersey, said:

I believe in segregation. They need a certain teaching that white children don't. They are like little animals. There is no civilization in their homes. They shouldn't hold up white children who have had these things for centuries. They are not as clean. They are careless about their bodies. Why should we contaminate our race? They are dirty and have skin diseases. Once I almost made a mistake and put a colored child in a white room. She was a dear, clean child; it seemed a crime to put her in with those colored children.

The church represents an area in which the Christian and the racial ideologies, both dominant in America, come into conflict. An incident in the South brought out the conflict of attitudes back of racial separation in the churches. In a conversation between an upper-class white man and a bishop, the question of admitting a Negro to church membership arose. The bishop, true to southern casuistry, explained that the church is a divine institution, and the congregation must accept the edict that all men are created equal before God;

but that the church is, nevertheless, also a social institution, and Negro membership in a white church would be the opening wedge to social equality. If the races came together at a church meeting, there was no escaping social equality. Thus it was decided to reject the Negro membership.

It is explained in other instances that the Bible insists upon racial integrity. In Moses' time, according to one informant, this was a principle of both the laws and the religion, and it was a cardinal sin to associate with other tribes. "Christianity," one zealously religious woman declared, "sometimes puts a strain on our southern way of life. God knows the darky has his place and we have ours."

Contacts in public places are more frequent in the North than in the South because there is less formal segregation. Nevertheless, it is not unusual to find pronounced attitudes on the part of whites against this contact and association, even though these attitudes do not always result in crisis behavior. Much of the discussion by white informants in the North centered around such contacts. Indeed, in some cases contact was limited to this impersonal level. Ordinarily, on the subways and crowded streetcars no one appears to pay attention to the presence of Negroes unless they are conspicuous by their large numbers. If a Negro enters a public vehicle and sits down beside a white person, there is little likelihood that the white person will move, although this happens occasionally. If a white person enters a vehicle and has the choice of sitting beside a Negro or a white person, the latter is more often selected. The impersonal character of these public contacts and the great variety of backgrounds keep the issue of race largely submerged.

In closer associations the attitudes are more clearly defined. A businessman said, "The Negro is not a good patron for our buses. People don't like to sit with them." In Philadelphia the manager of a motion-picture theater said, "A good class of white people can't degrade themselves by associating with them." The wife of a former white professor in a Negro college, now living in New Jersey, noted the embarrassment of public association. She said, "I don't care what people say, you can't help being conscious of it. It's like walking along the street with your petticoat hanging; it's no crime, but a little embarrassing."

The emotion-laden doctrine that it is dangerous for colored men and white women to be associated in any situation is widely prevalent. A woman in Montclair, New Jersey, who was ordinarily regarded as quite liberal and who did not object to eating with Negroes, declared:

I don't think they should be segregated. Just the same, I don't suppose I would want my daughter in a sleeper with a colored man; though, for that matter, there are a good many other people I wouldn't like her to be with.

It is not unusual for members of the white upper class to claim a great concern for the Negro's welfare, but to blame the masses for the conditions requiring segregation.

Merchants and businessmen have their own defenses for not catering to Negro trade. They may claim that they have no prejudice but must take account of the prejudices of their white patrons. It sometimes happens that a few of the dogmas are used in support of a point of view in an area into which the ideology as a whole has not diffused. Thus, a druggist in a suburb of Newark said:

My only contact with them is in the store. About half my patrons are colored. They are good people. They pay for what they want without any question, and they are pleasant. You know they have a body odor. It's unpleasant. Other customers don't like that. Many of them are diseased. That's why I use paper cups and containers. I couldn't ask other customers to drink out of the same glass. It wouldn't be sanitary.

In areas where Negroes are recent arrivals the whole series of resentments may be summed up in one or two fictions, such as "Negroes depreciate property." In the North the swimming pool frequently becomes an acute point of difficulty. A Y.M.C.A. secretary in a Pennsylvania city said:

They have both separate schools and those together. On the whole things are friendly here. The women in the Y.W.C.A. are very advanced. They look to the day when they will all be in one building. The leaders are optimistic. They are expressing themselves rather than the mind of their members. I don't think even the most ardent one would favor going in the swimming pool with a colored girl. As far as mixing with them in many things, we have our conferences and go as far as to even have one colored man in a night school class. But it is not to our interest to have them in the same gym or pool.

The various devices adopted for evading the civil rights statutes are reflected in the comments of several informants. A city official in Atlantic City said:

I think the southerners handle them better because they can't assert their rights. They are not permitted in the bars, etc. This equalization law is not a benefit for the man who runs the place. In New Jersey they have a state law that they are to be admitted to restaurants and theaters, but the courts wouldn't recognize it here. It is seldom a sensible colored man will thrust himself in where he is not wanted. In New York they have hired lawyers and prosecute such cases to the bitter end; they do not succeed in getting very far, not for the present time. I was in a restaurant in Philadelphia one time and a colored couple came in. The manager told them all the tables were reserved. They walked out. That's what overcomes the law. I kept a hotel for thirty years. They knew I didn't care for their trade, and they never came. I told them, "you know it is not fair to make me lose my trade." You can't throw them out, but the majority are satisfied to keep to themselves. They understand in the moving pictures that they are to sit on the left side. Our colored people are a nice class.

A newspaper editor in another city expressed himself as being in sympathy with the evasion of the laws designed to safeguard the civil rights of Negroes, and added, "What most Negroes call civil justice is so closely akin to social equality it is impossible for them to divorce the two."

Both in the South and in the North, especially in the latter section, there are equally deep-set attitudes in conflict with the racial ideology implied in the comments above. A public relations official in Boston pointed out that in this country the Negro has been set aside and made a special group; and this, in turn, has made him self-conscious and "martyr-minded." This man was critical of the tendency to "let the South assert what it knows to be wrong." A minister in New York observed that the apparent retardation after reaching fifteen or sixteen years of age was due more to social self-consciousness and an oppression psychosis than to heredity. He said, "The sensitive ones withdraw into a lonely isolation. It is practically impossible for a white person to get into a better class Negro home." The same point of view is implicit in the statement of an executive of a social agency in New Jersey:

One difficulty in this situation is the terrific sensitiveness of educated Negroes who have been snubbed so continuously because of color. It develops almost a persecution mania. One of my colored workers says that the difficulty is that they have grown so accustomed to snubs they get to expect them, and say it is always caused by color when it may not be.

ATTITUDES SUPPORTING RESIDENTIAL SEGREGATION

Attitudes similar to those supporting separation in schools are expressed in justification of segregated residential areas. The question usually takes care of itself in the South and seldom reaches the

level of action. For example, in a city like Charleston, South Carolina, with its back-yard pattern of Negro segregation, no pronounced
aversion to such proximity is expressed. An upper middle-class white
woman said:

The richest people in town have them living in their back yards. There
are some bad ones down the street, and I wish they'd move. But I don't
mind having my maids sleep in the same house with me. Lots of people
in the South have the nurse sleeping in the same room with the children.

In this instance Negro propinquity is associated with the prestige of
wealth and standing, and the practice continues. In general, however, the opinion is that "Negro quarters" are dirty, disease laden,
and dangerous. Moreover, it is held that "Negroes are happier in
their own neighborhoods."

A woman in the same state explained that:

Negroes get the small end of everything—poor houses, old churches,
and so forth. It happens to anybody who is lazy and shiftless and dirty.
I contrast them with the Italians whose homes I have been in. The
Italians have tidy kitchens, fresh starched aprons, snowy linen, but the
Negroes are dirty, sloppy and greasy. Some of them are all right. But
most of them are dirty and unsanitary. Their houses and yards smell.
They have dogs all over the house. You know it smells. They don't know
how to take care of things. Of course there are some white people who
don't too, but most Negroes don't know how.

It is not uncommon to hear, "The attitude of the community
toward the town across the tracks is rather low. It is a hangout for
thieves and convicts." These informants, in characterizing Negroes
as unclean, have voiced a general attitude toward the people.

The taboo against social equality and intimate association
apparently takes care of the problem of residential propinquity in
southern communities, where there have always been Negroes and
their place is so well defined in social space that their location in
ecological space does not loom as a great issue. In the North, however, where their social status is more anomalous and where they
have no customary place in the community, the residential location
of Negroes becomes an issue. Their appearance as newcomers in
white areas arouses the typical reaction to the stranger, which in this
case is greatly accentuated by the prevailing mythology.

A New Jersey resident who was acquainted with the southern
system presented a comparison between the North and the South and
at the same time illustrated how accommodations are made in resi-

dential areas. She lived in Montclair, where the problem of interracial adjustment caused by infiltration of Negroes was being experienced at the time of the interviews. She said:

My husband is a Southerner. I went South with him once to visit. The Negroes are segregated there and they get along better. They have no problem there. They have separate schools, cars, trains, everything. It's much better. They know their place. My husband doesn't like to live next door to them, but this is my mother's house and we get it cheaper. He speaks to them but it's hard for him. He doesn't like the children to play with them and he doesn't want me to send the boy to the nursery school with them, but I have to, he's so bad.

In the same city an upper-class woman who exhibited a rather sentimental attitude toward Negroes said:

I think they should have certain sections to themselves with as fine housing as in other neighborhoods. It will make them happier, because white people are so unfriendly; they are that much more exposed to it. I don't mean the city should force segregation on them, but I feel it would be wiser for their sensitive souls. I would not object if a colored family moved into this neighborhood if they had the same standards I demand of my other neighbors. I can't understand the terrible things people do to drive them out. I heard a story at Trenton of a colored woman minister who bought a house in a white neighborhood and when the neighbors found it out smashed windows and almost demolished the place. I was very indignant about it. She sold the place since she wasn't wanted there.

Various persons declared that Negroes were not desired in white communities because they are "bad neighbors," and "they depreciate property values since they do not keep up their property." A middle-class housewife in a New Jersey town said, "There is a type of Negro that lets things run down, but they are no worse than the same class of white people. I would not object to a real nice Negro family living next to me."

The basis of the antagonism in the majority of the cases is apparently class difference. This was frankly stated by the superintendent of employment in a public-service corporation in Newark, who said, "I live in a highly developed residential district and I would suppose if anybody were able to move in they would be our sort and acceptable. It's a class not a race distinction." The popular feeling is cryptically expressed in a remark made by a social worker in Newark: "When my uncle gets mad at the neighbors he threatens to sell the house to Negroes."

ATTITUDES SUPPORTING OCCUPATIONAL SEGREGATION

The Negro's place in the occupational structure is also explained by the ideology. A popular belief is that the black man—better known as a "buck nigger" in this connection—can do heavy work, but "must be driven to it like a mule," an analogy always on the tongue of the white man when talking of the Negro laborer. Negroes are regarded as best suited for manual labor, and hardly at all suited for technical or clerical work. Many dogmas of the racial orthodoxy are reflected in an interview with the manager of an oil company in Louisiana. In characterizing the Negro laborer he said:

The Negro is like a mule; a stolid sort of creature. He plods along, does his work well at his own speed, and doesn't wear himself out like the emotional white man. The southern nigger never worries about anything. Give him a full stomach and he's happy. I have worked all my life on the farm, and I envy him that. The Negro is too sluggish mentally for work in business. He just drifts along at a pace of his own. If you put him on a team he just lets them walk to town. Once in a while you get a good one as a mechanic on a truck, but they are exceptions.

We have a lot of good Negro carpenters, brick masons, etc. Industry hasn't availed itself of the Negro to any degree. The Negro's mind doesn't act quickly enough. They are afraid of injuries, and that's expensive. Where they are employed in large numbers they hurt themselves. They are not mentally alert. We had a few working class white people. They had a deep-seated prejudice against certain kinds of work; they like to have the Negroes do the menial things; they don't like to see white men do that. The Negroes make ideal servants; there are none better.

The last remark suggests the basis of the "caste" stratification of labor. An official in the open shop association in Arkansas gave evidence of the same sentiment:

There is very little displacement of Negro workers here. There is a certain line of labor particularly fitted to the Negro race and not the white, that not one white man in a thousand would do. That's true of the South in general. Such work as ditch digging, servants, gas work and utilities, section men, porters, bellhops, etc. The Negro is not a mechanic. The average one hasn't the mentality of handling any mechanic contrivance. Of course some are very skilled. The trend of their minds isn't mechanical. That's the reason why they have so many traffic accidents in the South. They are speed demons. They are careless as a class, and don't check up on their brakes or lights. They are not systematic.

According to the view of a white carpenter in Georgia, Negroes are naturally unfit for mechanical or technical trades:

The nigger's not as good a mechanic and never will make as good a one. You know the old saying, "He'll show the nigger in him." It can be proved. I've seen two nigger carpenters who were as good as any white, but they were above the average for niggers, and as a rule they mess up anything they do; one of them in the local is a well-read man, well up on all the rules of the trade. He knows how to work, but he has no idea of how it will look when it is finished; he has no forethought.

When asked about competition between Negro and white laborers, a union official in Georgia said:

The Negroes around here are not capable of doing the more skilled work. They are often helpers. The men prefer them to white helpers; they are more humble, obedient and strong. They know their place and keep it.

In reply to the same question a union official in Louisiana said:

I never heard of that around here. They don't come in competition on the jobs. The colored man does the heavy work. I have been in construction work all my life, and I have found the white man worthless on manual labor. The floating element of whites who will do that work are worthless. In the first place, you always have to feed them before they will work, and then as soon as your back is turned they run away. Contractors tell me it is very questionable to give white men jobs as common laborers.

The feeling against whites and Negroes working together and the racial stratification in labor appear to be related to the conviction that Negroes are incapable of certain work. A South Carolina editor voiced both sentiments in the same breath:

Colored people don't work in the mills at all. They are not capable of doing mechanical work such as is involved in spinning and weaving. Public sentiment is against the mixture.

THE RATIONALE OF RACIAL ETIQUETTE

What Makes a Situation Socially Significant

A white man reared in Georgia attended a school in New Jersey where there were also a few Negro students. On one occasion when he had been playing basketball with a Negro, he was asked if that did not violate the principle of social equality. He replied, "My wife was not present and I avoided an introduction to him." Being a thoughtful person, he attempted to analyze further the distinction which he automatically drew: With so few Negroes in the section there was little possibility that they would get the ascendancy; they were on sufferance and could be treated as exceptions, curiosities or guests without threatening the supremacy of the whites. They were the recipients and not the demanders of the contact. He would not invite a Negro to his home or introduce him to his wife. In the practical working out of relations between whites and Negroes there could be good friendships, wonderful family loyalties based on common work and trust; but this did not include shaking hands.

The Conventional Use of Titles of Address

The self-consciousness and social evaluation felt by whites in interracial situations is further reflected in the conventions surrounding the use of titles in addressing Negroes. The etiquette is dramatically expressed in the statement of a South Carolina attorney. When asked about etiquette in dealing with Negroes, he replied:

Respect is not what you should feel but what you do feel, and the white man does not respect the colored woman. I would find it difficult to treat the Negro with the same courtesy; it would be embarrassing to me. I would help an old woman across the street, but I would cut off my hand before I'd offer that courtesy to a younger one. I would not tip my hat to one. It would hurt me in the estimate of people I care more about. My personal reaction would be that it was indescribably unpleasant. That's imbued in us by tradition. I wouldn't even want to see a white woman sitting by the side of a servant in a car. I'm conscious of the same prejudice against the Chinese. It must be racial because they have as strong a feeling in the North. Certain animals have certain dislikes and so have people.

There is a modification of the taboo in the case of an executive of a large social organization who said:

I had a very astounding experience with a colored Y.W.C.A. secretary. I was willing to give her the title of Miss before her group in public, but not in private. I called her by her first name one day and she asked me if I wasn't making a mistake. She said the national office said she should be called Miss. I told her the southern women ought to know better how to treat Negroes than the national office. I think she was working for social equality. I have met all kinds, light and dark, but she was the first who wanted social equality.

A lawyer in Virginia explained why he could not bring himself even to use the title "Mr." He said that the fact of not doing it was a recognition of a different social status. Further, he could not think much of his own title after calling a Negro by it. A young middle-class man of Savannah said:

You can't get a white man in the South to call them "Mr." I don't say "Mr." because it makes me feel uncomfortable. I know that's prejudice, but it's instinctive and not reasoning.

It is apparent that individual practices in regard to etiquette vary, and that social constraint varies in intensity in different areas. Thus in the deep South a woman executive of a social organization reported that the compulsion to follow the custom was so strong that she had adopted it, and that Negroes expected nothing else:

You are not allowed to call them—"Mr." The attitude of Negroes down here is different, they would be surprised if you did. They would look at you and drop dead. They would think you were sarcastic.

In the same region, a secretary of the chamber of commerce had no inclination to call a Negro—"Mr.":

If I were inclined to call him—"Mr.", it would ruin me to do it. I have seen it done by some people. It didn't hurt them, but they were independent; it would make me uncomfortable. You must remember that there are generations of that feeling in me, but I do think I am fairly liberal. I played with them as a boy. You see little children five years old bossing them around. They know they are boss.

In a North Carolina city an elderly man of some standing was asked if he used formal titles when addressing Negroes, and he replied:

Invariably. I don't see why people hang on to that. These prejudiced people have never studied the Negro and don't know what he is thinking about. We ought to call them "Mr." and "Mrs." I don't think it has a bad effect on them; that it makes them disrespectful. Not at all. There is a wonderful colored woman at the colored institute who has commanded the respect of all the people. She insists on being called "Mrs." Most people wouldn't stand up for it, but she thinks it helps her in her work. Once we were all to meet in Boston for an educational conference. I asked one of the other men what he was going to call her. He said, "Mary," as he always had. She told me to tell him he had better call her "Mrs. Jones" in Boston or they would think he was familiar with her, calling her by her first name. And he did. I would tip my hat to any colored woman. There are twenty-five or fifty people here who would do the same. When it happens with a colored girl who is not known, people sometimes frown.

A clubwoman in the same area reported that those who don't use formal titles "simply haven't been educated above their prejudice and haven't got over the old servant idea of the Negro."

Other rationalizations of practices of etiquette were offered by a school official in New Orleans, who felt a strong public reaction against his work with Negroes. He said:

The new generation doesn't inherit so much of such prejudice. Contact breaks down some of it also. Of course, the sensible thing is not to shake hands with them. I have no feeling about it. I have done it. Sometimes I don't as a professional rebuff. I don't consider it has any significance except as a thing socially disapproved. If you pinned the average layman down he would say he wouldn't call any nigger—"Mr.", but in practice in some situations he would. He would affect the pose that all niggers look alike, but there would be some he was attached to. They all make exceptions. In our correspondence we sometimes do and sometimes don't, depending on the stenographers. Some of them don't care about doing it. It is only the conventional usual thing. There is no reason for making a point of it. I can call them "Mrs." if they are respectable people, without any qualms.

The Conscious Adjustment of Etiquette and Expectations

It is often pointed out that white people do not find physical contact as such repulsive, but only the social implications of certain types of contact. Then the important factors are the ideas or expectations in the minds of white and colored persons; their conceptions of the roles to be played give significance to the contact. The *definition of the situation* also determines the emotions involved. Thus, shaking a black hand may be very repulsive to a white man if he surmises that the colored man conceives of the situation as implying equality. White informants have reported that the presence of Negroes at dinners and dances may go unnoticed until it is discovered that they are not there as musicians or butlers, but as social equals. When the Negro was chattel property any relation of the most intimate degree could be entered into with impunity. Servants may still approach as close to the person being served as necessary. It is clearly the conception that makes the difference. An editor in North Carolina gave the following illustration of the manner in which the social situation is defined:

I just think we should give them some help like any other underdog. But that doesn't mean that I want to associate with them. It's just uncomfortable physically. I don't know in what way, but I don't like snakes either. It's partly pride. I wouldn't like to associate with someone who is my inferior. The old masters took intercourse as a matter of course: the Negro was their chattel, just like their property. They used the women like they used their bath, to satisfy their senses. Now the association implies, since the Negro is not property but human, that you put yourself on the same level because you can't deny them certain qualities of intellect and personality; thus the association implies a give and take and that means that you have lowered yourself to their level.

Interracial Dining

Eating and drinking together are universally symbols of intimate association. To eat with an outsider is indicative of his acceptance into the social group. Thus, it is not surprising to find that there are prohibitions against such close contacts. In Negro-white communities, especially in the South, the sentiments supporting these taboos are quite strong, as is evident from the remarks of a lady who is prominent in public life in the South:

I would feel that I was a traitor to my traditions, to those of my adopted city, to the Anglo-Saxon in my veins. It's not that I think Anglo-Saxon is the finest in the world, but it is undoubtedly superior to the Negro, and all races should preserve their integrity.

Indeed, this interdict is so generally accepted that the idea of contra vening it hardly occurs to anyone in the South. When a woman in Savannah was told that children evidently do not have race feeling, she quickly responded:

It's acquired from the social atmosphere. The Negro is not only separated by race but also by class. You wouldn't think of asking your Irish servant to sit at your table and eat with you and in the same way you couldn't ask a Negro to your table, because his ancestors have been slaves. It's a class as well as a racial difference. You can't overcome prejudice. Our racial attitude is so emotional. I, for instance, simply couldn't bear the thought of any contact with them. They are personally objectionable to me, most of them. They all have an odor, unless they have more white blood than they have any moral right to have. The president of the Negro college is a fine man, but I couldn't imagine him in my parlor; it is just utterly repulsive to me. This feeling couldn't be understood any place but in this section of the country. It's a hard problem to know how to be fair with them when you feel this way.

In striking contrast with southern white sentiment, in the North interracial dining is normally a personal affair. Those who approve may indulge; those who oppose it may refrain. The situations which focus attention on the issue are occasions of public significance when interracial dining appears to be given tacit approval by public officials. For example, when in the normal social routine of government Congressman DePriest and his wife were invited to the White House, considerable discussion was precipitated throughout the country, but not so much as was occasioned the first time a Negro, Booker T.

Washington, was invited to the White House during the administration of Theodore Roosevelt. This was violently opposed in the South, and there was some opposition in the North.

STEREOTYPES OF NEGRO PERSONALITY AND CHARACTER

The myths surrounding racial types furnish valuable insight into the human side of race relations. Comments relating to the more familiar stereotypes, which are an intimate part of the active thinking on the race question in the South, indicate how the Negro is expected to fit into the race system.

The Faithful Good Negro

One of the stock stereotypes of the racial ideology is the faithful old Negro whose name is traditionally enshrouded with pathos in such songs as "Old Black Joe" and "Uncle Ned." This stereotype is significant because it reflects much of the philosophy of race relations. It pictures the "good nigger" in his place and the sentiment white people have for him. Its representation of the intimate social bonds and rapprochement between the races and the Negro's acceptance of his position stands as a vindication of the social system. When any aspersions are cast upon the southern way of life, this portrayal of "our darkies" may be presented in defense.

The channels through which the waters of human kindness may flow are conventionalized. An upper middle-class Virginian, who spent his youth on a plantation, expounded his racial philosophy as he reminisced about his Negro "mammy":

As a boy I played with colored children. I loved my Negro mammy and kissed her as I would my white mother. The social side has nothing to do with the human side. I wouldn't have gone to school with the colored boys, but I was in sports with them, camped out with them, ate and slept with them. I remember one old friend, Jim, who had been a body guard to an old general. I saw him in back of the house when I was home last—he almost opened his arms to me. I shook his hand, just as familiarly. That's the human side of your old type Negro. If he came to my house he'd go around to the back door; he wouldn't think of going to the front. The South can get along with this type, but the northern type is an anathema to us.

It is not surprising that the Negroes thus characterized are the servants, who are said to be "the most reliable as a group." "His contact with white people has made something of him" is a frequent assertion. Thus in Virginia it was contended:

There is no danger of any friction here. The reason is that the Virginia Negro has been a house Negro. He has been in constant and intimate relation with white folks.

A woman residing in a city in the plantation belt of North Carolina expressed the same idea in explaining the character of a favorite servant:

There was the case of old Aunt Winnie. She was one of the old time ones and the salt of the earth. She had been trained by a white woman. There is a great difference between the old and the younger generation. The old ones carry their hats or take them off when you pass.

The faithful Negro man stands as a guard over white women and protects them. A club woman in New Orleans recalled a familiar myth:

During the Civil War, when the women were left alone in care of the nigras (it is hard for us to say Negroes) they never once betrayed that trust. They were faithful and we owe them something for that.

When a woman in Little Rock was asked if she feared Negro men, she replied, "No," and illustrated her attitude by saying, "Take that old janitor going through the hall. We have known him for years. The club inherited him along with the building. He is so faithful, he never leaves the place." With such a person one may be quite free. Furthermore, it is recognized that they, like all servants, learn how to manage their masters.

The type is also a proponent of "good race relations." Out of his mouth flows the white man's knowledge of how to get along in this world. Frequently a Negro leader assumes the role imputed to him by white people. In a Georgia town the secretary of the chamber of commerce reported:

I once went to a colored community to speak. There was a pretty smart man there and he got up to give a talk. He said he was going to tell them the difference between a white man and a nigger. "Brothers," he said, "if a white man walks down the street with a big cigar in his mouth, you know that looks natural, but if a colored man walks down the street with a cigar in his mouth, you know there's nothing behind that cigar but a black face. You must remember all the time it takes to develop civilization." He was a smart duck. I met another nigger once. He was a preacher and had won all the official honors in school, but he was most humble and knew his place and always took his hat off when he came in.

Of another such person in North Carolina it was said:

> We have a Negro college with a colored man at the head. He is really superior to Booker T. Washington and I don't know a more charming man. He is tolerant; makes no assumptions for himself. He teaches them that there are certain things which they have and they must develop them and not be imitators. He is a lovable leader. If we weren't so prejudiced, we would think he should associate with the educated people in town.

One of the things white people appreciate about such individuals is that they do not embarrass their white friends. If the two groups must meet together, "they don't presume anything but sit off to themselves."

The Servile Personality

Some informants noted that Negroes who "stay in their places" develop a servile personality corresponding with the attitudes they exhibit before white people. A New Orleans school official, who claimed to be liberal in his relations with Negroes, said:

> The Negro has an innate sense of courtesy that is quite remarkable. Maybe he has had to develop it. I find them very satisfactory people to work with. They are anxious to please and they will do anything they think you want them to do. There are very few unpleasant occasions.

The superintendent of Negro education in a southern state also noted this type and gave some insight into the social origins of the behavior pattern:

> I had a letter not long ago from a man who had been brought up on a slave farm. He signed himself "Your obedient servant." I am more or less conscious of this kind of man, who feels he owes more or less obeisance and respect to me because I belong to the race that at one time owned his forebears.

To some business and professional persons who have official and commercial relations with Negroes it appears that they sometimes overdo the ritual observance. Some young people imbued with the intemperate spirit of the efficiency expert find that business and racial etiquette are incompatible. Furthermore, those who are acquainted with the "new Negroes" suspect that the Negro is currying favors and honors. An attorney in a Virginia city said:

> My experience with the permanent Negro here is that they are too submissive rather than too officious. A couple of years ago there was a move for a Negro hospital. I prepared the brief for them. The brilliant

Negro president of the aid society impressed everyone with his very submissive, pleading manner.

The editor of a Richmond newspaper declared:

I think it is pitiful to see how submissive some of them are. There was a colored real estate man came up to see us; he stumbled over several words. Then he would apologize and say he couldn't pronounce those big words. Now I know that man was educated and besides a word like "actuary" is very common in his business. He was just flattering us by implying that we were more intelligent than he was. I think it's too bad when a situation develops that kind of manhood, so that they just try to please the white man.

Assumption of the servile attitude has a pronounced effect upon the Negro's social status, according to the observation of a merchant in Portland, Maine:

The very fact that the Negro realizes that the whites look on him as an inferior has a tendency to keep him there. A man will live up to the expectations of the best class of people. Nobody expects anything of the Negro and so he lives up to that.

"The Bad Nigger"

The greatest menace to race relations in the South is the Negro who "breaks loose and runs amuck." A North Carolina businessman said:

Disturbances are usually caused when some wild nigger gets wild and does something white men won't stand, and then he loses his head. We don't berate the nigger much for ordinary crimes; we expect servants to take things from us.

"The White Nigger"

The feeling back of the dogmatic conviction that racial mixture is socially dangerous and evil, the interdict against intermarriage, and ostracism of those who mix are extended to include persons of mixed blood. This sentiment appears to be the unconscious motive back of the widespread defamation of mulattoes. A southern social worker stated it thus: "The white people resent the mulatto because they know he is their wrong. That has built up a wall of antagonism." Frequently the paternalistic southern gentlemen, who assert that they have a high regard for the "real nigger," react strongly against the cross-breed who does not fit into the traditional stereotype. Pointing out the evils of miscegenation a North Carolina banker said, "They spoiled a good nigger; he's tainted. The crossing of two races has a bad effect; it's the most unfortunate thing about the past race relations."

Many informants recognized the marginal position of the mulatto, who differs from the Negro in looks and actions but, worst of all, presents a serious dilemma in the treatment accorded Negroes. When asked about the difference between mulattoes and blacks, a Little Rock attorney explained:

As a rule the black nigger is ordinarily a real nigger. He hasn't any exalted ideas of his own importance, and he is not uppity. The lighter ones have enough white blood to resent what they are or are ambitious to be something else. They talk back to you, or dispute your word, argue with you in a way that any good white servant wouldn't do. They carry a chip on their shoulder; they are looking for insults and slights because they are niggers. It's their general air that irritates you more than it would from a white person because you know you have more sense than they have.

The opinion that "mulattoes do not fit into the standard pattern" was concurred in by several informants. Thus a United States congressman from the South declared:

If you made a study of the younger generation of the colored race that are clamoring for social equality, you would find they had white blood in them. They think they should have white recognition. With the older generation we had very little dissension.

It is a fairly general assumption that the mulattoes are responsible for much of the disharmony in race relations and are the leaders of such "radical" organizations as the National Association for the Advancement of Colored People.

The Northern Negro

Few members of the "opposite race" bring down the scorn which southern white people hold for the "northern nigger." He is the epitome of what ought not to be, the counterconception of the accepted ideal Negro; and some Southerners say they cannot bring themselves to deal with a northern Negro in the role he assumes. One Southerner said:

When I was at the University of Illinois there were seven or eight niggers. It was quite a shock to me. But I didn't have to sit with them. One day I drove my car to a garage and I asked a nigger there if he could drive my car back to the campus for me. He said he couldn't drive my car anywhere, in such a snotty way. I told him he could at least keep a civil tongue in his head. He made some other remark. That's what they're like up North. No white employee would talk that way to you. If they take a chip around on their shoulder, they're unbearable.

The following characterization was given by a man from Ohio who had lived in Fayetteville, North Carolina, for twenty years:

The northern Negro class, if you give them an inch, will take a mile. They are a little arrogant and want to push themselves forward; want to run for office. I told them it had taken the white race two thousand years to get where they are and the colored folks were getting in too big a hurry.

It is also interesting to note the Southerner's reaction to situations where Negroes move through society unrestrained by racial mores and conventions. A newspaper man in a town in Georgia related the following incident to illustrate how "northern Negroes" get out of place:

I lived in Boston for several years. I used to eat my breakfast in a cafeteria. One morning a colored man came in and out of a whole row of empty seats, took the one next to mine. I got up and moved further. It's not social subjection but social separation that ought to be encouraged and aided in every possible development on all lines. I believe in encouraging their businesses, professions, lodges and churches. One of the greatest means of assuring friendliness between the races is ownership of property. It gives them a feeling of responsibility. They should be encouraged to the limit to build up their own social life of a high and proper sort, but the line between the races must be drawn, and the best Negro leaders agree to that. They realize that lack of social mixing doesn't imply inequality or inferiority.

In the South, where a racial accommodation has been worked out, the customary has become confused with the natural. It is assumed by some that any other system of relations would be un-natural and even sinful. In many instances it is evident that the social personalities of the informants have become so thoroughly integrated with the prevailing system that their sentiments and atti-tudes would be incompatible with a system of equality. Their habits of thought are based on the prevailing social structure and customs and are impervious to radical change.

The Outside Radical

Some whites consider Negro "radicals," "from the outside" or "from the North," especially dangerous. Indeed, it is quite symbolic that white people generally believe that any Negro who protests against the race system is "from the outside," for local Negroes are thought to be satisfied. It is said that respectable and competent professional men are the real Negro leaders, and "these leaders without exception are not striving for social equality or intermixture." In some places "outside leaders" are the subject of grave consideration and are given special attention. Thus, in a North Carolina city a newsman remarked:

We have no friction, especially on the Negro side, except when outsiders come in and begin to try social equality. We have a Negro paper here edited by someone who does not belong here; he is constantly crying for Negro representation on school boards, the chamber of commerce, the police department, and for equal treatment in the theaters. They have got some, but they want more. The better class of Negroes don't feel that discontentment, but the ignorant Negro gets his mind influenced. The white people have discussed it on the inside as to how to offset that paper's influence. We don't want to turn the man out of town, but both sides agree he does more harm than good. We have a fine type of Negro here and have confidence in them. The best friend the Negro has is the white man here, notwithstanding all the propaganda sent out. The dangerous element is in the radical from "the outside."

The "Rising Negro"

Many of the beliefs concerning the younger and better educated Negroes and the resentment expressed toward them are typical of attitudes manifested toward the newcomer, the parvenu, wherever he is found. Those who are "stepping up" may be admired as individuals, but as a group their entrance into higher social classes is resented. Such a feeling apparently prompted the following statement by a housewife in Georgia:

I never really tried to analyze my feelings. I want them to advance, but what will come of it, I don't know. It makes them better mannered and behaved, but the Negro men are much easier to live with than the women. They get a sort of attitude, especially the lighter ones, of trying to impress you with their equality. It is a disagreeable attitude of assumed poise; you know they're not really that way. The men seem to be more agreeable. Yet my experience has been so limited that I can't really say.

There is also evidence that in the minds of upper-class whites the "rising Negro" and the "climbing poor whites" are being bracketed together.

These attitudes should not obscure the fact that there probably would be unanimous agreement that Negroes have progressed since emancipation, and white people everywhere take pride in the im-

provement of the race. Frequently an informant frankly recognized
the portents of present trends toward equality, and some accepted
the logical conclusions with equanimity:

There is a more instinctive feeling among the whites, though even that
is less than it was. The individual makes a difference. The average Negro
of thirty years ago was a different looking creature. Now he is better
dressed, more educated, less of a mere animal type; he has improved in
appearance. Whether his mental and moral make-up is improving too
is a question.

The "Modern Nigger"

The "modern nigger" was described in more detail by an attorney
in Little Rock:

There is an old ice man here who is really respectful and feels his
place. I pay him to do some of my business for me. He is a smart old
man. The typical modern nigger is not worth killing. I don't know why
they got that way. Some of them are black, so it's not just the white
blood. The modern nigger has bought an auto for twenty-five dollars;
made a little easy money somewhere and thinks he's about it. They have
no feeling of responsibility; they want the white person's privileges
without their obligation. I don't object to them having nice things, but
they wouldn't be satisfied with the finest theater in the world if it was
for niggers only. They don't want things for themselves. They are like
social climbers; they want to be with white people. Some of these niggers
would give a million dollars to walk down the main street with a white
woman. They have business and professional equality, what more do
they want? Of course, you are a Northerner, you wouldn't ever understand how we feel.

The executive of a welfare department in Charleston gave some
additional insight into the emotion aroused by a Negro who escapes
from the traditional role of the slave:

Attitudes here vary with the different groups. There is an interracial
committee the members of which are considered by their opponents as
almost erratic in their sympathy for the Negro. That's because we have
left over here the feeling the Negro is still a slave, and when he is a
slave he is in his place. People are sympathetic with him and very kind,
but they just "see red" when they see the "new Negro." The literature
about him is loathsome to them. The Negro's place is where he was.
They think he should have education, but he is not capable of more than
a grade school training, and that more makes him no good. I believe in
giving them education and advantages as high as they can go, but don't
force them to take it; let them develop gradually.

An architect in Savannah distinguished the two types as follows:

There are two groups of Negroes, one is the younger element with a little education; they haven't the stability and moral character to carry their education; they are obstreperous and obnoxious. The old ones born before the Civil War, like my old nurse, are different; white people are very kind to that class. They are quiet, ambitious, and have the same high tradition as white people.

A common complaint is that "the younger generation doesn't know how to treat white people." Thus, a Virginia editor remarked:

The older ones are content to let things go on, but the younger ones are not. To illustrate, the Negro domestic's educated daughter demands to be called "Mrs." The old woman would never have questioned it. That is largely the outgrowth of the superintendent of schools who calls them "Mr." and "Mrs."

Frequently one hears that the new freedom is taken for license; and white people are prone to interpret any behavior not in conformity with conventional etiquette as rudeness and insolence. A former mayor of Charleston remarked, "The average nigger who is impolite thinks rudeness and insolence are evidences of racial superiority."

The "educated niggers" also belong in this class of "modern niggers." This stereotype not only symbolizes the resentment against the upstart, the one who breaks caste, and the parvenu, but epitomizes the orthodox dogmas on Negro mentality and temperament. A corollary of the tenet that Negroes do not develop mentally states that "education ruins him" and creates a superficial person. Thus, a banker in Raleigh said:

The educated Negro wants the shine, the uniform, the plume in his hats and the parade. They are not capable of working together; there is too much prejudice between them.

The judgment of a businessman in Macon, Georgia, against the educated Negro was much more severe:

As a general proposition, the educated nigger is offensive. He is impudent. He will knock you off the sidewalk. It is just like the Negro congressman saying, "If those boys I sent to the Academy fail, next time I will appoint bigger and blacker ones." Of course, this is an exaggerated example. There are some fine educated ones. As a general proposition education improves everyone. The impudence is a step in nigger evolution. He is human and we should do the best we can for him. Somebody has to take the manual position and we'd better train him to do it as well as possible.

Another indictment of educated and middle-class Negroes is that they exploit their people and are not a credit to the race. The manager of a machine shop in Newport News said:

You will find the middle class, educated Negro thinks he should live on the poor, ignorant Negro and take all kinds of advantage over him. If you could keep the educated Negro from exploiting the ignorant ones the race would be better off in the South. We get better support among the white people than the colored. We have only had two outlaw meetings, and both of those were caused by the middle-class Negro. They get impudent.

THE SEX TABOO

It is evident that one of the most potent stereotypes supporting the interracial taboos is the symbol of white womanhood. The strength of this symbol must be emphasized, for it underlies the whole ideology concerning miscegenation, intermarriage, and amalgamation, and forms the point of departure and the rationale of interracial violence and white supremacy.

The style of thinking may be illustrated by the following remarks of a policeman in a Georgia city:

In the South a lady is next to God. It's God, woman, and country with us and no niggers are going to touch our woman. I seen niggers in Kansas City, dirty, nasty men from the fertilizer factories, shoving the girls out of the way on the streetcar to get to their seats. If I could have set that car down in Georgia I would have been content.

The last remark is typical of reactions to the disregard of "caste" patterns. Resentment of race association is denoted in the reference to contacts of black men and white women. The president of a woman's club in a North Carolina city expressed the sentiment against such contacts. She said, "Horror and indignation is the first thought in any white mind when a Negro touches a white woman." Everywhere one hears of the absolute sanctions back of the taboo. A newspaper editor in a South Carolina town said:

That's the one thing the South is solid on, and I don't believe it will ever change. It's as good as a Negro's life is worth to look at a white woman in a certain way; he might as well snap his fingers at death as touch a white woman. The Negroes here know that if they look at a white woman or touch her, their life is as good as gone. That is one thing we will not tolerate. An outbreak could happen any time if a Negro did that.

In the same town a lawyer remarked:

One thing you might as well know; the South will not stand for anything like social equality. Any Negro who crosses that line is as good as
dead around this part of the county. We don't have any trouble; we get
along very peaceably, because they understand that. If they didn't, that's
where the trouble would start. We have a high regard for womanhood,
if not for the personal case, at least we treasure the idea. Any idea of a
Negro touching a white woman simply makes us want to kill him. I
would myself.

The feeling is not confined to the South, however. In the City of
Brotherly Love the manager of a movie theater declared:

When I see the "Our Gang Comedies" where that nigger gets fresh
with the white girl, it makes me boil. The idea of a nigger touching a
white girl!

The Sin of Miscegenation

In dealing with the nature of ideologies and the role of beliefs, it
must be noted that some beliefs are symbolic and are to be understood with reference to what they symbolize rather than as exact
blueprints of personal or social action. Thus, while miscegenation
continues, the racial orthodoxy proscribes such contact and from
the point of view of the doctrines it is sinful. These beliefs, however, are only a reflection of the strong interdict against intermarriage and the latent fear of amalgamation. Under the intense heat
of the puritanical racial mores interracial sexual contacts are placed
under a ban—albeit a theological one which merely preserves the
principle without preventing the practice.

The rationalizations offered in explanation of past and present
miscegenation throw considerable light upon the folkways and mores
of the interracial situation. An attorney in Richmond said:

The southern man has always held his wife and sweetheart in a place
of high devotion. He has been stern with himself where they are concerned. And then they take it out on colored women. Colored women are
more passionate, more satisfactory physically. Then there is also the
factor of isolation from one's social group. I once met a woman from
Louisiana who was very beautiful and lovely. She said she hardly ever
saw her husband. I found out he had a plantation and seven or eight
mulatto mistresses. He said he respected his wife so highly but for pleasure he had more beautiful mulattoes, and did his drinking and cursing
with them. The South just accepts that as the nature of men. They are
brought up to think so. When Thomas Jefferson planned the University,
he established boardinghouses with regular mulatto women around the

campus. Now boardinghouses are very rare. Then each man had one or more women of his own. Sometimes the colored women really love their men; they would die for them; but sometimes they compromise them. The boys learned to use colored women from their fathers and other men and thought nothing of it. That is changing now. The younger generation is more intelligent, and the question of social equality puts intimacy on a different plane from when they were chattels and property. ￫

A clubwoman in a North Carolina city was asked, "If there is so much racial difference, how do you account for the mulatto?" She replied:

I don't account for it, it's a disgrace, the fault of white people, a terrible blot on our name, and not to be excused for one minute. I don't know if it is going on now or not; I wouldn't be surprised. There's no reason for it now. I don't see as many light children now as I used to. I should think it was most repulsive. I don't see how a decent white man could lower himself to that extent. I think the Negroes themselves are developing some pride against that. That's a disgrace now. You can't trace it back. When people lived on plantations they were isolated and there was not a great deal for the young people to do. Satan always finds some work for idle hands you know, and I suppose that's how it happened.

An upper middle-class businessman from Georgia, when asked about the origin of mulattoes replied, "Oh, those are the sins of the older generations. That doesn't happen now, except with a few debased people."

Under the prevailing social system miscegenation not only leads to an increase of Negroes but it is regarded as degrading to the white persons involved. According to the popular judgment, "the white woman who engages in such relations steps out of her place"; but in the case of white men it is surmised that "their animal nature gets the best of them." The distinction is significant, for it is by means of this bit of casuistry that the social logic can be preserved while a deeply rooted custom continues. It is also affirmed that there is no real affection between the white man and the colored woman: "It's a matter of sex, not . . . love."

The Interdict against Intermarriage

Intermarriage of Negroes and whites was universally and completely proscribed by the persons interviewed for this study. Apparently, from whatever premise the informants started or whatever the grounds of their interpretation, they always led up to the accepted orthodoxy. Evidently there is no end to speculation on this grave issue; but here again the fashions of thought are so conventionalized and the obsessions so compelling that the collective mind runs in a groove. However, the rationale of the taboo varies in its complexity and in the sanctions that enforce it. Thus in the South, where such alliances are incompatible with the racial system, all the sentiments, attitudes, and beliefs operate to prevent them. In this culture area the proscription involves not merely a "climate of opinion" but a total ideology incorporating moral perspectives. This explains why the interdict is interpreted in terms of cultural values and theology. A minister in a Georgia city declared:

The white race has never recognized the propriety of intermarriage. It's a sin to marry a Negro or to mix with them, just as it's a sin to peddle dope instead of teaching school. Such a man throws away his opportunities and debases himself by failing to use his opportunity as a white man and sinks to a lower standard. He allows his creative capacity, his traditions, his descendants to be corrupted. He pronounces a curse on all his descendants. He no longer has pure white blood in his veins. He has produced a mule in the human family.

Usually the doctrine of white supremacy and the avoidance of Negro-white intermarriage are closely associated in the minds of informants. It appears that in the racial ideology identity of race stands as the last bulwark in support of the status quo. A member of the upper class in Savannah declared:

It is just impossible for white people to associate with them. It's just racial antipathy. Of course I have analyzed it many times. The white race is determined to be a white race and it's utterly impossible to make the colored race their equal or superior. Mixed blood means degeneracy. The pure Anglo-Saxon is the strongest in the world. If you would mix it with any race, especially a race that has been for centuries savages, you can't imagine the mixture would bring any helpful results. If you lower the standards of the white race by blood mixture, you can't maintain the same standards of living.

The same conception was voiced by informants in the North. Here, however, the beliefs are less orthodox; and the rationalization is couched less in terms of the traditional stereotypes and more in terms of scientific dogmas. In Boston an elderly newspaperman who was active in humanitarian work said:

I can't go so far as to believe in intermarriage. I think that is unwise. It is a great tragedy for the children. It is not race but the social environment that makes it difficult. There is such strong feeling against it; that criticism is so difficult to meet. It might cause unhappiness between the two. They would have to be big people to live through it. There is great prejudice among the colored people against intermarriage. My laundress says no decent person—colored or white—would intermarry. I heard someone say it was a theological problem. She said she had no prejudice, but she wouldn't entertain one in her home. I wouldn't have any feeling about that.

The comments of a high-school principal in Salem, New Jersey, show evidence of conflict between the melting pot philosophy and the conventional beliefs about the Negro as an element that cannot be assimilated. His opinion was thus expressed:

I am not qualified to make a statement as to the effects of intermixture, but from the general idea of America as a melting pot it would seem that mixture is advantageous. That might be different with races so widely different. I would think the mixture gave a better grade. Intermixture is not desirable or wanted by either black or white. The social consequences are undesirable. What mixture there is is not a case of admiration or any real motive but sex. Personally, if I were confronted with it, I would not want my daughter to marry a German, an Englishman, a Japanese, or any foreigner, or a Negro. Their social standards are so different. My feeling would be stronger against the Negro than the Japanese. The color element is great. The consequences are more difficult for mulatto stock.

The same point of view was expressed by a man in Portland, Maine:

I object to it because they belong to two different races. Even in the South, if a Negro married a white and the children were octoroons they would be despised by the Negroes. They are as averse to intermingling as whites. I have travelled South with the Governor of the State. We had close contact with many. We found that the light colored person was despised by their own blacks; they called them mongrels. It is not good to intermarry. It is the same way with Jews and Christians. They are a different race. Their characteristics are different, their likes and dislikes, their nature. There wouldn't be so much objection to intermingling if it weren't for prejudice. They are made aware of the general difference of feeling, and their children suffer for it. It has always been that way and it always will be. Education, making better citizens, living together, and then less and less racial differences will change that opinion. I don't think intermarriage will ever be widely prevalent. The difference in looks is a constant reminder of that thing. In this section they are as nearly eradicated as in any section. This is due to the very pleasant relations here. There are several very faithful, honest Negroes here. Sometimes they are as shiftless as the whites, but mine are nice help. My trip South didn't influence me to disfavor them.

A public health commissioner in New Jersey was close to skepticism on the matter of intermarriage. He was of the opinion that it would not be harmful to children; on the contrary, he had heard it was beneficial to them. Then he told of the case of a local family to illustrate the natural outcome:

One boy married a white girl. They had twelve children, all of whom married white people. They were all fine specimens, both boys and girls, and strong. The girls all married respectable white people. You can't prevent those cases. I wouldn't want to speak of it; I haven't studied enough about it. But you know you can't keep the sun from shining.

A publicity man in Boston represented the rare instance in which a person revolts against the most sacred conventions of his culture. He said:

Of course discussion of the race problem always gets down to the problem of intermixture. The arguments always come down to that. I try to take a sane and civilized attitude toward intermarriage. When they ask me would I want my daughter to marry a Negro, I say, "Damn right if he were a fine man." As a father I would tell her as an intelligent individual what the penalties would be. Yet I know all those considerations would not matter in comparison with the immediate fact that you loved a person.

THE SOCIAL BONDS BETWEEN NEGROES AND WHITES

In defending the racial system against attack, white informants frequently refer to the web of intimate social bonds that have grown up between the races. The allusions are significant in that they indicate the values running through the system. They reveal the general conception of ideal relations, but in indicating that there is a racial rapprochement and that the Negro accepts his place, unconsciously betray the "false social consciousness" underlying the ideology. These fictions are intended to show how natural the system is and how smoothly it operates.

White Paternalism

Within the biracial social order, as white people conceive it, there is a certain amount of reciprocity. While the colored man looks up to the white man, the two are bound by a web of human relations, and the white man looks out for the colored man. The philosophy of good race relations extols *noblesse oblige*. As described by white informants, the system is a patriarchal one. Many believe that Negroes are satisfied with their lot and accept the social status assigned them: If they were not satisfied, "they wouldn't respect

and love the white man the way they do"; and "If they weren't satisfied to remain as slaves, they would have risen up and massacred
their masters." Informants in the South and North alike frequently
remark that "people in the South know how to get along with the
Negro." This belief is imputed to Negroes—a corollary of the
assumption that they are contented in the South. In reviewing their
record in handling the Negro many Southerners are satisfied that
they have worked out the best accommodation and should be left
to deal with the problem unaided.

The Rapprochement between the Races in the South

The logical implication of such ideas is that a rapprochement has
been worked out between the white and colored people in the South,
and that a mutually acceptable set of relations binds them together.
Conflict is thus reduced, and "the race problem is solved" or "is being
worked out":

Things social just don't occur to the right-thinking white Southerner
and the Negroes don't want equality.

Again it was said:

We never have any trouble here because the Negro absolutely knows
his place, just as the white man does, and neither oversteps. You just
have to live here to understand that. There is only one way to handle
them. Feed them, work them, and make them stay in their place.

THE TRANSMISSION AND DIFFUSION OF THE ORTHODOX IDEOLOGY

One of the most revealing aspects of the racial orthodoxy is the
process of informal education by which the tradition is communicated
to the young and to newcomers. This is an intellectual phenomenon
that is no longer dependent upon primary social experience. Evidently
the ideology has taken on a semi-independent character and now
exerts a compelling influence upon all who come into its vortex. The
preceding survey has indicated some of the manifold ways in which
social evaluations may be affected.

Even the rationale of the social system has become customary and
appears natural. A minister in Winston-Salem said, "That is our
tradition. We just absorb it." In Savannah it was reported that
"it's acquired from the social atmosphere." Some of the media by
which the pervasive beliefs are borne along and transmitted were
suggested by a professor at one of the southern universities:

I have a great respect and affection for Negroes, partly traditional
and inherited, partly simply sentimentality. I heard stories from my

father about his slaves which were part of my general consciousness
before I was aware of having any consciousness. I had a Negro companion as a boy of whom I was very fond. The literary tradition, the
old functions and traditions of the ante-bellum South may have much
to do with it.

The general tone of the traditional plantation stories, which form
a conspicuous part of the folk heritage of the South, upholds the
"caste" order.

The unconscious process by which the tradition is absorbed was
alluded to by a professional woman in Montclair, New Jersey, who
said, "I have always felt a sense of superiority to them. I got it
from my father. It was in the very atmosphere of our home." The
logical premises of the social philosophy are assumed unconsciously.
Debate and discussion are not a prominent part of the process by
which the situation is defined. Commenting on his experiences upon
first going to the North, a southern sociologist said:

They wanted to talk about the Negro question, and it was one which
I hadn't given any thought to. I came to realize the significance of certain
phrases which I had always accepted without question. It made me conscious of the race problem as I had never been before. I had accepted it
as one does the sunshine—a fact not to be quarreled with. It was the
traditional southern viewpoint, when cornered, to put the question,
"Would you want your daughter to marry a Negro?"

The racial mores are the accepted standards of behavior and
beliefs that are not subject to discussion. The mores constitute
the way things are and the way people feel and think, and they
have their own *raison d'être*. Obviously, people in the South pick up
the mores having to do with race just as they do other phases of the
moral order. This is why some informants think of the racial mores
as part of "everything sacred" and speak of conformity to racial
customs as "adherence to the social religion." To newcomers they
say, "You will begin to feel about it as we do if you stay here."

Yankees who come South soon feel the pressure of opinion. One
who was residing in Fayetteville, North Carolina, said:

You gradually work into the habits of the place where you live. There
will never be a change in the South. They teach their children their attitude, and it is born and bred in them. It will take generations to change.
There is no crumbling of the color line.

There is evidence which suggests that even the radical social reformer
succumbs to the pressure of opinion. A social worker from the North

working in Richmond was convinced that "we should do something about it," but she felt compelled to comply with the rituals:

One has to adjust to the situation here. In Toledo I knew a colored attorney whom we occasionally had to dinner. I couldn't think of that here. There might be one or two Negroes here whom we would like to ask to the house but we couldn't think of doing it. I am willing to admit that I feel a little different toward the Negro since I have been South. With my mind I feel the same way. Yet I have a good deal of sympathy with the southern person who is afraid to give him the same opportunity because there are so many of them. I know it is illogical and emotional but there it is.

Many of the opinions and attitudes expressed by people in the North suggest that some of the orthodox southern beliefs have been diffused through that area. This is not surprising and, indeed, is to be expected since people in both areas have shared so much of the tradition and experience out of which the ideology has grown. Furthermore, migration of Negroes to northern cities has brought Yankees firsthand experience, which is reflected in the interviews quoted previously. This face-to-face contact, however, is not essential for the diffusion of the ideology; for symbols and beliefs migrate as well as people. The literature dealing with the Negro provides an experience world for persons who have never seen Negroes and communicates the general ideological conception, the pseudo understanding, and the feeling of "acquaintance with," which make the folk beliefs seem all the more real.

The ubiquitous color line in the United States thus traces a varied and complex pattern. It is less often seen and defined than discreetly or defiantly sensed by Negroes, and imperiously or indefinitely felt by whites. Irrational and intangible in many relationships, devoid of defensible logic in a theoretically democratic society, it is, nevertheless, one of the most positive realities in American life. It is uniquely, persistently, and universally an American institution.

PART II
BEHAVIORAL RESPONSE OF NEGROES TO SEGREGA-
TION AND DISCRIMINATION

Chapter XI

PERSONALITY AND THE RACIAL ROLE

The foregoing chapters have attempted to present objectively the formal institutions, social conventions, legal codes, and ideology supporting racial segregation and discrimination in three broad regions of the United States. Attention may now be directed to some of the subjective aspects of these racial codes as expressed or betrayed in the personal attitudes, sentiments, and behavior of Negroes. In the first place, several important factors which condition the responses of Negroes to racial institutions and practices must be taken into account. These factors include: (a) the regional and cultural setting, (b) the social stratification of the Negro population, (c) the situational factors involved in a given response, and (d) the basic personality type of the Negro involved in a given racial situation.

The attitudes and behavior of Negroes vary in a general way according to the cultural region in which they reside. As has been shown, there are marked regional differences in the racial institutions, and one would expect responses to be influenced seriously by the variety and intensity of types of racial segregation and discrimination. Negroes as well as whites grow up with conceptions of their role in a given racial setting, and they tend to act accordingly; but Negroes within each of the areas vary widely in their attitudes and behavior, and this suggests consideration of other factors such as social class, age, sex, education, appearance, occupation, and degree of intimacy.

Social class is a major factor contributing to differentiation of responses to segregation and discrimination; and some consideration should therefore be given to the structure of the Negro population and some of the influences responsible for the stratification into more or less self-conscious and recognizable groups.

The Negro *upper class* is made up of persons having at least two generations of established family organization, education, a profession or its equivalent, property and economic security, and a family tradition that associates the individual with some real or assumed past distinction. Important criteria distinguishing the members of this class include their conception of themselves as members of an exclusive class and the recognition of their superiority by other Negroes and, to some extent, by whites. The members are exclusive and meticulous in their intraracial associations and are sometimes referred to by other Negroes as "clannish"; actually they are closer to persons of like class in various parts of the country than to Negroes of another class in their own locality.

The recognition of these upper-class Negroes is often freighted with sentiments intended to disparage and, in effect, minimize the social distance. Derogatory statements of other Negroes about the value of education for Negroes and about the ability of the race to "stick together" are frequently protests against the superior class position. For example, a lower-class woman declared that "educated niggers is just educated fools"; and a lower-class man complained that "you can't get colored people together." The latter added:

You see in our race it is a lot of big men who think they are better than anybody else, and they don't want to look at you unless you're in their class. The only way to get them together is to put them in the graveyard. . . . The doctors and things like that think they're better than anybody here, but I think I'm good as anybody even if he's so high up he's in a aeroplane.

Lloyd Warner and his associates have suggested a useful and important horizontal distinction in the vertical classification: on the one hand, the upper-class "respectable" and, on the other hand, the upper-class "shady," the latter including persons who achieve the semblance of upper-class status through "conspicuous consumption" based on incomes from less respectable sources.[1]

The Negro *upper middle class* has most of the characteristics of the upper class but the members lack either a family history of some prestige or a profession or enough wealth for security. In this class may be found business executives, public-school administrators and teachers, some insurance executives, some professional persons, social work executives, and the like. Members of this class stress the possession of the external marks of "culture and refinement"; they make much of receiving special privileges which are interpreted as public recognition of their social position and inherent quality. They are extremely sensitive, both to the subtler forms of racial

[1] See especially Allison Davis, *et al., Deep South: A Social Anthropological Study of Caste and Class* (Chicago: University of Chicago Press, 1941).

discrimination practiced by whites and to the behavior and appearance of lower-class Negroes which influence general opinion about the Negro group of which they are, inescapably, a part.

The Negro *middle class* is made up of persons whose main characteristic is an active desire to be recognized as "respectable." In this group are skilled artisans, successful hairdressers, some ministers, clerical and white-collar workers, postal and other routine government workers, Pullman porters, and occasionally, more prosperous personal and domestic service workers, such as barbers. Their characteristics include homeownership, church membership, and regular employment. Awareness of class is evident in the statement of one man who thought the upper-class Negroes should build factories to give other Negroes employment: "Instead," he said, "if you go to one of them for a job the first thing they ask you is what do your parents do, and if they aren't lawyers or doctors or something like that, you won't get a thing." In this class are many of the self-conscious Negroes who patronize Negro businesses as a matter of race loyalty and condemn other Negroes, upper and lower, for not doing the same. A Negro man of this class commented upon the lack of race loyalty of some members of his race:

I believe in my race and do everything I can to help any of them along. I never buy anything from a white man I can get from a colored man. Everybody don't do it, though. Not everybody in this block buys papers from colored boys, but [referring to an upper middle-class Negro] Professor —— across the street, he gets his from a white boy. He's making his living off the colored people and gives the white boys his money.

This same person told of a Negro undertaker who contracted with a white builder to erect a large new house. When he was ready to build, some Negroes reminded him that "his business would suffer if he ignored the competent Negro contractors." The undertaker was forced to "pay off" the white contractor and deal with a Negro.

There is contempt in this class for the Negroes in the lower social brackets who have the protection of whites in their class resentments. A middle-class woman commented upon this type of situation:

There was an old nigger woman—you know some folks are colored and some are just niggers—she was a nigger woman and if she had occasion to wait on you she'd just throw the things out at you and cuss at you if you didn't like it, and if you said anything to her the white boss would defend her.

This class often accepts segregation but resents discrimination and makes much of the unfairness and injustice of this discrimination.

The *lower middle class* is one of the largest in numbers both in the South and in the North. It is made up of tenants and renters, unskilled and semiskilled workers, the more secure domestic and personal servants, train and store porters, day laborers, and others in similar occupations. The distinction between this class and the *lower class* is in the matter of standards: lower middle-class standards are considerably lower than those of the other middle classes, but there is ambition to improve, which is not found in the lower class. Lower middle-class Negroes have little education but are anxious about the education of their children. A common boast is that they "stay out of trouble" or "stay out of jail." They generally seek the associations and consolations of the church and, in religious language, condemn the social and religious looseness of the lower class. A good example of the lower middle-class Negro is the man who boasted that he was a "self-make" man. He said, "There never was a dollar spent on me in education in my life." But he had his estimate of the lower-class Negroes:

You know darkies got to have a boss over them. They will follow if there's a good boss, but when it comes to real principle, not ten in a hundred ever gives it a thought. They are getting just like the children of Israel. . . . You turn a nigger out of church now, and he just like a rabbit in a briar patch.

In referring to some of the behavior traits of the lower class, both Negro and white, another southern Negro from the lower middle class remarked:

These niggers here got Jim Crow pistols. They won't kill nobody but a nigger. If a white man come up, he'll drop it and say, "yes, sir, boss," and do anything that white man tells him to do.

Speaking of the religious traits of the lower class, he continued:

They ain't got no sense. Now they took that dead woman to church last night, and there was the biggest crowd following the corpse around; if it had been something uplifting you couldn't get them together. They stayed in that church all day.

In the North this class is represented by the hard-working, unskilled and semiskilled laborers, many of whom are now labor union members and voters. The small-time racketeers and policy handlers appear in this group, on the "shady" side.

In the South this class accepts segregation and much of what is regarded as discrimination by upper-class Negroes; but economic discrimination frequently causes reactions.

The *lower class* is another large group made up of rural and urban unskilled workers, with little or no education, and a low level of living, as a result of both low economic status and low social standards. In this class are the chronic relief cases and those who are unemployed because of lack of skill and general ability. In the South in particular they are economically dependent upon the whites and frequently accept this as normal. Members of this class accept segregation and are frequently resentful of the "pretentiousness" of the upper Negro classes. An undeveloped appreciation of the professional abilities of members of their own race is the result of long dependence upon whites and acceptance of white value judgments. One southern urban woman of this class said:

A nigger ain't got sense enough to be a doctor. He'll come in pattin' his foot, "uh huh, uh, huh" and whining like a cat.

The servants who gossip about Negro life to their white employers are in this class, and their employers seem curious enough about this life to prompt this gossip. One lower middle-class Negro, commenting upon this class and trait, said:

We got a *Black Banner* [newspaper] and the white folks know everything that goes on among our people. They don't have to come down here to find out what's going on, the *Black Banner* will tell them. When they ask me I just tell them I don't know. I ain't going to play no Black Banner for them.

The "race problem" is not an urgent issue with the lower social classes. They "know their place" and in their social isolation from the whites enjoy considerable freedom in domestic relations and personal conflicts within the group. Their problems are largely those of poverty. Occasionally they show an interest in the higher education of their children as a means of escape from an uncomfortable and oppressive economic status, but more often they regard education beyond the elementary grades as unnecessary and useless. They emphasize the church; and they largely make up the membership of the "cult" churches.

The *"folk Negro"* is another important category that cuts across the lower and lower middle classes. The distinction here is largely cultural. The traits, standards, and values of this class reflect the "Negro folk culture" nurtured by the cultural isolation of the southern plantation. Many of their attitudes and behavior traits evolved from the necessities of a life outside the general stream of American culture.

The rural "folk Negro" differs from the urban "underworld" Negro in that the traits of the former in their appropriate setting have achieved a kind of integration, equilibrium, and meaning in the life of the group, despite their differences from the general social norms; whereas the "underworld" life is merely disorganized and irresponsible. In the latter category are the "hellions" and "bad niggers," the prostitutes, pimps, and gamblers who have both personal freedom and immunity from the normal social restraints upon other classes. Whereas the folk Negro may have "naïve" notions about domestic life, "illegitimacy," and sex generally, the lower-class and underworld Negroes are indifferent to the accepted standards for other reasons.

The folk Negro is in a sense a "domesticated" part of white institutions in the South and, with the lower-class Negro, feels more secure in segregated institutions. They are frequently resentful and uncomfortable when Negroes of higher status protest segregation and discrimination, feeling that the latter are creating problems about which they do not care to worry. The folk and lower-class Negroes aspire to a certain amount of personal privilege within the racial mores; and if such privilege is denied they may register their protest by quitting a job without notice, by gossip intended to cause embarrassment, or by deflecting their resentment from the whites, who were responsible for it, to the Negro group in some form of personal violence.

The underworld Negro is often involved in violent encounters with other Negroes, usually of the underworld, but when he comes into contact with the police, his behavior is highly unpredictable.

Another factor conditioning the responses of Negroes to segregation and discrimination is the specific situation. Individuals of the same class and region may respond differently in various situations involving interaction between a Negro and a white person; while regional mores and class distinctions may define one's racial attitude in a general manner, the actual responses of a white person and a Negro toward each other depend on the nature of the particular occasion, personal characteristics, sometimes even on the mere number of persons present, the degree of intimacy between the interacting parties, and most important of all, their individual attitudes. What actually takes place may or may not correspond to what is generally expected. For example, whites in the deep South often deviate considerably from the common racial mores of that region in situations like a private drinking party; and in labor or farmers' unions interracial hostility is sometimes subordinated to interclass struggle. Again, eating with Negroes is generally the last thing that the "caste-minded" whites will do in the South; but the exceptions to this rule are not necessarily found only among whites who are free from race prejudices. A North Carolina farmer related that a white man once ate with him while his wife was away. An informant in a northern city reported that, while Negro men might be refused service in some white restaurants, Negro women might be waited upon. Still another informant in another northern city, a light-brown woman of fine build and refined manners, observed that when she went alone to a white restaurant she was often served, but whenever she had other Negroes with her she was discriminated against. In cases like these, sex and the number of persons involved in an interracial situation seem to enter into the determination of responses.

That the degree of intimacy existing between individual whites and Negroes and the racial attitudes of whites affect the Negro's response to discrimination is an even more familiar fact. Domestic servants who have been in the service of white families for long periods, and who are on intimate terms with their employers, may disregard the usual restriction about the use of the front door of the employer's house, even in the South.

Situations, or the environment as it is generally understood, may mean very different things to different individuals living in the same region or community and under the influence of the common mores, or even involved in the same immediate situation. If we carry the analysis a little further, it appears that what actually determines an individual Negro's response to discrimination is not only the external, or objective, environment but the internal, or subjective, environment. Individual attitudes and traits condition one's definition of a situation.

That individual personality factors are important determinants of responses to discrimination can be clearly seen in cases in which varying reactions to similar or externally identical situations are shown by Negroes who were either brought up together or so closely associated with each other that they shared a common social status and cultural tradition.

A common laborer and his wife in South Carolina could not see eye to eye in dealing with their white neighbors and had moved to their present place because of the husband's wish to avoid them. The difference between their responses was expressed by the wife in the following words:

I lived up yonder 18 years and 7 months. Them white folks live around me and they was nice. I like living up there. I like my own color, but I just got used to them. They was real nice people. Stayed there 18 years and 8 months and we never had a cross word. My house was always full of them. They came there and I'm in the yard washing, they get them a chair and set there and talk 'til time for me to cook dinner. They get they chair and come inside and set in the kitchen. They just like colored folks. Never was no difference. I was nice to them and they was nice to me.

My husband can't stand them. I don't know how come my husband hate white folks so bad. He gets so mad he cusses. Up yonder he'd come to dinner and see them and turn 'round and go back, and wouldn't eat his dinner. He say, "I can't eat a square meal for looking at the damn ol' po' white folks." They're nice to me, and like me, and I can't be mean to them. He just don't like to look at them.

Personality differences of a similar kind were shown by a couple belonging to a slightly higher social stratum, participating in a common cultural life. A Pullman porter in Georgia described himself as "a rough man sober," who would allow nobody to mistreat him, drunk or sober. Once a stationmaster wanted to rub out an entry which the porter had made in his book but "pulled in his horns," according to the porter's story, after he was dared to do it. The porter's wife, on the other hand, considered her white employer as "just like a nigger woman," who never hesitated to sit down and eat with her and to lend her money whenever she needed it.

A professional Negro in Tennessee related an interesting experience at a filling station. When he and his wife drove up to the station intending to park their car, the manager called an employee to serve the "boys." The Negro's wife resented the way they were addressed and asked him to drive on, even though the car was out of gas. Luckily, they found another filling station nearby; otherwise they would have had to return to the first station.

A Negro policeman in Maryland described the difference between his and his wife's responses to discrimination:

I have heard Negroes say they wouldn't accept certain jobs because white people call them by their first names. Take my own work, most of the men there call the Negroes arrested "darkey," "nigger," "shine," anything. I could get mad and put up a fight and make them resentful. It wouldn't do any good. I'd only be out of a good job, and they'd still go on calling Negroes whatever they please.

My wife has different ideas. She tells me to forget I'm colored and take seriously my authority to deal with whites. Well, she hasn't been in this man's land long. She can't take a lot of things I put up with because her viewpoint is that she's as good as anyone else, and she'd cuss them out. I think I'm as good as some of those Irish cops, too, but I've got enough sense not to make an issue out of it. I got to eat, you know, and jobs are scarce. [Speaking of segregated parks] My wife would look like a fool driving out to a park like that, subjecting herself to humiliation and trying to be with whites.

The secretary of an Urban League in a border state had a woman co-worker, good looking and well educated. They worked for the same cause in the same cultural area and were of practically the same socioeconomic status, but their reactions to seemingly identical racial situations differed markedly. Commenting upon her entering the white man's home by the back door, and comparing his own reaction in the matter with hers, the secretary said:

I just couldn't understand it when she came back and told me of having been invited to the back door of homes which admit me freely to the front. But I realized that she was so afraid that the servant did not respect her enough to admit her [to the front door]. There is some psychology here which we don't always understand, but it operates nevertheless. Why when I realized that this girl didn't have the goods, I had to let her go. It seems to me the important thing is one's own attitude, one's own confidence in oneself.

As to his own reaction to the same situation, he added:

Now, I had the thing happen to me once. It happens occasionally, of course. I had been invited by Dr. ——, a minister here, to his house for a conference. The colored maid invited me to the back, but I told her that I was here at Dr. ——'s invitation. I said it very graciously, yet with an air of authority. Immediately she seemed to say to herself, "I must recognize the superiority of this man." She let me in the front door, and I've been back several times. Never again did she make that first mistake. I am convinced that whatever it is it is within one's own self.

The secretary further described himself as one who seldom hesitated to assert himself, and who would never allow a white man to abuse him. Thus, when his first name was used in introducing him in conference with whites, he insisted that he be called by his full name. He felt so keenly about discrimination by whites that he had to resort to what he termed the "weekly escape," that is, complete self-isolation from any social contacts on Sundays in order to save himself from explosive acts. While the external conditions confronting the two were practically the same, psychologically the difference between their reactions was great: in the one, the aggressive impulses toward whites were obviously liable to be expressed, while in the other they were suppressed.

It is possible that the sex factor plays some part in this type of situation, although our experience suggests that there are almost as many instances in which the woman is more aggressive. One lower middle-class woman described a conversation with her white woman employer, who had asked her to come earlier one day and prepare dinner for her husband. This was reasonable, but the white employer had added, gratuitously, that the Negro woman's husband ought to prepare his own dinner. The Negro woman replied:

I love my husband just like you love yours, and your husband lays up in bed all day when he feels like it, and he don't cook his own dinner.

The employer said she was "the sassiest nigger" she had ever seen, and the Negro woman replied that she was talking "just as one woman to another." This was her significant comment: "She can't do nothing to me. *A colored man can't talk back to a white woman, but a colored woman can.*"

Two further illustrations involve persons of the same sex and same family background. The younger of two sisters in a small Arkansas town, a schoolteacher, kept her insurance book hanging just back of the front door so that she did not have to ask her white insurance collector to come in; she would let him wait on the porch, even on a very cold day. Her sister acted quite differently toward the white world. These are the schoolteacher's words:

My sister thinks that these people [whites] are just grand. She is a spiritualist and reads for all of these white people. She goes to their homes, and they help her with her canning club, and any projects she has. They all call her by her first name, and they think she is just fine. There are a few of us around here who don't go in for that.

The sister, when interviewed, spoke favorably of the white people with whom she came in contact. She thought that there had been progress in race relations, as indicated by the public school that had just been built for Negroes. The younger sister ascribed this difference in their racial attitudes to the difference in education. The younger had been to college; the older, only as far as the fifth grade. This explanation seems plausible, but there is evidence that educational differences alone are not sufficient to account for differences in racial attitudes and behavior.

Two brothers, brought up in the same family and now in college, since their childhood days have shown marked differences in their modes of response to frustration by family authorities or the white world at large. The older one early began to conform to authoritative requirements and to resort to substitutive expression of his hostile impulses, while the younger one equally early developed the pattern of forcing his demands upon the environment by open and unrestrained expression of his feelings. Thus, the former invariably ran away from white boys when they came threateningly close to him; the latter, though younger, took almost every challenge without hesitation. At present one is literally engrossed in intergroup aggression, while the other seems to be relatively free from race feeling.

These cases point to the importance of differences in individual personality in racial response situations where all other factors are at least externally the same; for cultures or social situational factors as ordinarily dealt with, in Sapir's words, "are merely abstracted configurations of idea and action patterns, which have endlessly different meanings for various individuals in the group."[2] What personality is, how situations are defined differently by different individuals, and in what ways cultural and personality factors interact upon each other are questions which naturally arise in any consideration of Negro response to segregation and discrimination if analysis is to be carried anywhere near a satisfactory conclusion.

The sociological approach to personality emphasizes the individual's conception of his role in society as the basic component of its organization, and seeks to understand his behavior in terms of his conceived role in a specific social situation.[3] From this point of view, to understand a personality it is necessary to explore the situational factors that condition an individual's conception of his social role. In a recent attempt to study the personality development of southern rural Negro youth the writer recorded various responses of the youth to the white world, and among other things took into account such factors as the community, class position, family training (in regard to race relations), individual experiences (also in regard to race relations), age, and intelligence.[4] A limitation of the sociological approach as it is ordinarily understood is that, while findings about social and cultural conditions may be true of a group of individuals, they are not necessarily true of any one particular

[2] Edward Sapir, "The Emergence of the Concept of Personality in a Study of Culture," *Journal of Social Psychology*, November, 1934, p. 411.

[3] Robert E. Park and E. W. Burgess, *Introduction to the Science of Sociology* (Chicago: University of Chicago Press, 1924), p. 70.

[4] Charles S. Johnson, *Growing Up in the Black Belt* (Washington: American Council on Education, 1940).

youth; for under similar social and cultural conditions such as common family traditions, including in this case the family training in race relations, markedly different personalities appeared, and seemingly identical racial situations often called forth different individual reactions.

In the studies of Davis and Dollard there is a serious attempt to go beyond the usual sociologist's interest in personality, for here the socialization by the family of an individual's biologic impulses from childhood days is given a great deal of attention. The chief emphasis, however, seems to be on the controls exercised by social class upon personality.[5] Negro families of different social classes were found to bring up their children in strikingly different ways; and one is led to infer that the children's personalities vary according to class position. But at the same time it is stated that "personality is perceived in that behavior of an individual which distinguished him from other individuals trained by similar social controls,"[6] and that "It is not apparent that personality, in the sense of the emotional and adaptive disposition of the individual, is principally typed by social classes. . . . It is simply held that they reveal the interplay in personality formation between those factors which arise from the general family, age, and sex controls, and those which are systematically reinforced by the class or caste environment."[7] In other words, according to the authors, the influence of the social class or even the caste, greatly emphasized in this and other studies of Negro youth, may or may not be important for the development of personality in any particular case or, at least, is of varying degrees of importance for different individuals. Just what the relation is between personality as defined and the "social controls" and how the family and other factors, on one hand, and the class and "caste" factors, on the other, actually interplay in the personality formation of a particular individual still remain matters to be formulated.

The study by Davis and Dollard does show with great clarity that there seems to be a more or less stable personality element that apparently is not directly connected with obvious cultural forces, such as those represented by social class or common family traditions; that the fundamental traits of a personality seem to take shape rather early in life; and that, once formed, these traits tend to

[5] Allison Davis and John Dollard, *Children of Bondage* (Washington: American Council on Education, 1941). Cf. Allison Davis, "The Socialization of the American Negro Child and Adolescent," *Journal of Negro Education*, 8:264-274 (July, 1939).
[6] *Children of Bondage*, p. 11.
[7] *Ibid.*, p. 16.

persist and manifest themselves in various situations. In terms of our present study it can probably be said that, if a Negro is essentially aggressive, he will be so in his relations not only to whites but to Negroes as well, and not only in one particular situation but in many situations, although the overt manifestation of his intent may vary according to external circumstances. Similarly, if one is essentially nonassertive or submissive, one may be expected to reveal it in more than one situation.

Whatever the strength of such factors as individual and racial temperament, as yet not clearly isolated, two things are reasonably clear: (1) basic psychological factors play some part in the differential responses of Negroes to segregation and discrimination, and (2) the role that the individual has learned to assume in the course of his participation in primary group life during his formative years is most important in his total personality structure and in his behavior in subsequent contacts with the white world. This stresses again the vital roles of the family, community, and general cultural setting into which Negroes are born. It is significant that older Negroes in the South, who are accommodated to the social and racial structure, take into account the differences between their own responses to these factors and those of the younger generation and of Negroes born in other parts of the country.

We may now examine some of the characteristic modes of responding to the race structure and its institutional and psychological implications. These modes, as indicated, are as varied as the Negro personalities themselves, but in a general way these personalities have been influenced by the very institutions to which they are reacting. Any broad category of response will include behavior varying widely in degree of intensity and in motivation. Characteristic racial experiences may develop "racial types." Although many responses may reveal some latent underlying hostility, they represent some form of adjustment of impulse and feeling to the race system.

In this process of adjustment and accommodation at least four major patterns are recognized. They are *acceptance, avoidance, direct hostility and aggression,* and *indirect or deflected hostility.* These types of response may be motivated by desire for personal security, self-esteem, economic well-being, sexual recognition, or various other factors.

Chapter XII

ACCEPTANCE

Acceptance by Negroes of the racial status defined in the institutions and in the etiquette is a form of accommodation. The race system and the behavior expected of Negroes are well known to all Negroes reared in the South; and their personal, emotional, and economic security are frequently based upon conformity to the expected modes of behavior. A marked degree of accommodation would consequently be expected in this region, where four-fifths of the Negroes still reside, and where overt clashes involving large numbers of the population are infrequent; in fact, social relations would be exceedingly difficult if a substantial number of Negroes did not either accept the expected status or seem to accept it. It is, of course, possible to conform externally while rejecting the race system mentally and emotionally; and there are evidences in Negro behavior of widely varying degrees of acceptance. A distinction should be made between unconscious conditioning to acceptance, which is an aspect of socialization in this environment, and rational acceptance of a role as a measure essential to survival in the environment. Differences in degree of acceptance by Negroes are based chiefly upon their individual conceptions of themselves in terms of their racial and social careers; and these conceptions, in turn, are largely dependent upon class position, educational and general cultural level, and the type of situation involving interracial behavior.

THE RURAL SOUTH

In the rural South relations are more intimate and custom-bound than in the urban areas. There are fewer class distinctions within both white and Negro groups. The rural economy supports a white population consisting of large and small landowners, middlemen, and tenants. Among the Negroes there is little room for large landowners or professional persons. As a result a large element of the Negro tenant population is dependent upon the white owners and

244

planters; and dominance and subordination are a part of the fixed social and economic pattern. Changes in agriculture, in the relationship between workers and their bases of subsistence; changes resulting from internal modifications of the Negro social structure; and the introduction of commercial and technical innovations of various sorts have brought about new relationships demanding definition, but on the whole the basic patterns survive.

The shadow of the racial mores penetrates deep into the intimate life of the Negro population in these areas. Perhaps the most striking fact about the biracialism is that there is greater social distance and less communication than in other areas, despite the greater control of racial institutions through personal contact. This is particularly true of the emerging Negro classes above the level of the common agricultural laborer or tenant.

The "folk Negro" is not, except in cases of helpless conflict with the white world, consciously aware of racial segregation and accepts it unemotionally as a part of his social world. The mobility of members of this group is within a narrow radius; they do not read and thus cannot make comparisons between their status and that of other Negroes elsewhere. For them the racial situation is not, as a rule, generalized but is conceived in terms of their personal relationships with good or bad landlords. The "white folks" are the ones who record their ages, see that they get "advances" for living, get them out of trouble, and get attention for them when they are sick. They know their world and have worked out sufficient satisfactions within it to permit life to go on without complaint, except as to "physical ailments," poor crops, church standing, and occasionally the wild behavior of those of their children who get dangerous notions in their heads about how they ought to act toward white people. Some folk Negroes do not consider the question of relations with white people important enough to discuss, or perhaps safe to discuss. The answer is usually, "We git 'long fine with our white folks—'course them po' whites [or peckerwoods] make a lot of trouble."

The increased mobility of rural Negroes and the beginnings of a new education for their children are having their effect upon the "Negro folk society" as it continues to emerge from the cultural isolation of the plantation; but the basic folk patterns of life persist in some areas and in some individuals transferred from this setting to an urban environment.

The response of this type of southern rural Negro to racial institutions is well illustrated in the case of a tenant-farmer family. None of the six children has gone beyond the fifth grade in school; the father has had no schooling, and the mother only about three years. One girl in the family, in explaining the peculiarity of the school ethics, said:

Some of the teachers talk about you—like if you get ready to have a baby and ain't married. And they talk about girls who stay out late with boys; and if you walk up the roads late at night, drunk and cussin', and if you beat your wife.

The baby in the family wears four strings about his neck: one holding a mole's foot (so that no harm can come to him), a rabbit's foot (to bring good luck), a piece of wood (to keep away evil spirits), and asafetida (to keep him healthy).

The family has no consciousness of racial separation or discrimination and describes white people generally as "nice":

They give you food if you need it, and if anyone is sick they will help you.

The father, commenting upon himself, said:

I ain't had no trouble getting along, and it don't make no difference to me if the chillen go back to school or no. . . . They need to know how to read and write; but 'long's they can do that it don't matter 'bout the rest. . . . Some people don't need no education. [On this point he said some, but when he described whom he meant, it was simply "colored people."]
I seen a whole lot of folks with book schooling, and they don't make sense. A man's got to be satisfied with what he's got, and some people get a lot of education in they head, and you can't do nothin' with 'em.

Through their personal relations with their paternalistic white employers some of these families are at times more closely attached to them than to other Negroes. One such couple discussed their relations with their white folks. The man said:

The white folks look out for you. When I was sick I went to the hospital, but they say I couldn't get in. But Mr. —— hisself went back wid me and tole 'em yes I was gonna get in; they have to find a place for me; and they did, too. And they sho' treat me good too, they gimme the care of a baby—better than the care some babies git. They lift me in they arms, and sho' did treat me good.

The wife added:

They sho' did, 'cause I went to see him and I know 'cause I see it myself. When I leave they ask me, "When you coming back?" I say,

"I don't know," and I slip back dere all kinda times, and every time I get dere dey sho' had him sweet and clean and nice. They sho' did.

In the same tenor are the remarks of another woman who said, without any apparent feeling of resentment:

White folks all right. White and colored get along all right. White folks just whup you when they get ready.

A man, instructing his son out of his own experience, said:

When I goes to a white man's house I stands in the yard and yells, and he comes to the door. If he tells me to come then I goes up to the door to talk to him, and I don't go in unless he tell me. If he tell me, then I goes in, but I don't set down lessen he tell me. And I don't talk to white folks direct like I does to colored. I lets him do the talking, let him take the lead. That's what he wants, and if he says something to me that I don't like, I says, "Now, Mr. ——, don't you think I oughta do such and such a thing," and then mos' likely he say "yes," but you better not go straight at the thing with a white man, he'll think you're smart. Yes, suh, I tells my chillen to do lak that. That's the way to get along.

As has been indicated, there is no clear-cut line distinguishing the "folk Negro" category from the simple lower-class Negro. Many of the behavior traits are the same, but the meanings differ. The racial concern of lower-class Negroes is not so often with the issue of segregation and discrimination as with personal security in their accepted sphere. A youth of 16 said:

White children call me nigger sometimes. I don't say nuthin' 'cause I know I'm a nigger and I don't want to get in no trouble. My daddy always tol' me not to pay any attention to white children when they meddle me, less'n I was gonna tell they parents, 'cause he didn't want me to git in no brawl and trouble.

A lower-class mother, in explaining how she brought up her children, said:

I tell them to be mannerable and stay in they place, and if they see some white children who want to be nice and play with them to go ahead and play with them; but if they are snarly and act mean to go ahead and not bother with them. . . . Here in Jonestown [Mississippi] it used to be a time when white people would hardly want to speak to a colored person in the street. But I raised up myself to speak to people, and when I'd pass by them I'd say "Good morning," whether they speak or no. Now it got so when a white person passes you they's most likely to speak.

Lower-class rural Negroes, like the group described as "folk," make a distinction between "white people" and "peckerwoods," or poor whites. There is little hostility toward the former and a fairly general acceptance of their racial position, without question, especially among the adults. In respect to the latter, there is acceptance of the racial role and a rigid conformity to it out of both fear and contempt. One young farmer said:

'Course I never have any trouble with the peckerwoods because I stay in my place, never get fresh, and always mind my own business.

In many parts of Mississippi and Louisiana there are Italians, Syrians, and Armenians. Of them it is said:

They are nice and treat colored fine. . . . They ain't like peckerwoods. In fact they a whole lot like colored.

There are only a few points at which lower-class rural Negroes are likely to infringe upon the white man's social world. They do not question the residential segregation, nor the segregation and discrimination in schools, transportation, personal facilities, churches, and associations of various sorts. It is largely for this reason that there is little conflict with upper-class whites. Points of conflict appear most often in status issues involving some lack of deference to lower-class whites. The careful observance of the codes is, thus, a matter of personal security:

I like some white people all right. I just don't want to have no trouble with them. If I did get in trouble with 'em, I wouldn't do nothin'. I couldn't do nothin'. They'd kill me. White folks don't play with no colored folks. You have to do what they want you to do or else your life ain't worth nothin'.

The pervasiveness of this fear and the almost physiological, as well as psychological, adaptation to the segregated Negro world appear in the story of a lower-class Negro girl:

The other place we live some white folks live right in front of us, and they were good. They had a well and let us use it. We'd work for them sometimes, and they'd give us clothes and money. We played with the children and fussed with them too if they didn't do what I wanted, but they liked me and when I'd come after water they'd tell me to take it home and come back and play with them. I was a big girl before anybody meddle me, and I was living up here then. They would say, "Look at the little black nigger." I wouldn't say nothing to them; just act like I didn't hear 'em. Some white people are just as hateful, and some are just as good as they can be. Sometimes some old hateful ones would throw rocks at me, and I'd get mad, but I wouldn't say nothing. I know if I said or did anything all the white people would get after me. I don't know nobody they got after, but I think they would get me anyway. My uncle and aunt always said go on and don't pay 'em no attention.

White children have a lot of things I don't have. They have movies and I have to go all the way to Greensboro to see the movies, just because I'm colored. Colored can't go in the drugstore and eat nothing either. Nobody tried, but they say they can't. I reckon they'd lock them up if they tried. If I had a drugstore I'd treat them all alike. *'Course, I'd have a section for the white and a section for the colored, because maybe the colored wouldn't want to be with the whites, and maybe the whites wouldn't want to eat with the colored. If I had to sit down and eat with whites I'd feel funny, 'cause I know white folks are mean and they might not want me. I wouldn't like to go to school with white children,* I'd be the only one there dark, and they'd be picking at me and calling me black. I'd just rather be with my own color. Even if they were nice I'd still rather be with my own color. I didn't think so much about things I couldn't do until one day I went downtown and stopped by a movie house to look at the picture outside, and I thought I'd like to see it, and I looked for a sign for the colored, and there wasn't any; just a sign for the "white," so I knew I couldn't go.

The significant point is that in the rural South segregation is fairly generally accepted, either unconsciously as an unquestioned matter of fact or consciously as a matter of expediency. In the latter case acceptance may be motivated by fear or by desire for economic or personal security; but for this there would be many more racial disturbances in these areas. However, not all of the acceptance for reasons of expediency is placid and resigned. It may cover most areas of Negro contact and extend throughout a lifetime, but a particular crisis experience may bring out a violent response. A young man in one of the Mississippi counties said:

An' every once in a while you'll run acrost a peckerwood that's all right, but I'm just like my daddy when it comes to them. I'm scareder of colored folks than I am of white. If a white man cuss me, I'll cuss him back, and if air' one ever try to lay a hand on me, I'm gonna kill him.

There are comparatively few rural Negroes who by reason of education, occupation, or income are sufficiently removed from the mass to be classified as upper class. Usually this small upper-class group is made up of teachers, doctors, extension workers, larger farmers, owners of businesses, undertakers, and insurance men. The largest single group is that of schoolteachers and principals; since most, if not all, of them hold their jobs at the will of white school officials and politicians, they are extremely careful to observe the racial etiquette as far as possible, while discreetly showing enough self-respect to keep the respect of the Negroes for whom they are expected to provide leadership. Even among the upper and professional classes of rural Negroes there is no expectation of anything approaching equality of provisions or treatment. In some of the cities of the upper South there has been discussion of teachers' salaries and argument for equal salaries for equal preparation, experience, and responsibility; but in the rural areas this is unthinkable. A school principal in Johnston County said, "There's supposed to be a 30 per cent difference in white and Negro teachers' salaries now, and we are asking that the difference be cut to 20 per cent for the coming year." In other areas the question of readjusting salary schedules to the level of white salaries is not regarded as proper for discussion.

The middle and professional classes of the Negro population in the plantation counties have few privileges. Those who remain in, or elect to move into, these rural areas know what to expect and live accordingly. They simply take the customs for granted; and when they cannot escape them they accept them, some without thinking about it unless a stranger is present, some with tolerance, and some with such completeness as to make them impatient with others who try to resist or evade prevailing customs. These Negroes also make distinctions between white persons, which is one way of minimizing the problem and preserving a superior conception of one's self in relation to such situations. For example, a Negro undertaker in Poinsett County, Arkansas, explained:

The white people here are pretty nice. They don't bother you on the street. . . . Of course there is a certain element—these ignorant poor white people—they think they are better than the colored people. If you attend to your business, you don't have trouble.

This man was driving his Buick automobile on the highway when he overtook a white man in a dilapidated old car, chugging along with painful slowness. The Negro blew his horn and tried to pass. The white driver saw that the man behind him was a Negro and deliberately pulled over to the left to prevent his passing. The Negro simply trailed along behind. After many miles of this he finally "lugged his motor," and when another white man forced both of them to make way, he was ready for a fast pickup behind the passing car. He said:

He cussed me, but I kept right on going. He didn't have a chance to catch me. But that doesn't happen much.

The younger Negroes were giving him some concern with their occasional indifference to the established etiquette. There is a drugstore in one of the towns that serves as an informal social center for white rural youth. The practice in these places is for Negroes to purchase soda water or ice cream at the counter and then go to the back of the store, or outside, to consume it. These young Negroes sometimes forgot to put a respectful distance between themselves and the counter while drinking their soda water; and this man feared a disturbance of race relations as a result.

The strength of the etiquette is such that it is frequently embarrassing to Negroes of sufficient economic status to own a car to accept the ordinary services of filling station employees. A schoolteacher said:

I'd rather put water in my own car than have anyone else do it. But they insist.

In one of the counties a Negro extension agent, whose duties were heavy and had required contact with many farmers over a considerable period, found that he got along best with the white people by "taking few liberties." He handled his work from his home and assured himself that he really did not need an office, although the white extension agents found it necessary to have this convenience. The rational basis of acceptance for most of these Negroes was put simply by a Negro undertaker in Mississippi:

In this part of the country a Negro can only go so far. I know that, and that's the reason I am able to stay out of trouble. They know you are a Negro and I know I am a Negro, and I know that there is a certain way white people are going to treat a Negro. They want you to stay in your place, and if you get out of it too much they are going to put you back in it. I mean by this that the white man is the boss in the South and you got to talk to him like he is the boss. It don't make any difference how much money you have or how much education you have, he won't look at you as his equal, and there is no use in you acting like you're his equal if you want to stay here.

THE URBAN SOUTH

Several generalizations can be made regarding the general patterns of Negro response to segregation in urban areas, although there are variations in responses as in segregation patterns. Segregation is generally accepted by Negroes of the lower and middle classes. Discrimination in most institutions is fatalistically accepted by the lower and lower middle classes, and they do nothing about it. The middle and upper middle classes resent discrimination in work opportunities, schools, libraries, transportation, parks and other public facilities and seek modification within the limits of the "separate but equal" principle. Any conflicts are usually in situations involving economic and personal security and status.

One attitude is that there are good and bad white folks and good and bad Negroes. "Among classible white people," one woman said, "it is really good to be among them." She impersonally attributes segregation to the law: "I know that according to the law of the land we ought to be divided."

Others resent the attitude and behavior of whites and advocate segregation. One woman expressed herself strongly on this point:

White people hate to see the colored man come up, an' they's comin' too fast to suit him. They got as nice houses on 11th Avenue as they got in West End. White folks don't like that an' they do everything to put the colored folks back. You know they ought to have colored police out here, but you see we ain't got 'em. I don't like to 'sociate with white folks. They's some good ones but they ain't many. I believe we ought to all the colored folks be in one part of town an' all the white folks be in another part; all the colored folks together.

For some there is economic security in segregation:

Some folks fuss about white folks' ways, but we get all we got from them, and about half of us got to work for them, so I don't see no need of fussin'.

The physical security of the Negro community appeals to some who do not enjoy association with whites. With present white attitudes and behavior it can be understood how many Negroes would prefer segregation to the uncertainty and discomfort of association with whites who menace their personal safety. A Negro man in one of the southern cities protested:

I don't like this idea of mixing. I want to be with us colored people. I work for them [whites], get their change, and go right on.

Speaking of the whites, another Negro declared, "They're all right in their places." There is a suggestion that this attitude of acceptance of segregation is deep-rooted in the personality. A woman who had been North confessed that even there she could not feel comfortable among whites:

I feels funny 'bout settin' next to them. Up North I never got use to them settin' 'round me.

The comment of a southern woman whose sister lives in Cleveland, Ohio, shows a similar shading of the acceptance attitude, namely, that since there is segregation and discrimination in both sections it is better in the South where one's feelings are not hurt by having association rejected:

I don't see where our people in the North make any more than we do. I am expecting my sister from Cleveland to visit here in a few days, and she always talks about she can't see how we live down here. I tell her I guess she doesn't think we are living, but I don't see where they have any more privileges. There is prejudice there, too. They can go in places and sit down beside white folks, but they don't want them any more than they do here. When I am up there I tell them, "Down home, if we know that they don't want us, we don't go."

An "adviser" on the problem of contact in the South said:

Let the Negro stay to his self and the white man stay to they self, and they never be no trouble.

A mother, in concern over the safety and comfort of her children, accepted segregation inferentially as a safeguard:

I don't want my children to mix with white children. It just ain't good for white and colored children to mix. It just ain't right for the two races to mix, and I'm going to see that my children stay away from them.

Members of the lower middle and middle classes accept segregation for personal security; but there are numerous indications that members of the lower class are indifferent to it or unconscious of it. Expressions like these are heard:

I never think about them. I just takes life as it comes, and goes on.

I ain't studyin' 'em.

They don't bother me none.

Some feel no resentment in the personal adjustments that have to be made in transportation:

I'd as soon ride in the rear as in front. I get up and move if I'm sitting front and some whites come in. You see I can handle myself enough to get along with any of them.

Another said:

They're just people so far as I am concerned. As long as they are nice to me I don't give them a thought. I don't expect anything from them, and I don't worry and get my feelings hurt. On the streetcar I sit back, and if a seat gets empty, I move back to that.

Acceptance Based upon Identification

The simplest and one of the more common types of acceptance of the Negro role, as traditionally conceived, is that based upon identification with a white primary group as a domestic, or retainer. "White folks," said one woman, "is fine people. I was reared with them." This relationship provides a basis for personal and economic security on a level compatible with the role, where loyalty and dependence inspire a sense of protection. Since the privilege and power of protection go along with high social status and wealth, the dependents themselves become symbols of the power and prestige of the protectors. One of the more creditable heritages of slavery has been the continued paternalistic benevolence of son of master to son of slave. It has bolstered the social prestige of the one and the personal security of the other.

Neely Stephens is a nonunion carpenter who came to Nashville from a rural area in the state twenty years ago. He takes pride in the confidence white people have in him:

When I work on a job I go all over the people's house. I tell them if you want to go away, go on and leave all the doors open if you want to. I'm here. They go off and say, "Neely, I'll be back such-and-such a time." I say, "All right, everything's going to be all right, because I'm here." They trust me. There ain't many men can say that.

He knows the racial etiquette and believes in it and is convinced that he has made and retained white friends within his range of association with them. Although no white person has ever shaken hands with him in Nashville, when he goes to his home in the country for visits it is different because he is better known there:

I walk down the street and they all come by and shake hands. The white people ask me, "Where you been, Neely? What you doing, Neely? How you getting along, Neely?"

Regarding the matter of titles, he says:

I call them "Mr." and "Mrs." except them I was raised with. White people call me everything. Them that know me call me "Neely," and them that don't call me "Hilliard." Sometimes one calls me "Uncle." I know how white folks is and I understand their ways. I always stand fair with my white people. They always been fair to me, and I been good to them. I always been a man to use my manners.

The reward for this loyalty and understanding came in an emergency in which any Negro of his class would need a friend. He was arrested on a whisky charge. Accommodatingly he had allowed a white friend to order some whisky in his name, and at a time when the state was "dry." Without funds for a lawyer he explained to the judge how he had been misled. Commenting on this crisis situation he said:

The judge questioned me hisself. He said, "Neely, you got a wife?" I said, "Yes, sir." He said, "How many children you got?" I said, "One, Judge." He said, "Neely, who raised you?" I told him Tom Beasley raised me. He said, "I know Tom Beasley and he's a straight man." He told the jury, "This man ain't guilty of no crime I can see. If you go out and convict him I'll overrule you." He told me, "Go on home, Neely, and don't come back before me no more."

He can get along with white persons who do not like most Negroes because he knows how to conduct himself. Relations with minor white officials are less pleasant than relations with the "boss," and in his working life there have been encounters with these minor officials in which the "boss" supported the Negro. The range of his contacts with whites is limited to personal relations on a basis acceptable to the whites; and it never occurs to him to want anything that it is regarded as improper for a Negro to have.

In the lower middle class identification is sometimes carried to the point of rejecting other Negroes entirely. A middle-aged widow revealed this in giving the reason why she moved from a Negro neighborhood to the back yard of a white family although not employed by the white family:

They've always been friends to me; they are nicer than colored sometimes; I have had them to cry after me when I left a neighborhood. That old trash from Cedar Street [a Negro street] just make me shamed I am colored. They just throw themselves away. I am sick of colored people; colored people done graduated me.

Acceptance Based upon Belief in Negro Inferiority

By implication in statements and in behavior many lower-class and lower middle-class Negroes reflect their belief in the inherent inferiority of all Negroes to all whites. They accept the stereotypes of Negro mentality and character without serious challenge, frequently reinforcing them from their own experiences. Their limited range of communication with other Negroes precludes any important modification of their assumptions. Indications of the refusal of other Negroes to accept their role are interpreted as foolhardy delusions, as unwarranted attempts to get out of their place, or as supercilious social gestures designed to humiliate their kinsmen. This attitude is typified by a Birmingham millworker who said, "I always respect the white man and go into his home by the back door."

It is disturbing for him even to think about social relations on any but a basis of dominance and submission:

No telling what I would do if I had to set down to the table and eat a meal with a white man. I wouldn't enjoy it. I would be wondering what everybody that sees us would say. I tell you it would be hard. I would much rather wait until they finish if I had to eat at the same place with them. They would feel better, and I know I would.

His philosophy is made clearer in his attitude toward voting:

I can't read and write, so I don't need to be voting just to be doing something. Ain't much need of these Negroes getting in that voting business, anyhow. The white folks running the country, and he can't do no good. That's the way it looks like it is to me.

In spite of full acceptance of the Negro status and belief in his own inadequacy, there is a tinge of self-pity and even resentment in his estimate of this disparity. "Sambo," he said with an exaggerated gesture of emphasis, "sho' has a hard time. He got to make it easy for everybody else." He occasionally held jobs under Negro sub-foremen, but he could not take them seriously. "They wasn't much," he said. "We didn't pay much attention to them. It was the white man who could do the hiring and firing. That was the man to watch." Conceivably, his low educational status, illiteracy, and rural background may have contributed to his conception of himself, and to his almost complete racial submission and humility.

There is acceptance of white standards of professional competence which transcends race pride, discounts personal relations based upon the expected Negro role, and expresses distrust of the Negro's professional abilities. Mrs. Freddie Collier of Houston is a domestic but nevertheless fairly comfortable, economically. For her health consultations she goes to a white doctor:

They have a different room where they take the colored patients. I have sat there all day and waited and waited. Some of the white people who came in after me was waited on first. I don't know whether he has special hours for colored. Dr. Ray always calls me "Freddie." I have colored doctors come to the house unless the case is serious, then I have a white doctor. I had a white doctor to come to see Sonny. I didn't want to trust a colored doctor. I don't think they know as much as a white doctor, and you can't depend on them. I just ain't got no faith in a colored doctor.

Acceptance Based on Desire for Personal Security

There is an insistent urge to conform to the pattern of expected behavior in the desire for personal security; and the resultant acceptance behavior may conceal varying degrees of resentment, hostility, or sheer fatalistic resignation. Although this type of behavioral response appears in some form among all classes of the Negro population, it finds widest and most pronounced manifestation in the lower middle class. It is explained in the expression of an Atlanta Negro laborer who said, "When you in Rome you got to act like it."

Elliot Easter is a general handy man in Nashville. He is about sixty-five years old, and came to the city from a farm in Alabama thirty years ago. Since then he has spent a few years in Ohio working in a foundry. Now he independently makes a living by selling small orders of ice and coal. He is in this business because he does not want to work for a white employer. He has no difficulty with white persons for two reasons: his contacts are limited to a minimum; and when he meets them he knows what they expect, and he conforms:

I don't remember any trouble I have had with them. If they say something, I just go on, and say nothing, unless I just have to.

He has never entered a white home except for work, and he always goes to the back:

When they come to our house by the front door, I don't try to make them come around to my back door.

He removes his hat when talking with a white person, as a matter of caution, but thinks it is no more than common respect and courtesy to remove his hat when in the presence of white women:

It is another reason for respecting them when you know that they will get you killed for disrespecting them.

His contacts with white people are definitely limited, partly from choice and partly because of his cultural and economic position. It is part of his philosophy of race relations to keep out of situations where one is likely to have trouble with whites; but he thinks that every man should protect himself from abuse by whites, although with some discretion. He says that there is "no use cutting off your nose to spite your face"; and that you are in the South, "so act like it." That does not mean that you have lost all of your rights; when you have a right to demand respect from the white man, you "ought to be straightforward about it. If he does not respect your right, then quit dealing with him. At times you are liable to be abused if you come in too close contact with white people." Then the informant steers clear of them. His philosophy seems to be to get everything possible out of the situation when he has the advantage; to accept the inferior role when that is definitely expected; and to avoid clashes of any kind when there is the slightest possibility of unfavorable outcome.

Acceptance with Reservations and Latent Racial Resentment

The real sentiments concealed by careful conformity to the expected role are best observed when some crisis situation dissolves the protective pattern and releases the more active feelings. Marie Pendleton is a large, stout, dark-brown woman whose years of domestic service in the homes of wealthy southern families have given her a certain dignity and poise, despite her 239 pounds. Her competent hands are always busy, and she suggests, for all the world, one of the pre-Civil War black mammies whose ample arms and resourcefulness brought unfailing comfort to the children of the southern aristocracy. For most of her forty-five years she has lived with white people, first on the farm and later in their city homes. She knows their habits and has shared their sorrows and joys, managed their children, and got her satisfactions from their recognition of her skill in pleasing their taste with her cooking, and from her evidences of loyalty. Even when employed as a cook at good wages, as wages go in the South, she would spend late evenings sewing for her mistress.

Marie Pendleton experienced an incident that scratched the surface of this relationship and threw her back on her race. The incident is significant because it helps to explain certain traits commonly associated with Negro domestics whose characters are presumed to be thoroughly understood by their employers. She has decided to live by day work from her own little cottage and by occasional catering for parties. She said:

Now I know that white folks like to talk about how much they loves you, how much they care about you. Mrs. Emmons used to say she loved me as much as she did anybody in the world. But she wasn't fooling me. She didn't love me, Marie, she loved the work I done for her. I knowed when she was doing all that talk if anything ever happen she'd turn on me just as quick as she would on any other colored person. But as long as she pretended like and went on, I went on too. And sure 'nough I liked her as well as any white person I ever seen. But color do make a difference. You just can't love other folks like you do your own color. These white folks say they love you, but it ain't you they's in love with, it's your work—what you can do that they love. If you don't believe that just stop work and see how long they love you.

Her experience proved the point. When she was working for an insurance executive he gave each of the servants a sickness and accident insurance policy on which the benefit payments amounted to $11 a week. After leaving his employ she kept the policy paid up, although she was apparently well and strong. During her second year of work for Mrs. Emmons she discovered that she had an abdominal tumor and that she must have an operation. She told this to her new employer, who arranged for her to have an operation at the city hospital and had her examined by her own physician; and he arranged for a well-known surgeon to perform the operation. Mrs. Emmons was active in all the arrangements and, according to the servant, "wanted to manage everything." She assumed this responsibility for her cook just as she would have done for a child. The rest of the story is more revealing in the language of the informant:

You know Mrs. Emmons is a fine woman, she's all right as far as she goes. But she just looks like she want to ask you the last question. She just got to know everything about you and some things you wants to keep to yourself. You just don't want to tell everything. Well, she made all the arrangements for the operation; just took charge. That was all right, but I didn't ask her, she just done it herself. Then she said, "Marie, I'll pay your rent for you while you're in the hospital; how much rent do you pay?" I told her she didn't have to do that, but she say she wanted to; so I told her how much rent I pay for the room where I live once a week and in the summertime when she go away and I has my vacation. Then she asks me, "Marie, do you have any money?" and I say, "Yes'm, I've got a little money." But she wanted me to tell her how much money I had in the bank, and I wouldn't tell her. I just said to her, "Mrs. Emmons, I don't want you to do no more for me than you just wants to. I can get along all right. If you just look after the operation and the hospital, I'll get along all right. I can look after myself." But she just wasn't satisfied, that woman wanted to know all there was to know about you. She didn't want you to keep nothing. So she says to me one day, "Marie, do you have a sick benefit policy?" Well, I was just struck, so I says, "Yes'm." "How much is it, Marie?" she says. "It's enough to take care of me while I'm sick, Mrs. Emmons," I says to her. Well, she still wasn't satisfied, so she says, "How much will you get every week from your policy, Marie?" Well I had to tell her something, so I say, "Five dollars a week."

Well she seem to be satisfied with that, and things went along all right. But right then I was ready to tell her that it wasn't none of her business how much I got from my policy. She had just about pushed me too far. Well, she took me to the hospital and made all the arrangements and everybody treated me just fine. You know she came out there to boss that hospital. She didn't fool with no nurses, she told Dr. Manier what to do, and he had to see that it was done. But she carried it too far. The morning I was operated on she come to see me, and she said, "Marie, how do you feel?" "Why," I says, "Mrs. Emmons, I has a headache this morning." And she says, "Ain't they give you your breakfast this morning, Marie?" And I says, "No'm." Well, that woman went right to Dr. —— and says, "Now you got to give Marie her coffee this morning. She ain't had her coffee, and her head hurts. Every morning at eight o'clock Marie has her coffee, and you got to give it to her." Of course the doctors said, "Yes'm, we'll give her her coffee right away." But they didn't. They knowed better; they knowed better than Mrs. Emmons about that coffee. But she thinks she know all about everything. And she seen to it that I got the best of everything.

But one day she come in, and I could see that she was mad. She says to me, "Marie, didn't you tell me you got five dollars a week from that sick policy?" And I says, "Yes'm." Then she flew into a fit, she was mad. She had been to see Mr. Wells and found out that the policy brought $11 a week, and she was mad enough to fight. She said, "Marie, I just can't understand why you would lie like that to me. I went to Mr. Wells and he told me that the policy brought you $11 a week. I didn't want to believe him, but he showed me the policy. Marie, it just hurts me to think that you would lie to me like that. I just can't have confidence in you no more."

Well, I said to her, quiet like, "Now, Mrs. Emmons, I tried to let you know that I didn't want you to know all there is in the world to know about me. I think I got a right to have some privacy about me about some things. You remember I told you that you didn't have to do nothing for me, no more'n just what you wanted to. Of course, I'm just a poor colored woman and I needs everything I can get, but, Mrs. Emmons, I didn't ask you to pay my rent or keep up my insurances or anything. You say you done this jest because you wanted to. And I don't think it was fair for you to ask me all about my insurances and things. I tried to let you know I didn't want to tell you, but you just insisted, so I said five dollars. I think my insurance policy is my business. I done paid it all myself. Ain't nobody paid my insurance but me. I work hard and pay for it."

Well, after a while she cooled down and she said, "Well, Marie, I'll take you back if you tell me you're sorry and apologize." That did make me mad. I said, " 'Pologize to you for that? No'm, I ain't done nothing wrong that I can see." But she says, "Can't you see it was wrong for you to lie to me like that Marie?" And I says, "No'm, I can't see that. If it was the first lie I told, it would be different. But I been lying for you ever since I come to work for you. I done told lies to all your friends for you. Now what's the difference if I tells you one lie for myself? I can't see that because it's for me, that it's so bad I has to 'pologize for it. No, ma'm, I ain't going to 'pologize. You hadn't ought to ask me that question. I'm a human being. I can keep some things to myself if I wants to. You didn't have no right to go asking all about my business."

You know I can understand why she didn't send for me no more. I got out of my place, and I sassed her. White folks ain't got no use for you when you do that; don't care how much they love you before. As long as you lets them do your thinking you can get along all right. But ain't nobody going to ask me the last question and treat me like I was a child. After I go so far, I quit. 'Cause if you do good work you can get a job most any time. Ain't no trouble to get a job if you can do all the work they want.

In this instance there is full acceptance of the pattern of expected behavior, but a desire to preserve privacy in respect to the more intimate personal affairs. An energetically possessive mistress penetrated this last citadel of self-esteem and personal independence and, instead of being diverted by artful deception, was deeply offended by it. Such possessiveness reduces the object to the status of an irresponsible child; and in the case of this domestic, consciousness of her ability to get another job precipitated a break in relations. But for this type of crisis situation the limits of acceptance would not have been revealed.

It is fairly common for lower- and lower middle-class Negroes consciously to make all the external gestures of acceptance, although feeling differently, not only when they wish to escape a conflict situation, but when they want something. A Negro restaurant keeper in one of the smaller cities made this comment about obsequious removing of the hat by many Negroes:

Now that is the way a lot of these Negroes here get what they want from the white man. They keep their hats in their hands as long as they are talking to him. A man does not need to lose all of his self-respect in order to get some of the things he wants from the white man, even in this little old town.

Another Negro in the same town confessed his use of this device in response to the demand of certain whites, not only for recognition, but for flattery:

They want all the Negroes to jump and pull off their hats when they are talking to them. The only reason that this is so is that these big niggers keep their hats in their hands when they are bowing and scraping to "Mr. Charlie" trying to get something out of him. Then he expects all niggers to do that. I know that is what they want, and since I am in it I can do it. When "Mr. Charlie" has something that I want there is nothing that I can't do to get it.

The behavior of the so-called "big nigger" is here used as a rationalization by a lower-class Negro. The small Negro professional or business man is more likely to employ an avoidance device, which neither offends the white by behavior that would be interpreted as impudent, such as keeping his hat on, nor offends his own dignity too greatly, as would be the case if he removed his hat. He may not wear a hat at all, or he may remove it before meeting a white person, or wipe his brow to suggest that his head is too warm with a hat on.

Some of the more race-conscious Negroes on a different social level resent the reservation of white sections at Negro dances for which "name" bands play. They also condemn those Negroes who carry acceptance beyond the limits of necessity. One of these, an insurance man, said, "These Negroes have been kicked so much by the white folks they like it, I believe."

Acceptance of Sex Taboos

The small number of incidents dramatized by violence is evidence of the acceptance of the sex taboos. This is an issue on which there is so much feeling that the behavior of Negroes is frequently exaggeratedly negative. The interracial sex mores prohibit relations between Negro men and white women and tend to condone relations between white men and Negro women. The latter relationship has been increasingly censured by both Negroes and whites in recent years, but it is by no means discontinued as yet. A Birmingham miner said:

It ain't right according to the law for them to marry. You don't see none of it. They do all they want without that though. What is the use of a white man marrying a Negro woman when he can have a lot of mariny babies by her and don't have to marry. He gets the best of the deal and she gets left holding the sack. I can't see how some of them can be such fools; but they do it.

Another said:

I know that they got us Negro men all wrong. We don't want "Miss Ann." All that we want is a chance to get the things that a man is supposed to get. They keep us in the background because they say that we want them to give us equality. All that means to them is that we want to take "Miss Ann" out and have a good time with her. That is the wrong way to look at it and you can't tell them any different. If we do want their women, it is only because we can't get our own for them. Our women are really some pretty things and they are crazy about them.

It is assumed by some of these men that the fear of sex relations between Negro men and white women is responsible for unnecessary restrictions; and this is resented at the same time that the desire is denied:

> They think that is all we want, anyhow [sex relations]. Every time some white woman say somebody bothered her, they say a nigger did it. I, for myself, don't have no desire for none of them. It ain't worth what they try to make out of it.

Rationalization of Acceptance

In the southern cities the racial behavior of upper middle- and upper-class Negroes is a compound of selective acceptance, avoidance, and rationalization for self-respect, and is basically resentful or even hostile. Their central purpose is to preserve their self-esteem in an environment which makes demands incompatible with this aspiration. Perhaps few white persons would deprive Negroes of self-esteem as such. Broadly speaking, every person should be satisfied with himself; but the points of view differ with respect to the basis of this self-esteem. The Negro who has acquired some education, property, and a sense of values which controls his social behavior in a generally approved manner, seeks recognition of these qualities because such recognition gives security and stability to the status itself. Hence, if recognition is denied, there is resentment. The issue is met in various ways, but there must be a minimum of acceptance in order to live in the environment at all.

As with other classes of the Negro population, the extent and character of acceptance vary with individuals. At the same time there is a marked difference between social classes in the aspects of the race system accepted. For example, practically all southern Negroes *accept* racial segregation. The lower-class groups as a rule pay little attention to it, or take it for granted. The upper-class groups accept it, but resent it. When they cannot change it, they try to turn it to some advantage in a business or professional way. They may attempt to rationalize segregation as being in the interest of racial solidarity. Occasionally it is accepted and condoned as necessary because of the still uncontrolled behavior of lower-class Negroes. Again, segregation may be resented not so much because white persons object to association with Negroes on a physical basis as because these upper-class Negroes object to contact with the great unwashed masses of their own race. A Negro school supervisor in Mississippi expressed such resentment of his "unhygienic brethren," indicated sympathy with the white attitude, and accepted his personal isolation from the whites. He said:

The only place that Negroes can go that whites go for amusement is to the movies. They can go to all of the theaters here. They go into the balcony, of course. The white man comes up there to try to keep the Negroes straight sometimes, and I don't blame him. The Negroes need to be kept in line sometimes. A lot of them have not been used to anything and they get up there and pay their dimes and they think they own the place. I tell you, it is awful up there sometimes when you go up there. I can see why the white man segregates Negroes then. A lot of the trouble the Negroes have they bring on themselves. It doesn't worry me to sit by myself, that is with my own people. That is all that I have ever done. Besides, the place is nice and the fare is not as high as it is when you go to a place where you sit with whites.

A Negro real-estate man in Atlanta, who has a fairly large business bringing him in frequent contact with the institutions of the white community, said:

At the Court House they have a colored elevator, but that don't bother me. *It runs like the rest of them.*

Regarding the matter of voting, he said:

I'm a Republican and in Georgia they don't have primaries. They have a convention. *I never go, but I could if I wanted to.*

The Negroes decided to run a man for Alderman too soon and the white folks saw they were going to elect him, so they changed the ward lines. My name was not where I'd been voting. It was away out in the West End somewhere. *I saw what happened and I let it go.*

This man made numerical estimates of contact problems. "Dealing with white people," he said, "you find 99 per cent of the upper white people are all right and 80 per cent of the poor white folks likewise. It's just 20 per cent you find hard to deal with."

It is not uncommon for upper-class Negro professional persons to assert ignorance of the behavior expected of Negroes. Back of this attitude, however, there is frequently an awareness of the situation which is accepted at the same time that its existence is denied. A Negro professional man in Houston, for example, in referring to contacts with whites in public places, said:

I haven't seen anything special that a Negro is expected to do. If he is I must have been wrong a number of times, because I don't even know what it is.

He was critical, however, of the "old mossbacks" among lower middle-class Negroes who "start getting their hats as soon as they see the white man." Eating together, he remembered, was "one of the sore spots":

They just don't seem favorable to that kind of thing. In most of the meetings that we may happen to have with the white dentists, eating never comes up. *It may be we could eat if we tried.*

He did not indicate who would try, nor did he suggest that the subject never came up because it is taboo. It was more comfortable to believe that it might happen if it was suggested, and more comfortable to accept the taboo than to raise the issue to test the possibility of change.

The inadequacy of the schools was not in his judgment a question of racial status but of the perfidy of the "Uncle Toms," those Negroes who openly conform to the expected patterns of racial behavior in order to profit personally. Of them he said:

They have put the Negroes here at a terrific disadvantage. They have fixed it so there is not much chance of the Negro's getting anything without a terrific fight.

The secret of his adjustment is that he knows where to go and how to act to escape embarrassing situations. He has little trouble in any of the places where he trades:

I look for places where I can get value for my money. I rather know where to go to get the best of service.

Such places are those tested by someone else and found agreeable in their racial attitudes. In transportation he has no difficulty because he uses his own automobile:

I rarely stop at stations where I am not known. . . . I have regular routes that I travel.

Regarding professional organization, he has made the same mental adjustment to separation and convinced himself that it is advantageous rather than disadvantageous:

We do not belong to the same organizations as the whites, *but they co-operate with us* in anything that we attempt in our little organizations.

At least three attitudes appear to be behind acceptance of the racial pattern by the various classes of the Negro population whether in the urban or the rural South. There is the group that believes in the inferior role of the Negro whether as a temporary or as a permanent status. They act on this belief and have no difficulty. Their wants do not stray beyond the limits of what is permitted. They are

seldom aware of a race problem and are irritated by other Negroes
who presume to seek more than is intended for them. They instruct
their children in their appropriate racial roles; and they enjoy the
measure of tolerance and security which this status ensures.

There are those who feel, mildly or strongly, that there is uneven-
ness in the balance of privilege and opportunity, but for greater
comfort and safety they accept the pattern without protest or deep
indignation. They do this and so instruct their children in order to
stay out of trouble.

There are those who resent the restrictions on Negroes as discrimination; but when they cannot avoid situations, they accept them
without articulate protest. This attitude is well expressed by the man
who said, "I don't like it but the best thing I can do is keep from
worrying about it."

Chapter XIII

AVOIDANCE

The most common type of response to the personal implications of the race system is that of *avoidance*. Although this is most conspicuous in the efforts of upper-class groups to preserve self-esteem, it is a fairly common phenomenon among all classes and varies in degree with the situation and with the motivations involved. There is manifest in this behavior not only a precautionary effort to avoid certain types of racial contact, but an attempt to avoid conforming to the patterns of expected behavior.

For those individuals of all classes whose behavior falls outside the category of acceptance, segregation and discrimination constitute in some degree a frustrating situation. There are various ways of dealing with this kind of situation. One is by careful planning of personal behavior so as to circumvent the situation, or if this fails, to protect oneself by devices designed to "save face." Impulses are controlled in the process; and a crisis situation is avoided by preserving, externally at least, the semblance of conformity to the expected behavior. In some cases the resentment or aggression may be directed away from the object of provocation to other personal or impersonal objects. In other cases, depending upon the personality of the individual, the impulse may be expressed without restraint in direct hostility and overt aggression. In both instances there is latent hostility, but the mode of expression differs. This chapter deals with the devices employed in avoiding direct contact with racial institutions or resolving conflict situations with a minimum of damage to the ego.

In a general way the large majority of the Negro population, particularly in the South, is accommodated to the race system. Behind bland conformance with etiquette, however, sentiment and behavior range from accord without a qualm to overt hostility. Feelings of resentment among all classes find expression in avoidance of those situations in which violations of the mores carry severe penalties.

267

Some Negroes are able to avoid contacts with whites in a great many areas of relationship. This is especially true of the upper classes, whose work and social life require only occasional contacts, and who have developed certain compensations for privileges denied. However, for the vast majority of Negroes the daily routine of life and work makes frequent contact inevitable; and as a result they have developed a wide variety of individual techniques, often subtle and calculating, for minimizing the area of effective exposure. The specific techniques employed are usually influenced greatly by the individual's education and experience, which contribute to his conception of his role. Further, the areas of avoidance differ greatly with social position; and there is a marked regional variation in the methods employed.

THE SOUTH

The social structure of the rural South is such that it is difficult for Negroes of any class to disregard the etiquette governing contacts between the races without running serious physical risks. Relationships in this setting are so personal and intimate in character that anyone who challenges the moral order becomes suspect; and few Negroes who plan to continue living in the section are willing to take the chance. There are, of course, many areas of personal relations within which contacts and communication occur without consciousness of insecurity. The general state of caution, however, prompts a limiting of the area of relationships whenever possible, thus reducing the possibility of conflict situations that may bring out latent hostilities and preserving self-respect in those actual situations where resentments, if aroused, must be suppressed.

Avoidance of Direct Physical Contact

Among the lower-class rural and urban Negroes the reaction to whites is dichotomized by the two extremities in the white class structure, namely, the upper class and the lower class. While there is a relative sense of security with the upper-class whites, which is concomitant with dependence upon them, the competitive aspect of the relations with the white lower class and the long history of mutual animosities create a totally different situation. If a lower- or lower middle-class Negro has an upper-class white man for a protector, this is security for the Negro in his relations with the courts and in matters of credit, illness, or financial crisis; but it helps little in his relations with lower-class whites. Most of the antiwhite sentiments expressed by these Negroes concern chiefly lower-class whites, or

whites of lower-class origin who have achieved positions of authority
on the police force or as foremen and overseers in industry or agriculture. Contact with them in these roles is limited, but inescapable.
The policy of a Negro farmer in Marked Tree, Arkansas, seems
fairly typical:

I found that the best way to get along with white folks is to just be
pretty careful and come in contact with them as little as possible. There
are times when you have to take a lot of things. Those things that you
can avoid, you ought to. I am not a white folks' "nigger," and I try to
keep out of trouble. I know, though, that I am in the South, and I know
they can make it hard for me, so I just try to attend to my business and
see if I can dodge a lot of trouble.

A Mississippi farmer, in describing his method of "getting along,"
expressed practically the same sentiment, and added:

If I decide that I want to back against somebody, I am going where
Negroes have a little more voice in politics.

The most common expressions of the lower- and lower middle-class
Negroes are:

I stay as far away from 'em as I can,

or

The farther they is from me, the better I like it,

or

When I see them, I let them have they side of the street, and goes on.

This desire to restrict contacts with whites to a minimum is also
revealed in the experience of a Negro mechanic in a rural North
Carolina town. In his daily routine he has to go to the post office,
where white clerks have an opportunity to remind him of his status.
He said:

They treat me all right, but I hear they treat some colored people bad.
I get my mail at my own box, so I don't have to say a word to them.

The desire to escape contacts with whites is one of the incentives
to farm ownership, even though this objective is not often achieved.
One independent Negro farmer said:

I have never done much work besides farming in my life. I would not
want to work for one of them [white persons]. If I can't have my own
little land without supervision, I don't want to farm. I like to work for
myself. I have always worked with Negroes in the South. I never did

have white people working for me. I don't think I would particularly like to work with them. I think I could get along with any of them.

In the urban South avoidance is facilitated by residential segregation, which is in part imposed and in part accepted as much from the desire to avoid contacts as from the desire for physical security. The problem is one of avoiding situations that can become racially critical. One concern of the lower-class groups was expressed by the woman who said:

I don't want 'em around me. First thing you know they be putting something on one of my boys and hanging them. I like them in their place.

Middle-class families do much of their shopping in neighborhood stores, where they are known and the merchants have sound financial reasons for being courteous, or at Negro stores, if such stores are reasonably adequate, even if their prices are higher. An upper-class Negro woman said that she did much of her routine shopping by telephone since her voice and diction could get more consideration than her face in the store.

In transportation, both local and long-distance, lower- and lower middle-class Negroes accept segregation and frequently inferior facilities without much question. Whenever possible middle- and upper-class Negroes adopt the substitute arrangement of automobile travel. It is often more expensive, but the emotional satisfaction derived from escaping humiliating treatment is considered worth the extra cost—and at the same time the carriers lose a fare. In one interview a middle-class girl confided:

I just can't ride these streetcars. I'm so glad dad has a car now and we don't have to be bothered with them.

In another instance a middle-class man saw a certain advantage resulting from the intent to segregate Negroes:

White people are helping us and don't know it. We tour in our own cars now more than by rail. We don't have to stand their insults on trains now. . . . That segregation is to our advantage.

An upper-class Negro in rural North Carolina, who had traveled for a great many years by railroad, explained his method of expressing objection to the "Jim Crow" coach:

Of course Negroes ride in the Jim Crow coach here. Everybody knows that. You'd better ride in the Jim Crow coach. But I don't ride in it; I just don't ride trains now. I use my car and drive anywhere I want to go. That's one of the reasons I have a car; so I can go when I please. I feel sorry for Negroes who have to ride trains and busses.

It is a frequent and proud boast of many Negroes of this class that they have never ridden in a segregated streetcar or bus.

Middle- and upper-class Negroes have other devices for avoiding direct physical contact with whites. In the southern cities the "collector" is a familiar figure, normally used by firms doing a large credit and installment business. Many white insurance companies carry large Negro debits which are handled by white agents. They are a familiar sight in Negro neighborhoods, standing in the doorways smoking, with their hats on, and adopting either a familiar mood or one of punitive severity. Middle- and upper middle-class Negroes object to this conduct and frequently make their payments by mail, or discharge the obligation with the fewest possible contacts, or use Negro companies. The limited range of policies and the cost of insurance with Negro companies, as well as the prestige and credit standing acquired by being insured in one of the larger standard companies, together encourage the antithetical desire for insurance with white companies but no contact with white agents. If the agents adopt an acceptable role they are tolerated; if not, the business is handled impersonally through the mails.

The Negro upper classes in the cities acknowledge a considerable educational and recreational loss to themselves in their refusal to attend theaters which segregate them and impose other humiliating conditions, such as entrance through back streets and alleys and restriction to the frequently dirty and poorly kept balconies with one class of seats. If the all-Negro theaters and auditoriums are not adequate—and they seldom are—these Negroes defer such satisfactions until a vacation or visit takes them to a northern area. In general, they will attend public meetings in the South only if they are equitably segregated or not segregated at all, although some fail to adhere to this pattern, reasoning that the educational value transcends the effects of the personal compromise.

Liberal Southerners interested in formal interracial meetings have been surprised that Negroes, and particularly young Negroes, do not like to attend them even when the object is to improve race relations. This lack of interest is merely another example of avoidance behavior, which is conspicuous among Negro college students and upper-class Negroes. A frequent and unsatisfactory result is that interracial youth meetings bring together upper-class whites and ambitious but less talented Negroes who lack both an intellectual and a cultural common ground. The adult interracial committees attract more responsible Negro membership and leadership; but the atmosphere of their meetings is frequently strained with mutual fears of transgressing some phase of the mores, the experience is unpleasant, and accomplishments are very limited, at best.

Behind the avoidance behavior of urban Negroes are many of the fundamental motives that condition behavioral responses in the rural environment; but the larger variety of institutions in the urban Negro community and in the city as a whole make urban Negroes less dependent upon any particular institution or set of institutions. Moreover, a larger proportion of urban Negroes are not directly dependent upon whites for a livelihood; and contacts with white persons may therefore be held to a minimum. It is possible for one who knows the devious paths of this "ultraviolet" world to travel through the South without encountering the blunt and menacing reminders of the race system. The Negroes who live there in a particular locality know what can and what cannot be done; the stranger from another city of the South is less certain of details but knows the broad pattern; the Negro from the North is lost and, unless escorted by a native, is almost certain to get into trouble.

Avoidance Based on Desire for Personal Safety

Violation of the etiquette of race relations in the South, especially in the rural South, carries the threat of reprisals which may take the form of physical injury. The inability of Negroes to achieve reasonable protection through the courts against the danger of injury to person and property is a source of deep-lying and permanent feelings of insecurity. Situations holding such dangers are, therefore, consistently avoided. When complete avoidance is not practicable, extreme care is necessary to prevent conflict. A Negro farmer in a rural Arkansas county pointed out that Negroes must be particularly careful in the use of an automobile:

You have to be pretty careful driving on the streets here in town. They [whites] drive so wild and crazy here that you have to be on your toes. I drive naturally, and watch out. The white women drivers are not as careful as they might be, so I keep close watch out for them. You know how far you would get with them in any kind of argument about right or wrong. The best thing I know is to stay on the right side, and as far out of the way as possible.

The fear that leads to avoidance when confronted with "ticklish" situations was expressed by a Negro insurance agent in a town in Mississippi:

It is an old saying that if you play with a dog he will lick your face. That is true as far as I am able to see. If you stand around and talk to those old peckerwoods they will be ready to do something to you if you act like you don't like it. I keep away from them as much as I possibly can.

Lower-class whites are particularly sensitive to any suggestion of Negro "arrogance" and are quick to suppress it with violence whenever it is safe to do so. Because this group is in most direct economic competition with the lower classes of Negroes, any conspicuous improvement in Negro status is easily interpreted as challenging the economic privileges of these whites, without regard to the exigencies of free competition. A Negro farmer in Alabama who had managed to save enough money to build a good home was advised by his upper-class white friend that if he built the house as planned, he should not paint the outside because this would provoke the envy and enmity of the lower-class whites, and the house would probably be burned down. He did not paint the house. When a rural Negro group wanted a better school, they offered to help with the work on a white school first, in order to reduce the pressure of objection to a new Negro unit.

Avoidance behavior is observed in the occupational sphere, especially in the case of middle-class Negroes. Where there is actual competition above the unskilled levels for jobs usually thought of as "white jobs," some Negroes will of their own choice accept symbols of lower status while performing work of higher rank. Thus a shipping clerk will wear overalls and accept the pay and title of a porter; a clerk will take the title and pay of a messenger; a nurse will permit herself to be called a domestic; and a chiropodist will enter the homes of white persons by the back door at night.

Sometimes Negroes must avoid certain jobs altogether. Thus for many years Negroes were employed as firemen on the Illinois Central Railroad line which runs from Illinois to Louisiana. However, a wave of ambush killing of these firemen and brakemen by whites who wanted their jobs had the effect of discouraging further Negro aspirations in this direction. A Mississippi Negro said:

They used to have Negroes braking and firing on the roads. The only reason that they are not there now is that they are afraid they will be shot off like dogs. So many of them did that in the past that few of the Negroes try to get those jobs now.

This avoidance is not restricted to potentially dangerous situations. Negroes and whites may occasionally develop a great deal of mutual

satisfaction from personal relations on a social level. It is a part of
the unique system of relations in the South for white persons to
extend to individual Negroes considerations which are categorically
denied the masses of the race. The "unnaturalness" of the relationship when other whites or Negroes become involved is liable to
prompt the Negro ultimately to withdraw. A Negro carpenter living
in Johnston County, North Carolina, related the following experience:

The white man across the street from here is just as nice to me as he
can be. He calls me over there and begs me to play checkers with him;
and he sells candy and drinks and things like that, so while we play he
insists that I eat with him. He carries the thing so far that sometimes
I get scared. He'll fix ice cream up for me any time, and both of us eat
there. I just stopped going over there so much because I didn't know
what those other white folks would think. You know they can get some
crazy things in their heads sometimes.

The experiences of a high-school principal in one of the states of
the upper South might be regarded as fairly typical. His school is
located near a white school. Boys from different schools, meeting
in groups going to and from school, not infrequently engage in fights
that take on the nature of informal sport. Such fights between white
and Negro boys, however, were more or less serious in their implications. They involved the security of the Negro community. The
principal solved this by keeping his boys at school until the white
boys had reached their homes.

When the Negro boys needed a basketball, they raised the money
and ordered one from New York. It was not received in time for a
scheduled game, and so one of the boys borrowed a ball from the
white high school, through a member of its team. The game was
played and the ball returned. The principal promptly brought the ball
back, saying, "My boys don't want the ball back. You keep it." The
Negro principal said of this, "That made me feel funny. I knew he
didn't want the white boys to use the ball after the colored boys had
played with it." Later the real concern appeared in the white principal's remark that he did not object to this type of co-operation, but
some influential white families might. These influential white
families included members of the school board who could make and
withdraw appointments; and their objections might actually mean
a loss of the principal's job.

In referring to voting in the community this Negro principal
said:

In —— I could have voted, because I probably would not have been noticed. Here [a smaller town] I would be too conspicuous. I might run into a board member at the polls, and since I don't know how he wants me to vote, I might not be voting the right way. So I just let it alone.

Another type of insecurity prompts avoidance of white contacts or even business with white people. This was brought out in the case of a Negro insurance agent for a company serving both Negroes and whites. He is sensitive and cautious in regard to certain limitations in his position. He said:

This company I work for is a pretty nice one. It is for Negroes and whites, but I never sell the whites any insurance. I always send them to one of the white agents. They would want me to be doing something that wasn't right. If I did not do it they would all be angry with me. The best thing that I can do under those circumstances is to stay out of their way. I do that by not writing any of them up.

Avoidance Based on Desire to Maintain Self-respect

Lower middle-class Negroes occasionally resort to avoidance as a method of striking back. A common laborer living in Marked Tree, Arkansas, severed his relations with several white insurance companies, and gave this as his reason:

I used to belong to two or three white insurance companies, but they have been dropped because they did not do right by me. I belong to a Negro company now, and I think I will remain with them and let the whites go their way. The Negroes need some help anyway. We have to do something to show these peckerwoods that they ought to respect us.

Another informant, a domestic servant living in the same area, goes fifty miles to Memphis to consult a Negro doctor because the local white doctors show so little concern and respect. This strongly motivated type of avoidance of white services has been one of the most important factors in the building up of Negro professional practice and business. Failure to show proper respect is sometimes carried to extremes, as in the case reported by a Negro carpenter in a small North Carolina community:

The white dentist here makes a difference between whites and colored. He's the only one here who does it, and I guess he wouldn't if there was a colored dentist here. You know he has special hours for colored, and he lets them all know they're colored. He insults the colored women so that none of them won't even pass his door. He's crazy about colored women. One of the colored teachers here didn't know about him, and she went to him to get some work done. He told her he would do the work and she wouldn't have to pay him a penny because she was just the girl he had been looking for. Of course she came away and told what he said. She was as mad as a hornet.

Any contact that results in personal insult or suggests group dis-respect may provoke avoidance behavior, especially in situations in which Negroes suffer no serious disadvantages. Since the Negro's own church institutions can be attributed as much to choice as to exclusion from white churches, no sacrifice is involved in avoidance of contacts in this sphere. There are not many church denominations in the South in which Negroes and whites worship in the same build-ing. The Catholic churches permit or encourage biracial worship more often than the Protestant. The Primitive Baptists continue the prac-tice of joint worship in some small southern communities. A Negro farmer in North Carolina described conditions in one of these churches and at the same time revealed the personal resentment that prompted his avoidance of them:

Down at the lower edge of Wayne county is a Primitive Baptist church with white and colored. It's been going on for years. My sister was a member. It has a white minister. It ain't nothing. It wouldn't happen here if I could help it. Why, it's very embarrassing. Take the preacher—you can't take him home to dinner with you. What kind of a preacher is that, if he can't be close to you? And the Negroes sit behind the preacher in the church. The white people are facing the preacher. Then they had a sign up on the wall, "Negroes drink at the spring." I went to their church and saw it and tore it down, and throwed it on the church. I never went back. But I talked to some of the white members about it, and I told them they ought not to have Negro members; but they said the old folks done it and they have to carry it on. But I think it's a mess. Any colored person that has any sense wouldn't go there.

A similar conflict between tradition and the newer self-conceptions of Negroes is illustrated in another informant's comment on mixed cemeteries:

When I was a boy I understood that Negroes and whites were buried in the Riverside Cemetery. That's a white cemetery. I can't explain it, unless it was on the basis of slaves. I guess they were just colored families which were attached closely to some white family ties carrying over from slavery. And then you know these new Negroes don't want all of that close tie-up. They want to do things for themselves. That may account for Negroes using their own cemeteries. Nowadays a Negro wouldn't want to be buried in a white cemetery. That's how most of us feel about it. I know I wouldn't want to bury any of my people in a white cemetery.

It is interesting that this informant who carefully avoids current tension situations finds stimulating emotional release in objecting to a situation which is harmless and no longer important. Nevertheless, it appears to play a part in preserving his balance and, accordingly, his self-respect.

Negroes avoid situations in which they fear embarrassment and humiliation, even though no physical danger is involved. Upper-class Negroes are especially sensitive to these situations because of the loss of prestige that may result. Quite as important, however, is the simple fact of discomfort in the presence of white persons with whom there is no common bond of interest or sentiment and hence no effective communication. Upper-class Negroes refuse invitations to participate in social activities with white persons, even those with whom they are well acquainted, because of the community pressures that would develop if the practice were carried on over a protracted period of time. Lower-class Negroes are more likely to avoid similar situations because they feel uncomfortable in them. They "just wouldn't feel right," especially with middle- or upper-class white persons. This is probably a class as well as a race reaction. A Negro brickmason, the only Negro worker on a construction job on which numerous white workers were employed, received an invitation to a semisocial event to which all his fellow workers were invited. He described the incident as follows:

> The owner of the hotel gave a big barbecue while the hotel was building. He invited everybody, and he invited me. I went to him and told him I couldn't come. He suspicioned something, and he said, "You won't be the only colored there. The boys tending the barbecue will be there, so you won't get lonesome." I thought fast and I told him, "You know, I'm uneducated and it takes a long sleep for me to read these blueprints for my next day's work. If it was on a Saturday night, when I had Sunday to read the blueprints, I would go." That night about 12 o'clock somebody knocked on the door, and there was a nigger with a dishpan full of barbecue and a pot of Brunswick stew. We had a big time. I hadn't seen them blueprints in a week.

There are, of course, some personal relations between Negro and white members of the lower classes, but these relations show marked evidences of social distance which hamper them and make them only tolerable and strained. With so much caution involved, the Negroes of all classes tend to be suspicious of the friendly gestures of whites. A Negro printer in one of the southern cities said:

> I do quite a lot of work for white people. Some of them come out here,

and they act too nice. I get suspicious when I see a white person acting too nice around a colored man. We have been doing business with two or three wholesale paper companies for about fifty years. When any of their salesmen come out here, or I call any of them, they treat me as nice as you could want. Several of the fellows down here asked me to go fishing with them. I didn't go because I don't believe in getting too thick with white people. I know this is the South, and I'm not a social climber, so I don't go in for anything like that.

The question of interracial dining is often a difficult one for middle- and upper-class Negroes. The influence of the taboo on the behavior of whites is so unpredictable in this situation that the Negroes prefer to avoid it. A Negro farm agent in a North Carolina county reported that he occasionally found himself in a rural home at mealtime in company with white farm agents, and commented on this situation as follows:

There's not much eating together. They'll put you at a separate table in the same room. I've never eaten with a white person. Now, only once was I in a tough spot. Mr. ——, extension agent, came here while we were finishing dinner. He asked for something we had, and I fixed him a separate table to eat on. I never offered him dinner with us; but other colored agents say he eats with them. I find they'll eat at your house if you ask them. But I'm as much above eating with them as they are with me. I don't ask them.

Their experiences with theaters and other commercial amusement places reveal the tendency of Negroes of all classes to seek compensatory satisfactions in the less adequate institutions of the Negro community. The values may be less, and adjusted to the most numerous element in the population, but they afford greater security and relaxation. In most of the southern cities there are the larger theaters with segregated and usually inferior accommodations for Negroes in the balconies; and there are all-Negro theaters, with inferior productions. This combination of facilities has peculiar results. The lower-class and less sensitive Negroes see the better productions from the balconies of the superior theaters, while the more sensitive and better educated Negroes attend the inferior shows.

A Negro physician who regards the side (alley) entrance by which Negroes enter some white theaters as a cause for embarrassment explained his position:

I never go to the theaters in the South. I just think that if I am not good enough to go in the front door I am too good to go in the alley entrance. I have had invitations from the management of these theaters to see certain movies, and I have written letters about the alley entrance on a number of occasions. I had an invitation from the management of Loew's when the movie *Men in White* was playing there. In the letter he was telling me what a fine picture it was, and that it was something every physician ought to see. I wrote him a letter telling him that I never attended his theater because I object to the entrance in the alley. I told him that we don't want to eat with white people and we don't want to sit with them. We are satisfied with our own people. But what we want is a respectable entrance in front of the movie house. I said that it should be embarrassing for him to receive this letter, but it is not embarrassing for me to write it. I appealed to him as an intelligent person not to insult Negroes by inviting them to come to a theater where they have to go through an alley to get inside.

The policy of exclusion in many cases and the practice of discourteous treatment in a great many others have not often provoked aggressive efforts by Negro citizens to correct the circumstances. This does not imply that all Negroes resignedly accept these discriminatory practices in all cases, but rather that there has been no organized effort to correct them.

In both rural and urban settings one of the situations most frequently avoided, notably by middle- and upper-class Negroes, is that involving modes of address regarded as disrespectful. In fact, the promptness with which instances of failure to use titles of respect are mentioned, whenever the question of racial discrimination is raised, suggests that this offense to personal self-esteem might be considered more acute than the fact of segregation itself. Avoidance of being addressed by one's first name has been called "a middle-class pattern." A Negro executive of a social organization in a southern city said:

The clerks give all Negroes who seem to ask for it their titles. Of course you know our middle class pattern. Our accounts are in the name of Mrs. J. W. Jones, or something like that, never Mrs. Mary Jones. We force the issue by avoiding the giving of the first name. The clerk has no alternative except to call you nothing.

Negro women of this group resist the white clerks' practice of calling all Negro women by their first names by using only their husbands' initials. One informant reported:

I always give my name to the clerks as M. F. Jameson, so they can't call me by my first name, Mary. One old girl was selling me some face powder, and I told her, "Mrs. M. F. Jameson." She said, "What's *your* name?" I said, "M. F. Jameson." She said, "What's your first name?" I said, "M. F." She said, "That's a funny name."

Contrarily, Negroes avoid the established pattern of addressing whites in many instances in which no real respect is felt or when feelings of status are involved. Interestingly enough, it is not so often the members of the upper classes who are disposed to avoid giving titles of respect, or to omit titles altogether, as it is those of the lower classes in relation to lower-class whites. Upper-class Negroes regard the use of titles of respect as a dictate of their superior training, while some lower-class Negroes appear to derive revengeful satisfaction from the omission of a title, or the substitution of another title than that required by the etiquette. A Negro in Nashville, who had worked for a period in a foundry in Ohio, made this admission:

I remember I had a hard time getting back in the swing of things after going up North. I don't call all of them "Mr." Some of them don't merit being called that. If I think that some of these crackers want me to call them "Mr." I just don't call them nothing. I just say "hey" and talk right loud to him without calling him anything.

The substitution of titles other than "Mr." and "Mrs." by Negroes suggests retaliation for the whites' practice of addressing Negroes as "professor" or "doctor" instead of the more appropriate "Mr." The use of these exaggerated titles by Negroes in addressing whites permits sly retaliation without incurring serious risks. The white man is flattered and the Negro is amused. This device was well described by a Negro porter in Houston:

I usually say "judge," "lawyer," or "colonel," just like they do to us. I know that none of them are judges, and some of them I call lawyers are not lawyers. I just do it because they do us that way, and they like it. They think I am just fine. Where I work I call a lot of those fellows "editor." Some of them aren't any more than reporters or just office help; but I call them "editor" anyhow. They like to be flattered. Some of the boys I know very well I call by their first names. We have some down there who belong to the National Guard, and I call them "captain." They like to be impressed that they are big shots.

An unskilled laborer in Birmingham explained how he carefully estimated the white person and the situation before deciding upon his method of address. Whenever possible he avoided using a title:

If I am out and I don't care whether I get what I want or not from one of these old crackers I might call him anything. Like if I want a cigarette, I may say, "Hey, buddy, give me a smoke." I would just about get it if he was the only one around. He would not get mad. If he did I would not care; I know that he better not start nothing about calling him "Mr." I do like they do to me. If I think it is best for me to say "Mr." I say it. I don't have to say it to these old "red necks" unless I want to, though. That is the stuff that burns me up.

There are situations in which upper middle- and upper-class Negroes employ elaborate indirect methods in order to escape the personal impact of discrimination, or to respond to it in a socially acceptable manner. A Negro physician in Nashville on an emergency case parked his car too long, and when he returned a policeman approached him. Officers have the right to give tickets for violating traffic rules if warranted, and with less authority they sometimes upbraid careless or indifferent white drivers; but in the case of the Negro physician the officer threatened to "beat hell out of him" if he violated a traffic regulation again. The physician said:

I just felt like waiting for that fellow and getting him. When it happened I promised myself to get even, but after I cooled off I just forgot it. I know this is the South and you might just as well recognize it.

What he actually did was to make a formal complaint to the chief of police, a very proper procedure, but one that in this case had no more likelihood of bringing satisfaction than responding directly to the officer. However, the southern police system was given the opportunity to correct itself.

This dependence upon the institutions to aid in avoiding direct encounter in matters affecting the self-respect of Negroes appears in the hopes of southern Negroes with respect to the ballot. A Negro lawyer in one city expressed his conviction in these words:

The future of the Negro in this town is dependent on his using the ballot. There are 120,000 Negroes here in this town. That is enough to make anything that we want out of any white man. I am looking forward to the time when I will be able to have a hand in an organization that can elect the governor of this state and tell the president whom we want for a district judge. When you get that strong there won't be any little problem about the place that Negroes can sit on the car and that kind of stuff.

An able Negro in Houston, a politician, barber, and college graduate, expressed his belief in the ballot in these optimistic words:

If we can get it [the ballot] there will be a decided change in the way that the Negro gets along here in Houston. . . . If we can get some of the things done that we plan, it won't be long before the present barrier to voting is removed. I think that with close to a hundred thousand Negroes here we ought to get the things that we need, in proportion to the representation that we have in the general population.

In his case words are accompanied by deeds. He has set in motion a political organization in Houston which has a membership of 1,700, and which has been suing officials who showed discrimination against Negroes; and it is actually conducting a factual study of the Negroes' standard of living in that city as a basis for their future campaign.

It has sometimes been suggested that Negroes who make it a policy to avoid occasions for discrimination often have an absorbing interest in improving their own status. Instead of spending their energy on making complaints or taking other retaliatory measures, they spend it in ways which will eventually advance them to a superior class position and give them a certain measure of compensation for their inferior caste status. This is well illustrated in the case of an automobile mechanic in Johnston County who turned aggressive impulses into constructive work for self-advancement. He was first employed in a garage at a salary of $10 a week. After a white man asked if he could do "real good" work on his car and not "nigger-fashion" work, the mechanic said he resolved to do only first-class work in repairing cars. He patiently learned the trade and in the course of eight years finally succeeded in securing a much better job; and he was running a garage of his own at the same time. He refrained from voting, in order to avoid trouble with whites; and he once declined to tell the truth about the bad treatment he had received at the county hospital for fear that, while his boss was away, "they'd try to kill" him.

Somewhat similar is the case of an unmarried domestic servant who said of herself:

I worked awhile in service and then was able to begin a course in beauty culture. I didn't want to spend my life working in white people's kitchens, and I knew I could never go to college, so I thought if I could open a beauty shop I could make a good living.

In response to discrimination she consistently avoided such public places as parks and large stores where Negroes were not welcome; and at the time of the interview she had not been downtown for months, "because," she said, "I don't put myself on them when I know I'm not wanted."

It has also been suggested that Negroes who adopt the avoidance pattern in response to discrimination often transfer their aggressive impulses toward whites to Negroes of the lower class. Instead of holding the whites responsible for caste barriers, so-called lower-class Negroes are blamed for the discrimination that all classes have to share. The following statement by a senior postal clerk in Indianapolis seems to be typical. In explaining to the interviewer the necessity of his wife's chaperoning their daughter, he said:

We have a very low class of Negroes in Indianapolis. That is one reason why it is difficult for us to insist on all of our rights. We can't go to the white people and ask that certain Negroes be admitted to places and others refused. I can't blame white people, though, for drawing a line.

In his actual relations with whites he practices avoidance; and he is one of the leaders of the Negro community advocating a separate school system and a separate wing for Negroes in the city hospital. He gives as his reason the desire to secure more jobs for Negroes; but the more aggressive Negroes do not agree with him in this.

A successful elderly carpenter of Johnston County made it a practice to go to the market himself every Saturday in order to keep his wife at home and thereby protect her from whites. He had this to say about lower-class Negroes:

The lower-class Negro don't respect himself. He does so many things to show that he don't respect himself that you can't expect the white man to respect him. Our people will get drunk and beat their wives and fight each other like dogs. Then they expect the white man to respect them. How can he when he knows all about them.

In his actual dealings with whites he practiced avoidance except in his place of work; and he said he would not mix with whites even in the church, "for I want to be where everybody is colored."

Diversion Tactics of Avoidance

Other forms of avoidance utilize well-conceived diversion tactics that might be referred to as "positive indirection." A lower-class Negro about fifty-five years of age drove a very disreputable car with defective brakes as well as an uncertain motor; shortly after dark one night at a highway intersection he drove into a new and expensive car carrying a white man and three white women passengers. The new car was badly dented and scarred, and one of the women was slightly injured about the face. Promptly the Negro began in a loud and terrorized voice to abuse his old car for having no better sense than to bump into "a white man's pretty automobile." He pointed to the damage it had done to the new car and to the passengers; stroked the crushed fenders and side with his hat; elaborated on the stubborn and sinful recklessness of his "no-count" vehicle; threatened to take an ax and beat it into scrap iron. An upper-class Negro chanced to be passing shortly after the crash; and when he saw the cars in difficulty, stopped his car a short distance away and walked back to see if he could be of any assistance. In the midst of the tirade against his "ole fool of a nothin'," the old Negro without shifting the tempo of his speech signaled frantically to the other one to go back. Misunderstanding the signal, the upper-class Negro came closer, and without looking directly at him the other whispered, "Man, go on out of the way befo' you git me in trouble." The upper-class Negro withdrew to a distance and observed the remainder of the drama. In the end the white owner of the wrecked car helped the Negro push his old wreck off the highway, and the incident was closed.

"Clowning" is, in the same sense, a lower-class avoidance method. If it is suspected that a racial situation is impending, the Negro may resort to the diverting device of entertaining the whites. Among potentially hostile whites such Negroes will affect exaggerated physical response to tickling; wear their hats on their heads upside down; cut fantastic openings, for comfort, in their shoes; cut fancy jig steps; laugh loud and infectiously; roll their eyes; make wide gestures of fear and fright; or sing ludicrous songs.

The diversion type of avoidance is not wholly confined to the lower classes. One middle-class Negro, when stopped by a menacing officer for violating a traffic regulation, pretended to be illiterate and incapable of reading signs and, after appropriate recognition of the racial and personal vanity of the officer, got off with a mild reprimand. This is not unlike the shrewd Negro who ran through a red stop light and explained to the officer that he saw the white folks going through the green light and thought that the red light was for colored folks. This was utilization of the segregation theme to escape possible danger.

Upper-class Negroes have reported that they can sometimes throw a suspicious and possibly dangerous white officer off guard by facing him directly and asking a question. In certain other circumstances they escape problem situations by speaking a foreign language. A party of four Negroes, including one who spoke Spanish fluently, had trouble with their car in a small town. The one who spoke Spanish went to a hotel patronized exclusively by whites and asked in that language for a room for himself and his party. Since no one could speak Spanish and he apparently spoke only enough broken English to convey the point of the request, the party was accommodated as possible South Americans.

Avoidance of Mixed Labor Organizations

Some reference should be made in this connection to the situation in the organized labor movement in the South. Members of the Negro minority have joined the union standards in large numbers, especially the Congress of Industrial Organizations with their official advocacy of democracy in labor circles and their emphasis upon rank-and-file control. Despite these ideals, however, the strength of custom in the South is such that local organizations have not yet succeeded in translating many of their principles into practice. As a result many Negro workers have failed to lend general support to the union cause and have avoided these relations, preferring to work as independents or in separate unions. The short but descriptive view of the situation expressed by a Negro carpenter in Atlanta may be regarded as typical:

In Atlanta I never joined the union because of segregation. All of the big jobs were awarded to the union and they won't let a union Negro work on the job.

"Passing" as a Form of Avoidance

Negroes with physical traits closely resembling those of the white race may represent themselves as white and be popularly and consistently treated as whites. In the vernacular this is called "passing," but it is another method of avoiding discrimination and segregation. Although some distinguishable Negroes accept this practice for those able to carry out the deception either as a simple matter of personal choice or as a vengeful vindication of their race philosophy, there are others who object to the practice and regard such persons as race traitors whose just punishment is denouncement to the white group. Negroes may "pass" in an effort to get away from their race, or they may "pass" merely to escape its more acute handicaps. In the latter case they retain, so far as possible and practicable, their social relations in the Negro world.

To prevent detection, however, those who "pass" do not associate with other recognizable members of the group while playing the white role. A Negro woman living in Houston, who "passes" on occasion, tells of the manner in which it is done, and of the satisfactions derived therefrom:

To prevent things like that [failure to be waited on when accompanied by other Negroes] I don't go to these places much with any other Negroes. The only places where I do not get the same treatment as whites are those where I am known. I don't try to slight my color, but

I don't see why I ought to deny myself things I can get. I have been to some of the best shows downtown. They would not think of letting all the Negroes go there. I am not usually afraid, because I can put up a pretty good front. They are pretty careful before they call a person a Negro. I look somewhat like a foreigner, so I can get by without a great deal of trouble. I like to put one over on them occasionally.

One would think that, considering the presumed risk of "passing," only exceptionally bold persons would attempt it. This is either not the case or there are more bold Negroes than is usually assumed. In rural areas and small towns where everyone is known, "passing" is not safe. In some southern cities it is easy in public places because of the number of swarthy whites. The intent is not always to deceive even in situations in which deception would be readily possible.

A well-known Negro poet boarded a train in Georgia and turned toward the Negro coach. When the conductor shouted to him to go into the white car, he paid no attention. Later when approached again by the conductor and told to move, he replied that he belonged where he was sitting. Puzzled, the conductor examined the man's hair and hands, but without any helpful clues in his association of speech or dress, had to take the word of the passenger. The conductor then became ingratiating and explained that he had to watch for white men who came into the colored coach to "meddle the girls."

Another upper-class Negro, the son of a well-known executive, answered a call to military service and reported with some of his friends and classmates at a Negro camp. The white officers in charge were so convinced that he was white that they had *blood tests* made and "proved" it. It required much documentary evidence and persuasion for him to remain in and with his race.

Under the circumstances it is not difficult to understand how casual contacts can place the presumption on the white side, with or without personal design. The difference in treatment and in available facilities is quite considerable. The practice is, thus, as constant as the pressure of the whites makes it, and this is usually in the direction of classification of the person as white.

Sex Avoidance

The powerful sex taboos, particularly as they affect Negro men and white women, prompt behavior of the avoidance type where members of the opposite sex and race are concerned. There is the popular belief among the white group, especially white men, that Negro men have more or less chronic sex designs on white women; this is the stereotype that is commonly used in defense of the practice of lynching. So active is this fear that some of the more sex-minded of the white population assume proximity and opportunity to be tantamount to insult or assault, or threat of assault. In any such situation the burden of proof of innocence is on the pair; but in the case of a Negro man and white woman it is never proper to suspect the woman, and thus the burden of proof is on the Negro man, or the circumstances. Further, any attempt of the white woman to assert the innocence of the man raises the question of interest in protecting him. To escape this equally uncomfortable suspicion it is easier for the woman, unless she has a pronounced and self-sacrificing interest in human justice, to accept the chivalric protection of the men of her race. Negro men of all classes are aware of this mentality and studiously avoid all situations that place them in lone contact with white women.

For some Negro women the sex taboo on Negro men has been a satisfying motive for retaliatory repulsion of the advances of white men. A Negro domestic, in response to overtures from a white cab driver, promptly replied that she could get black, brown, and yellow in her own race and did not care to be bothered with white men. The assumption of the "easy virtue" of Negro women exposes all of them to the sex designs of whites who seek safe adventure across the line of race. As a result many Negro women have found it necessary to avoid all situations favorable to these unwelcome advances. When they cannot avoid the situation, they repel the advances with the most embarrassing allusions and retorts that come to mind.

THE BORDER AREA

In many respects the border areas are not very different from the upper South. There is an absence of formal and legal segregation in some areas, but the racial discrimination is more acute, if anything, because it is unexpected. In these areas there is frequently more consciousness of the problem of keeping the Negro in his place, and less certainty in the Negro group about what that place is. The atmosphere surrounding interracial contacts is thus considerably more tense, although both the formal and informal penalties for infringement of the mores are less severe. In spite of the existence of more occasions for free association, there is in the state of uncertainty a stronger disposition on the part of Negroes to seek emotional security in racial institutions of their own making. Avoidance behavior in these areas is more often in the direction of escaping the total situation and tends to develop aggressive race-mindedness rather than petty devices for circumventing individual situations.

Avoidance in Personal Relations

There is not much personal contact in homes although the taboos are less rigid than in the South. Lower-class Negroes behave substantially as in the South, and the middle and upper classes maintain a social distance by avoiding contacts. Protection of person is the motive underlying this avoidance pattern in both races, and this is an indication of the tension-laden atmosphere surrounding such relationships. In referring to his attitude regarding the visiting of white homes, a Negro barber living in Indianapolis said:

I never go to their homes to visit. I don't have no business there and I don't want them visiting me. We don't have that social visiting around here and it's best not to because if anything happens like a falling out, or any trouble, sure as you're setting here, the Negro he's going to come out at the bad end. I never seen it fail.

In the same city a respected Negro of the upper middle class enjoys the reputation of having been the only Negro to hold a certain government position. He grew up in this community and as a boy played with white children. Some of these childhood friends still live there and treat him with cordiality. Two of them are now prominent merchants in the city and occasionally call at his home. Despite frequent invitations to return these visits, he has never done so. He said:

My wife and I don't visit among white people. These friends of mine drive by here once in a great while and stop in but we don't go to their homes. They have invited us but of course I don't expect their families and friends to accept us. I don't push in because we happened to be friends as children. I don't think the respectable Negro wants to be entertained in white people's homes. We ask that we be treated courteously and that we be given all the rights any citizen should expect.

In this avoidance behavior the conditioning factor is fear of injury to self-esteem.

An interesting view of social intercourse between the two groups was given by a Negro waitress in a white café in Baltimore. She explained her refusal to allow her son to play with white children as follows:

Here colored children play to themselves and white children play to themselves. I think it ought to be like that. I don't let my kid play with white ones. There aren't any white people living near us anyhow, but if there was some I'd not let my boy play with them. I think we should teach them that while they are small and there wouldn't be any trouble later on. Soon as children get to fighting the parents get into it and trouble starts. I intend to teach my kids they are as good as anyone but let them know white people don't think so and don't want them about.

Avoidance in Professional Relations

In the border area the social distance evidenced in general relationships between the races carries over into professional and upper-class relations. The white professional men lack that element of southern tradition that tolerated a properly respectful Negro clientele; and many Negroes feel that these white professionals are not interested in them as cases. As a result the Negro professional has his best opportunity and is encouraged in this area. The general feeling of "not being wanted" carries over into the hospitals, where some Negro patients assert that the white nurses take a "disdainful" attitude toward the patients in their care.

The general point of view regarding the use of white doctors was expressed by an informant in Indianapolis:

I prefer Negro doctors. I never called a white doctor in my life. The only reason I had one to operate on me was because I was forced to. They don't permit Negro doctors to do operations in the hospital. I understand most of the white doctors ain't so particular about Negro patients. When I am sick I want someone who is interested in me to be my doctor. The colored doctor is interested in his patients. He can't wait on no white folks, so he gives Negroes extra care to make a good name for himself. I go to Negro dentists, too. We got a whole lot of Negroes who just like to brag that they go to a white specialist or some white doctor. Ain't nothing to it. These doctors don't get them well. They don't even want to bother with them, yet they go to them and get overcharged.

The same point of view was expressed by a Negro physician living in that city:

For a doctor, I stay pretty well and seldom have to use one [a doctor]. If I do I call a Negro. I don't use white doctors. Even in consultation, if I can't get the best white man in whatever field I happen to need conference on I don't bother with them. White doctors do not want to treat Negroes here. They don't mind when they are just getting started and need experience and money to establish themselves. They will open up their offices in a section outlying a Negro district. They are very polite and courteous to the Negro while they need him. As soon as they get established down town they ignore Negroes. They even refuse to make home visits to former patients.

The same reaction to white doctors was reported by Negroes in Baltimore, where there is a decided preference for Negro doctors.

One woman who had had experience with both Negro and white
doctors gave her reason for calling on Negro doctors when in need
of medical services. On one occasion she had been advised to go
to a white specialist. Although he had no separate waiting rooms,
he seemed quite perfunctory and unconcerned about her physical
condition; according to her, he "seemed like he got tired of answering questions and he ain't told me what was wrong yet." She then
went to a Negro doctor who told her that she had low blood pressure and ordered a special diet, which improved her condition. The
experience was more a social than a professional one in her estima-
tion. She added:

I know some white doctors don't like to touch bad-looking Negroes.
Some here won't even go to a call if they know it is a colored home.

She told of a Negro friend who called a white doctor. When he
learned that the patient was colored, he left abruptly, stating that
the wrong doctor had been called.

The experiences reported may be slight exaggerations, but the
fact remains that the Negro medical profession flourishes in the
border cities, where there is less competition than in either the
South or the North.

Avoidance of Embarrassing Situations
in Department Stores

As has been shown, in the border areas the large department
stores are more explicit and positive in their segregation and discrimination practices than are the stores in the South. Negroes
of all classes, and particularly of the middle and upper classes,
are sensitive to the obvious unfairness of these practices and avoid
them whenever possible. Some of the more financially able ones
make their purchases in near-by northern cities where the policies
in dealing with Negro customers are different. The great majority
of the Negroes, however, in avoiding disrespect and embarrassment
in the downtown department stores, turn to the inferior shops in
the Negro communities. These enterprises are most often operated
by Jewish owners, and the managers make a special effort to secure
Negro patronage. The number of these stores and the manner in
which they expand in size are evidence of the extent to which they
are used by members of the Negro group.

In describing the attitude of the larger firms toward Negro
customers and her reasons for not visiting these establishments,
the wife of a Baltimore longshoreman said:

I ain't been downtown for over five years. I know they don't want Negroes, and I ain't one to push myself on them. Some stores is awful. I stopped at the door of one store downtown, trying to decide to go in, and they come outside before I made up my mind and told me they don't 'low no niggers in them stores. They wasn't polite about it. Just as hateful as they could be. Certainly did say "nigger." That happened to me several times, then I stopped going. Some of the places won't let Negroes try on nothing. We got a store not far from here, and I been over to buy, but they come right out and say, "You ain't 'lowed to try nothing on." Down at the May Company Department Store they only let Negroes go in the basement. They don't even let them stop on the first floor to look around. They got a special man there just to tell Negroes to go to the basement. Hultzer and Kahn is one of the biggest stores downtown, and it's run by Jews, but they don't permit Negroes to go in. I ain't never tried Bonwit-Lennon. It's one of them high-class places, and I know they ain't got colored trade. I just don't bother in them stores. They treat you so cool I rather not go. I don't intend to try any more either. It hurts my pride to spend my money with white folks that don't want it.

This attitude is not unusual. The chief objection is to what is described as the insulting behavior of the clerks under the policy of segregation. A young woman of light-brown complexion went into a store and asked for flesh-colored hose. The clerk brought out a pair of heavy black stockings and told her she could take them or leave them. It was embarrassing enough to keep the girl from ever returning there to shop.

In some of the stores Negroes are allowed to try on hats only after placing a small white pad on their heads to prevent soiling. One of our informants regarded this practice as a gross insult, and it led directly to avoidance thereafter. She said:

I went in there one day and was going to try on a hat. The clerk come giving me a little white cap. I turned to her and looked her straight in the eye and asked her what was she giving me that for. I told her, "I don't want to buy no white cap, I want a hat." She come telling me Negroes got grease on their hair and soil the hats. I said, "I ain't got no more grease on my head than you. I wash my hair just like you, and don't put no grease on it, and I'm just as clean as you." I wasn't buying no hat that I had to try on over a white cap. Well, she looked at my hair, and then she looked at me and said, "All right, go ahead and try them on, only please be careful." I decided I wouldn't buy from her, and went back on down to Pennsylvania Avenue and got me a dollar hat.

Sex Avoidance

The sex taboo is as strong in the border area as in the South, even though the penalties for violation are not always so severe.

Most Negroes avoid situations that might suggest sex intimacy. A Negro domestic worker in Indianapolis said of sex contact between Negro men and white women:

> That's dynamite in this man's town. Didn't you read about that Negro who got lynched right here in Indiana? Sure, they caught him with a white woman. They didn't do nothing to her, but they sho' nuff lynched him. They will send Negroes to jail if they catch them talking to white women too much. These men are too scared to run with white women. Some of the cheapest crowd may but they go to jail if they are caught.

There is perhaps less sex contact between white men and Negro women than in parts of the South. The Negroes are in better position to demand and enforce mutuality of avoidance in this respect.

Avoidance and Negro Personality Development

We have referred to the fact that segregated institutions and discriminatory treatment have some discernible influence on the personality development of Negroes. Many of them are aware of the damaging effects on personality and shield themselves as far as possible against situations involving segregation and discrimination. Negro parents are particular in many instances to have their children avoid situations offering any opportunity for sensing the inequalities of the racial system. The mother who refused to allow her child to play with white children through fear of later disillusionment is a case in point. Similarly, the suggestion of a Negro executive of a large insurance company, who lives in Indianapolis, regarding discrimination in colleges may account for the migration of increasing numbers of Negro youth to southern colleges. Speaking of the situation obtaining in a college in Indianapolis and of its effect upon students of the Negro group, he said:

> I think most Negroes do better in their own schools. When they get into white schools they aren't welcomed and they begin to feel self-conscious. I've never been to a white school but I've met people who have attended mixed schools and they have told me they couldn't enter into things. We've got a college here in the city called Butler University. It's a church school, supposed to be liberal and religious and they have been awful hard on Negroes. They are forced by the law to have a few Negro students if they apply but if you've been reading the papers you've seen how bad they have been treating them. They have been trying to put them in a special place to eat and give them a separate rest room, and one girl out there told me they tried to make Negro students sit together in classes. When they have all that to fight they can't give themselves to their work. At a Negro college they feel they belong.

This type of sentiment supports the argument for separate Negro schools in border states, where by law the elementary and secondary schools may be either mixed or separate.

In summarizing the avoidance behavior of Negroes in the border areas, it should be emphasized that avoidance in the critical areas is more complete than in the South. In the border areas Negroes are more or less accommodated to the racial system, which demands their exclusion from many areas of possible relationship. The hostile attitude of whites toward any attempt on the part of Negroes to alter the mores places a negative value on measures designed to correct existing inequalities. Direct discrimination and greater immunity together have stimulated the formation of associations whose programs aim at reduction, or punishment, of racial inequalities. Illustrations are found in the fight of Negro teachers in Maryland for salary scales equal to those of white teachers and the aggressive measures employed by Negro citizens of Indianapolis in appealing to the municipal government, and eventually to the federal government, for justice to the Negro citizenry in the construction of a Negro wing of the city hospital. There is evident, however, a lack of individual aggressiveness in meeting discriminative situations, and though at times shrewd methods have been devised to achieve the satisfactions which the folkways of the area deny, there is a disposition to avoid completely those situations which are laden with possibilities for conflict.

Chapter XIV

HOSTILITY AND AGGRESSION

Hostility is regarded here as the active expression of an antagonistic attitude. In the preceding chapter it was noted that some forms of avoidance also reveal antagonistic attitudes in relation to segregation and discrimination. The essential difference is that in one instance the expression is controlled, whereas in the other it is either unrestrained or deflected. There is an abundance of evidence, from all classes of the Negro population, suggesting that some element of resistance, or resentment, or hostility is present in responses to critical interracial situations.

A general distinction may be made between covert and overt expressions of hostility. In the first, antagonistic attitudes are expressed, usually vocally, to a person or other social object believed or known to be outside the range of communication of the person or group toward whom hostility is felt. Comments made by Negroes to other Negroes are usually in this category. In the second, antagonistic attitudes are expressed, vocally or physically, directly to the person or group toward whom hostility is felt, or to another social object believed or known to be within range of communication. For example, if a Negro makes an insulting remark to a white person in a face-to-face relationship or about him to another white person, either remark may be regarded as an overt expression of hostility. The two expressions belong in the same category as actual physical conflict, although they are less violent. In general it may be said that overt expression of hostility is intended to provoke definite reaction on the part of the object of the hostile attitude, while covert expression gives vent to the hostility while avoiding reaction.

The different types of hostility may be classified as personal hostility, group hostility, and impersonal hostility. In the first, the object of a hostile attitude is a person, although the social agent may be either a person or a group. An example, which will be documented hereinafter, is found in a southern rural county where Negroes as a group have a hostile attitude toward a white relief administrator whom they hold personally responsible for what they believe to be obvious discrimination in the administration of relief. This type of hostility is more likely to be based upon specific experiences of a social agent than the other two types. Where the object of hostility is a group of persons, their general attitude may arouse hostility, although the social agent knows of no specific experiences upon which it is based and even admits to exceptions within the group toward whom hostility is felt. The hostility of a social agent is impersonal when directed toward a geographic area (the South, the county, etc.) or a social situation in which he cannot or does not individualize or personalize members of the group as objects of his hostility.

Hostility may be classified also according to the basic motivating factors of physical safety, self-esteem, economic well-being, and sexual recognition. Hostility may arise (1) as a means of maintaining these basic "rights", (2) as a device for obtaining them, or (3) as an expression of resentment because of being deprived of them.

THE SOUTH

Overt Hostility and Aggression

Hostility and aggression are closely related as forms of response to the race system. They are most often in evidence in crisis situations. Few Negroes in the South go out seeking occasions for the release of their feelings of antagonism; but there are those who, after utilizing the ordinary avoidance devices, resign themselves to conflict without regard for consequences. In some cases release of hostility is prompted by the reflection that there is no more safety in one mode of behavior than in another; that defense lies in taking the offensive. In other cases, in which status and education play a part, overt expression of hostility may be prompted by concern for self-esteem.

The Negro's usual mode of expressing hostility toward whites in the South is covert, the factor of physical safety being paramount in regulating the mode of expression. Recognizing that their physical safety is constantly threatened by both public and private agents of the race system, Negroes restrict their actions and expressions accordingly. Individual temperament, however, plays some part in determining the form of expression of hostility. In an encounter with a white neighbor of her employer a Negro domestic threatened to "wring her guts out holding her hair" and so frightened her employer that she fainted. A young Negro schoolgirl in Memphis confessed that she hated all white people, explaining that she hated them because they hated, and were mean to, Negroes. She said, "I want to be true to my race and I can't be true to my race and like white people too, can I?" She had knocked down a white girl who called her smaller brother a "nigger."

The most frequent instances of direct hostility occur in minor situations, usually involving an infringement of personal privacy in the Negro home. When action is taken in such cases, two things are generally insisted upon: (1) the white person must remove his hat, and (2) he must use titles of respect in addressing the Negroes. Such situations are not as common among lower- and lower middle-class Negroes as among middle- and upper-class Negroes; but occasionally there is such insistence, especially if the white is also of the lower class and entering the Negro home for business reasons.

The dependence of white agents on Negro business is a strong weapon in the hands of Negroes who are disposed to express their general or personal hostility. A white agent selling bedspreads in a Negro community in Atlanta entered the home of a Negro brick-layer, who is a church member and normally regarded as a peaceful man. For a few moments the bricklayer watched the salesman standing with his hat on in the presence of his wife and then exploded:

What's the matter with your hat—glued to your head?

The salesman, surprised and confused by this unexpected defiance of the etiquette, replied half defensively that his company would fire him if he "took off his hat in a nigger's home." The Negro shouted, "Well, I'm going to fire you right now. Get out of here." When the man tried to argue, the Negro moved menacingly toward him, and the white man left. If the salesman had chosen to make an issue of this, he would have damaged his chances for further sales in that neighborhood. If he had chosen to accept the rebuke, he would have had to remove his hat in other Negro homes or run the risk of a similar physical encounter elsewhere.

It is quite common for a Negro to express direct retaliatory aggression by talking back to a white when discriminated against, voicing his complaint, and in many cases effectively demanding respect, or at least the external manifestation of it, on the part of the offending white. Thus when a clerk in a Nashville store suddenly left the wife of a professional Negro to wait upon a white customer who appeared, and a second clerk asked the Negro woman whether she could afford to open another account, she spoke back directly to both clerks and threw the things she was buying to the floor. She had no hesitation in expressing her anger at the treatment she received.

Another upper middle-class Negro woman, a high-school teacher in Atlanta, was examining some articles in a store. When a white woman customer pointed to the article she was examining and said, "I want that," she retorted promptly, "I am buying it." A clerk in the store once insisted on knowing the first name of the same Negro woman when accepting her payment; but she complained to the floorwalker, and the salesgirl later had to apologize to her. On another occasion a white man moved ahead of this teacher in a line at a post office, where discrimination is not supposed to exist since it is a federal institution. She quickly stepped in front of him saying, "Do you know what you are doing? Don't you know you are supposed to be behind me in this line?"

There are examples of more direct and violent expression of hostility among the "unprotected" lower-class Negroes. In one of the southern cities a Negro named John Brown was greatly but discreetly admired by other Negroes. He was a quiet, slow-moving man of medium stature but with powerful arms. He hated all white people and, although he seldom attempted to provoke a conflict, seemed always to welcome any opportunity for an encounter. At the age of eighteen he had received a severe and unwarranted beating by police officers and since then had been piling up a record of successful encounters with them and with any other white men who took liberties with him. On one occasion when an officer sought him on suspicion of committing a minor offense, he pulled the officer from his horse, took his pistol, badge and cap, beat him and sent the personal equipment to the chief of police with his compliments. Later two officers were overpowered, disarmed, and beaten by John Brown. He was an object of interest to "bad white men" and to officers with a bad reputation among Negroes, because of his dangerous fearlessness rather than because of his crimes. He refused to fight other Negroes, even though there were some who sought to bolster their reputations as "bad men" among Negroes, and their standing with the white police, by beating up John Brown. He maintained this role for some fifteen years and, finally, was shot in the back without warning by a rookie white officer seeking personal distinction.

Direct impulsive aggression toward whites, as has been pointed out, is characterized by physical violence without consideration of consequences. One of the most interesting cases coming to the attention of this study was that of a lower middle-class Negro waiter, who had numerous conflicts with whites. On one occasion when he was on a streetcar, he saw an elderly Negro woman who was sitting in one of the front seats being hurled and slapped by the motorman. She had paused to get her breath before moving back. His instantaneous reaction to the situation in his own words was: "I was boilin' and before I knowed it I had him by the throat. I was on top of that peck just cutting him with my long bowie knife." Later it cost him $400 to get out of the police station.

At another time the streets were flooded and streetcar passengers had to get off at a certain place and transfer to a bus. When he was getting off, the motorman thought he was too slow and kicked him. He threw the camera that he carried at one of the white men near the motorman and then went and got it back. Then he threw bricks at the car and broke the windows. This time he escaped arrest.

At his place of work, a roadside house, he made friends with some of the lower-class whites and used them to beat up one of the white managers. He stole the wife of the next boss and finally engaged him in a fight. In the end, according to his story, the boss was poisoned by his own wife.

This waiter seems to be quite typical of lower- and lower middle-class Negroes who forcibly revolt against the racial position imposed upon them regardless of consequences. Their aggressive impulses once aroused, they defy both external and internal restraints, for along with the intensity of their hostile feelings there is a relative immunity from ordinary moral and legal restraints.

The feelings here reflected have been described with a great deal of insight by Richard Wright in his novel *Native Son*. The lawyer who was defending Bigger said:

The all-important thing for this Court to remember in deciding this boy's fate is that, though his crime was accidental, the emotions that broke loose were already there; the thing to remember is that the boy's way of life was a way of guilt; that his crime existed long before the murder of Mary Dalton; that the accidental nature of his crime took the guise of sudden and violent rent in the veil behind which he lived, a rent which allowed his feelings of resentment and estrangement to leap forth and find objective and concrete form.[1]

Many other so-called acts of crime on the part of Negroes may be considered in the same light.

[1] Richard Wright, *Native Son* (New York: Harper & Brothers, 1940) pp. 330-331.

The badge of police authority gives lower-class whites freedom to bolster their socially impoverished egos which has contributed, perhaps more than any other factor, to the generalized hostility of southern Negroes, particularly of the lower and lower middle classes. There were very few Negro informants who could not relate from either experience or hearsay instances of police brutality to Negroes far out of proportion to that warranted by the situation; and there were always some instances of unrestrained expression of hostility. The situation has created the phenomenon of the "bad nigger," the dramatic exemplification of hostility in the South. The "bad nigger" is one who lacks the restraints of middle-class "respectability" and by virtue of his lack of status and personal security disregards the racial etiquette defining his sphere and role. He will fight and take no thought of consequences because he has no recourse to either whites or Negroes for protection of his person. He is his own and only protection. Strangely enough, the "bad nigger," despite his unfavorable status with whites and his lack of support from Negroes, is secretly admired by Negroes.

The question "Where are the 'bad Negroes'?" frequently brought from respondents the half-serious, half-tragic observation that they sooner or later meet their end. In every city, however, there are always new characters, bitter, silent and sullen, who are in some respects a check upon indiscriminate white aggression. Incidents called to the attention of this study illustrate the individual methods of physical defense used by these hostile and overtly aggressive Negroes when subjected to white aggression. They strike fast and furiously. One such incident involved a Nashville Negro who was threatened by an officer with a drawn revolver in a downtown district. The Negro knocked the gun from the officer's hand, felled him with his fist, removed the shells from the chamber, threw the gun across the street, and walked away.

A young Negro mechanic with little formal education, a bitter resentment of whites, and a reputation as a prompt and rugged fighter was overheard in a Negro barbershop lamenting the mass impotence of Negroes and the puny impression made on the total situation by his physical combats. He said:

The thing that kills me is I ain't got enough education. If I had a lot of education I would be a Communist or something so I could do something about it.

Middle-class Negroes can avoid many critical situations because the routine of their lives holds them close to the institutions of the

Negro community. Moreover, one mark of their status is the security which they ensure for themselves by avoiding situations in which it might be seriously threatened.

The situation is different for upper middle- and upper-class Negroes whose professional duties frequently carry them beyond the usual Negro institutions. In this group there are a few who lack the disposition or skill to avoid crises resulting from the prosecution of lawful missions, despite the restricting etiquette. One example involves a Negro college instructor who holds a Ph.D. degree from a northern university. While living in Atlanta, he had occasion to go to St. Louis. It had been customary for Negroes to secure Pullman accommodations through a certain Negro who was connected with one of the social organizations; but Dr. ——— had steadily refused to use this method. He had gone to the ticket office and insisted that he be sold Pullman accommodations, reminding the agents that he could not solve the race problem every time he took a ride on the train, and that they might as well sell him Pullman tickets because he would continue to pester them. They had occasionally sold him reservations, indicating that they regarded him as "queer" or "crazy."

The train on which he wanted a reservation to St. Louis was an all-Pullman train from the Florida resorts. He was told that no reservations were sold out of Atlanta. This assertion was obviously false; and he told the agents that they were not telling the truth, that the statement was absurd, and that if they would come down to the train the next evening they would see him enter the Pullman. They did not argue further. Just as he stepped out of the ticket office he met a blond, blue-eyed Negro friend. He told this octoroon his problem and gave him the money to buy the ticket, which he secured without difficulty.

Dr. ——— boarded the Pullman train the next evening. It was not until the train reached North Georgia that the Pullman conductor and the train conductor reached the car in which he was seated. When they saw him, they stopped suddenly and engaged in conversation. Then the train conductor said to the Negro, "You will have to get out of this place. We will lock you up there in the drawing room, which is empty." When the Negro passenger asked why he would have to get out of his seat, he was told, "You know colored people can't ride in trains with white people in Georgia." The Negro replied that he "was not riding with white people in Georgia." The Pullman conductor continued, "We know you are an interstate passenger, but you will have to get out of this seat."

The Negro replied that he would not get out of his seat. Then the conductor asked, "Are you defying us?" The Negro passenger answered spiritedly, "No, I am not defying you, but you are meddling with a peaceful passenger." To this the conductor replied, "So you refuse to do as we tell you, and you are not going to get out?" "No," he replied, "I am not going to get out," and then he added, "Yes, I might get out, but I will not get out alive." They walked away. After they had left the car a Pullman porter came to the Negro passenger and said, "Mister, I'm sure glad you talked back to those white folks. Don't you be afraid. If anybody starts to do anything to you tonight I'll let you know." However, nothing further happened.

The following incident reflecting underlying hostility involved an upper-class Negro of national distinction who expressed active and open racial hostility:

One day I went into the bank to draw $125. The clerk sent a note back, as was evidently customary, to see what my balance was. While he was waiting he said to me, "Jackson, you don't come in often." I said nothing, but turned my back and began to look at the decorations on the ceiling. When I turned around to the window again to see if my money was ready, the clerk repeated, "Jackson, don't you hear me, I said you don't come in often." Again, I turned my back and moved a step or two from the window and began to look at the decorations on the ceiling. Once again I turned around to the window to see if he were ready to give me the money. As he counted out the money, he said, "Jackson, I said you don't come into the bank often." I noticed that his name was Italian. I said to him, "In Italian, you are Signor C." He said, "Yes, yes," smilingly, and then I added, "And in English, I am Mr. Jackson." He appeared a little startled and then said, "Oh, excuse me, I thought that you were a colored man. What are you?" In reply I said, "Can't you see that I am a colored man?" Immediately he blew up and said, "Do you mean to tell a white man to call a colored man 'Mr.'?" In the meantime he rushed from his cage to the desk of the vice-president and blurted out, "He tried to make me call him 'Mr.'" The vice-president told him to quiet down. I said to the vice-president that he was calling me simply by my name and was enraged because I said I was "Mr." to him. The vice-president said that the teller did not mean any harm and that he was only trying to be pleasant. Then I said that perhaps I had been a little hasty, and added that when he calls me "Jackson" I will call him "Cornelli." The vice-president said, "Oh, no, I don't mean that." Then I said there was no power in heaven or hell that could make me call a white man "Mr." who did not put "Mr." to my name. The vice-president then told the teller not to call me anything, and I said that I would not call the teller anything either.

The same individual was involved in another situation which approached a critical point. His general racial point of view and distrust of whites had prompted him to instruct his wife to be careful about admitting white men to the house and to insist upon their removing their hats if they entered. One day when he returned from his office he found his wife standing outside the house and he asked her why she was there. She said that a white man had come into the house and told her that he wanted to look at the gas range. He asked her if she had let him in, and she stated that she had refused admittance, but the man had insisted upon entering. The husband immediately rushed into the house and, encountering the man in the kitchen, asked what he was doing in the house without being properly admitted by his wife. The man said that he had come to look at the stove and asked, "What about it?" The informant said, "Moreover, you have your hat on in here." To this the reply was "I don't take my hat off in any nigger's house." As this remark was made, he lifted a large wrench which hung at his side. The Negro reached for a butcher knife which was on the drainboard, and as he did so the white man rushed from the kitchen and out of the house, shouting, "Nigger, if it's the last thing I do, I am going to bring my gang out here and hang you to the highest pole." The Negro replied that if he tried it he would be the first to get shot. Then he telephoned the gas company and reported what the man had said about not taking his hat off "in a nigger's house" and his threat to bring a gang to his house; and he repeated his own threat that he would shoot the leader of any such gang. The next day he wrote a similar message in a letter to the gas company, but nothing further was heard of the incident.

The overt expression of hostility seems to be limited to the so-called "bad niggers" and the more aggressive upper-class Negroes, in situations which they are unable to avoid by reasonable means. Members of both classes are aware that they expose themselves to violent reprisals, but they are willing to take the chance.

Covert Hostility and Deflected Aggression

The weapons employed by lower-class Negroes in expressing hostility covertly may take the form of petty sabotage, unexplained quitting of jobs, gossip, pseudo-ignorant malingering. Middle-class Negroes are in better position to use the economic weapon of controlled purchasing power. Upper-class Negroes may use this also, but in addition they find it effective to use the method of indirect attack on the offending institutions by arousing outside public opinion.

One of the milder forms of indirect aggression is the use of one group of whites to punish another. Connection with influential whites may serve not only to protect lower- and lower middle-class Negroes from lower-class white annoyance and police interference, but in the absence of Negro political participation it often provides the only means of redress once an injury has been perpetrated. A barber in one of the plantation counties cited a case in which Negroes got redress for certain indignities:

The police are pretty brutal in the way they treat Negroes. Most of them whip you when they arrest you. One of the night "laws" went to one of the colored churches one night, got a colored woman, dragged her out of the church and whipped her. Some of the better class of white people got behind it and he lost his job. The woman worked for some good white folks and they had him arrested.

In the rural South covert hostility motivated by the desire to maintain or to achieve physical security is by no means limited to situations involving police officers. There are manifestations of Negro hostility in other areas of contact: on the highways, in personal encounters in business, and in other personal relations.

Indirect aggression is generally resorted to by Negroes who for various reasons have found it expedient to conform to their caste role externally but who privately nurse intense hostility toward whites. Owing partly to external circumstances and partly to personality predispositions, the ways in which hostility is expressed are often indirect and subtle and in some cases so ingenious that discrimination itself is turned into a channel of aggression toward the oppressor. Instead of fighting wherever they are discriminated against, Negroes adopting this type of response choose their own battleground.

Those who can afford to own an automobile have a way of expressing their hostility toward whites in a more or less indirect manner. A furnace worker in Texas said of his own experience, "I drive in a way that makes it look like I'll run over them if they walk in front of me when I have the right. I act like I don't see them. I have had some of them to curse at me for this, but I just laugh at them and keep on driving." In such cases the automobile not only gives the Negro a sense of power and prestige but shares the blame for any damage that occurs. Thus, there is little wonder that only a few years ago the possession of a car by a Negro was considered something of a criminal offense in the deep South.

One of the most interesting and in some instances quite effective ways of expressing hostility, used by Negroes in different walks of life, is that of being polite and courteous enough to guard oneself from being insulted and at the same time inflict pain on the white person. This is the "gentleman's way" of getting even with whites without incurring further aggression. An insurance agent, after relating how he asked a group of white men to come into his house when the latter came to inquire about his wife's pay and asked her to come out, said, "I spoke to them in a firm manner and I was courteous all of the time." As to his general policy, he added:

I come in contact with some of the toughest of them, but I always try to be courteous with them and nothing ever happens to me. That is the best thing that you can do to get the white man's nerves. If you can still be courteous and let him know where to get off and don't get all excited and scared when he blows up, you can handle him pretty well. They get all excited quick and if the Negroes do not get scared too, they think that they had better be careful.

This is a Negro's use of the "war of nerves" strategy, but it is adopted primarily for self-defense.

A schoolteacher in Arkansas has her way of using politeness as a weapon. Referring to white insurance men who, according to her, "are the talk of the town among colored people," she said:

Sometimes when they come here and act so smart—they always have some nasty joke to tell you—I make them stand out on the porch, and when it's cold it is not so comfortable. You know there is a way of being so polite to white people that it is almost impolite. I say polite things, but I look at them hard and I don't smile, and while what I am saying is polite the way in which I say it isn't.

A slight variation of the same technique is the private differentiation some Negroes make in using such terms of address as "Mr." and "Mrs." An elderly Negro school principal in South Carolina, whom white people used to call "professor" not because they had any special respect for him but because they did not want to address him as "Mr.," described his way of addressing whites:

I address older white men as "Mr." and white woman as "Miss" or "Mrs." when I know them and "ma'am" otherwise. Young white men I give "Sir"; I reserve "Mr." for settled men.

The differentiation made here is obviously not at all common to users of the English language or even to any large number of Negroes; it is private and is used to express and at the same time to hide hostility toward certain white persons.

An interesting expression of covert hostility is revealed in the experience of a rural Negro school principal who in most respects managed to remain acceptable to white people. This principal knew how to behave well enough to survive seven white superintendents. They all had about the same attitude in the matter of limiting the financial allocation to the Negro school program, although their methods of accomplishing it varied. On one occasion when he went to visit the new superintendent, the Negro principal was greeted as follows: "Well, uncle, how many students you got in your school?" Some time later, when asked by a member of the school board how he liked his new boss, the principal said:

It speaks bad for a man who's been to the highest schools in the state, and occupying the position he does, to call me "uncle" at this late time. "Uncle" belongs to a plantation time. When masters wanted their children to show some kind of respect they taught them to call them "uncle," but it's too late for that now. He went back and told him, just as I wanted him. The next time I went there he said, "Good morning, Jenkins, come in and have a seat."

One method of defeating a situation that is resented is to be clever enough to take advantage of the competing self-interests of white officials and supervisors. In one county, for example, a member of the school board owned a paint store; and it was not difficult for him to be persuaded to look favorably upon the idea of painting the school. In another county, after completing his term of office, the ex-superintendent of schools opened a hardware store. When he approached the Negro principal about the need of oil for his school floors, the principal replied apologetically, but with sly intent to convey his real feeling:

But, Mr. ——, you know how hard it is to get a little oil for our floors. Even you turned it down when you were superintendent.

In conversations between Negroes open hostility toward whites is frequently expressed, but it becomes covert in face-to-face situations between Negroes and whites. The white person is not always aware of the depth or character of this feeling. A Negro worker in a South Carolina soft drink plant went into a store to make a purchase and was followed by a white person. The clerk passed the Negro and waited on the white customer. When the Negro started to leave the store, the clerk shouted, "Wait and I'll wait on you"; but the Negro went on out. In commenting on this he said, "I'd die before I'd go back to them." But the clerk thought he had merely lost a sale.

Similarly, a construction laborer in Birmingham reported encounters on streetcars that kept him enraged, but he could only express his hostility in wishful thinking. His report of the following incident is illuminating:

They have a conductor on the car that carries a gun sometimes. He tries to treat you in a pretty rough way sometimes. It is because he has a gun that he is so rough. There is one Negro who burned for stopping him from being so rough one time. I reckon that there are more than that that let the conductor have a dose of his own medicine. One guy left one of them laying right there in the door, and I wish that more of them would do the same thing.

There is a type of covert hostility that takes the form of destructive gossip. A Mississippi Negro informant, commenting about a prominent white political figure in the state, said:

This is the way old —— got rich working prisoners on a farm. He had all of his prison farm where you had to work. They did not do anything but raise cotton. They made plenty of cotton, too. Old —— was too slick to let anything happen to him like that stuff that happened down in Louisiana. He would do almost anything for money that you asked him to do, but he never would take any money directly. One time he was asked by a man to pardon his son. He offered him a thousand dollars. He got mad with the man, but told him to sit down.

Then they went out and looked at some stock that he had. He told the man that he ought to buy one of his bulls. He offered the man the bull for a thousand dollars. The man was a long time catching the point, and said that he had no way of getting him home. B —— told him that his son could drive him home. He was a slicker, that ——.

Covert expressions of hostility among middle-class Negroes may be prompted by factors beyond purely personal considerations. Generalized hostility toward whites may be aroused by injustice in the local administration of federal programs. Interest in the schools of the community, for example, may make this class of Negroes sensitive to local policies of discrimination resulting in disparities in financial support. Referring to a Negro school, one such informant said:

It has a mighty poor rating, and gets hardly any consideration. The colored teachers get very little money and they are greatly underpaid compared with white teachers. The superintendent, being white, looks after his race first. So the school building over there isn't fit to raise pigs in.

Sexual jealousy is also responsible for hostility that remains covert. "White men have their fun with colored women," said a Birmingham Negro. "It's against the law, but who says anything about it. Anything goes but the nigger, they say." The interest in the celebrated Scottsboro trials of Negro boys for alleged rape drew out some hostility, which was expressed in sympathy for those youths. One informant, in a burst of indignation, said:

Look at those Scottsboro boys. They spent all that time in the jail and the penitentiary. What for? Those boys did not have any more to do with those women than I did, and I was not even there. How in the world could they take on all of those boys? Why in the world anybody would lie like that, I don't know. It seems like the white folks get to thinking about making the nigger suffer, and they lose all human nature. They don't think at all. Ain't no way that they can make me see any excuse for what they tried to do to all of those Negroes just because they happened to be on the train with some white whores who decided to turn a trick with some white fellows. I tell you, it makes a man feel pretty hot sometimes.

Some Negroes who are helpless and dependent on the dominating whites have a way of expressing hostility that is perhaps universal with any people in the same predicament. They deliberately play the role of parasites and often in the name of loyalty or submission live or prosper at the expense of their victims.

An unskilled laborer in Cleveland, Mississippi, has developed almost to perfection the art of submission for aggressive purposes. The superficial character of his accommodating behavior and the intensity of his inner resentment may be seen in the following statements:

I have had it pretty easy with these white people here since I have been here. . . . I know just how to get along with them. I can make them think they own the world. It is nothing but a lot of jive that I hand them. If I was a little better off, I would get away from around here and all of the white folks could kiss where the sun don't shine. This place is all right in a way, but a man has to be less than a man to get along most of the time.

Commenting on the whites' entering Negroes' homes at will, he added:

That is why I wish that I was where they didn't want to mob a fellow when he stands up for his rights. I would really bust some of them down. As the saying goes, I would make black look just like white. I would cut some of these red necks down my size.

His means of retaliation for discrimination is described in these words:

They want all of the Negroes to jump and pull off their hats when they start talking to them. I know that is what they want, and since I am down here in it I can do it. When "Mr. Charlie" has something that I want, there is nothing that I can't do to get it. That is because he has something, and if I don't get it from him where can I get it?

In other words, surface observation of the racial etiquette in order to get things from whites is his way of aggression.

Perhaps the lowest type of passive aggression is exemplified by the pimp or the pimplike character. The author of the statement just quoted made a keen observation on this point when he said, "Now in regard to a Negro marrying a white man's mistress, all that had happened was that the white man had another Negro to support." It should be noted in this connection that in some places in the South some Negro men are reduced to such low economic status that resort to this parasitic form of aggression is probably due more to external circumstances than to their own psychological inclinations. Others, however, deliberately set out to make "suckers" out of the white men, as one Negro put it, by enticing them to the lure of Negro women, and make this a regular business either in houses of prostitution or in private night clubs. The psychology of this sort of behavior may be complex, but the destructive motive behind it is self-evident.

Telling jokes is another indirect method of expressing hostile impulses. A factory hand in Cleveland, Mississippi, reported that at the place where he worked the white foreman and the Negro workers often exchanged jokes. One morning he told one of the boys, "Hurry up there, you son-of-a-bitch. Your mammy must not have given you any breakfast." The colored boy retorted, "You skinny bastard, look like your mammy never gives you anything to eat." Then they all laughed. In fact, he said that those colored boys played the "dozens" with that white fellow any time.[2] Games and jokes of this sort make life a little easier for all parties involved in a strained relationship, for they give a certain amount of sanction to the expression of impulses that are suppressed only with great difficulty. Even among Negroes themselves the proverbial laughter and light-

---

[2] John Dollard, "The Dozens: Dialectic of Insult," *The American Imago*, 1:1-25 (November, 1939).

heartedness are not without aggressive import. James Weldon Johnson made a shrewd observation in this connection. After having
studied the phenomenon for some time he concluded:

But I did discover that a part of the laughter, when among themselves,
was laughter at the white man. It seems to me that for the grim white
man in the backwoods of the South the deep laughter of the Negro
should be the most ominous sound that reaches his ears.[3]

In still another form of indirect aggression, hostility toward the
dominant whites is deflected toward other peoples having less capacity for retaliation. Examples include the resentment toward
upper-class Negroes felt by certain lower-class Negroes who can
neither avoid contact with whites nor assert themselves in any adequate manner when they are the victims of discrimination; and the
resentment of those who are economically better off but are so weak
and helpless in expressing their hostility toward whites that they
"take it out" on other racial groups such as the Jews, the Chinese,
the Mexicans, the West Indians, and those whom they call "Dagos,"
"Polacks," and others.

It has been noted that there are Chinese merchants in several of
the Delta towns in Mississippi and that Negroes patronize them
because they "feel freer." This situation offers an opportunity for
some deflected hostility, since the nonwhites provide a substitute for
Negro counteraggression. A lower-class Negro reported this experience:

A bunch of us went in one of them Chinese stores. I asked for a
match, and he got mad because I didn't say "Mr." We was about to
turn the joint out. He called me a son-of-a-bitch, and told me to call him
"Mr." I don't 'low no man to call me a son-of-a-bitch. I called him a
Chinese son-of-a-bitch, and started to get him. One of them other
Chinese said for him to let it drop.

In some cities this hostility is deflected toward the Jewish merchants in Negro neighborhoods who, for business and other racial
reasons of their own, are less likely to use forceful measures in retaliation for Negro aggression.

At the other social extreme is the Negro college teacher whose
reaction to discrimination is one of avoiding scenes. He refrains from
expressing resentment toward the white man when he is discriminated against; but he confessed that he took a certain delight in embarrassing whites who visited the college as guests and who were not
informed about the amenities of upper-class Negro life. Since whites

[3] James W. Johnson, *Along This Way* (New York: Viking Press, 1933), p. 120.

who visit these schools are usually friendly ones, they are a safe outlet
for aggression on the part of a Negro who avoids direct conflict in
a potentially dangerous racial situation.

The complexities of Negro status in the North are commensurate
with the intricacies of the northern cities where Negroes live. The
population of a large city not only has well-defined classes but many
interest groups with characteristic reaction patterns. The large concentrations of Negro population in New York and Chicago offer a
wide range of positions within the Negro status, from those who
live in a world almost entirely Negro to those who "pass" and have
only casual and infrequent contacts with the Negro world.

In the northern city there is preoccupation with class both within
the Negro group and between race groups. In the former case concern for the upper classes of the Negro population is a reflection of
the basic opposition to the popular tendency to confuse Negro status
with servant status. Acute consciousness of class is an oblique recognition of the existence of "the Negro status"; and the attitude of
lower-class Negroes toward the Negro is one form of indirect expression of hostility. Preoccupation with class in interracial situations appears to grow out of the need for a common defense of
economic interests, strong enough at times to cut across race lines.

There is a considerable amount of racial discrimination in the
North, but it is a common observation that the Negroes who discuss
these discriminatory practices most frankly are those who originally
came from the South. The Negro pattern of behavior outside the
Negro residence areas is carefully molded to permit maximum freedom within the vague margins of acceptability. Within the Negro
areas there is more realization and sense of both security and possession. Buried racial antagonisms can easily be called to the surface,
however, in a variety of overt expressions with or without strong
provocation. Migrants from the South in particular, who have stored
away memories of deep-cutting offenses discreetly tolerated in the
South, may reveal undue aggressiveness in the areas of open competition.

Personal-Racial Aggression

In the North the Negro escapes many of the more obvious forms
of segregation and discrimination, and little of the racial etiquette
is in force. When discrimination occurs it is more subtle, and hence
most of the experiences recorded were reported by middle- and upper-

class Negroes. Occasionally it happens that an institution or relationship may involve personnel with a southern background, and difficulties may develop; but usually some form of redress is possible through formal channels. Where such redress is not possible, the situation may result in physical conflict.

The most common form of aggression in the North is vehement verbal assertion of rights. Some temperaments lend themselves to this more readily than others. The tendency to talk back to offending whites and to resort to every possible means of aggressive retaliation, short of physical violence, is illustrated in the case of an accomplished woman lawyer in Chicago. On one occasion she went to shop in a fashionable district. First, the elevator girl refused to take her upstairs, and then after she got upstairs nobody waited on her. When a man finally came to order her out, the lawyer attacked him verbally with great violence. She reported the story in part:

I really shouted then. I was pointing my finger in his face and I said, "If you touch me again [the man had touched her hand while she rang for the elevator], even my little finger, I'll have you arrested, and I've practiced in the courts long enough to have just enough influence to do it. Why," I said, "I kick your kind around every day in court. You've been used to Negroes who tuck their heads and run when you scowl. Well, let me tell you, this is a new kind of Negro and there are plenty more like me, so you'd better watch out. If I were a man I'd knock you down."

A more formal, and sometimes quite effective, way of expressing aggression directly is to sue the white offenders. This type of response is consistently practiced by a real-estate man in Chicago. When he brought a charge against a white woman, the owner of a restaurant on the South Side, she was fined $25, and the story of the lawsuit was carried in the local newspapers. As a result he felt that some other restaurants in the city had changed their policy toward Negroes. One interesting aspect of this Negro's policy toward whites is his constant readiness to challenge any white establishment in which discrimination is practiced contrary to the law of the state,[4] and to bring suit whenever he can procure the necessary evidence. On one occasion he purposely went into an "exclusive" bar in the Loop. The very reluctant bartender gave him the glass of gin he ordered and charged him $1.25 instead of the usual price of 15 cents. He immediately took issue with the bartender and followed this up with legal proceedings against the owner. This Negro is an out-and-

[4] It should be noted that this legal weapon against discrimination is not effective in all states. For statutes on this matter see Chapter IX.

out fighter, but he uses means that are socially approved and relatively effective.

Some middle- and upper middle-class Negroes in northern areas
make a point of seeking opportunities to assert their resentment of
discrimination. An upper middle-class Negro woman said:

I wish I had nothing to do but float around and let myself in for it
because I like to fight. They don't put a lot over me. I don't care where
I am or who is around. I know I am as good as anyone. I know I've got
something most white people haven't got even if I belong to a minority
group, and I know my rights. I'll fight for them with anybody or any
time.

A contrasting case was that of a woman real-estate agent in Chicago.
One of the main topics of her conversation was her disagreement
with a Negro man in the same business with respect to his petty
attitude toward discrimination. She said:

Mr. ——, who is in the kitchenette business like I am, believes in
fighting these old white people any time he gets a chance. Now he went
up here on 60th Street and bought a building in the white section. They
had to get cops to guard the place. The white people were going to try
to run them out. They threw rocks through his windows. . . . I can't
understand why he wanted to do that. . . . He is always going to some
place where he knows he isn't wanted. I don't believe in that.

Following her own policy of avoidance, she always goes to places
where she knows she is welcome, does not eat out, and has never tried
to eat in downtown drugstores although she believes that they would
serve her.

Except in cases of southern Negroes who have recently migrated
to the North, there is not the same frequency or variety of devices
substituted for direct aggression. Cases are reported of southern
Negroes who had restrained their impulses in the South out of consideration for personal safety, but in the North were prompt to resent
violently any attempt at personal discrimination on racial grounds
or any insult from a white person. Such encounters have been frequent in the thickly settled Negro sections of northern cities.

When a Negro redcap in Chicago was assisting a passenger who
happened to be from the South and called him "darky," he had to be
restrained from doing violence to him. A Negro passenger on a bus
struck the white driver in a trivial argument over change and accused
him of trying to import "crackerism" into New York.

Where racial segregation and formal discrimination do occur in
the northern cities, they are so strongly supported that it is difficult

for individual Negroes to make any effective protest. As a result they either tend to ignore the areas in which discrimination is known to occur and content themselves with thinking that they could receive the service or use the facility if they tried, or they use their collective strength to attack discrimination through formal channels. The ballot is perhaps the most effective means of combating discrimination in the North. This has been the weapon most used and most relied upon by Negroes of all classes who were interviewed on this question. In fact, it may be said that it was the voting power of the Negro populations in northern cities that brought about the new civil rights bills.

Race Riots

Several cities in the North may be listed in a description of a type of collective resistance to white aggression—race riots. Where these have occurred, the underlying problem has been that of racial segregation and discrimination in recreational areas, residence areas, and industry. In East St. Louis, Illinois, during the first stages of the northward migration of southern Negroes in 1917, there was a race riot which resulted in the death of 39 Negroes and 8 whites. The Chicago riot in 1919 started over an apparently trivial incident at a bathing beach. White bathers objected to a Negro boy's crossing an imaginary line dividing the two races in the water. They stoned the boy and he drowned. In the racial clashes that continued for several days 22 Negroes and 16 whites were killed, while 342 Negroes and 178 whites were injured. There have been riots in Springfield, Illinois, Washington, D.C., and New York City, although that in the last-named city was only partly racial in motivation. A race riot is differentiated from a lynching in that in the former there is direct, violent, and collective resistance on the part of the Negroes.

Organized Aggression

Direct action in opposition to racial discrimination has been attempted by several organizations with some measure of success. The more aggressive Negroes have directed their resentment of personal and group discrimination through these organizations which have more power to effect changes or to punish. One of the earlier efforts to combat racial discrimination was the so-called "Niagara Movement," organized in New York by W. E. B. Du Bois in 1905. Out of this, in 1910, grew the National Association for the Advancement of Colored People, which is the most effective of the present organizations combating discrimination. It is supported very largely by

Negro membership throughout the country. It has an impressive record of successful court battles against racial discrimination in social, civil, legal, and political relations. It has won practically every case carried to the Supreme Court, and each of them has involved the protection of the fundamental citizenship rights of Negroes.

In 1931 the success of the boycotting and picketing movement against white merchants who discriminated against Negroes as employees was recognized; and the movement began to spread through northern and a few southern cities.

The National Urban League, using more pacific methods, has sought to combat racial discrimination in industry. It has been active since 1911 and has branches in many cities, chiefly in the northern industrial areas.

The most recent of the combative organizations is the National Negro Congress, which has attempted to unify local movements in protest against injustices, on a united front principle.[5]

The Negro press should be mentioned in this connection, notably those newspapers published in the North and having a national circulation. Racial discrimination is news of high value and appeal, which has kept Negroes alert and helped to solidify opposition to any and all forms of segregation and discrimination. In notable instances the Negro press has been effective in bringing about changes. It has served two useful purposes: it has been a direct weapon of attack on segregation and discrimination; it has been a medium through which individual Negroes could relieve their aggressive feelings, both through reading it and through contributing to it.

One of the more recent forms of racial aggression in the North is the consolidation of racial issues with economic and political disaffections of non-Negro groups, usually to some punitive end. The case of the Scottsboro boys helped to arouse northern Negroes and Communists to action. The food riots in Harlem during 1933, although precipitated by economic frustration of both Negroes and whites, nevertheless revealed a residue of racial hostility in the bitter fury of the Negroes toward the objects attacked and the immunities.

In Chicago residence problems cause more friction and conflict situations than in New York. The battle for living quarters has called forth antagonism, violence, and court action. Refusals to sell or lease property to Negroes, reinforced by court action, are used to

[5] "The Programs of Organizations Devoted to Improvement of the Status of the American Negro," *Journal of Negro Education,* 8:539 (July, 1939).

keep Negroes out of some residential areas. The wrecking of buildings and personal violence toward Negroes who get into a building in an area considered as restricted to white families are not as common as formerly.

The hostility of the Negro must be expressed through various intricate procedures which do not always dramatize the situation. The conflict in its indirect action is intense, often because of emotionally charged considerations of status. In general, it may be said that, although there is greater freedom for overt expression of racial hostility in the North, there is actually less of it than of covert hostility in the South.

Chapter XV

RETROSPECT AND PROSPECT

The foregoing chapters have attempted to present characteristic patterns of Negro segregation in the United States as the effects of sociological and historical processes. Numerous variables are involved, for personal and group relations have varied in response to time, place, class, and personality factors. It remains now to view this practice in a broader context, in its relation to: (a) other group relations in American society, (b) trends in race relations of which segregation is a function, and (c) the basic democratic ideology of American society.

Although Negro segregation has arisen in response to cultural and biological imperatives and has become a deep-seated characteristic of the social organization of American society, the practice is not limited to racial groups. National and cultural groups are not wholly exempt. It is currently customary to refer in sociological literature to the Negro-white relationship as one of caste. There are, indeed, similarities between Negro-white relations and a caste organization of society; but this identification fails to reckon with responsible forces that are actually breaking up such caste organization as exists in the United States as well as in other parts of the world where caste has been part of an accepted and established social order. The Negro population is actually the largest of the American minority groups, and the essence of minority status is self-consciousness and a struggle for status. In this respect the Negroes are like other minorities, such as the Jews, Orientals, and Mexicans, not to mention those transient minorities, the European immigrants.

In one way or another, minorities are excluded from full participation in the life of the community and the conduct of the state. This immediately raises the question of the relation of this circumstance to the democratic theory of the state, which assumes complete participation of all who are capable of functioning economically or politically as members of society. The essential fact is that the actual

316

practices of the dominant majority are, for whatever reason, in direct conflict with the ideals and professed objectives of the state. It is this fact that gives reality to the minority status of the Negro and other groups. It is the necessity for struggle that forces upon them the solidarity by which alone they can gain the status that is assured them.

The theory of the democratic state assumes, with respect to the different racial and cultural units of which it is composed, a degree of cultural assimilation corresponding to their equal status in citizenship. In actual fact, however, the democratic theory is frankly qualified by the dominant group's value judgment of assimilability. Racial groups that are physically and culturally similar to the dominant pattern or ideal are acceptable; racial groups which differ markedly from the norm are less acceptable. In their case adjustment or accommodation within the framework of the democratic society is demanded rather than assimilation. The policy of segregation and the permanence of the pattern differ for groups regarded as assimilable and unassimilable.

The segregation of the American Indian is both the most complete and the most effective, inasmuch as it is maintained by a reservation or preserve, which puts this minority totally outside the cultural framework of American society. The Mexicans present a mixed pattern, depending upon the social judgment with respect to assimilability. In sections of the country in which there are large numbers of Mexican laborers they are classed racially as nonwhite and, thus, are automatically segregated. The attitude back of this is a compound of many elements embodying, according to one student, aversion to color, social pressure against intermixture with an "inferior" race, disdain of the conqueror for the conquered, hatred of frontiersmen for those who are or who have been at some time in their way, the revulsion of the Protestant and puritanical Yankee against Roman Catholicism and Latin folkways, contempt of the higher economic class for the lower.[1] Where Mexicans are regarded as white, as in the instance of persons of Spanish-Indian mixture, or are persons of official status from adjoining states whose good will is essential to hemispherical solidarity, factors that might otherwise determine attitudes toward the strangers are in abeyance. Although Mexicans are still racially segregated in the Southwest, they are no longer nonwhite by census definition at least.

The Orientals are similarly segregated and, by the strength of

[1] B. Shrieke, *Alien Americans* (New York: Viking Press, 1936), p. 54.

their own institutions, segregate themselves. As a result, their lives are only slightly affected by American institutions. Segregation in the cases of all these groups applies most commonly to residential areas, schools, churches, and various semipublic and public institutions and services. With respect to the Orientals, social unassimilability is associated with political unacceptability for citizenship.

There are three groups which for one reason or another are acceptable for citizenship but upon whom the shadow of segregation falls. These are the foreign-born, the Jews, and the Negroes. The segregation of the first two groups is temporary and considerably influenced by economic factors. The Negroes as a group experience the most persistent and the most pervasive forms of segregation, based upon economic, social, traditional, and legal considerations.

The laws prescribing racial segregation are based upon the assumption that racial minorities can be segregated under conditions that are legally valid if not discriminating. Theoretically, segregation is merely the separate but equal treatment of equals. In such a complex and open society as our own this is, of course, neither possible nor intended; for whereas the general principle of social regulation and selection is based upon individual competition, special group segregation within the broad social framework must be effected artificially and by the imposition of arbitrary restraints. The result is that there can be no group segregation without discrimination, and discrimination is neither democratic nor Christian.

The legal enactments of the southern states with respect to the Negro represent an attempt to crystallize separate racial spheres by subjecting violations to punishment. The degree of punishment varies with the social significance attached to the violation. The laws are designed, apparently, to serve as a substitute for a caste organization of society. However, the fact that these laws exist suggests that custom is not enough to regulate human relations between the races in a highly mobile society. The presence of these laws, moreover, indicates that the caste sanctions are subject to, or in process of, change.

Segregation laws tend to appear where there is erosion of custom. In the South this erosion may come either from the amenities of personal relations or from the impersonal force of technological or economic or social change. In the border and northern states, where the dominant customs are more favorable to the personal and civil freedom of Negroes, the erosion is affecting the more liberal traditions. This is one of the inevitable results of the movement of large numbers of Negroes and whites from southern backgrounds to these areas and the increased visibility of the Negro in the areas.

In theory the laws are designed to separate without discrimination. However, both in legislation and in practice there is discrimination; in equity any segregation that is not mutual or voluntary is discrimination. No thoroughgoing tests of the constitutionality of many of these laws have yet been made; and both the advocates and the opponents of segregation now seem reluctant to have them tested. On the one hand, it is quite possible that a Supreme Court decision could introduce violent repudiation of custom, as in the famous Gaines decision that established the right of Negroes to enter the southern state universities formerly regarded as being exclusively for the training of whites. On the other hand, an average of the present practices of the states would show the status of the Negro crystallized below the level of manifest possibility.

It is well to observe that traditional racial practices and ideologies which have developed over centuries cannot usually be dissolved within a decade. Since most racial attitudes and all prejudices are nonrational, they are seldom affected by reason or even by humanitarian doctrine. The forces most likely to effect changes in the future are those which gradually have been eroding custom and the idiosyncrasies of the racial etiquette during recent decades. These are, indeed, the forces that have made it necessary to employ the instrumentality of law to re-establish and reinforce custom with respect to expected behavior and the distance that custom decrees between races.

Urbanization and industrialization have contributed measurably to the gradual disintegration of certain features of prevailing custom. The Negro population of the South, for example, largely as a result of its historical connection with commercial agriculture has been a rural population. Race contacts have been influenced by the extreme cultural isolation incident to this rural setting and by the unique social status of Negroes in the plantation economy. In all the southern states, however, there is evidence of the gradual disintegration of these culturally stagnant "black belt" communities, a spreading of the Negro population into southern cities and towns and, subsequently, to northern industrial centers. In 1880 there were 300 counties in which over half the population was Negro; in 1930 there were only 187 such counties. Over this period the Negro population in northern states grew at a rapid rate, notably after the economic disturbances induced by World War I. During the decade 1910–1920, for example, the Negro population in Ohio increased

67 per cent; in New York, 50 per cent; in Illinois, 67 per cent; and in Michigan, 251 per cent. Over the forty-year period from 1890 to 1930 the rural Negro population increased only 12 per cent while the urban Negro population increased 251 per cent.

The profound cultural shocks involved in the mass movement of Negroes have been more significant than the population increase per se, and it is here that we can readily observe noticeable shifts in the patterns of interracial behavior. In the first place, new associations arise in urban centers. The races are more often together in public meetings and institutions, in schools, and in places of commercial amusement. They work together and they are incarcerated in the same penal institutions. The breadth, strength, and variety of these contacts have tended constantly to break down and rearrange the behavior patterns conditioned by custom and tradition in the rural setting. Legal codes of northern and some border states, even though not always seriously enforced, have been designed to safeguard the rights of the Negro minority in each new area of contact. Other corollaries of urbanization and industrialization may be observed in the substitution of impersonal control over free labor for the control of custom and in the increasing occupational stratification which has been dissolving the caste pattern.

Following closely in the wake of urban exposure is the increased sophistication which has engendered dissatisfaction with the social as well as economic status quo. More active participation in a literate world has increased mobility within the city; and this in turn has increased the range of communication and helped to develop stronger personal relations across race lines within a class framework.

The improvement and extension of Negro education, the raising of the economic level, and the social and cultural differentiation within the group, in spite of the drastically retarding effect of the traditional racial policies of the country, have altered the patterns of behavior and compelled modifications in the attitudes of certain elements of the white and Negro populations toward the institution of racial segregation itself. Moreover, the white majority's insistence upon Negro segregation in such a dynamic society as that of the United States has had the effect of creating among Negroes a sense of racial solidarity and a consciousness of struggle for status, which is a requisite of effective collective action. In this sense segregation has been an advantage.

Donald Young, in discussing the traditional antagonisms underlying present patterns of racial segregation, observes: "The inevitable conflict is one between ideals—ideals of justice, humanity, and immediate sacrifice for the gains of posterity—and the practical exigencies of personal interests which may not be dismissed by an accusation of selfishness."[2] This is essentially a sound observation. However, it has happened that the "practical exigencies of personal interests" of the dominant white group, or elements of it, have been in conflict with the rigid policy of segregation itself. The most conspicuous recent example of this concerns the southern white and Negro miners in the Birmingham area. Over the whole history of their separate competitive bargaining with industry and management, neither racial group achieved substantial economic improvements. In fact, the more intense the racial competition the weaker the wage structure became. It was not until the policy of racial segregation was made secondary to common economic improvement that gains for either were possible. There are now, despite the tradition of separation, over a hundred unsegregated unions in the area.

It is not inconceivable that the tremendous costs of a racial dualism in the many-faceted social structure will operate to reduce the policy of segregation eventually to a mere symbol. Pointing in that direction are the early results of the Supreme Court decision in the case brought by Congressman Arthur W. Mitchell against a railroad company for not providing equal accommodations. The contention of the railroad was that few Negroes used the Pullman and dining car service, and thus it would be costly to provide dual service. After the decision that it was unconstitutional not to provide equal service, it was provided in the way that involved the least cost: A curtain was hung in the dining car, and it was exposed only enough to indicate the intent to segregate.

The present excess costs of the separate school system in the South have been adjusted by diverting funds to which Negro children are legally entitled to white children, in the effort to give them as much education as possible. Equalizing the system would involve tremendous financial costs or lowering the present provisions for white children. The possible legal pressure has not yet been seriously faced. The most desirable solution would be equalization with federal aid. However, at the higher level of education, where the admission of Negroes to graduate departments of white institutions has become an issue, there is serious temptation to avoid the overhead costs of complete duplication of expensive facilities, especially where the number of Negro applicants is small. In two separate-school states in the upper South the problem has been relieved by admitting Negroes

[2] Donald Young, *American Minority Peoples,* (New York: Harper & Brothers, 1932), p. 592.

to existing institutions. In none of these situations has the question
of ideals and justice been dominant, or a controlling factor in the
modification of the pattern.

With reference to the future status of the Negro population in the
United States, speculation has taken several possible directions, most
of which are romantic and outside the current of world realities.
There is the status of wardship, as established historically in the case
of the Indians. Fugitive white and Negro groups have toyed with
the idea of an autonomous separate state. There is the ideal, difficult
of realization, of mutual segregation without discrimination. There
are historical precedents for a frankly accepted caste structure if it
can be maintained through force, vigilance, and modification of
world economics. There is, further, the possibility of the integration
of diverse physical types in our national background in a common
culture, without social or political penalty for physical divergence.
Such is the official theory of the American state.

Social democracy is referred to most commonly as an ideal to be
achieved; and our political democracy, as a theory still in process of
experimentation. In times of crisis, particularly when the theory is
challenged by other political forms, there is a revival of the democratic *doctrine*. The same type of revival in the religious sphere
should be expected, for example, in any outright challenge of the
theory of Christianity. Neither in normal nor in abnormal times, however, is democracy a political or social fact, however long it has been
in the American tradition; and we tend to speak of America as a
democratic nation in about the same spirit that we refer to America
as a Christian nation.

It would be exceedingly illuminating to have a comprehensive
study of the actual functioning of the democratic process in normal
and intimate social relations. There is an abundance of descriptive
material available on social relationships, but this is seldom related
to the social standards which alone give meaning to the organization
of a democratic society and a democratic state.

It is not, of course, by any means certain that the nation has any
fundamental desire to become a thoroughly democratic society, despite its formal political designation as a democracy. Great Britain,
the chief democratic associate in the present war, has its India and
its Africa, in which little semblance of a democratic organization of
society is permitted even under the emotional stress of fighting a
world war for the preservation of the principle.

Similarly, America has its racial minorities which were frustrated
and disillusioned as a result of their participation in the last war to

preserve this principle. As one writer has put it, in describing the inner contradiction of democracy, "Somehow they [the practical men who manage our affairs] must avoid the apparent chicanery of appearing to defend something which we do not possess, and which we do not wish to possess."[3]

Liberty and equality have been described as mutually exclusive and contradictory conceptions. Liberty is an individualistic notion which gained ascendancy when modern society superseded feudalism. Equality is something else; it is a notion, however, that is implicit in the conception of socialization—socialization of medicine, socialization of industry—toward which government, under the necessity of regulating our increasingly integrated and centralized economy, has for a long time been tending.

It is possible that under the pressure of the present necessity of organizing for war, socialization, which seems to be a principle at once ethically sound and politically effective, will receive an increasingly wider application. In any case it seems more obvious today than at any previous time that a principle is operating in society, though not always effectively, which tends to reconcile liberty with equality and to bring about a social order which permits wide differences among individuals and groups, and at the same time to ensure for each the understanding and respect of every other.

Reconciliation of conflicting group interests, in conformity with a policy of racial segregation, has frequently been responsible for a form of education which Oswald Garrison Villard has impatiently characterized as "the last refuge of the frustrated reformer." Education is, at best, a slow and faltering process, subject to all the divagations and distortions imposed by a fundamental "will to believe," namely, the will to believe that the man of a different race or color is a little less human than ourselves.

From the beginning of our history two fundamental principles have been active in shaping American institutions and the American way of life: free individualistic economic initiative, and racialism. In a virgin country with an unlimited frontier and vast natural resources our capitalistic economy, with its emphasis upon free competition and exploitation of both men and resources, seemed the most efficient and quickest method of developing the country. With the closing of the frontier and the "settling down" of the world, it became evident that unrestrained competition leads to excesses that have seemed to benefit a few but have worked hardships on vast numbers. In the logic of this system, freedom of opportunity meant

[3] Buell Gallagher, *Journal of Negro Education*, 10:50 (July, 1941).

eventually the freedom of the strong to survive at the expense of the weak. In the end the free play of individual and economic forces has come near to destroying the economic and political system it created, along with the individual freedom which it was designed to ensure. To preserve the democratic principle it is now necessary for the government to impose rigid controls and regulations, to determine the conditions under which the competitive principle may operate, to provide safeguards for small industries, to preserve the economic security of labor, and to protect women, children, and the handicapped. Labor legislation, the Fair Labor Standards Act, Social Security, the National Labor Relations Act, antitrust legislation, farm security, and the regulation of the stock exchange are all examples of this necessity.

The second principle, that of racialism, beginning with the introduction of slavery, has traced a broad pattern across the history of the country. Slavery was as important to the early development of the country as free competition itself. The two principles have been closely linked; and only in such enactments as the Thirteenth, Fourteenth, and Fifteenth Amendments have legislators sought to regulate race relations to ensure equality of opportunity in the schools, industries, or civil life. Indeed, the Fourteenth Amendment has been more frequently employed in the defense of corporate "persons" than of Negroes, for whose protection it was originally designed. The effects of the unrestrained operation of the principle of racialism are conceivably as dangerous to American society as the unrestricted play of free competition in the economic sphere.

Logically, it would be appropriate for government to impose controls and regulations, as mandatory as those imposed on its economic life, to ensure to all its racial minorities not only free but equal participation in the economic and political life of the country. In fact, before the present war is ended, such action may become a political necessity.

INDEX